Advance acclaim for

GOOD AND EVIL

"Farley has written a creative synthetic account of human existence. He draws upon a rich variety of sources in both parts of the book. The first, a multidimensional interpretation of the human, provides a basis for the second, an account of sin and redemption. Religious symbols in the second part interpenetrate the more philosophical account of the first to provide a distinctively novel understanding of human limitations and possibilities. Readers of traditional theology will find ways to relate their interests to a store of contemporary knowledge; nontheological readers will see how traditional religious symbols can deepen a secular understanding of human life."

—*James M. Gustafson*
Henry R. Luce Professor of Humanities and Comparative Studies
Emory University

"Edward Farley's newest book, *Good and Evil,* is a comprehensive, authoritative, and original contribution to contemporary philosophical theology. In this remarkable volume, the central issues pertaining to the ambiguity of human passions as entwined forces of creativity and self-destruction are addressed in a manner that is at once rigorous and profound. Farley's approach is that of a critical and reflective ontology that marks out a passage between the Scylla of traditional logocentrism and the Charybdis of a postmodern disparagement of the resources of reason."

—*Calvin O. Schrag*
George Ade Distinguished Professor of Philosophy
Purdue University

GOOD AND EVIL

Interpreting a Human Condition

EDWARD FARLEY

FORTRESS PRESS Minneapolis

GOOD AND EVIL
Interpreting a Human Condition

Interior design: Publishers' WorkGroup

Cover design: Terry Bentley

Cover art: Tate Gallery, London/Art Resource, N.Y. N 5057 William Blake, "The Good and Evil Angels Struggling for Possession of a Child," 1805

Library of Congress Cataloging-in-Publication Data

Farley, Edward, 1929-
Good and evil : interpreting a human condition / Edward Farley.
p. cm.
Includes bibliographical references and index.
ISBN 0-8006-2447-5 (alk. paper)
1. Man (Christian theology) 2. Good and evil. 3. Sin.
4. Salvation. I. Title.
BT701.2.F37 1990
233—dc20 90-44380
CIP

The paper used in this publication meets the minimum requirements of American National Standard for Information Sciences—Permanence of Paper for Printed Library Materials, ANSI Z329.48-1984.

Manufactured in the U.S.A. AF 1-2447

3 4 5 6 7 8 9 10 11

To David G. Buttrick, H. Jackson Forstman, John R. Fry, George H. Kehm, Leon Pacala, and Robert R. Williams: scholars, teachers, and friends of three decades, with appreciation.

CONTENTS

ACKNOWLEDGMENTS

Excerpt from *Opus Posthumous* by Wallace Stevens is copyright © 1957 Alfred A. Knopf, Inc. and used by permission of the publisher and Faber & Faber, Ltd.

Excerpt from "Wilderness" in *Cornhuskers* by Carl Sandburg is copyright © 1918 by Holt, Rinehart and Winston, Inc. and renewed 1946 by Carl Sandburg. Reprinted by permission of Harcourt Brace Jovanovich, Inc.

Excerpt from *Faust* by J. W. Goethe and translated by B. Taylor is copyright © by Washington Square Press, New York, and used by permission.

Excerpt from "Blue Squills" by Sara Teasdale from *Collected Poems* is copyright © 1920 by Macmillan Publishing Company, renewed 1948 by Mamie T. Wheless. Reprinted by permission of Macmillan Publishing Company.

Excerpt from "Dirge without Music" by Edna St. Vincent Millay from *Collected Poems* is copyright © 1928, 1955 by Edna St. Vincent Millay and Norma Millay Ellis. Reprinted by permission of Elizabeth Barnett, Literary Executor.

Excerpt from *Troilus and Cressida* by Geoffrey Chaucer, translated by G. P. Krapp, is copyright © 1932 Random House, Inc., renewed 1960 by Elizabeth Krapp. Used by permission.

Excerpts from "Choruses from 'The Rock'" in *Collected Poems 1900–1962* by T. S. Eliot is copyright 1936 by Harcourt Brace Jovanovich, Inc. and copyright © 1964, 1963 by T. S. Eliot. Reprinted by permission of the publisher and Faber & Faber, Ltd.

Excerpt from "John Brown's Body: A Poem" from *Selected Works of Stephen Vincent Benét* (New York: Holt, Rinehart and Winston, Inc.). Copyright © 1927, 1928 by Stephen Vincent Benét, copyright renewed 1955, 1956 by Rosemary Carr Benét. Reprinted by permission of Brandt and Brandt Literary Agents, Inc.

Excerpt from "The Man with the Hoe" from *The Man with the Hoe and Other Poems* by Edwin Markham (New York: Double, Page & Company, 1920).

PREFACE

This book is a theological account of a human condition attested to in religious faiths of the Hebraic and Christian heritage. What makes the account theological is its attention to the paradigm or vision of human evil and good (sin and redemption) present in some form in the primary symbols of these faiths. The account pertains to a human condition because it attempts to discover how elements of this paradigm enter and transform three spheres of human reality: agency, the interhuman, and the social.[1] This is why the volume begins with a depiction of these spheres, including various dimensions of human agency (Part One), thus postponing its specifically theological moment (Part Two). The central aim of the volume is to understand how human evil and good arise in relation to these tragically structured spheres. I have included brief introductions to each part to call attention to its major themes and contentions. The propositions in these introductions may help the reader to follow and assess the movement within each part.

Overall the volume is both a series of discrete explorations (concerning, for instance, courage, wonder, subjugation, and interhuman violation) and a comprehensive theory of human evil and good.[2] It is also a self-conscious attempt to address some of the problems of

1. Throughout this essay, I use the terms *human reality* and (a) *human condition* more or less interchangeably. They do, however, have slightly different connotations. *Human reality* is the comprehensive term for the human form of life in which converge the three spheres of agency, relation, and the social. *Human condition* is the term for the same thing when approached from the perspective of its tragic situation and its encroachment by evil and redemption.

2. In this essay, the term *evil* means *human evil.* This is a somewhat narrower usage than evil as anything that deprives something of what it needs or seeks. Thomas Aquinas defines evil in this broader way and argues that moral evil is a specific instance of this with its own distinctive features. See Thomas Aquinas, *Disputed Questions Concerning Evil (Selections)*, trans. R. Ingardia, Parma Edition, privately distributed, Question 1, Art. 1. On the other hand, I am not using the term so narrowly as to mean simply agential evil, treated in this essay as the dynamics of idolatry. Because human evil has distinctive dynamics in all three spheres of human reality, it cannot be identified simply with the dynamics of agential motivations and acts.

theological ethics and anthropology that have been around for centuries or have arisen under the impact of modern (or postmodern?) philosophies, psychologies, and social sciences on the ancient Christian paradigm. For instance, the volume addresses problems created by the dualism of the individual and the social, the problem of human evil and phylogenetically rooted aggression, the difference and relation between good and evil and the tragic, the problem of a revised theory of virtues and vices, the role of beauty and aesthetics in moral life, and the place of the will and the involuntary in good and evil.

This volume is a monograph and as such stands on its own. It is at the same time one piece of a larger project. That project began with two books of theological prolegomena, one of which addressed the epistemological question of faith's relation to reality, the other methodological matters of criteria and procedures.[3] This volume applies some of the ideas and procedures advocated in *Ecclesial Reflection* by exploring the way a portrayed paradigm of a religious faith and its determinate universals modify more general enduring features of human reality. This present volume is the theological anthropological part of a more comprehensive treatment of the Christian paradigm that includes its vision of the sacred and its way of understanding the historical conditions of redemption.[4] There will be those who worry about starting an inquiry into the Christian paradigm with anthropology. They will see such a maneuver as proposing anthropological grounds or foundations for whatever else remains. I must confess that I do not see this undertaking in that way. Because the Christian paradigm is an interwoven pattern of sorts, its interpretation has no absolute or self-evident beginning. I begin

3. See *Ecclesial Man: A Social Phenomenology of Faith and Reality* (Philadelphia: Fortress Press, 1975), and *Ecclesial Reflection: An Anatomy of Theological Method* (Philadelphia: Fortress Press, 1982).

4. There is a question whether *theological anthropology* is the proper term for this essay. In traditional Protestant theology, the two themes of the *imago Dei* and sin constitute the locus of human being. See Wolfhart Pannenberg, *Anthropology in Theological Perspective*, trans. M. J. O'Connell (Philadelphia: Westminster Press, 1985), 20. But since the time of the old Protestant theologies, theological anthropology has undergone gradual expansion. Charles Hodge expanded it from the two motifs to include themes of the origin of human being, the nature of human beings, free agency, the original state of human being, and the question of the soul. See Hodge, *Systematic Theology*, Vol. 2, (New York: Scribner, Armstrong, and Co., 1874). Reinhold Niebuhr's *Nature and Destiny of Man: A Christian Interpretation*, 2 vols. (London: Nisbet, 1941), and Emil Brunner's *Man in Revolt: A Christian Anthropology*, trans. O. Wyon (Philadelphia: Westminster Press, 1947), were two of the most important theological anthropologies of the neo-Reformation theology, and they both continue the expansion of the scope of anthropology. In Wolfhart Pannenberg theological anthropology undergoes yet another broadening into spheres of history and the social. See Pannenberg, *Anthropology in Theological Perspective*, 1985, Parts 2 and 3. What I am attempting is both narrower and broader than these texts. It is narrower because of the many anthropological issues it omits, especially philosophies of will, freedom, and issues of body and soul. It is broader because it takes up the redemption of human reality.

with a description of evil and redemption for strategic, heuristic, and pedagogical reasons. I propose, in other words, a way into the paradigm, not a basis for its truth.

Such a project would appear to be a systematic theology. It is not. This project falls somewhere between the independent volume on a theological theme and a comprehensive *summa, Glaubenslehre,* or systematic theology. One reason this project does not fall within the genre of a systematic theology is its tendency to cross the borders that demarcate the theological disciplines. According to traditional mappings of the territory of theology, systematic theology is a specific discipline set off from ethics, history, and practical theology. But the reader of this work will soon realize that these explorations have as much to do with ethics and moral theology as with systematic or philosophical theology, and they have much to do with pastoral theology and psychology.

I have said that this is a theological work. I mean by this that it uses a retrieved paradigm of a major world faith to interpret a human condition. It does not interpret human good and evil simply by collecting materials from various sciences and philosophies into a general ontology of human reality. The reason why the paradigm of a specific religious faith may help to interpret what we are up against is that wisdom about these things rarely has to do with something utterly generic or formal. Profound insights into persistent and widespread features of human reality arise from the collective experiences of peoples. This is why we can learn from Buddhist reflections on suffering, Native American attitudes toward animal life, and Chinese ways of relating to ancestors.

The style and language of these explorations may be too theological for those who think theology is passé, irrelevant, or even dangerous, and insufficiently theological for those who think theology can only be done under purely traditional or ecclesial norms. The latter group may be bothered on two counts. First, they may think that the cognitive style of reflective ontology is insufficiently biblical and historical. This presupposes that a work is theological only if its claims are directly traced to the primary texts of a religious tradition (scripture, creeds, the works of the great theologians). I must acknowledge that pertinent texts of this sort do remain in the background of these reflections. I did spend many years studying these texts, but I have only asserted, not established, the yield of that study in a retrieved paradigm. I can only acknowledge this deficiency. Although the work would surely be clearer and better if an encounter with classic and contemporary texts were interwoven into the explorations, it would also be interrupted by digressions and far too long.

Second, some will see this work as insufficiently theological because of their assumption that a theology is Christian only to the degree that it explicitly appeals to christological criteria. But it is my conviction that much of what is called Christianity persists more or less without change from the faith of Israel and has eloquent expression in the Pentateuchal, Prophetic, and Wisdom literatures of the Hebrew Bible. The Christian movement neither reversed nor significantly altered the vision of evil and redemption in these texts. Early Christianity does, of course, extend these themes in certain directions (eschatology) and develop new emphases (*agapē*). To be sure, a careful historical study of the themes of evil and redemption would uncover distinctive interpretations in any specific text, differences between Qoheleth and Amos, between the Psalms and Paul, and between Paul and the pseudo-Pauline tracts. I have glossed over these differences in order to address what appears to be a paradigm of evil and redemption that each one in its own way embodies. It may also be the case that evil and redemption will be interpreted differently if one attempts to subject them to a christological center (cf. Karl Barth). I have refrained from doing so in the hope that the content of this paradigm would be more generally available than it would be if Christocentrism were made its necessary presupposition.

From an opposite perspective, some may judge these reflections to be far too theological. They assume that to retrieve a religious faith's paradigm either violates the integrity and truth of other faiths or provincially excludes those faiths as legitimate sources of insight into human reality and its condition. The first concern is what prompts me to speak of a human condition. Although it does appear to be a condition very widespread in human history, possibly even extending to all of history as we know it, I do not want to assume its universality as an anthropological *a priori.* I want so to describe it that peoples of other traditions can recognize something like it in their own experience and history. I do speak a good deal about redemption and the experience of the sacred in these chapters, and since I am explicating the Christian paradigm of these things, I have in mind redemption as it is experienced in that specific historical tradition. In no way, however, do I want to contend that the redemption described in these pages is not available to or outside the experience of other peoples. A religious community can attest to the sacred as it experiences it. It cannot attest to the absence of the sacred in other communities. As to the second consideration, the issue of "world theology" raised by W. C. Smith, I can only acknowledge that a study of other religious faiths as paradigms of evil and good would surely correct and extend these explorations.[5] I do not explicate other

5. Wilfred Cantwell Smith, *Toward a World Theology: Faith and the Comparative History of Religion* (Philadelphia: Westminster Press, 1981).

paradigms for reasons of limited competence and limited time, not for reasons of methodological commitment.

Although this is a theological work, it is not just for theologians or Christians. I do hope, of course, that these explications will help active participants in the Christian community to think about the paradigm that has shaped their existence. But I also hope that they will help those who have little or no interest in religion to discern how the dense symbolic world of an ancient faith might illumine their own condition. Friedrich Schleiermacher addressed his first work to a small circle of friends he called the "cultured despisers" of religion; in other words, to intellectuals for whom religion was both scientifically passé and a corrupting influence on human culture. The attitudes toward religion of present-day cultured despisers, secularized intellectuals, range from sublime indifference to aggressive antipathy. Antipathy to religion, an attitude I frequently share, comes easily in a society where mass media keeps religion's most fanatical and fraudulent extremes constantly before our eyes. Indifference to religion comes easily when the primary socializations of a society fail to transmit the powerful and rich narrative traditions of communities of faith. I have this portion of our population especially in mind when I adopt a thin theological style and make minimal use of the standard discourse of Christian doctrines. I have also tried to avoid technical and esoteric expositions that presuppose narrow specialization. The text, I fear, is challenging, and its vocabulary is academic and philosophical. The purpose, however, of this vocabulary is to assist reflection to move into different paths, and I do try to define terms as I go along. The reader will also find highlighted in the index to the volume locations where my use of specific terms is explained or defined. The result is neither a popular nor a technical piece but simply a serious attempt to make sense of a condition we all face.

The cognitive style of these explorations is reflective ontology. I call it *ontology* because it is directed not to contingent events or discrete entities but to perduring features that constitute the being of something in its region or situation. In this usage the *being* of something is not a static or timeless essence in contrast to process or change but its characteristic powers or ways of existing in the typical and extended situation of that thing. This is why there can be an ontology of a human condition and not just of human nature. I call the style *reflective* because the being of this human condition and reality is not grasped in straightforward perceptions, logical derivations, or experimental repetitions but rather in ways of thinking that embody modes of experience and practical interests. If we use Jürgen Habermas's mapping of cognitive interests and undertakings (technical, practical, and emancipatory), reflective ontology clearly falls in the second type.[6] The cognitive style of reflective ontology is not absent in the Western theological tradition. One thinks of St. Augustine, St. Anselm, Blaise Pascal, Friedrich Schleiermacher, and Paul Tillich. As a style it appeals to a broader set of evidences than simply textual authorities. In these pages I avoid as much as possible arguments based on authoritative texts and appeal rather to consensual norms operative in mutual human interactions. I attempt not so much verifications and demonstrations as the confirming approximations of human wisdom.

How is this project located on the map of contemporary theologies? Continental philosophy of the last hundred or so years is its primary philosophical location. This does not mean, however, the rather technical deployment of Edmund Husserl's phenomenology that was prominent in *Ecclesial Man* but rather an interaction with a literature that ranges from Maurice Blondel's *Action* (1893) to the works of Emmanuel Levinas today. If phenomenology is present in these pages, it is in Gabriel Marcel's sense of an explication of reality rather than the caricatured sense of subjective idealism, indifference to reality, or Immanuel Kant's transcendentalism. Continental philosophy then informs the cognitive style of this reflective ontology.

As to the many ways of going about theology on the present scene, my tendency is irenic and pluralistic rather than polemical and school-oriented. My approach is undoubtedly in the liberal and revisionist line of nineteenth- and twentieth-century theology, but I see no necessary reason why many of these reflections would contradict the convictions of evangelical and Barthian theology. Planted in Scripture, a confessional tradition, or in Christology, these theologies will want to say much more than I do about these themes, but they also inherit from the past many of the puzzles addressed in these pages. Furthermore, the general orientation in this work toward the larger contexts of human life (nature, living things) depends very much on Alfred North Whitehead and process philosophy. As to liberation, feminist, black, radical, and deconstructive theologies, I have introduced this volume by taking up the anti-ontological criticisms of these movements, contending that the relation of these movements to reflective ontology is not one of direct and absolute repudiation. Some readers will not be interested in the issue of reflective ontology and its critics, discussed there. To them I suggest that this preface is a sufficient introduction to this book.

6. See Jürgen Habermas, *Theory and Practice,* trans. J. Viertel (Boston: Beacon Press, 1973). See also Richard Bernstein's *The Restructuring of Social and Political Theory* (New York: Harcourt Brace Jovanovich, 1976), Part 4.

Although my theological posture tends to be irenic in relation to other approaches and schools, the project itself does embody some rather severe criticisms of certain positions or tendencies in present-day theology and philosophy. The method of reflective ontology is an implied criticism (explicit in *Ecclesial Reflection*, Part I) of methods that make direct appeals to texts whose truth is presupposed in some *a priori* way. It also implies criticisms of those theologies that so proceed inside the circle of a privileged discourse, logic, or community, that they are released from all broader criteria or explication of broader regions of reality. To say that human evil and redemption can be understood without any use of philosophy, biology, sociology, linguistics, or psychology is tantamount to saying that human beings need no bodies, selves, societies, or discourse for their evil doings or their redemptive change. This volume is critical of all binary conceptual schemes: individuals and society, theology and ontology, authoritative Scripture and reason, praxis and theory. This includes what may be a new binary system, deconstruction, with its list of rejected and accepted epochs and categories. This book is critical of theologies ancient and modern that have tried to understand human evil and redemption apart from the tragic element in human existence. It resists those forms of theology and philosophy of religion that assume that knowledge, reality, truth, and the like occur above the historical determinacies of history and actual faiths. It also resists those forms that assume these things only have to do with what is utterly concrete.

Finally, this book originated more than ten years ago when I gave the Schaff Lectures at Pittsburgh Theological Seminary on a related topic. I am grateful to that school for that invitation, which gave me the chance to begin. But the years of further study were able to be translated into a written text on the occasion of a full year's absence from teaching. This was made possible by the leave policy of the Divinity School of Vanderbilt University, by grants from the Association of Theological Schools and the Research Council of Vanderbilt University, and by a faculty development grant given by the Lilly Endowment, Inc., to the Divinity School of Vanderbilt. To these benefactors I am exceedingly grateful. My gratitude extends also to another group of benefactors. The reflective explorations of these pages began in the situation of teaching. This means that a number of students were patient enough and interested enough to join in the explorations, raising critical questions and supplying their own insights. In some cases dissertations that students wrote on these themes have contributed to these pages. And although I attempt to give credit to these sources when they are used, I am sure that many other student contributions are here that I have now forgotten. These too are benefactors to whom I owe much.

GOOD AND EVIL

INTRODUCTION

ON COGNITIVE STYLE

> I wonder if I lived a skeleton's life,
> As a questioner about reality,
> A countryman of all the bones of the world?[1]
>
> *Wallace Stevens*

> The end of humanism, of metaphysics, the death of man, the death of God (or death to God!)—these are the apocalyptic ideas or slogans of intellectual high society. Like all the manifestations of Parisian taste (or Parisian disgusts), these topics impose themselves with the tyranny of the last word, but become available to anyone and cheapened.[2]
>
> *Emmanual Levinas*

I attempt the reflective explorations of this book with a guilty conscience. Academics experience this sting when they submit their finished projects to a readership knowing that their insights are already surpassed if not discredited. The Furies are especially familiar to those who write philosophical and theological treatises. Works of this sort tend to freeze a changing and complex world into concepts and systems. But my guilty conscience is prompted also by something else. These reflections are, frankly, ontological. They are purportedly about human reality and a persisting and widespread human condition. In the sphere of agents, I explore postures and desires at work behind acts and beliefs. In the sphere of relation, I attend to the way people are together face-to-face and to the violations and alienations of their being together. In the sphere of the social, I try to understand how institutions lend their awesome powers to subjugation and liberation. Whence the guilt? It may be simplistic to think there is a prevailing ethos in these pluralistic times. Yet there do appear to be widespread consensuses about some things, and one of these consensuses is deep suspicion of "ontological" theology. On this issue,

1. From the poem, "First Warmth," in Wallace Stevens, *Opus Posthumous* (New York: Alfred A. Knopf, 1957), 89–90.
2. From Emmanual Levinas, *Collected Philosophical Papers,* trans. Alphonso Liugis (Dordrecht, Boston, Lancaster: Nijhoff, 1987), 140.

biblicistic, historical, structural, semiological, narrative, Barthian, deconstructionist, liberation, therapeutic, political, and linguistic theologies join hands. Accordingly, I have an intense sense of submitting something whose immediate destination is not a living dialogue but the museum. The experience is not one of being creative or ahead of one's time but of being a theological atavist who works in the cognitive styles (though unfortunately without the genius) of St. Augustine, Friedrich Schleiermacher, Martin Buber, and Paul Tillich. My mood is, however, not only moribund but also hopeful. I hope that this book is not a mere reliquary of a forgotten and discredited way of thinking. If the following two claims are true, then this hope collapses under the weight of powerful discreditings. First, ontological thinking is intrinsically and inescapably unhistorical, a violation of the concrete and mutable character of whatever is actual. Second, deconstruction and other anti-ontological movements of thought have in fact discredited and displaced the epoch of ontological thinking. I shall explore these two claims in the two sections of this introduction.

IS REFLECTIVE ONTOLOGY UNHISTORICAL?

The cognitive style of the following chapters combines a rather general retrieval and interpretation of the Hebraic-Christian paradigm of evil and good with what I am calling reflective ontology.[3] This combination serves the overall aim of this project, which is to explore the sense in which this paradigm of a human condition describes and illumines what is actually happening in the everyday worlds of human beings. In other words, it explores the sense in which this paradigm is true. The hermeneutic retrieval is more assumed than explicated. It occurs in the form of a few general motifs pertaining to evil and redemption, motifs I introduce into the text only after separating them from ancient forensic, cosmological, and psychological conceptual frameworks. But the prevailing cognitive style of the essay is reflective ontology.

The book itself is a series of reflective explorations of the way human reality is distorted by evil and is open to redemption. The term *ontology*

3. The qualifier, reflective, shows the connection of this cognitive style to what Paul Ricoeur and others call reflexive philosophy. Accordingly, reflective ontology is not simply the inquiry into the structures and features of regions of being (cf. Husserl's regional ontology) but an analysis in which the philosopher's own locus, situation, and condition are one aspect of whatever is under consideration. Thus, for instance, an ontology of the features of the human body should be differentiated from the reflective ontology of the lived body or embodiment. The cognitive style of Gabriel Marcel is a clear instance of reflective ontology. See, for instance, the essays in his *Homo Viator: Introduction to a Metaphysic of Hope,* trans. E. Craufurd (Chicago: H. Regnery, 1951).

may well be inappropriate here. I do not use it for one side of a binary analysis, like biblical faith versus ontological reality, or biblical and theological styles versus philosophical and ontological styles. Philosophical ontologies of human reality that pay no attention to the paradigms of major world faiths have been around for centuries. Part One of this work attempts just such an account, that is, a philosophy of human reality and its condition. The theological explorations of Part Two are ontological in the sense that they exhibit characteristic and enduring features of a human condition. In this volume, ontology is not an alternative to, but a feature of the symbol systems of world faiths. Their primary symbols pertain to recurring, typical, and perduring features of our condition as it is tragically structured, goes wrong, reduces freedom, and is open to redemptive change.

Because this ontological reflection is not one level of a two-tiered exchange between theology and philosophy, the cognitive style of this volume is not a method of correlation. I am not trying to show how the deep questions of the philosophy of human reality correspond to the deep answers of the religious tradition. Nor am I trying to show how the general ontological structures of human agents, relations, or societies correspond to the particular historical contents of the symbol systems of a religious faith. These explorations at first sight may look like this sort of thing. I do distinguish the primary symbol systems of faith from the generic and formal features of human reality and its condition. For example, the symbolic differentiation between primal innocence and historical corruption (Genesis 2) is not simply a generic feature of the human life-form, like temporality or embodiment. But while human reality can be interpreted in a great variety of abstractions, it is not simply a two-layered affair consisting of an overlay of ontological features on the historical concreteness expressed in religious texts. Accordingly, we do not grasp the insights of these texts by simply correlating some ontological generic layer with some historically specific layer.

Any living thing as concretely actual is an ever-changing and contextual convergence of many interrelated but irreducible systems, any one of which can be the target of focused study. We can, accordingly, select and study the skeletal system simply in itself. We can abstract for the purposes of study human individuals as organic systems, as socially shaped systems, or as personal agents.[4] Focusing, abstracting, and

4. In this text I follow Alfred North Whitehead and Charles Hartshorne in using the term *abstract* to mean a cross-section of a larger totality. Concreteness, then, does not mean simply individuality but rather actuality, and what is actual is the totality of multiple systems and relations. Given this sense of abstract and concrete, all cognitive apprehensions, because they are selections, are abstractions.

selecting is in fact the only way we human beings obtain knowledge of anything that is actual. We are simply incapable of apprehending all of the interacting, interdependent, and constantly changing aspects and relations of a thing in one simultaneous, synthetic act.[5] Furthermore, because these various systems and spheres are interdependent and open to each other's influence, the only way we can understand how something about human reality is real is to grasp how it occurs in and has an influence on these interacting systems. If there is no way whatsoever that human evil shapes human agency and its historicity, face-to-face relations, or the dynamics of social institutions, then we suspect that there is no such thing as human evil. It is merely a vacuous symbol. And if evil and redemption, idolatry, freedom, interpersonal violations, and *agapē* are in some sense real, that is, are a modifying part of the spheres of human reality, then to exhibit their reality calls for some knowledge of how these various systems work and what happens to them under the impact of evil or redemption. Accordingly, I begin this volume with a general account of human reality and its condition (Part One) in order then to explore how various spheres and dimensions undergo and contribute to evil and redemption (Part Two).

The theological moment of this work (Part Two) proceeds ontologically by identifying generic human features in order to exhibit how they are receptive to, and the bearers of, evil and redemption. What are identified for reflection are not so much unhistorical essences as features of a life-form that perdure over a very long biohistorical period. This in fact is the sort of ontology one finds in the prophets of the eighth century B.C.E. or in the Gospel of Mark. The question is whether or not this discourse about what historically perdures is unhistorical, and whether exhibiting these perdurings violates the axioms of determinacy, concreteness, change, and relativity that Charles Darwin, Friedrich Nietzsche, pragmatism, history, and the social sciences have forged onto modern consciousness.[6] I shall respond to this question with the following three observations.

5. According to Wallace Stevens, it is poetry and not the sciences that is concerned with concreteness and therefore corrects the tendency of knowledge to focus on abstracted aspects of things. "Poetry has to do with reality in that concrete and individual aspect of it which the mind can never tackle altogether on its own terms, with matter that is foreign and alien in a way in which abstract systems, ideas in which we detect an inherent pattern, a structure that belongs to the ideas themselves, can never be." From "On Poetic Truth," in Stevens, *Opus Posthumous,* 235–36.

6. *Unhistorical* occurs in these passages more or less in its Heideggerian sense. It does not mean a mode of thinking that represses history in the sense of the location of something in relation to its past. Rather, the counterpart to unhistorical is the historical in the sense of historicity (*Geschichtlichkeit*), an existential of human being-in-the-world that expresses the mortality, temporality, and world participation of *Dasein* or human being. Thus, to think unhistorically is to propose features, essences, or predicates that occur above this world participation and are not subject to it.

1. First, the philosophy of human reality is concerned with matters that we human beings simply take for granted, however radical our anti-ontological perspective. Human beings cannot avoid being cognitively serious about the typical and persisting things in the everyday world that are the very conditions of life and well-being. These entities and processes are the contents of everyday speaking and writing. The purposive activities of everyday life (discernments, communications, and physical efforts) rest on at least some continuity or persistence of things and on our capacity to grasp that continuity and translate it into discourse. If everything that was actual, from molecules to planets, exploded every billionth of a second to reform into an utterly different thing with nothing at all enduring over time through patterns of organization, there would be no entities, facts, features of things, events, or processes. Nor would there be what we call experience, discourse, or thinking. Nor would there be human beings themselves.

The actualities we experience may, in fact, reform themselves every billionth of a second. Nevertheless, this movement into novelty retains sufficient past contents for types of entities to persist over time and for types of events to recur. Types, patterns, and continuities apply to everything from granite to complex, self-transcending individuals of higher mammalian species. Furthermore, nonhuman living things survive, mate, and feed only by grasping the persisting, characteristic features of things in their environment. Much of human discourse has to do with these persisting patterns. And when we direct our speaking, thinking, and writing to actual individuals, artifacts, social complexes, and past events, we are addressing things whose continuity, patterns, and features have sufficient continuity to be recognized over time. Predicative language, the language of features of things, likewise has to do with perdurings over time. When we say that someone is angry, religious, jealous, or has a good sense of humor, we are speaking about some sort of perduring.[7]

The explorations of these chapters presuppose this commonsense conviction that we human beings do experience the world as a complex of patterns, continuities, and recurrences, that these experiences are to some degree sharable and communicable (and intersubjectively verifiable); and that some kinds of discourse function reasonably well in this cognitive sharing. In other words, I do think that there are such things as agents, face-to-face relations, and social organizations; events, processes, and

7. I have elaborated this notion of perduring as necessary to truth intentions and to the concept of truth in an essay, "Truth and the Wisdom of Enduring," in Daniel Guerrière, ed., *Phenomenology of the Truth Proper to Religion* (Albany, N.Y.: SUNY Press, 1990).

entities; agential features such as temporality, emotions, and postures; and social features such as power and subjugation. Since all of the philosophers I know about (including Friedrich Nietzsche, Jacques Derrida, and Richard Rorty) act and speak out of these same convictions, I conclude that, however radical their repudiation of ontology, metaphysics, truth, representation, and the like, the repudiation retains and even requires these convictions. What is repudiated cannot then be the mere fact of continuity, recurrence, and pattern or the working discourse in which this fact is shared.

These chapters also proceed under the conviction that the experience, sharing, and voicing of world continuities at work in everyday life, reality negotiations, and the sciences is open to reflective inquiries that do not simply repeat the experiments of focused research or the formal analyses of logic and mathematics. If there are such things as agents with their own distinctive ways of perduring over time, a kind of thinking should be possible that attends precisely to that characteristic enduring. This rather strange, reflective thinking attends to the *being* of the specific continuity rather than its external causal conditions or the empirical operations of one of its constitutive systems. Accordingly, we human beings not only experience and talk about such things as our language-acts, malice, face-to-face violations, and social oppressions, we also self-consciously attend to and try to understand these things. We can and do converse with each other about what is and is not subjugation or wonder. The explorations of these pages make no attempt to prove the existence of these subject matters. I know of no way to demonstrate by logical derivation, appeals to sense experience, laboratory experiment, or historical-hermeneutical exposition that agents exist, that we human beings do violate each other, or that wonder is a possibility. These things are always already there in our world in a variety of fashions. For readers who require their demonstration or who think that all commonsense discernments and discourses are now utterly discredited, these ontological reflections will have little appeal.

2. A second reason why reflective ontology may be unhistorical and thus a discredited undertaking is that its stock in trade is the universal. Most of the seminal philosophical thinkers and movements of this century, (Ludwig Wittgenstein, vitalism, empirical-linguistic philosophy, Martin Heidegger, pragmatism, deconstruction, etc.), have turned their considerable weapons against universals. These assaults have many roots, but two of the most important are the shift Darwin effected in the way nature is understood and a similar alteration by the social sciences in the way history is understood. Darwinism disabused us of any notion that actual living things existed in the world as fixed classes

with fixed features.[8] Since nature is an ongoing panorama of ever-changing, ever-adapting entities, taxonomy can be no more than an arrangement of family resemblances for practical purposes. But the taxonomical structures of class, genus, or species are not world constituents or even a "mirror of nature" (Rorty). Both modern physics and microbiology extended this picture of an ever-changing (though not necessarily progressing) flow of events, and Alfred North Whitehead weaved all of this together into a comprehensive speculative metaphysics of world process. History and the social sciences reinforced the displacement of universals with their own version of an ongoing, mutually influencing (and therefore relative) network of events. History, societies, and social systems display forms of organization, epochal features, influences, trends, individual entities, and macro-movements, but not universals. Anglo-American philosophers of language argued that the notion of universals as references or states of affairs is a linguistic mistake and Continental philosophers like Heidegger contended that what comes to illumination on the plane of human being is not an entity with a fixed nature but an ever self-surpassing way of existing.

As far as I know, the ontological reflections of these chapters do not propose or assume universals as world constituents. I join with criticisms of modes of thinking that posit words as representations of immutable realities behind the flow of change. At the same time, the function of language cannot be reduced to the voicing of difference. To speak of malice or play is not to speak of mere difference but of something in which differentiation is ever at work. And to acknowledge that human beings are not simply aggregates of essences or contingent mirrorings of a universal essence is not to say that human beings are utterly undifferentiated in the midst of living things (which would be to say there are no human beings) or that human beings have no characteristic features, distinctive possibilities, or ways of being corrupted. Living things are ways of being, and this includes ways of surviving, struggling, opposing, desiring, responding, and even creating.

Natural and social sciences attempt to understand the various life-forms, including human beings, by studying selected aspects in specified causal environments (molecular, chemical, societal, behavioral, etc.). Ontological reflection, as I understand it, neither contradicts nor duplicates these efforts. It resembles these attempts insofar as it too would grasp human beings as a differentiated form of life. Unlike them, its focus is not on the various explanatory internal and external causal

8. For the battle between Darwinism and taxonomy and the impact of a Darwinian approach to nature on structures, concepts, and the like, see Steven Jay Gould.

environments of the human being, but on the differentiation itself. Older ontologies express this differentiation in terms like soul, reason, and will.[9] Except for narrow empiricist approaches, most modern philosophical anthropologies are not utter displacements of the descriptive programs these concepts served. Even concepts like the historical, the play of difference, discovery, openness, and writing are not about fishes or figs. Like the older programs, they indicate cognitive interest in human being as a differentiated form of life.[10]

In these chapters I propound a slate of terms that could be taken as unhistorical universals. I speak of three interconnected spheres of human reality (agency, relation, and the social), dimensions of human agents, and features of a widespread historical condition. None of these terms works as a universal in the sense of a constituent reality. I use the terms to describe the human way of existing in the world, the human form of life. And I use them to describe characteristic or possible powers or capacities of that existing, including the capacity to undergo and perpetrate evil and good. Ontological reflection means in these pages a focused way of inquiring into enduring features of human experience that is already part of commonsense discourse, including the commonsense discourse of Derrida, Rorty, and others. I attempt to reflect on the differentiated way that human beings suffer and subjugate, and develop postures of malice and of wonder. If there are no such things whatever, then these reflections are unhistorical. If there are such things, then philosophies are unhistorical that suppress that which makes human beings historical beings.

Closely related to the problem of universals is the matter of universalism. Does reflective ontology intrinsically and necessarily promote a false universalism? Universalism is now one of philosophy's most ambiguous terms.[11] Many kinds of universal statements make no appeal to unhistorical universals. Biologists who assert that no human infants are born without the genetic component, DNA, are making a universal claim. Statements about the universality of human temporality or embodiment may be of this sort. In this sense of universality, a universal

9. These terms are not utterly displaced in modern philosophies, even in philosophies that are major departures from the ancient schools and movements. *Soul* continues as a working notion for some philosophers. William Barrett sees the displacement of the concept of soul as a human and philosophical impoverishment; see *The Death of the Soul: From Descartes to the Computer* (Garden City, N.Y.: Anchor Books, 1986). See also Steven Strasser, *The Soul in Metaphysical and Empirical Psychology* (Pittsburgh, Pa.: Duquesne University Press, 1957), and Anna Teresa Tymieniecka, *Logos and Life: The Three Movements of the Soul*, in *Analect Husserliana* (Dordrecht, Boston, and London: Kluwer Academic Publishers, 1988).

10. Through these chapters I use the phrases *human form of life* and *human life-form* to explicate the term *human reality*. I am not self-consciously appropriating Wittgenstein's well-known and somewhat technical expression, *form of life*.

11. For analysis of some of the senses of universalism, see my *Ecclesial Reflection: An Anatomy of Theological Method* (Philadelphia: Fortress Press, 1982), 309.

feature is one that is a *sine qua non* of a particular form of life. The human life-form thus has an internal skeleton, DNA, sociality, emotions, and temporality. Insofar as any life-form is epochal and not everlasting, its *sine qua non* features are also epochal and therefore changeable and changing. The ontological reflections of these chapters are open to a wide variety of construals as to their universal reach. Many of the descriptions of human reality and its condition in Part One are so general as to apply to the human life-form as such. Accordingly, the chapters on the biology of human beings and on historicity would apply equally to archaic and postarchaic human beings. The chapter on sociality is likewise general but applies only to human reality as it exists in the form of societies and social systems. As to the historically determinate paradigm of human evil and good in Part Two, it is not a universal *a priori* of human reality. This paradigm is universal only to the extent that it applies and I make no effort to make that application. Such things as idolatry and subjugation seem to me to be very widespread in human history, so much so in fact that one can only suspect individuals and societies that insist that they are immune to them. But I have no desire to make this case in some *a priori* way.[12] I prefer simply to describe these things and leave the issue of their historical reach to rest with their power to evoke recognition.

3. Before us is the question whether reflective ontology is intrinsically unhistorical. I have contended that it addresses what the commonsense convictions of philosophers and scientists take for granted, the world continuities at the root of ordinary discourse, and that reflection on these continuities does not require the positing of unhistorical identities or transcendent universals. I must now qualify these contentions. I have distinguished between commonsense discourse oriented to world continuities and ways of pursuing ontology that translate recurring features and continuities into world-transcending universals. I have thus implied that the reflective ontology of these chapters attaches itself to the former and avoids the latter. But this distinction assumes that our commonsense world negotiations and discourses are, because they are unavoidable, normative. I do think there is something to be said for this position. I do not mean by this that the opinions (*doxa*) of the commonsense world are normative and thus should never be subject to rigorous correction and inquiry but rather that the commonsense world as a sphere of convictions, illuminations, and activities oriented to reality is itself necessary to even the most technical of scientific or philosophical undertakings. Thus, if the

12. I have tried to express this non-*a apriori* sense of the universalism of the primary symbols of major religious faiths in the notion of determinate universals. See *Ecclesial Reflection*, chap. 13.

cognitive convictions of the commonsense world are absolutely falsified, no cognitive styles survive whatsoever. When absolute cognitive skepticism is victorious, it loses the possibility of being aware of itself or making a case for its own preferability.

On the other hand, the cognitive convictions of the commonsense world come at a price. Paradoxically, we must distort reality in order to know it. I realize that one way to avoid this paradox is to translate all cognitive claims about knowing into practical functions. I myself prefer to live in the paradox and to acknowledge the provisional successes of our cognitive life, our partial and ever-changing grasp of how things are, and the distortion this knowledge always perpetuates, because to be knowledge it must select, focus, abstract, and de-contextualize what is always larger, interconnected, and changing. Reflective ontology does not avoid but embodies this paradox and limitation. Even the briefest and simplest event or entity in the world is dense, relational, complex, and involved in a move toward novelty. Thus, no actuality is synonymous with its continuity, the enduring patternings of commonsense discourse. This means that the most precise and disciplined cognitive style perpetuates what is false in its very attempt to be true. The history of human cognitive efforts is a history of continuing heroic attempts once and for all to correct this. Plato would move from the *doxa* of the everyday world to true knowledge (*epistēmē*). Recent corrections seem to offer a promised land "beyond metaphysics," a land untroubled by presences, representations, and even truth. In my judgment this correction will always be called for, and the land will always remain promised. This is because all of these correcting agendas require the cognitive convictions of the commonsense world and the presences, representations, texts, and continuities on which to work their disruption. To return to the question whether reflective ontology is unhistorical, I must now say that it has no built-in immunity from unhistorical distortions of reality. By the very act of claiming, describing, distinguishing, and focusing, it violates the density and mutability of things as much as any other cognitive style. Its preoccupation with "the bones of the world" (Wallace Stevens) calls for ever-new disruptions of its terms and insights.

IS REFLECTIVE ONTOLOGY DISCREDITED BY "POSTMODERNISM"?

Maurice Blondel, Franz Rosenzweig, Gabriel Marcel, Martin Buber, Paul Tillich, Paul Ricoeur, and Emmanuel Levinas all explored issues of religious faith in the cognitive style of reflective ontology. What contemporary critics of this style may sometimes forget, is that reflective ontology is itself a polemic, negation, and disruption of other cognitive styles, especially those that quantify knowledge and reality, which have arisen with advanced industrial societies. Reflective ontology attempts to think human reality from its very center. It would make the way it thinks reflect the dense and mysterious requirements of this life-form rather than make that life-form fit the requirements of a method selected in advance, or reduce its reality to some broader classification, such as an organic system or a group of behaviors. Reflective ontology's correction is not directed to the scientific study of human beings as such but to philosophies of human reality that use some specific science as the sufficient, comprehensive, and exhaustive model of human reality and its condition. This negation has a moral and political aspect. If human reality is merely an object that occupies this or that causal system of its environment, there would seem to be no criteria by which subjugation and violation could ever be recognized, much less opposed. Thinking from the mysterious center of human reality, reflective ontology works to uncover what violates and corrupts human reality. Hence the critical disruption it perpetrates not only targets quantifying reductions of human reality but exploitative social systems that would profit from obliviousness to the density and mystery of human beings.

There now have arisen philosophies and theologies that purport to be alternatives to reflective ontology. Many of them identify themselves by the elusive term, *postmodernism.*[13] The rhetoric of these movements is one of opposition against a family of undertakings: academic theology, foundationalism, theology, onto-theology, metaphysics, onto-philosophy. These terms are not strictly identical, but they are code words for a kind of thinking or cognitive style that appears to have fallen into disrepute. Are these postmodern movements really antitheses to reflective ontology? We should not be too quick to answer affirmatively because: (1) all three major kinds of criticism of ontology are at the same time ranged against the oppressions of advanced industrial societies and presuppose certain anthropological criteria for that opposition; (2) there are passages in the literatures of these movements that explicitly deny an oppositional relation; and (3) there appear to be retentions of certain elements of reflective ontology in these literatures. What then can we make of the opposition to reflective ontology in the light of these three

13. Once a descriptive, historical term becomes attached to a polemical or constructive agenda, it takes on features of the slogan. This is now the fate of this term. Furthermore, because it is a good word, it functions as the slogan of almost opposite theological agendas. It is used for an essentially conservative theology by George Lindbeck to describe a theology content to explicate the affairs of a specific religious community over against older, liberal theologies. And it is used by deconstructionist theologians to describe the demise of what Lindbeck would retain, the Western theological tradition. See Mark C. Taylor, *Erring: A Postmodern A-theology* (Chicago: University of Chicago Press, 1984).

considerations? Is reflective ontology discredited and displaced by postmodern philosophies and theologies? I shall pursue this question by examining three different though frequently interrelated movements, each of which mounts a characteristic opposition to reflective ontology: opposition on behalf of the primacy of praxis, opposition on behalf of epochal displacement, and opposition to logocentrism. All three criticisms are found in the literature of philosophical and theological deconstruction. Both liberation-oriented and deconstructive thought exemplify the first; radical theology (e.g. Thomas Altizer) the second; and French deconstruction (Jacques Derrida) the third. My aim is to place this essay in relation to these apparent oppositions.

Ontology and Oppression

Both political theology and deconstruction oppose reflective ontology on the grounds that it is hopelessly entangled in and the dutiful servant of some long-running social oppressions. These movements expose two quite different dangers of ontology: First, ontology violates the concreteness of experience and the world openness of the human agent, and second, ontology lends itself to co-option by socially oppressive social systems. The first criticism has historical roots in that strand of Western culture (romanticism, religious pietism) that opposed experience to ratiocination and metaphor to concepts. The second criticism is rooted in that strand of the Enlightenment tradition (I. Auguste Comte, Karl Marx) that opposes all thinking, that by suppressing its own contextuality, legitimates its indifference to praxis and world change.

1. The first criticism of ontology as a freezing of experience is present in both feminism and deconstructionism. According to deconstructionism, the very act of discerning a presence and distinguishing it from something else perpetrates an oppression. Built into this act of distinguishing is a preference, a ranking of one side of the distinction in relation to the other. The result is to filter the world, including its ideal possibilities, through a fixed system of preferences. This filtering produces a binary structure of oppositions in which one column of concepts dominates the other.

What is problematic about distinctions, preferences, and concepts? Why is the flow of presences into representative concepts oppressive? Such a claim would surely puzzle some representatives of the early Enlightenment, for whom conceptual objectivity was the liberating alternative to the ability of authoritarian systems to oppress because of their isolation from criticism. The first reason is the disruption between the concepts of ontology and reality itself, a familiar theme in the poetry and fiction of the Romantic movement. The Romantics sensed in an acute way the disproportion between precise conceptualities and the intensities of experience. Walt Whitman listens to the "learned astronomer" but finds the real thing in a stroll under the stars. The poet e e cummings describes nature as prodded and poked by philosophers only to answer them with Spring.[14] According to these texts there are ways of living in concepts that deprive human beings of nature, experience, beauty, and reality.

But deconstructionists trace this disproportion into a way of negotiating with texts that violates the differentiation at work in everything that is actual.[15] The flow of reality (presence) into privileged categories suppresses the play of difference ever at work in texts, writing, human beings, and the world.[16] Conceptual hierarchies are intrinsically oppressive because once preference is bestowed on a concept, the flow is subject to it. So begins a dynamics of resistance to whatever would undermine, reverse, or eliminate that concept. This dynamic represses the intrinsic openness of the human being and the perpetual differentiation at work in anything and everything. And because reflective ontology facilitates this flow of reality (presence) into concepts by proposing distinctions, laying claim to insights, contending for the real, ontology can only be something intrinsically repressive, something from which we need liberation.

2. Contemporary feminism and liberation theology pick up the social strand of the Enlightenment to expose a second reason that ontology is repressive. Expounding the dynamics of social and political oppression, Marx saw that the flow of reality into conceptual systems is not just an agential act but a sediment of history. Conceptual hierarchies pervade societies and exercise hegemony over whole epochs. The reality or privileged side of these binary systems confirms hierarchies of actual social power and privilege. The hegemonies of conceptual systems are also hegemonies of patriarchalism, racism, and classism. Concepts are suspect because, like so many other things, they lend themselves to subjugating uses of power. Ontology as conceptualizing falls under this suspicion.

This second criticism of ontology contends that ontology is intrinsically repressive because it subverts the urgency of reform in concrete contexts. A contextual understanding of human endeavors and the moral passion for social reform converge in this criticism. According to contextualism, human knowledge is both socially located and driven by human interests,

14. e e cummings, *Collected Poems* (New York: Harcourt, Brace and World, 1926), 21.

15. On the relating between deconstruction and politics, see Dick Howard, *Defining the Political* (Minneapolis: University of Minnesota Press, 1989), chap. 5.

16. For an excellent account of the concept (or nonconcept), difference, both in its historical roots (Nietzsche) and its twentieth-century proponents (Heidegger, Derrida, Foucault), see Charles E. Scott, *The Language of Difference* (Atlantic Highlands, N.J.: Humanities Press International, Inc., 1987).

and there is an important correlation between the two. Those who would know things are always located in time and space, that is, in specific historical periods and social systems. They occupy universities, governments, and corporations. They work as males and females, minority members, affluent suburbanites, and in varying stages of their careers. They receive their cognitive agendas (research projects?), styles, and warrants from a historically determinate past. However objective, technical, or self-evident their procedures, their results reflect their social locations. From these locations come their cognitive interests, selections, cognitive methods, and comprehensive world-views and paradigms of knowledge and reality. This is not to say that social locations simply determine in some simple causal way the evidences and procedures of cognitive endeavors. That notion itself is the offspring of a world-view and metaphysics. Yet cognitive undertakings influence and are influenced by their environment. Even those who would distance themselves from the political and social issues of the institutions of which they are part influence their environment by that distancing. They shape the environment by leaving certain themes untouched and unresearched, and thus they support the marginalizations and invisibilities that oppression fosters.

The other aspect of a praxis-oriented cognitive style is the conviction that the oppressions that structure societies place a primary agenda of resistance and reform on all members of the society, and this includes those who would press back the horizons of knowledge.[17] For all oppressive societies attempt to undermine potential resistance by disguising their own oppressive character. They thus co-opt institutions of knowledge for the agendas of oppression and work to render them irrelevant by diluting their influence. Accordingly, it is important that the members of these institutions resist this co-option and make their cognitive programs available to the service of liberation and societal well-being. In this view, ontology is especially suspect because what make it ontology is its preoccupation with the transcontextual and its suspension of moral and political concerns. It is easy to see how economics, political science, and history can be used by programs of social betterment but not reflective ontology.

I am not inclined to repudiate these criticisms. Concepts and their systems are disproportionate to experience. Schemes of conceptual

17. Michel Foucault contended for a new way for intellectuals to understand themselves and relate to society at large, a way that embraces social and political responsibility. See his essay, "Truth and Power," in *Power/Knowledge: Selected Interviews and Other Writings, 1972–77*, trans. C. Gordon (New York: Pantheon Books, 1980), 2. According to Ernst Becker, this is exactly the way the leaders of the Enlightenment saw themselves and their role in society. *The Structure of Evil: An Essay on the Unification of the Science of Man* (New York: The Free Press, 1968), chap. 3.

preferences do freeze the play of difference. And historically accumulated conceptualities do serve oppressive social systems. These criticisms, however, are not entirely unambiguous. Do they call for an absolute rejection of conceptual preferences (and thus reflective ontology) or a philosophical therapeutic of caution and correction? A closer look at both criticisms prompts me to think that these are relative criticisms rather than absolute negations. Consider the following.

First, all of the criticisms themselves use preferred concepts. Strewn throughout these texts are historical representations, preferential and non-preferential terms, commonsense and everyday world warrants, and appeals to textual evidences. The criticisms proceed by way of a constant flow of reality into conceptualities.

Second, like the whole genre of praxis-oriented criticisms, these criticisms perpetuate a binary rhetoric, an assault on *A* on behalf of *B*, an advocacy and preference for *B* over *A*. Accordingly, a new double-column takes form: concepts versus metaphors, absolutes versus relativities, identities versus differences, the ahistorical and timeless versus the temporal, certainty versus uncertainty, and metaphysical thinking versus non-metaphysical thinking. Are we to conclude then that only items on the rejected side of the column are corrupted and corruptible and that items on the preferred side are not? If that were the case, these criticisms would gather around them a new fixed conceptuality, a new personal piety, and a new social entity (a philosophical school) that, as the vanguard of liberation and difference, would be certain, self-righteous, and beyond criticism. It is painfully clear that oppressive social systems of racism and sexism co-opt and corrupt concepts. Do they somehow fail to corrupt a society's metaphors? Are human openness, doubt, and creativity somehow above being used to legitimate an entrenched and oppressive discourse? Both the Marxist and the theological-prophetic strands of these criticisms would apply corruptibility and the dynamics of legitimation to both sides of this new binarism.

Third, insofar as praxis, protest against oppression of various sorts, and liberation motivate these criticisms, the criticisms are on behalf of something. They prefer liberation to oppression. Accordingly, they possess criteria, however inexplicit, to identify when oppression takes place and to establish the basis for opposing it. What makes human beings able to be oppressed, what is it that oppresses, and what makes oppression something to be opposed? Does an oppressive system assault human rights, violate biological and personal life, impoverish culture, remove the conditions of human survival and development, treat human beings as objects, and rank them into hierarchies of superiority and inferiority? What is oppressive about Auschwitz, apartheid, and the absence of an Equal Rights Amendment? If these sorts of concerns motivate these criticisms, then all sorts of things are being assumed about the human form of life that are the concern of reflective ontology. In other words, as oppositions to oppression, these criticisms contain a covert reflective ontology. They work for some kinds of treatment of human beings and against other kinds. If they are really indifferent to such things as rights, justice, and dehumanization, one can only suspect that the criticisms will end up as new legitimations of oppressive powers.

Fourth, is it the case that reflective ontology necessarily subverts the primacy of praxis and the urgency of reform? Here too the case of political and liberative thought against ontology is not entirely unambiguous. But directed against philosophies and theologies that deny their own contextuality or pursue a type of scholarship that has little or no relation to the desperate problems of our present-day world, the criticisms are direct and unambiguous. They apply both to traditional theological approaches that see their subject matter as floating above the movements and relativities of history and contemporary professionalized scholarly disciplines that are indifferent to their social locations and the issues of a threatened planet. Do such criticisms discredit in an absolute way reflective ontology? One rather extreme form of praxis-oriented criticism would appear to have this in mind. It insists that cognitive endeavors are legitimate only to the degree that they explicitly thematize issues of oppression and serve as tracts for strategic change. In this view, ontology as such is either irrelevant or oppressive because its subject matter does not entail an explicit thematization of social injustices.

I am persuaded that reflective ontology along with other inquiries and pedagogies is not only inevitably contextual but should play a role in the ongoing struggle for a pollution-free planet, a peaceful international politic, and a just society. Whether reflective ontology can play such a role depends on what context means and on how social change occurs. Context is not the clearest of concepts. It owes its essential ambiguity to broader or narrower ways of defining its reach or scope. Radical theology, Michel Foucault, and deconstruction place us in the context of a whole epoch or in a shift of epochs. Some authors write tracts directed to very specific political struggles, for instance, the battle between developers and environmentalists for the votes of legislators concerning the use of a specific tract of land. Both an economist's arguments for a specific monetary policy before a government committee and a work that articulates the general dynamics of agroeconomics are contextual. And it appears that most of the writings of feminism, liberation theology, and black theology fall between these two senses of contexts. They are not contextual in the sense of strategic tracts written explicitly for the battles that occur in the corridors of power but are articulations of culture-wide trends and problems. The distinction here is between context and situation. Context is the total range of natural and historical influences. Situation is the gathering of elements that evoke strategies of action. In my judgment reflective ontology is contextual but not situational. To be concerned with the being of human reality and condition, with what makes subjugation a human violation, and with the relation between the tragic and evil, is contextual because it attempts to voice something about the human life-form that we need to understand so that our struggles for a better life will be successful.

An absolute rejection of reflective ontology may also presuppose that cognitive endeavors assist social change only when they promote thematizations of explicit social problems. If social change is as broad as a shift of epochs (e.g., from patriarchal to nonpatriarchal) and as narrow as the restructuring of a small committee, the cognitive work pertinent to it will cover a broad range of genres. The redoing of a society's primary symbols and its normative culture involves corrections and explorations that call for a variety of levels of work; specific historical studies, studies of the way language works, or the way social power works, resymbolizations, and thematizations of social injustices. If the only way that social ills are corrected is through explicit thematization, then reflective ontology has little role to play in that correction. But if intensified awareness of the general dynamics of human evil is helpful, then reflective ontology has its part to play in the struggle for social good. In sum, reflective ontology is contextual and praxis-oriented in a more general way than some explicit thematizations of social problems. But its attempt to reflect on the dynamics of human tragedy, evil, and redemption make it both contextual and pertinent to the issues of praxis.

I conclude then that these criticisms of ontology are relative rather than absolute repudiations. The primary mark of relative criticism is that it distinguishes between what it opposes (sin, oppression, injustice, evil) and the carriers of these things. Relative criticism opposes distortions rather than constituents of realities. Virtually everything in a racist society functions to promote and preserve that racism: discourse, political power, class symbols, educational policy, the medical system, family structures, religion, and the sciences. Relative criticism is properly directed against all of these things, not to eliminate them, but to expose them as vehicles of racism and to transform them. Few social reformers advocate the elimination of medicine, discourse, or families. Similarly, relative criticism is properly directed against reflective ontology not as an intrinsic evil but as an oppressive conspirator with other corrupted social movements. There are, we should recall, strands of Western history (absolutistic pietism, Manicheanism, some kinds of political communism) that would redeem by eliminating and destroying the carriers of corruption themselves. They oppose in an absolute way the body, leisure activities and pleasures, sexuality, and institutions as such. They mount absolute oppositions on the assumption that the mundane carrier is intrinsically and not relatively evil. But the critical programs of deconstruction and praxis politics do not appear to be this sort of thing. If they are not, they would reform not eliminate reflective ontology.

Ontology and Epochalism

Ontology is also suspected because it partakes of the thought world of a now-discredited intellectual epoch. According to this view, the epoch of Plato, Western metaphysics, and theology is now ending. Ontology has faded into oblivion along with God, the self, history, authority, body and soul, substance, and the medieval cosmology. It is as passé as subterranean worlds of demons and the practice of bloodletting to treat illness. Nietzsche, the early Heidegger, radical theology (Altizer), philosophical and theological deconstruction, and some kinds of feminism all have versions of this story. *Epochalism* as I am using the term describes efforts to discredit or establish philosophical claims by epochal contrasts. It is not so much a way of interpreting history as a use of history to make philosophical (or theological) points. It may look like intellectual history, cultural anthropology, or sociology of knowledge but its claims and conclusions have a philosophical character.

What appears to be epochalism often tends toward the way many intellectual movements interpret their own relation to the past. Phenomenology, process philosophy, Marxism, and linguistic-analytic philosophy can and do sell themselves as the movement that once and for all discovered and corrected the fallacy of all previous modes of thought. Accordingly, previous philosophies (or theologies) are objectivist, metaphysical, dualistic, bourgeois, speculative, or prescientific. They are passé for having failed to discover existence, time, language, oppression, and difference. But these examples of philosophical hubris display only a pseudo-epochalism because their criticisms are not based on simply epochal change. Their newly discovered truth establishes the epochal shift, not vice versa.

In theological deconstruction epochalism is not just simply a now versus then discourse but a historiography and methodology. Better expressed, it is a synthesis of historiography and methodology. The epochalism of theological deconstruction is rooted in two strands of thought which have a common historical root.[18] One strand is from radical theology (including the post-Christian-era theology of Dietrich Bonhoeffer), whose main present-day exponent is Thomas Altizer.[19] Its second strand is the post-Husserlian continental philosophies of Martin Heidegger and Jacques Derrida. Behind both strands is Friedrich Nietzsche's passionate account of the massive epochal shift that engendered modernity or post-modernity. The rhetorical structure of theological epochalism resembles pseudo-epochalism in that it puts forth a binary opposition between "then" and "now." "Then" is the dragon slain (or being slain); "now" is the slayer. A group of code words describes the then: the Western tradition, Western metaphysics, theology, onto-theology, logocentrism. Postmodernism describes the now. A set of terms, categories, or concepts unify the discredited then: presence, reason, "God," history, authority, certainty, absoluteness, intuition, representation, the self, and identity. Another set of preferred terms describes the coming now: art, metaphor, gesture, difference, temporality, uncertainty, play, and innovation. Epochalist historiography also includes seminal representative figures of the old epoch (Plato, Augustine, René Descartes), transitional figures that anticipate or help precipitate the now (Hegel, Nietzsche, Søren Kierkegaard, Edmund Husserl), and representative figures of the new epoch (Heidegger, Derrida). As a method, epochalism credits or discredits concepts by locating them in and showing their dependence on the conceptual hegemony of the then epoch. This presupposes either that the old epochal scheme has been shown to be untrue or oppressive or that it is nonfunctional as a powerful, persuasive, and useful interpretive scheme. The former procedure presupposes direct criticism of the epochal scheme and as such is not logically fallacious. Its logic is: *X*, *Y*, and *Z* have been shown to be untrue; *A* depends on *X*; therefore *A* is untrue. In this form, epochalist discourse is shorthand for a variety of direct criticisms. If this is what is going on in theological epochalism, its case against the Western tradition, etc., turns on the rigor and validity of a large number of specific criticisms. Likewise, its case against ontology is established by direct criticism rather than simply epochalist appeals.

18. Mark C. Taylor is at present the primary representative of theological epochalism; see *Erring* (1984); *Deconstructing Theology* (New York: Crossroad, and Chico, Calif.: Scholars Press, 1982); and *Alterity* (Chicago: University of Chicago Press, 1987). Taylor's program combines two forms of epochalism, that of Thomas Altizer and that of deconstruction. See also Carl Raschke, *The Alchemy of the Word: Language and the End of Theology* (Chico, Calif.: Scholars Press, 1979).

19. Epochalism is the primary framework and perhaps even method for Altizer's interpretive agenda, the making of a philosophical-religious point through literary and historical studies. The program began with *The Gospel of Christian Atheism* (Philadelphia: Westminster Press, 1966), and continues through *Total Presence: The Language of Jesus and the Language of Today* (New York: Seabury Press, 1980).

On the other hand, if epochalism proceeds on the assumption that epochal change itself discredits, a variety of questions is raised. And this is the ambiguity that gnaws away at epochalist discourse. It is either a shorthand discourse for direct criticisms made somewhere else, or which it is obliged to make, or it is a set of arguments based on epochal change. Some texts of this literature do appear to proceed in the second way. According to these texts, the Western tradition (and with it a whole way of thinking and writing) has simply been swept away, and this epochal shift is itself what discredits the content of that tradition. Let us restate the ambiguity. These texts do speak of endings in the sense of terminations. They do not so much directly refute the concepts of self, God, or presence as claim that their epoch is over. Do they identify epochal ending with refutation? Is this theological epochalism a soft relativism whose program is to describe the historical waxing and waning of primary symbols or a hard or historicist relativism that identifies the historical weakening of a symbol with its discreditation? The soft version of epochalism is closer to hermeneutics and the sociology of knowledge than a metaphysics of reality and meaning. It rightly contends that God, self, philosophy, knowledge, and history itself are thematics (meaning-clusters) of history. They arise with the experience and discourse of specific peoples. They can disappear from history, be transformed in meaning, and become marginal to the culture that engendered them. Accordingly, there is nothing eternal or universal about these thematics. Furthermore, they can be part of an epoch's or people's oppressive social structures. It is because the conceptual schemes and primary symbols are historical that they can be the focus of transvaluation (Nietzsche), de-struction (Heidegger), deconstruction (Derrida), and archaeology (Foucault). In their actual function in societies, these thematics disguise their oppressive roles, cover up their origins, and suppress their own relative, historical character. De-struction and its allies work to expose this historical character, which means also to expose both the oppressive element and the play of difference in these meaning-clusters. That is why these programs can claim to be liberative. They would break the tyranny of fixed contents and symbols over human societies and agents. In the programs of soft relativism, ending can mean historical termination, but its more characteristic meaning is the absence of sheer identity in any historically formed thematic or conceptual scheme.[20] God as a meaning-cluster of patriarchal and political

20. Epochalist expressions frequent Derrida's works. In most cases Derrida is not attempting to refute or establish simply by epochal location but is exposing a servitude to fixed meaning. He proposes a way of dislocating and interrupting certain epochal-wide concepts (presence, etc.). And what he has chosen as the region of this disruptive work are texts. Charles Scott interprets Heidegger's expressions about end in a similar way. Heidegger's aim

metaphors (sovereignty) can end with the epochs in which those metaphors are dominant.

Theological epochalism can also be construed as a hard relativism that collapses issues of facticity and truth into issues of meaning. A hard relativism identifies states of affairs, actual entities, and realities with meaning-clusters. In its extreme form it is at the same time a subjective idealism because of its reduction of reality to meanings. If a way of meaning something (God, mountains, self, disease, human beings, history, etc.) passes off the scene, the thing itself passes. Mark C. Taylor's treatment of the end of the self helps us test this issue.[21] When Taylor says that the self has disappeared, does he mean there are no more human beings who experience themselves as personal, violable, as choosing, making plans, and having desires? Or does he mean that identity-oriented ways of interpreting these things are discredited by direct criticism? On this particular theme, Taylor's arguments are not epochalist but directly philosophical. He makes his case by direct criticism of Augustine's philosophy of the self and replaces that philosophy, not with a nonself, but with a complex and astute phenomenological analysis of the self's essential temporality. He then continues to speak explicitly and referentially about the self. "In the effort to secure its identity and establish its presence, *the self* (italics mine) discovers *its* unavoidable difference and irrepressible absence."[22] Taylor speaks of disappearance, but what has disappeared (if he is correct) is an interpretation, not the self. The self remains to be reinterpreted by Taylor himself. If this meaning of end and disappearance carries over to the other themes in Taylor's book, *Erring*, then his epochalism is fairly close to that of Derrida and Heidegger, a critical disruption of ways of interpreting and fixed meanings. On the other hand, if Taylor thinks that these thematics are discredited simply because history has shifted, he is proposing a hard relativism. What problems attend hard relativism, the identification of meaning-clusters with states of affairs such that the historical ending of the former is the refutation of the latter?

1. If epochs and their thematics are absolute negative or positive criteria, so that mere epochal assignment can discredit, historical relativity itself is abandoned. If peoples and epochs really are relative, there is no reason why the views, concepts, and arguments of Augustine or anyone

is "to push metaphysical thinking to its fundamental existence, to its meaning. The effect is to de-structure this way of thinking by showing that it has missed its own origin and that when its origin—the question of the meaning of Being—is thought through as temporality in the context of finitude, the conceptuality and language of Being change, and, hence, we shall see, Dasein changes." In Scott, *The Language of Difference*, 61.

21. See Taylor, *Erring*, chap. 2.

22. Ibid, 50.

else in an epoch cannot be insightful and useful for other epochs, and no reason why the categories of postmodernism cannot be ambiguous, oppressive, or mistaken. Epochal contrast as a normative cognitive warrant simply glosses over the complexities, resemblances, perdurings, and relativities of history. It is in other words an absolutism.

2. The question and issue of God or the self can be utterly determined by epochal change only if there is no distinction whatsoever between images, language, meaning, and interpretation and the way things are. Such a view comes close to a statistics-oriented epistemology that sees the true, the right, and the good as whatever prevails. If issues of sexism and racism are simply matters of prevailing imagery, having nothing to do with what human beings are, desire, and need, then they are actually oppressive only if an epoch's prevailing images so define them. If prevailing meaning and the way things are coincide, there is no way that an epoch's prevailing sexism can be criticized. The alternative to this identification of meaning and truth is the capacity of human beings, ever present in history, to transcend the views, meanings, evidences, claims, convictions, and oppressions of their epoch and their socializations. If meaning and truth are identical, no critical stance is possible toward our epoch's prevailing imagery. Since philosophical and theological deconstruction presume and insist on such a critical stance, it would seem that, in spite of their epochalist rhetoric, they are not proposing a hard relativism.

3. The claim that God appears or disappears with cultural change and that there is nothing else but this appearing and disappearing assumes some form of Feuerbachian projectionist theory. But this theory is itself a metaphysical alternative based on the negative metaphysical claim that the total world system is sufficient unto itself. This position is a respectable one, is frequently argued, and now prevails among most philosophies of advanced industrial societies. Perhaps it is a tenet of postmodernism. If it is, postmodernism is a metaphysical position, a conviction about what is and is not the case about the nature and conditions of reality.

In the light of this distinction between soft and hard relativism, I can only conclude that the epochalist discourse of postmodernism is a soft relativism. If it is, its relation to reflective ontology is not an absolute opposition based on an appeal to epochal change.

Ontology and Logocentrism

Behind the epochalist discourse of theological deconstruction is a direct criticism of reflective ontology. It calls into question an intrinsic feature of the Western tradition, namely its logocentrism. Since logocentrism appears to be the very stuff of reflective ontology, it would seem that postmodernism (deconstruction) offers itself as a philosophical opposition and alternative to ontology. Although the criticism of logocentrism does not originate with Jacques Derrida, it does occupy a central place in his philosophical program.

What is logocentrism? One of Derrida's ways of exposing it is to analyze classical semiology (de Saussure).[23] According to Derrida, classical semiology translates into a formal structure the commonsense way of relating signs and realities that dominates our entire epoch. According to this structure, signs signify and are subject to things (*res*) whose intelligibility is always already there on the basis of the things' participation in a cosmic scheme (*logos*) whose basis is God. The primary concepts of this structure or model are presence, representation, meaning, and intuition. The "metaphysics of presence" is his shorthand term for this cluster of concepts. According to this commonsense model, realities, entities, meanings, etc., are contents carried by signs and manifested to apprehending subjects. For Derrida, at least three problems attend this commonsense model. First, entities as meanings must be simple identities in order to be so carried and so manifest, and he contends that there are no such identities. Neither are there contents that precede or float above the flow and network of activities that constitute our situation. Second, the model requires some ultimate (divine?) basis of world intelligibility, a metaphysical claim which at best is arbitrary. Third, the model obscures the play of difference ever going on in all contents, meanings, references, and the like.

Does this anti-logocentrism pre-empt and discredit reflective ontology? This would surely be the case if (l) logocentrism (the elimination of the play of difference), is a necessary or intrinsic feature of reflective ontology, or (2) anti-logocentrism is a direct opposition to and, if successful, a replacement of meaning, referencing, representation, and presence. At this point an ambiguity arises not unlike that of epochalism. Does the criticism of logocentrism entail an absolute rejection of the concept cluster of the metaphysics of presence or is it an introduction of critical and cautionary ways of using or personally incorporating those concepts? To put it another way, is logocentrism the mere facticity of presence, representation, and meaning in thinking and speaking or is it a way of thinking and speaking (construing) these things that represses the play of difference? I shall pursue this ambiguity as it attends the themes of presence, representation, and ultimacy.

1. Is the facticity of (a) presence, the theme of presence, or the appeal to presence identical with the metaphysics of presence? The term, *metaphysics of presence,* suggests they are not. It describes rather a form of

23. See Jacques Derrida, *Of Grammatology* (Baltimore: The Johns Hopkins University Press, 1976), 7–18.

thinking and speaking that withholds difference from presence or so privileges presence in relation to the flow and play of difference that sheer identity of meaning overwhelms novelty, relativity, and openness. If this is the case, the deconstructive criticism of presence is not an opposition, repudiation, or displacement of presence itself. This interpretation is borne out by the pervasive presences assumed and appealed to (the commonsense element) in the texts of deconstruction and in Derrida's repeated and explicit rejection of a logic of opposition or displacement.[24]

2. Does deconstruction propose to replace representation? Here we again meet ambiguity. If representation means an act in which a content or entity is distinguished from the term or image used to communicate that content to someone else, it is clear that deconstruction has no plans to eliminate it. The majority of deconstruction texts are about and directed to other texts and as such they represent, refer to, weigh evidence about, and interpret contents distinguished from the linguistic vehicles used to do these things. They represent the Western tradition, classical semiology, Christianity, religion, signs, views of various philosophers, features of millennia-long epochs, and even such things as the self and God. However, the target of these criticisms may not be representation as such but representative thinking, a kind of thinking that would simply be a channel for identities at the expense of the play of difference.[25]

3. Does deconstruction criticize, oppose, disprove, or displace all attempts to think or consider some ultimate reference or framework? The strongest criticisms in these texts concern the anchoring of meaning, truth, and presence in some ultimate intelligibility. Here again the criticism cannot be a mere displacement, else deconstruction becomes a metaphysical alternative, a positive nihilism, a counter demonstration of a godless finitude. Rather, its critical agenda is to display the epochal and historical character of discourse that contains an ultimacy reference and to argue for the play of difference even in that discourse.

To return to the question: Does deconstructive criticism of logocentrism oppose or displace reflective ontology? I can only conclude that this criticism is not a direct rejection of presence, representation, and ultimacy but a transgressive disruption of unhistorical modes of thinking these things. Accordingly, deconstructive criticism repudiates reflective ontology only if it can be shown that reflective ontology requires in a necessary way modes of thinking that eschew difference. It is the case

24. For instance, "This is why it has never been a question of opposing a graphocentrism to a logocentrism, nor, in general, any center to any other center." In Jacques Derrida, *Positions* (Chicago: The University of Chicago Press, 1981), 12.

25. For an account of Heidegger's and Foucault's criticisms of representative thinking, see Charles E. Scott, *The Language of Difference*, 98–99 and 145–46.

that reflective ontology directs itself to presences (e.g., human beings displayed in their temporality), that it represents (e.g., malice or subjugation), and that it is carried in meanings expressive of enduring features and powers. But as presence, representation, and meaning (though not ultimacy) are aspects of deconstruction itself, the criticism is surely not a repudiation of these things.

I must acknowledge, however, that reflective ontology is not just a repetition of the commonsense representations that occur in everyday life. It purports to explore the being of things, including the being of human reality. And it is clear that deconstruction as such has no such agenda. The issue is whether the being of things is or is not itself regional, epochal, and historical. I do not at this point see why it is not. If human reality is finite, a delimited species, and a provisional occurrence, surely it is an epochal and regional being. To explore the being of its reality is to explore what shows itself as enduring. I do not see why such an exploration is anymore a metaphysics of presence than Foucault's representation of the enduring features of a de-limited period, (e.g., the age of representation). Of course all thinkings and explorings are perpetually tempted to shut out difference, and as such they ever invite and need cautionary and transgressive philosophies like deconstruction.

Two concluding points are in order. First, I have dwelt on what I think to be deconstruction's philosophical importance and I have contended that deconstruction disrupts but does not repudiate discourses of presence. But what is the status of this program of textual transgression? Is deconstruction a prophetism directed to the idolatry of presence such that if it is successful, it brings the epoch of meaning and presence to an end? In other words, are such things as meaning, presence, and representation philosophical sins that, good pietists that we are, we must ever confess but hope that the new age will overcome? If this is the case, I must depart from deconstruction at this point. It is true that a certain way of existing toward meanings and presences subjugates, represses, and violates. However, it is also true that apart from meanings and presences, we have no world, no remembered experiences, no appreciated and valued things. Accordingly, I must construe deconstruction not as a philosophy that would (if it could) terminate presence and meaning but as an ever available therapeutic to the idolatry of these things.

Second, deconstruction as a philosophical therapeutic is a philosophy of liberation of a sort. What is the promised land into which we step when the prison gates are opened for us? It is the land of nonviolation, openness, novelty, and creativity. This therapeutic aim is deconstruction's genius and limitation. For human liberation is formal and even empty if it has nothing to do with courage, vitality, wonder, compassion, and obligation.

I understand why deconstruction's specific self-appointed task is to expose the play of difference in these things. But if it contends for a freedom that opposes or displaces them, it is only one more sign and instrument of the oppressive de-humanizations of advanced industrial society. These de-humanizations call for an exposure of what makes human reality violatable, what prompts it to violate, and what opens it to redemption. And these are the themes of a reflective ontology of human reality and its condition.

PART ONE

THREE SPHERES OF HUMAN REALITY

This interpretation of a human condition works from a paradigm of human evil and good carried in the symbols and narratives of Hebraic and Christian faiths. But paradigms of this sort are not the only pertinent sources for interpreting this condition. The term *human condition* describes not so much a collection of features of human nature, as what we are up against in our environment, the situation that evokes our typical efforts as living beings. Natural and social sciences, humanistic studies, and philosophies all explicate what we are up against. Accordingly, one way to depict and reflect on our condition is to appropriate these resources. Most such depictions turn to one of these resources for their primary metaphor, model, or conceptual framework of interpretation. When biology is the source of that metaphor, the exploration proceeds by proposing parallels between the human life-form and other living things, especially the higher mammals. When the social sciences are given prominence, the interpretive framework is taken from politics, economics, and history. Whatever the dominant resource, reflection on our condition never simply repeats the specific experiments and research of some science. That is because the problem itself, human condition, is intrinsically broader than the problems of specific sciences. Accordingly, the discourse of this broader reflection is not the argot of scientific and scholarly specialties but a discourse of action, reason, work, values, labor, *vita contemplativa,* the tragic, historicity, beauty, and interest. What we are up against, our typical efforts to live in our environments, are never simply chemicals, DNA, economic patterns, or pathological behaviors. Human condition is a category of experience and has to do with things we are perennially aware of, things that evoke our ongoing responses and deep postures: suffering, other-relations, uncertainty about our future, and death.

The term *human reality* describes the form of life that exists in this condition. A variety of biological, psychological, and historical sciences study this life-form in its difference from and continuity with other forms of life but do not as such describe what I have called its condition.

Human reality does not mean simply human individuals and their features. If that were the case, the study of this life-form could be multi-disciplinary, but the results would all pertain in some way to individuals. They would depict biological features of human individuals, features of subjectivity, even of the soul. As a form of life, human reality is more a species term than an agential term. Individuals thus constitute only one of the three spheres of human reality.

In Part One of this work, I attempt a brief account of human reality in its three spheres. The account draws on biology, the social sciences, and philosophy, but it is not a mere summary of the data or results of these resources. Such an aggregate of data describes neither human reality nor the human condition. Because these different resources are pertinent to our subject in quite different ways, my use of them varies from source to source. In chapter 4 on biological being, I expound some general and distinctive features of human reality as a biological life-form. In chapter 1 on the interhuman, I draw on and expound a wide variety of texts from continental philosophy. In chapter 3 on historicity or agential temporality, I engage in a reflective ontology whose background is certain twentieth-century philosophical texts. I summon the help of these sciences in order to describe the three spheres of human reality. But Part One is also a theory of human condition as a tragic condition. Accordingly, I attempt to expose in each of the spheres of human reality a constitutively tragic structure. I contend that, aside from the paradigm of evil and good, the tragic is the most general and unifying feature of our condition, that is, of the way we effortfully exist in our environment.

I am using the term *philosophy of human reality* for this attempt to bring to bear various pertinent cognitive resources on the broader questions of our life-form and condition. Philosophy of human reality and condition is neither indifferent to nor synonymous with these pertinent resources. It presupposes that the being of the human life-form is available in some way to reflection, but this availability does not arise from an indifference to the specific knowledge of these sciences. These cognitive resources (sciences, humanities, etc.), like all such resources, are abstractions that a more comprehensive and synthetic reflection attempts to correct. The result, however, is not a comprehensive objective anthropological science but a thematic portrait of human reality and its condition.

The following propositions summarize the major themes and contentions of the philosophy of human reality and condition.

1. *The human life-form or human reality is distributed over three interrelated and overlapping spheres, each of which is a necessary condition of the other two: the interhuman (chap. 1) the social (chap. 2), and individual agents (chaps. 3 through 5.)*

2. *Although each of these spheres is primary in its own order, the interhuman is primary to both agents and the social because it is the sphere that engenders the criterion, the face (Emmanuel Levinas), for the workings of the other spheres.* This primacy carries over into modifications of human reality by evil and redemption.

3. *Individual agents are irreducible, complex, and multi-dimensional.* Interpretations of human agency that ignore this multi-dimensionality not only invite oversimplification but lend themselves to violating and subjugating agendas. Historicity (transcending temporality), embodiment, and elementary passions are the primary agential dimensions. According to classical thought, reason, the power to discern, interpret, and understand the world, is a major agential dimension. I have treated this in a minimal way and under the theme of the passion for reality. Because all agents are also constituted by their participation in the sphere of the interhuman, it can also be said that intersubjectivity is a dimension of agency. However, I have chosen to expound intersubjectivity as an aspect of the second sphere, the interhuman.

4. *The human form of life, like all living things, actively strives, effortfully acts, and responds.* In the sphere of agency this takes the form of a phylogenetically rooted striving to survive and to seek the conditions of well-being. A broader reflection discovers human agents to be constituted by elemental passions. In addition, striving also structures the sphere of relation and the mechanisms of institutions. Passions push powerfully in all of the spheres.

5. *The spheres of agency, the interhuman, and the social are mixes of causalities (influences), perduring structures, and transcendings.* In this respect too human reality is an exemplification of and not an exception to other forms of life. This is why none of the spheres lends itself solely to causal or structural or deconstructive analyses. Reflective ontology of human reality is possible only because there are perduring structures and features of this human life-form.

6. *The most general feature of our human condition is its tragic character.* The term *tragic* refers to a situation in which the conditions of well-being require and are interdependent with situations of limitation, frustration, challenge, and suffering. Human condition is not tragic simply because suffering is an aspect of it but because sufferings of various sorts are necessary conditions of creativity, affection, the experience of beauty, etc. Further, all three spheres of human reality are tragically structured. Thus agents, relations, and institutions obtain and maintain their goods only in conjunction with all sorts of intrinsic limitations, exclusions, and sufferings. For reasons of exposition, I postpone the explication of the tragic aspect of the agential sphere as a whole until chapter 6.

1
THE INTERHUMAN SPHERE

Abstract what others feel, what others think,
All pleasures sicken, and all glories sink.[1]
Alexander Pope

Face is the positive feeling of self-warmth turned to the world for others' scrutiny and potential sabotage. Face is society's window to the core of the self. We can fully appreciate the importance of face when we realize that nothing goes deeper than the exposure of the self-esteem to possible intolerable undermining in the social encounter.[2]
Ernst Becker

In the epoch we call history, human reality or the human life-form is constituted by three interconnected spheres. These spheres are both ways we experience our reality and interacting realms that present themselves to be thematized and interpreted. We experience our own life-form as agents (thus as self-aware and acting individuals), as living in social systems, and as participating in interpersonal relations. We take all three for granted in our everyday-life negotiations, but only two of them have evoked widespread scientific attention. Natural and social sciences have accumulated massive data and interpretive schemes that pertain to the organic and psychological aspects of the human individual and to the workings of society and culture. Perhaps this focus on the spheres of agency and sociality reflects a prevailing dualism of Western thought, the dualism of the individual and the social.[3] At work in the everyday world and its

1. Alexander Pope, "Essay on Man," *The Poetical Works of Alexander Pope,* ed. A. W. Ward, (London and New York: Macmillan and Co., 1896), Epistle 4, 217–19.

2. Ernst Becker, *The Birth and Death of Meaning: A Perspective in Psychiatry and Anthropology* (New York: Free Press of Glencoe, 1962), 88.

3. Dualisms persist from ancient and Cartesian divisions between nature and body (studied by the sciences) and consciousness and the personal (studied by philosophy, religion, or the arts). In the sciences this dualism is promoted by the split between the biological and the cultural. A new dualism which now overlays both the Cartesian type of dualism and organism-culture dualism articulates the split between individuals and social systems. It results from combining the ancient tradition of philosophical reflection on human individual experience (thus the soul, the personal, *Existenz,* and freedom) and the modern thematization of the social and the collective (culture, society,

cognitive convictions is a third sphere which, compared to the other two, has gained only minor attention. This is the sphere of the interhuman, the sphere of (interpersonal) relation.[4]

Where do we find the interhuman? We will surely miss it altogether if we think of it as the social or as something deposited before us "out there." It resembles the personal in that it is a reality already at work in our cognitive and experiential transactions with what is out there. This is not to say that human beings have no awareness of the interhuman, that it is something merely hidden, something we hypothesize or logically deduce. But, since it permeates and shapes awareness, and since all awareness tends to be drawn toward specific things (themes, memories, persons, objects, tasks, etc.) the interhuman calls for a reflection that helps us to become aware of what we already know.[5] This reflection can be resisted. Some kinds of cognitive postures and methodological commitments work to obscure and suppress the interhuman. For instance, the interhuman can be obscured from the start by the assumption that human being-together is nothing but specific events of social interaction or patterns of social organization. But it is also hidden when it is reduced to I and Thou encounters or to a transcendental structure.

praxis, justice). I have described this new dualism in an essay, "Piety and Praxis: Hermeneutics Beyond the New Dualism," in Douglas Knight and Peter Paris, eds., *Justice and the Holy: Essays in Honor of Walter Harrelson* (Atlanta: Scholar's Press, 1989).

4. I have selected the English term, interhuman, among a number of candidates, a list which includes the intersubjective and the interpersonal. The English term, *interhuman,* translates Martin Buber's term, *Zwischenmenschliche,* sometimes translated as the Between. Buber uses the term to describe the actuality of the relation of human beings to others, something that occurs from time to time in genuine meetings. See his reply to critics in Paul A. Schilpp and Maurice Friedman, eds., *The Philosophy of Martin Buber* (LaSalle, Ill.: Open Court, 1967), 711. This volume contains an excellent exposition of this concept in Buber; see Nathan Rotenstreich, "The Right and the Limitations of Buber's Dialogical Thought." In addition, see Bernhard Casper, *Das Dialogischen Denken: Eine Untersuchung der religionsphilosophischen Bedeutung Franz Rosenzweigs, Ferdinand Ebners und Martin Bubers* (Freiburg, W.Ger.: Herder, 1967), Part III; and Donald L. Beer, *Mutuality: the Vision of Martin Buber* (Albany, N.Y.: SUNY Press, 1985). Casper notes that Buber uses the phrase, ontology of the interhuman, but argues that the Between can only be negatively articulated (299–300). In my appropriation of the term, the interhuman includes elements other than actual meeting and dialogue. In this volume, the interhuman is a fairly inclusive term for the basic features of human being-together presupposed by the institutions and sedimentations of the social.

5. Philosophies of the interhuman have widely differing explanations of the elusiveness of the interhuman based both on their specific analyses of the interhuman and their overall philosophical programs. For Husserl the interhuman means transcendental intersubjectivity and this calls forth the rigors and complexities of transcendental method. For Heidegger the interhuman means the being-with of Dasein, hence, bringing it to expression involves the break with ontically dominated thinking, the *Destruktion* of the history of ontology, and the allowing of the truth of the occurrence of *Dasein* as a being-in-the-world to be illumined. For both Marcel and Buber, the interhuman is obscured not just by its marginality to immediate awareness but by the depersonalizations and dehumanizations of a whole historical and societal ethos.

What is the *interhuman?* In order to grasp its several elements and to avoid a premature narrowing, I am using the term to describe a sphere of reality, namely the sphere of face-to-face relation or being-together in relation. My account of it in this chapter will be neither exhaustive nor systematic. I do want to include in the account insights which I shall use later to explore human vulnerability, human desire, and social being, and how these things function when transformed by both evil and redemption.

THE TRIADIC STRUCTURE OF THE INTERHUMAN

The interhuman is a recurring theme in nineteenth- and twentieth-century continental philosophy.[6] It is also present in Anglo-American philosophy in the form of the problem of other minds.[7] These literatures present to us a variety of approaches and proposals that at first sight appear to be exclusive of each other.[8] The controversies press us to choose among alternatives: the interhuman as structure of interpersonal intimacy, a structure of the social world, or an always already there being-with of human beings. But instead of being exclusive, these competing interpretations together express the complex structure of the interhuman. The essential insights of each approach turn out to be expressions of three elemental features of the interhuman.

6. There is no full survey of the total literature. The most comprehensive treatment is Michael Theunissen's *The Other: Studies in the Social Ontology of Husserl, Heidegger, Sartre and Buber,* trans. C. Macann (Cambridge, Mass.: MIT Press, 1984). A second study is T. J. Owens, *Phenomenology and Intersubjectivity: Contemporary Interpretations of the Interpersonal Situation* (The Hague, Netherlands: Nijhoff, 1970). This work is on Scheler, Sartre, and von Hildebrand. For an excellent account of the theme in German idealism see the forthcoming study by Robert R. Williams, *The Spirit of Recognition: Fichte and Hegel on Otherness.* Excellent introductions to the cluster of issues and to the literature are to be found in Theunissen, *The Other,* Introduction; Fred R. Dallmayr, *The Twilight of Subjectivity: Contributions to a Post-Individualist Theory of Politics* (Amherst, Mass.: University of Massachusetts Press, 1981), Introduction; and Calvin Schrag, *Experience and Being: Prolegomena to a Future Ontology* (Evanston, Ill.: Northwestern University Press, 1969), chap. 6. For a typology of the basic approaches, see Maurice Natanson, *The Journeying Self: A Study in Philosophy and Social Role* (Reading, Mass.: Wesley Publishing Co., 1970), chap. 2. The most comprehensive collection of essays on the subject that includes the work of a number of theologians is Marco M. Olivetti, ed., *Archivio di Filosofia: Intersoggettività, Socialità, Religione,* Anno LIV (Padova, Italy: CEDAM, 1986).

7. Because I am not construing the question of the interhuman as the basis for affirming other minds, I shall draw primarily from the explorations of continental rather than Anglo-American philosophy. For an important collection of the essays on this theme from early Anglo-American analytic philosophy, see John Wisdom, *Other Minds* (Oxford, Eng.: Oxford University Press, 1956).

8. Theunissen, *The Other,* offers a twofold classification of basic approaches, the transcendental in which he includes Husserl, Heidegger, and Sartre and the dialogal, thus Buber. In my judgment this typology fosters unnecessary incompatibilities between Buber and others, omits or plays down other important approaches which do not fit the two options, thus Scheler, Marcel, and Alfred Schutz, and glosses over senses in which Heidegger and Sartre are at odds with the transcendental approach.

Alterity

Much of the literature on the interhuman is preoccupied with the challenge laid down by *solipsism,* the idea that each human individual is so utterly enclosed in its sphere of consciousness that it has no true knowledge or experience of any other consciousness. Reality means the reality of my consciousness. Social solipsism has both an empiricist and idealist form. In the empiricist version, the possible objects of knowledge are either sense objects or empty, analytical relations, hence, the other mind can not possibly be known. The idealist version arises on opposite grounds, the centuries long exploration (from René Descartes to the present) of human *Geist,* (mind, consciousness, self, person).[9] This too promotes a solipsism because the more subjectivity is distinguished from the external and from whatever is external, the less the subjectivity of the other is accessible.

In most empiricist or idealist philosophies, solipsism is more a methodological path to the interhuman than a solution or conclusion. But we should not permit the overwhelming consensus against solipsism to eliminate the strange mystery of the interhuman.[10] For the very struggle with the problem of solipsism uncovers that without which the interhuman would have no reality. Solipsism articulates the irreducible and uninterchangeable "I" structure of human experience. This "I" is an embodied centeredness in the world and the foundation of the very notion of perspective. We never experience anything except in and through our own complex of sensations, thinkings, and feelings. Accordingly, we do not

9. Kant, Fichte, and Hegel are the main figures of this tradition. See Williams, *The Spirit of Recognition,* for expositions of intersubjectivity especially in Fichte and Hegel.

10. An older approach now opposed by almost everyone is a solipsistic account of the interhuman. It argues that human beings experience in an immediate way the body of the other and with that the gestures, communications, and expressed emotions, thus we know that there is another "I" behind these things, by analogy with our own gestures and acts, directed by our own "I." In other words we know the other "I" by analogical inference. Husserl offers a very complex version of this approach in the Fifth Cartesian Meditation. *Cartesian Meditations: An Introduction to Phenomenology,* trans. D. Cairns (The Hague, Netherlands: Nijhoff, 1960). Husserl's language of ownness sphere, analogizing transfer, and pairing all suggests he falls within this approach. On the other hand, he argues that there is an immediate grasp of the other as personal body (*Leib*), and this would appear to undercut an analogizing or inferential solution. Further, in Husserl's approach to intersubjectivity in the three posthumously published volumes of his *Nachlass,* empathy not analogy is the central category. For a brief but better organization of the *Nachlass* materials than the chronologically arranged volumes of *Husserliana,* see Gerd Brand, *Welt, Ich und Zeit; nach Unveröffentlichten Manuskripten Husserls* (The Hague, Netherlands: Nijhoff, 1955). Most interpretations of Husserl's philosophy of intersubjectivity rest almost entirely on the Fifth Cartesian Meditation. Thus, Sartre, *Being and Nothingness: An Essay on Phenomenological Ontology,* trans. H. E. Barnes (New York: Philosophical Library, 1956), Part III, chaps. 1, 3; Alfred Schutz, *Collected Papers,* ed. M. Natanson (The Hague, Netherlands: Nijhoff, 1962–66), 3 vols., vol. 3, 51–84; Paul Ricoeur, *Husserl: An Analysis of His Phenomenology,* trans. E. G. Ballard and L. Embree (Evanston, Ill.: Northwestern University Press, 1967), chap. 5; and Theunissen, *The Other,* chaps. 1–4.

experience anyone else's felt emotions, sensations, or immediate flow of thoughts. If we could experience these things, there would be no other and therefore no interhuman. For dialogue, intimacy, and empathy all require a genuine other. As a positive conclusion or solution, solipsism maintains that the centered "I" is an isolation from the world. It is important to distinguish this position from the insight into the solipsistic element in the interhuman; the negative fact that the other's experiences can never be experienced as such by me. That which makes the other genuinely other is not a temporary obstacle which a cognitive strategy will remove. Gathering more information, changing perspective, adopting different methods of inquiry, or developing a better technological instrument will not give me the other's experiencing as my experiencing.[11] The strange elusiveness of the other "I" is the solipsistic element in the interhuman. The solipsistic element in the interhuman is what makes this a sphere of relations between beings who are irreducibly other to each other; in other words, the sphere of alterity. The other, then, is what I do not and cannot experience in the mode in which I experience myself. It is an "I" which is not I.[12]

Alterity, however, is more than a mere negation, a term for the other's inaccessibility or for the non-interchangeability of positions between I and other. This negative formulation rests almost entirely on the problem of the knowledge of the other, and if alterity is reduced to that, the other is simply a failed cognition. But we do not experience others simply on the spectrum of cognitive efforts (believing in, hypothesizing, drawing conclusions, gathering evidences, etc.). The other is a source of acts directed at me and which involve me. The other as "I" is, therefore, an experiencing, interpreting, feeling center of its world. Two things follow from this.

First, to experience the other as other is to apprehend that one is experienced. It is to experience oneself not just as acting, interpreting, and autonomous but as interpreted, typified, and assessed.[13] This is the experience of being something in the other's world, subject to the other's perspectives, motives, and agendas. The existence of such an

11. Husserl's concept of the sphere of my own (*Eigenheitsphäre*) is one account of the solipsistic element of the interhuman. For it is the sphere of my own which is not interchangeable. For a similar point see Maurice Natanson's "Introduction" to Alfred Schutz, *Collected Papers*, Vol. I. His account stresses the hereness and nowness of the embodied "I" so that the other is always there.

12. Maurice Merleau-Ponty formulates this paradox of the other in *The Phenomenology of Perception*, trans. Colin Smith (New York: Humanities Press, 1974), 348.

13. The primary contribution of Sartre to the exploration of the interhuman is his explication of the experience of the other's objectification, or as he says, the other's look or gaze. See *Being and Nothingness*, Part III, chap 1, no. 4.

other disputes any claim I have to be the one "I," the only perspective, the autonomous actor.

Second, as an actor and self-initiator, the other has a privileged position of self-knowledge and self-interpretation which contests my assessments and interpretations directed to it.[14] The other as other resists my efforts to incorporate it into my world and perspective. Alterity, then, is both the uninterchangeability and irreducibility of the other and a resistance and challenge to my autonomy and its claims. Whatever solutions are proffered to the problem of intersubjectivity, they must incorporate this primordial structure of alterity at the heart of the interhuman.[15]

Intersubjectivity: The Always Already Thereness of the Interhuman

Philosophers disagree over whether the solipsistic element or alterity is an intrinsic element of the interhuman or a misconstrual based on a false premise. Those who argue the latter charge solipsism with trying to build a cognitive bridge from a known consciousness to an unknown other. Solipsism as a false premise is the positing of something that has no existence, the isolated consciousness. According to these critics, there is no actual "I" so cognitively isolated that it must discover proofs for the existence of the other "I." In my judgement this is a telling criticism, but what is eliminated by it is not what I have called the solipsistic element or alterity but a way of interpreting it which results in a private and isolated "I." The criticism of this position introduces us to a second element in the interhuman, its character as always already there.

According to these criticisms, the individual who wonders reflectively whether or how it experiences the other is already intersubjectively formed.[16] Accordingly, the so-called internal acts or mental processes

14. See Emmanuel Levinas, *Totality and Infinity: An Essay on Exteriority* (Pittsburgh, Pa.: Duquesne University Press, 1969), 195. For the resistance and the non-manipulatibility of the other, see Ernst Becker, *The Birth and Death of Meaning*, 84.

15. Maurice Merleau-Ponty expresses the solipsistic element when he says, "insofar as the other person resides in the world, is visible there, and forms a part of my field, he is never an Ego in the sense in which I am one for myself," in *The Phenomenology Perception*, 352. Levinas retains the solipsistic element in the following phrases, "Expression does not consists in giving us the other's interiority." See Levinas, *Totality and Infinity*, 202.

16. For Maurice Blondel this means that collaboration with others is one of the many layers of human striving which constitute human action as such. See *Action: Essay on a Critique of Life and a Science of Practice*, trans. O. Blanchette (Notre Dame, Ind.: Notre Dame University Press, 1984). For Alfred Schutz it means that the only human being we know is a being active in the world of everyday life already shaped by the reciprocities and structures of the social world. For Heidegger it means that *Dasein*, the privileged and primary field for the illumination of being, is always already a being-in-the-world which at the same time is always a being-with. For Merleau-Ponty, it means that the self-awareness and even world awareness of adult human beings comes about through interpersonal acts in the world of

such as considering evidences and arguments, constituting oneself as a self, and even raising the question of the other are activities which presuppose and use intersubjectively formed postures, deposited meanings of language, roles, and agendas. We can try to jump the gulf to the other only if the gulf is in some way already bridged by intersubjectivity.[17] Thus, intersubjectivity is always already there when individuals become aware of themselves or self-consciously reflect about their relations to others. Intersubjective entanglements are already present and presupposed when we engage in empirical, deductive, or reflective explorations.

The Interpersonal

Human being-together is not simply alterity and intersubjective entanglement. Alterity and intersubjectivity are necessary elements in the interhuman. But the interhuman itself is interpersonal relation. But alterity and intersubjectivity could be interpreted as mere structural elements in a being-together that is not a relation of persons. Correcting this notion is the philosophical lineage whose primary author is Martin Buber.[18] According to this tradition, the interhuman is more than a pregiven structure, more even than an existential. It is the interpersonal. Unlike the already present entanglements of intersubjectivity, the interpersonal is something disclosed in concrete human acts and relations. Thus, for Buber, it happens as a turning to the other and a becoming

infants. See "The Child's Relation to the Others," in *The Primacy of Perception and Other Essays in Phenomenological Psychology*, trans. J. Edie (Evanston, Ill.: Northwestern University Press, 1964).

17. Because of the multiple ways the terms are now used, the intersubjective, the interpersonal, and the interhuman could be used interchangeably to mean the inclusive sphere of the interhuman. In this essay the interhuman is the inclusive term but its primary meaning is that of the interpersonal, of which alterity and intersubjectivity are necessary aspects. The intersubjective is the always-already-social reality of the interhuman. If I understand him correctly, Theunissen places this aspect under the rubric of the transcendental, and thus includes Sartre and Heidegger along with Husserl among those who focus on the always already there of sociality. He can thus introduce the approach of dialogue as an opposition and competition with the transcendental. In my view it is not a matter of alternative approaches but of emphasized aspects.

18. For an extensive bibliography of the European literature spawned by Buber, see Theunissen, *The Other*, 4–7–429. An early account of the philosophy of dialogue is John Culberg's *Das Du und die Wirklichheit: Zum ontologischen Hintergrund der Gemeinschaftskategorie* (Uppsala, Sweden: Lundequistska, 1933). See also Bernard Casper, *Das dialogische Denken: Eine Untersuchung der religionsphilosophischen Bedeutung Franz Rosenzweigs, Ferdinand Ebers und Martin Bubers* (Freiburg, W. Ger.: Herder, 1967); and Gerhard Bauer, *Zur Poetic des Dialogos* (Darmstadt, W. Ger.: Wissenschaftlichebuchgesellschaft, 1969). An early work on the interhuman which is not simply a dialogue approach is Karl Löwith, *Das Individuum in der Rolle des Mitmenschen* (Darmstadt, W. Ger.: Wissenschaftlichebuchgesellschaft, 1928). For the experience of the "we" see Fritz Kunkel, *Das Wir: Die Grundbegriffe der Wir-psychologie* (Konstanz, W. Ger.: Bahn, 1972). An early expression of French personalism is Maurice Nedoncelle's *Reciprocité des Consciences: Essai sur la Nature de la Personne* (Paris: Aubier, 1942).

aware which breaks the order of mere observing or onlooking.[19] Gabriel Marcel thinks human beings are so oriented to the data, problems, and socializations of the sphere of the impersonal with its structure of egocentricity (*ecceity*) that awareness of the interhuman requires a reflective break, a kind of redemption.[20] But the reflective break called forth by the interpersonal must originate in concrete acts of commiseration, empathy, and dialogue. In other words, concrete existing relations mediate our awareness of the interpersonal.

We can discern, however, two quite different emphases among the philosophers of the interpersonal. The one sets its sights on certain acts in which the personhood of the other is present; the other attends to the relation of dialogue and mutuality. The search for the distinctive act in which the other appears as other goes back to Fichte and Hegel. The term both of them used, recognition (*Anerkennung*), gives primacy to the apprehending or knowing consciousness, and this approach continues in Edmund Husserl's description of the transcendental constitution of the other (*Cartesian Meditations,* V). Both Husserl and Max Scheler, the two dominant figures of the early phenomenological movement, ceased to give primacy to the knowing consciousness when they identified empathy as the basic act of human being-together.[21] But it was Scheler who moved the search for the act toward the other onto a new plane by his emphasis on the emotions.[22] For Scheler the other is directly present in such emotional postures as the feeling of sympathy (*Sympathiegefühl*), fellow-feeling (*Mitgefühl*), or community-feeling (*Miteinanderfühlen*). For Scheler it is only when we look beneath the apprehending acts of the intellect to the passions that we find how persons are present directly to each other. When we commiserate with the grief of the other, we are not just speculating about the possible inner workings of another's hypothetical consciousness. And when we are together by way of felt emotions, we are not two exteriorities in objective relation. There is, instead,

19. See Martin Buber, *Between Man and Man,* trans. R. G. Smith (New York: Macmillan, 1948), 10. See also his essay, "Distance and Relation," in *The Knowledge of Man: A Philosophy of the Interhuman,* trans. M. Friedman and R. G. Smith (London: Allen and Unwin, 1965).

20. Gabriel Marcel, *The Mystery of Being,* trans. Rene Hague (London: Harvill Press, 1950), vol. 1, chap. 9, and "The Ego and Its Relation to Others," in *Homo Viator: Introduction to a Metaphysics of Hope,* trans. E. Craufurd (New York: Harper and Row, 1962), 13–28.

21. For Husserl on empathy see Gerd Brand, *Welt, Ich und Zeit.* An interesting study of empathy is Edith Stein's doctoral dissertation written under the influence of both Husserl and Scheler, *On the Problem of Empathy,* trans. W. Stein (The Hague, Netherlands: Nijhoff, 1964).

22. Max Scheler, *The Nature of Sympathy,* trans. Peter Heath (London: Routledge and Kegan Paul, 1954), esp. chap. 2. For a description and criticism of Scheler's views, see Alfred Schutz, "Scheler's Theory of the Intersubjectivity and the General Thesis of the Alter Ego," in *Collected Papers,* vol. 1; also, Herbert Speigelberg's chapter on Scheler in his *The Phenomenological Movement,* 2 vols., 2nd ed. (The Hague, Netherlands: Nijhoff, 1969), vol. 1, chap. 5.

a genuine emotional participation in what makes the other, which is not just the perceiving of bodily acts and gestures.

At times Scheler carries this perceptual approach to the experience of the other so far as to say there is a kind of merger of two streams of experience which collapses the distinction of I and other.[23] This extreme version of direct perception and participation becomes self-contradictory when it claims both a genuine other and a merger that erases that otherness. But Scheler's extreme formulation of emotional participation need not discredit his basic point that human beings experience each other in immediate ways. This need not mean that we experience the other in the exact same mode in which we experience ourselves. It rather says that we are not so distanced from the other that all we grasp in immediate ways is a bodily facade or external behavior. Gabriel Marcel and others have rightly argued that the body of the other is never a mere corpse or external automaton but is a living, manifesting, expressing, and communicating reality. The possibility that the other can deceive us about its emotions or thoughts may be evidence for its irreducible alterity but it is not evidence for an utterly unmanifest personhood hiding inside a bodily machine. The accomplishment of Scheler and his lineage was to show how human beings are "available" (to use Marcel's term) to each other at the level of participative emotions.

The other emphasis in the literature of the interpersonal focuses not on the act or posture (recognition, empathy, availability) in which the other is present but on the mystery of personal encounter and dialogue. This is the line from Martin Buber to Emmanuel Levinas. The philosophers of dialogue explicate the interpersonal, but they differ from Scheler's emphasis in two respects. First, their fascination is not with the specific acts that yield the reality of the other but with the mystery of that yielding itself, the mystery of the thou. This is the theme of Buber's semi-poetic *I and Thou* and also the theme of the "face" (*visage*) in Levinas. Face articulates neither physiognomy (the plane of sensibility) nor acts which emotionally feel the other. It is the "infinitely strange" and mysterious presence of something which contests my projecting meanings of it, an unforeseeable depth which can evoke the act of murder but which cannot be cognitively or emotionally mastered.[24] Second, the theme of dialogue is about what

23. According to Scheler, "Our claim is, rather, that so far as concerns the act and its nature and the range of facts appearing within it, everyone can apprehend the experience of his fellowmen just as directly (or indirectly) as he can his own," *The Nature of Sympathy*, 256.

24. For the theme of the face in Levinas, see his "Signification and Meaning," in *Philosophical Papers*, trans. Alphonso Lingis (Dordrecht, Netherlands: Kluwer Academic Pub., 1987); *Totality and Infinity: An Essay on Exteriority*, trans. A. Lingis (Pittsburgh: Duquesne University Press, 1969), 187–220; and *Ethics and Infinity*, trans. R. A. Cohen (Pittsburgh: Duquesne University Press, 1985), chaps. 7 and 8. See also Thomas W. Ogletree, *Hospitality to the Stranger: Dimensions of Moral Understanding* (Philadelphia: Fortress, 1985), 45–51.

happens when the irreducible reality of thous occurs in ongoing mutual relation (*Gegenseitigkeit*). Dialogal philosophies focus their attention on the vicissitudes of the dialogal relation and the effect of that relation on everything from primal awareness to language.

Alterity, intersubjectivity, and the interpersonal describe three approaches to the interhuman. They also describe basic and interdependent elements of the interhuman. Hence, any comprehensive account of the interhuman must incorporate all three. Without alterity, the uncloseable distance between I and other, there is neither a structural intersubjectivity nor an interpersonal act and relation. Intersubjectivity, the always already givenness of the other that constitutes the very being of agents, is presupposed by interpersonal relation and dialogue. This givenness of being with others is not a cause or explanation of the interpersonal but a condition apart from which recognition, empathy, dialogue, and relation could never occur. Unless the human being is already drawn out of itself and conditioned by the other, it is incapable not only of availability (Marcel), encounter, and empathy but even of de-personalized and manipulating relations. Yet in its own way, the interpersonal is necessary to alterity and intersubjectivity. If mutual emotional participation and dialogue never occur, human beings will not really experience the distinctive otherness of the other. Further, all three aspects taken together show that the interhuman is neither a timeless essence of "human nature" nor a mere possibility. The interhuman is both a givenness and a task, and this is what has evoked analysis both of its givenness (Husserl, Heidegger, Maurice Merleau-Ponty) and of its task (Buber, Marcel, Levinas). Hence, like other spheres of human reality, the interhuman describes something human beings approximate, desire, forget, realize, or even try to suppress or abandon.

COMPASSION AND OBLIGATION

The interhuman bespeaks the mystery and depth of human reality. At the same time, the triad of alterity, the intersubjective, and the interpersonal is as such somewhat formal. Thus, the same philosophers who depicted the experience of the objectifying gaze, the being-with of Dasein, and the face have discerned in these things elements of the tragic and of the ethical. In other words the interhuman also bespeaks a problematic condition. If this triadic sphere had no such elements, theology would have little need to refer to the interhuman except as a formal condition of the ecclesial community. The interhuman is a necessary part of a theological vision of the human condition because it has to do with a distinctive way human beings are vulnerable and because it is part of what human evil corrupts and redemption transforms.

There are ways of interpreting the interhuman that preempt the tragic and the ethical. For instance, if the interhuman arises simply with the question of knowing whether there are other minds, it is reduced to a cognitive relation. This way of posing the question restricts the answer or solution to the level of knowledge. Thus, empathy, encounter, dialogue, being-with are all subsumed under the question of how we know an other exists. That there is a cognitive element in these acts need not be disputed. But cognitive acts and postures are not the heart of the interhuman. To make them so obscures the interhuman's primary offspring, obligation and compassion. A second approach which preempts the tragic and the ethical takes its start from the everyday world of social relations and posits need and utility as the heart of the interhuman. That is, the interhuman arises from and is based on a sensed usefulness of the other. Our everyday world negotiations show us that the other is like ourselves: needy, unpredictable, self-oriented, and dangerous. Thus, relations between others are negotiations of self-interests about power, status, and use. Both approaches distort the interhuman by suppressing the triad of elements which comprise it. And apart from alterity, the intersubjective, and the interpersonal, the tragic and ethical dimensions of the interhuman will remain hidden.

What actually occurs when human beings share emotions or engage in dialogue? Levinas, Marcel, and others contend that something happens in human being-together which is not just negotiating agendas or calculating how self-interests might be met. Something is going on that is irreducible to the negotiations of power and status. Levinas's thesis is somewhat startling. When we experience the face of the other, or when the face occurs in conjunction with being-together, we experience a summons, an invocation (Marcel), a claim, a call to commitment and responsibility. This primordial summons is the basis of the values in the normative culture: the normative culture is not the basis of the summons. What constitutes this summons? The following account is both an explication and a restatement of Levinas's theme of the face in terms of compassionate obligation. The summons from the other is something that evokes a response in which compassion and obligation converge. For purposes of exposition, I shall momentarily separate these two motifs from what is essentially a single act.

Compassion

Why does the face evoke compassion? We recall that the negative meaning of alterity is the impossibility of merging the immediate experiencings of human persons. Alterity is experienced when I experience the other's gaze, an interpretation of my being from a perspective and location not my own (Jean-Paul Sartre). But this has a counter side. I experience alterity when I experience the other's resistance to and contesting of my interpretation of her or him. Alterity, then, is not just the experience of the cognitive elusiveness of the other but a reciprocity of autonomies. Thus, human beings together are mutual interlocutors (Levinas). But this clash of resistances and contestings is at the same time a co-disclosure of fragility.[25] I experience the other as not only centered and autonomous but as fragile before my interpretations and actions even as I experience my own autonomy as fragile to the interpretations and actions of the other. As faces we human beings experience being exposed to and subject to each other's world. This is why this mutually discerned fragility refers not just to the other's physical contour, the other's body which can be injured, but to the other's personal being which can be objectified, disapproved, assessed, insulted, violated in a variety of ways, and murdered.[26]

What does this co-discerned fragility have to do with compassion? If the mutual discernment of fragility were the recording of a fact, as it would be in the cognitively oriented other minds view, then discerned fragility and compassion have no connection. But the sphere of the face is the sphere of empathy and emotional participation. In this sphere one can not respond to the face of the other as if it were a mere externality, a thing, or an artifact. We do not first cognitively grasp the other as fact and object and then infer its autonomy and fragility. The sphere of the face is the sphere of emotional participation, and the discernment of the other is an emotional discernment. And because what is discerned is the other's fragility or what Levinas calls its destituteness and nakedness, the other is experienced as a summons to compassion. It is important to remember that we are exploring here the summons invoked by the face and not compassion itself. But our exploration would miss the mark if we confused compassion with acts that are dominated by the ego's needs, for instance, pity. Genuine compassion is directed past or through the suffering that calls forth pity and attaches to the other itself in its fragile and destitute undergoing of that suffering. The summons then is an invitation to transcend self-preoccupation.

Obligation

The face is also a summons to felt obligation. That which distinguishes compassion from pity, namely being drawn toward the other's fragility, is also what gives the summons the character of felt obligation. When we are summoned by the face, we are alerted to the objective predicament of the other. This would be the attitude of charity in the cold-blooded sense of a

25. I have taken this term from Paul Ricoeur's *Fallible Man*, trans. Charles Kelbley (Chicago: Henry Regnery Company, 1965).

26. For themes of the vulnerability of personal being, see Ricoeur, *Fallible Man*, chap. 4.

self-serving act. Being summoned by the fragility of the other not only evokes a suffering-with (compassion) but also a suffering-for (obligation). Obligation is a posture or disposition that comes into being as a hearing and felt response to the summons of the face. As the disposition to join with the other in her or his fragile struggles against whatever threatens and violates, obligation is on behalf of. As the compassionate disposition directed to the other in its fragility, it is obligation-toward. But concretely and actually, there is only one posture evoked by the summons, compassionate obligation.

The face occurs in the sphere of the interhuman as that which summons to compassionate obligation. It is not, however, a feature or essence of that sphere. And because it is not, we human beings respond to the summons in a variety of ways. We may respond in postures of compassionate obligation. We may also reject the summons in dispositions of cruelty and malice. However, even in these responses, the face and the summons are present. For cruelty and even murder (as Levinas has argued) are possible only with the discernment of the fragile and summoning other.

INTERHUMAN VULNERABILITY

Vulnerability is the capacity of a living creature to undergo harm. Harm means both the frustration of the needs and desires of that creature and the pain and suffering that accompany that frustration. Each of the spheres of human reality has its own special vulnerability. As are living animals, we are organically and biologically vulnerable. As personal beings we can experience distinctive sorts of violations (insults, humiliations). Human being-together or interpersonal relation engenders two quite distinctive vulnerabilities: interpersonal suffering and benign alienation. These vulnerabilities arise in connection with our empathetic and emotional life and with the summons of the face to compassionate obligation. Accordingly, the vulnerabilities of the interhuman are not timeless essences but occur in the types, degrees, levels, and situations of human intimacy.

Interpersonal Suffering

Our subject is not actual human suffering in all of its types and complexities but the vulnerability to suffering as it occurs in the sphere of the interhuman. Interpersonal suffering occurs in two primary forms: the suffering that comes from commiseration with the other's suffering; and, the suffering that occurs when interpersonal relations themselves are wounded. We are able to suffer on account of the sufferings of the other because of the summons of the face to compassionate obligation. If we were unable to emotionally discern the other's inherent fragility, we would not be able to suffer over the sufferings of the other. The face plunges us into the sphere of the fragile other, the other who like ourselves is interpreted, subjected to another's framework, and subjected to an environment. Summoned by the face, we emotionally participate in the woundedness at the heart of the other. And this emotional discernment of and participation in the other's fragility makes human beings vulnerable to each other's sufferings. This is why suffering, because of the sufferings of the other, is not just the egocentric projection of what it would be like to undergo the other's misfortune. In that act, the face has not yet appeared.

A second form of interpersonal suffering occurs in conjunction with deep and enduring interpersonal relations. These relations all show the marks of the face and compassionate obligation. Respect, commitment, loyalty, affection, and love are the familiar examples. Sometimes they converge in certain types of enduring relations such as friendship, erotic love, and collegiality. These relations are neither *a priori* to the interhuman nor absent from it. It is clear that they are diminished or distorted by anything that diminishes empathy, the interpersonal, or the face. Two things about these relations make us liable to a distinctive type of suffering. First, the relations themselves are fragile, some more than others. They are subject to the vicissitudes of human society, personality, body, and physical environment. The loved parent can sicken and die. Lovers can quarrel and part. Second, the being and identity of human agents becomes defined by these relations. Their tone is one of passion and concern, not indifference and callousness. Even relations of enmity and apparent indifference can foster deep interdependencies. The interdependencies of some relations reflect deep biological and psychological needs. Furthermore, human beings are not objective entities external to their relations but are constituted by their relations. But interdependent relations are neither quantities nor categories. We human beings can live in patterns of independence, distancing ourselves from all intimacies, and when we do, we reduce our interpersonal vulnerabilities. And insofar as we passionately and empathically live in enduring, intimate relations, so we are vulnerable to the intense suffering that comes with their cessation or wounding.

Benign Alienation

Malignant alienation is a corruption of the interhuman that arises in connection with the dynamics of evil (chap. 14). Benign alienation is an intrinsic and tragic element of the interhuman.[27] Two well-known but

27. The terms, benign and malignant, come from Erich Fromm's distinction between benign and malignant aggression. See *The Anatomy of Human Destructiveness* (New York: Holt, Rinehart and Winston, 1973), chaps. 9–13.

quite opposite views of what we are up against either ignore or distort benign alienation. Some kinds of Christian piety and theology foster the view that benign alienation has no existence because human reality is essentially good. An opposing view interprets human being together as intrinsically evil, a relation of enmity and mutual destruction. Neither the rosy world of certain Victorian novels nor the "hell is other people" of Sartre's play express benign alienation.

The first view, a kind of sentimentalism, overlooks the effect that human self-initiation and autonomy have on the interhuman. What is that effect? Let us recall that alterity is intrinsic to the interhuman. Alterity means the uninterchangeability of individual experiencings and selves and the resistance and contesting of mutual interlocutors. Thus, the other is experienced as one who is in the world alongside me but who contests my version of it and pursues his or her own aims and agendas. In other words, the other is a center of needs, aims, and practical actions that I cannot possess, occupy, or replace. This means that at the heart of the interhuman is a vast set of incompatibilities that originate in the irreducible otherness of the participants. Incompatibility refers to the impossibility of harmonizing the perspectives, aims, desires, and agendas of self-initiating persons. Accordingly, incompatibility is a structural element in the interhuman.

What has this to do with alienation? Alienation arises between human beings when a benign antipathy of some sort displaces or reduces the summons of the face or distorts the relations that embody obligation. Antipathy can enter into and qualify friendship, sibling affection, and marriage. Hurt feelings, suspiciousness, and accusation are the signs of benign antipathy. The antipathy present in these postures is benign insofar as it does not arise from the dynamics of evil. Manichean or neo-instinctivist views distort and perhaps eliminate benign alienation by confusing it with enmity, malice, and the like. These benign antipathies do not so much reflect the workings of evil as the inescapable incompatibilities in the interhuman. Here we have the parent unable to simultaneously attend to the needs of all the children, the inability of an engaged couple to adjust their career plans to each other, and the impossibility of a firm to appoint all of its qualified people as its Chief Executive Officer. These incompatibilities effect misunderstandings, resentments, and suspected favoritisms, and with these things, benign antipathies. The incompatibility of aims and actions is a feature of the situation of all living things. But because the sphere of the interhuman is also the sphere of personal being, incompatibility is experienced in conjunction with self-understanding, self-valuations, and all the specific sensibilities of persons. Incompatibilities thus are not trivial but introduce antipathies into human interpersonal relations. As personal and self-invested, human beings do not respond dispassionately to displacement and competition. Our interests prompt us to resent, suspect, or accuse those whose aims and efforts are incompatible with ours. Thus, benign alienation and its antipathies is neither a struggle of tooth and claw nor a simple harmony but rather a sign of the finitude of interhuman being-together.

I would conclude this chapter not with a summary but with a new observation. In its own way, the interhuman enters into and makes possible all the other spheres of human reality. This is because all other spheres are ways in which the human life-form experiences reality and negotiates its existence with the world. In the sphere of agents, these negotiations occur in acts of value assessments, granting or withholding beliefs, making cognitive judgments at various levels, cooperating on joint projects, and interpreting to each other the flow of daily events. All of these acts presuppose a shared world. A shared world enables us to assume that the object I perceive is also the object the other perceives, that the person I remember as the president of my college is the same person my classmates remember as president. The hammer I ask for from my co-worker is the same hammer she has been using and hands to me even as the cabinet we are working on is the same cabinet. A consistent and absolute solipsism must deny common objects in a shared world. But it is only with the interhuman that a shared world arises. Thus, correlative with the reality of the interhuman itself is the reality of things and the reality of the world. Because of empathy, the intersubjective, and the interpersonal, the apparent perspectival isolation of human beings is something secondary and derived. The triadic aspects of the interhuman converge and with that convergence comes a shared world. This shared world is partly something given, something that develops with the development of the interhuman itself, and partly a perpetual negotiation and accomplishment. To say that we experience the same things in the same world does not mean a collapse of perspectives into each other or the elimination of the contesting that arises with alterity. No one person's act of perception or valuing is identical with another's. What the interhuman makes possible is a reciprocity of perspectives and a negotiation of differences so that collaboration on projects and the ascertaining of truth and reality are possible.[28] Apart from this discourse and collaboration, the self-interpretations of the individual person, the complex organizations and institutions of society, and even the sciences of life and cosmos would never arise.

28. The phrase, "reciprocity of perspectives," comes from Alfred Schutz. See *Collected Papers,* vol. 1, 11.

2
THE SOCIAL SPHERE

> Society is the form in which the fact of mutual dependence for the sake of life and nothing else assumes public significance and where the activities connected with sheer survival are permitted to appear in public.[1]
>
> *Hannah Arendt*

The interhuman is the sphere of being-together of genuine others in interpersonal relations. Yet, we never experience the interhuman simply in itself. This is because we never experience anything, including the spheres of human reality, in its merely formal or abstracted aspects. We experience the interhuman only in the incidents, interactions, and enduring patterns of life already organized by language, rituals, and institutions. In other words we experience the interhuman only in conjunction with the social. In the previous chapter I contended that the interhuman was primary to the other spheres, that both individual agents and social institutions require it. But in another sense, the social is the primary sphere. The social is the environment that is already present to shape individual agents and interpersonal relations as they come into existence. Accordingly, it constitutes the concrete context or matrix of all agendas, shapes all interpretations and generates all discourses. We human beings know ourselves and our world only through an already formed sociality that contains institutions, languages, customs, and norms. The social is also primary from the perspective of victims of violence and disenfranchisement, desperate for immediate release from victimization. There is no other first order of business.

THE SPHERE OF THE SOCIAL

What do we mean by the social?[2] Empirically speaking, the social is the sphere of specific human interactions plus all of the structures and

1. Hannah Arendt, *The Human Condition* (Chicago: University of Chicago Press, 1958), 46.

2. For a general theory of the social, see Gyorgy Lukacs, *The Ontology of Social Being*, trans. D. Fernbach (London: Merlin Press, 1978).

processes through which they take place. While actual interactions in the present are the observable reality or actuality of the social, sole preoccupation with them misses the very heart of the social. What occurs in actual human transactions? When we live and act in our social environments, we take for granted, make use of, and appeal to a vast complex of things that persist out of our past and into our present. To act in a social environment is to have already internalized a past legacy of customs, procedures, societal laws, values, and roles. From the individual's perspective, the social is a system coming out of the past that mediates values and knowledge and delivers needed resources for present action. And something has functioned to make this system of laws and social roles available to us. To be available for internalization, laws, values, and norms must find units that carry them over time from one generation to another. Societal roles, gender functions, gradations of value, and knowledge must be deposited in vehicles that bridge generations. These vehicles are such things as language, (the primary vehicle of the social), belief systems, institutions, customs, and rituals. If human reality were merely what is contemporary, if all things were ephemeral without continuity and duration, there could be no social. The sediments and vehicles of the social give quasi-permanence to what otherwise would be ephemeral. In this way resources for action are made available across generations. For example, myths, weapon-making lore, food procurement skills, and customs of sexual and reproductive behavior of the various peoples of the Kalahari desert in South Africa are sedimented into corporate memories and institutions so as to be available to the next generation. It is just this generation-bridging, sedimented, and available past that constitutes the Kalahari peoples as a social reality.

By what means does the ephemeral obtain quasi-permanence? How is it that past skills and cognitions become sedimented so that they bridge generations? That which bridges generations are vehicles that are not dependent on the efforts and existence of any one individual. These vehicles arise from the process of institutionalization whose offspring are agreed-upon roles, functions, relations, and acts that organize two or more people in some joint enterprise.[3] The recurring tribal dance,

3. Institutionalization is a broader concept than basic universal institutions. In the standard sociological textbooks, institutions are ". . . purposive, regulatory and consequently primary cultural configurations, formed to satisfy individual wants and social needs." See Joyce O. Herzler, *Social Institutions* (New York: McGraw Hill, 1929), 4. Frequently listed as institutions are family, education, religion, economics, and politics. But institutionalization is the creation of patterns of activity designed to endure through time. Thus, creating a committee or a task force is an institutionalization. Institutionalizations are what Pitrim Sorokin calls vehicles, patterns which enable a group to facilitate its aims,

marriage, and university committees are all examples of institutionalizations. Institutionalizations are agreed-upon ways of organizing social behavior so that values are passed on and aims are pursued and accomplished. Institutionalization is not simply one among many features of the social. As that which carries sedimentations over time, it is the primordial movement that brings the social into existence.[4]

As a generation-bridging patterning that makes various resources available to the present, the social has something to do with human needs. Most elemental are needs which we share with primates and other living animals; needs pertaining to the conditions of life itself such as safety, warmth, and reproduction. Because we are personal and interhuman, our needs and aspirations reach far beyond these elemental needs.[5] For instance, language enables us to symbolize the subtle dangers, beauties, and even possibilities of the world and this symbolization itself calls into being new needs and aspirations. But the relation between human needs and the social is not just a matter of needs engendering social instruments. The social does function to meet both elemental needs and the more subtle aspirations of the personal and the interhuman. But once the sedimentations and institutionalizations of the social are present, human reality takes on an immeasurable, many-layered, and unpredictable complexity that creates new needs and aspirations for play, creativity, invention, and communication. Human needs and the social exist together in a feedback system in which both needs and institutionalizations are ever being newly created. The social, thus, takes on a life of its own. It becomes, in other words, a sphere of human reality. Irreducible to the elemental needs of biological life, it brings into being what some call history.

realize its values, by objectification. See Sorokin, *Society, Culture and Personality: Their Structure and Dynamics* (New York: Harper and Brothers, 1947), chap. 21. According to Peter Berger and Thomas Luckman, "institutionalization occurs whenever there is a reciprocal typification of habitualized actions by types of actors." See *The Structure of the Social World: A Treatise in the Sociology of Knowledge* (Garden City, N.Y.: Doubleday, 1966), 54.

4. Whether the social in the sense being used here is also in the animal world is not easy to determine. Obviously, there is a social behavior of animals and there is continuity between that behavior and human social behavior. Instinct-based social behavior, for instance, the complicated nest building of the weaver bird, would not qualify as the social. Yet in some animal species, social behavior has a learned component. For this to be the social as it is being used in this book, this behavior would have to endure through time in a network of meanings sedimented in language and undergo institutionalization.

5. Ernst Becker argues that self-esteem is the primary and unifying need of human beings, and this is what brings about the complex ritual behavior between persons as they try to adjudicate the sensed mysteries and dangers of their relations. See Ernst Becker, *The Birth and Death of Meaning: A Perspective in Psychiatry and Anthropology* (New York: The Free Press of Glencoe, 1962), chap. 7; and *The Structure of Evil: An Essay on the Unification of the Science of Man* (New York: G. Braziller, 1968), chap. 14.

ELEMENTS OF SOCIAL REALITY

Power

In its concrete existence, the social is a sphere of the workings of power. The social as a sphere of power is evident both to the suffering victims of subjugating power and to those who wield or embody social power. Until the rise of the notion that the social can only be studied or understood in value-neutral postures, power and the corruption of the social was the primary reason for the study of the social.[6] One studied the social in order to change it. According to this strand of the Enlightenment, the social is an actual, contemporary, and problematic reality that calls forth a hermeneutics of suspicion and correction. This reality can be comprehensive (a global ecosystem, a nation) or discrete (the health care of the aging in a small city).

Although the value-neutral approach to the social dominates present-day social sciences, it is not without its challengers. Michel Foucault conducted "archaeological" investigations of social systems having to do with mental illness, health care, crime, and sexuality that traced contemporary networks of exploitation to suppressed or forgotten interpretative turns of the past. Herbert Marcuse exposed the way in which powerful institutions of both Western capitalism and Soviet communism function to disguise the exploitative character of their own systems to produce contentment with servitude, lack of awareness of exploitation, and thus the incapacity to oppose and change.[7] Robert Heilbroner and Jonathan Schell have offered gloomy assessments of the capacity of industrial societies in the nuclear age to reverse the lemming-like march toward ecological and political catastrophe. Many other studies have discovered links between the perils, instabilities, and corruptions of present-day social systems and continuing entrenched racist and patriarchal postures. All of these literatures exemplify what the Frankfurt School calls critical theory, the approach to the social as a concrete, contemporary, and corrupted system of power that sets tasks of social betterment.

The reality of the social is not simply social misery and corrupted power. Misery and oppression can pervade and co-opt the social only

6. Two excellent historical accounts of the turn in social science and philosophy away from the ancient view that practical interests must guide social inquiry to a value-neutral orientation are Richard Bernstein, *The Restructuring of Social and Political Theory* (New York: Harcourt, Brace Jovanovich, 1976), Part IV, "Background"; and E. Becker, *The Structure of Evil*, esp. chap. 4. Becker's account is especially helpful in showing that the original form of positivism, Auguste Comte, is in the Enlightenment tradition which sees the social sciences to be guided by aims for a better society. Thus, value-neutral sociology is a turn away from Comte and positivism.

7. Herbert Marcuse, *One-Dimensional Man: Studies in the Ideology of Advanced Industrial Society* (Boston: Beacon Press, 1964).

because of structures and processes whose functions as such are not to oppress. As the sedimentation and institutionalization of human reality, the social is a complex of characteristic types of corporate entities, functions, relations, and mechanisms. Since the nineteenth century, this complex has been subjected to extensive inquiry by history, sociology, cultural anthropology, political science, economics, and social philosophy. These sciences attempt to understand what is actual and contemporary by grasping what is characteristic, widespread, and repeated. One need not posit timeless essences to apprehend the characteristic cultural and societal differences between an Islamic village in the Arabian desert and a small town in mid-America. Furthermore, because it is just these characteristic structures and processes that are operative in social evil (subjugation), analyses of specific sociopolitical situations under agendas of change can not avoid making use of these inquiries into the characteristic structures and dynamics of social systems.

Society

It goes without saying that these structures and dynamics are attached to specific and self-sufficient social entities or units. The most inclusive social entity is a *society*.[8] Societies are social organizations which are more or less responsible for themselves and which do not depend on some larger self-sufficient unit. Further, a society is the social entity on which a number of subsystems and smaller organizations depend. The gatherings of tribes into the Sioux nation and the modern nation of Israel are both societies. Tribes, cities, clubs, and schools are all subgroups or ways of organizing life within a society. Two quite different perspectives and levels of analysis help disclose the workings of societies; society as a social world, and society as a collection of social systems.

The Social World

To understand human beings in the workings of societies is to face a formidable obstacle. The reason is that all social groups combine the open-endedness and mystery of personal agents with sedimented and repeating structures and processes. Accordingly, strong is the temptation to hurdle the obstacle by eliminating what renders society muddy and elusive, the agents whose actions (behaviors, relations, intentions) are the fuel for society's operations. Mimicking the mathematical and physical sciences in their quest for scientific legitimacy, the social sciences have often reduced society to a complex of objects. And the

8. This is Parsons's concept of society, "an empirically self-subsistent social system," which "meets all the essential functional prerequisites from within its own resources." See Parsons, *The Social System* (New York: The Free Press, 1951), 19.

anonymity, impersonality, and distances of the social appear to confirm this narrowing of the social to quantifiable causalities. Quantifying approaches may acknowledge personal agency but only as an isolated and unknowable sphere that has little to do with the understanding of society. Quantification thus perpetrates a new dualism of personal agents (either unknowable or reducible to non-agential laws) and societies. The sphere of social sedimentations is thus a flat world of perceived regularities knowable by statistical inquiry.

Whatever else societies are, they are spheres of human actions and interactions. The entities that make societies work are human agents as they both create and participate in generation-bridging sedimentations and institutionalizations. Thus, social inquiry sets the initial task of grasping how the life of interhuman agents undergoes sedimentation and how agents "construct" a social world.[9] Or, to put it conversely, social inquiry would understand how the deposits and institutions of the social world incorporate the actions of agents. When social sciences ignore this step, they reduce roles, functions, social change, and hierarchies to mere entities, objects, or causes. In other words, the social world, the shared world of agents, is an important aspect of the operations of social systems, and a society includes both the social world of human agents and their social systems.

The world of the social world is not simply the surrounding physical environment but a set of interpretations or constructs of meaning which a human group takes for granted. Thus, the social world of late nineteenth-century Plains Indians is very different from the social world of present-day Pennsylvania Amish. For there to be a social world at all, meanings must be shared and this sharing internalized and taken for granted by members as they interact with each other.[10] To obtain this taken-for-granted status, meanings must be deposited in the life of the group to

9. The major theoreticians of twentieth-century sociology struggle with the agential aspect of the social world. Becker thinks that the social question, "*Die Sociale Frage*," was one of two great intellectual questions of the nineteenth century and consisted of how to relate the two basic components of society, individuals, and the structure that holds them together. Becker, *The Structure of Evil*, 136. The figures who took up this question were Max Weber, Emil Durkheim, Alfred Schutz, Pitrim Sorokin, Talcott Parsons, Georg Simmel, and G. H. Mead. A useful original exploration of the agential "construction" of the social world is Peter Berger and Thomas Luckman, *The Social Construction of Reality: A Treatise in the Sociology of Knowledge* (Garden City, N.Y.: Doubleday and Company, 1967).

10. Alfred Schutz took over the Weberian problem of how acts of meaning found the social world. See his exposition of Weber in *The Phenomenology of the Social World* (Evanston, Ill.: Northwestern University Press, 1967), chap. 4. For his own proposals, see especially "Equality and the Meaning Structure of the Social World," in *Collected Papers*, vol. II, *Studies in Social Theory* (The Hague, Netherlands: Nijhoff, 1964), and "Choosing Among Projects of Action," in *Collected Papers*, vol. III, *Studies in Phenomenological Philosophy* (The Hague, Netherlands: Nijhoff, 1966).

endure over time, and the primary carrier of these deposits of meaning is language. In addition to language, shared meanings are deposited in repeated gestures, face-to-face ceremonies, symbolic acts, and rituals. The reason that shared meanings virtually create the social world is that they attend and constitute the primary acts that form social interactions into a world, namely the acts which Alfred Schutz calls typifications.[11] Only when human agents typify what they experience can they relate to each other through expectations of role, behavior, status, etc. It is through typifications that we recognize friends and enemies, genders, and dangerous situations and deal with these things accordingly. Because typifications are not just external causes but are acts which draw on shared deposits of ideal or general expectations, actual experience can overturn them. Our typifying expectations do undergo constant correction. Thus, even typifications sedimented deep in the structures of a society's corporate memory can be overturned. Accordingly, the social world is not a mere structure but a fluid and open-ended reality in which adaptations and creative responses to new situations engender new shared meanings. Because of this flexibility of changeable meanings and typifications, a society can develop an unfathomable complexity of structures, roles, and functions. Further, flexibility and open-endedness has produced an immense variety of societies with their social worlds and social systems in what we call history.

The deposit of shared meanings especially in the form of typifications is the basis of the other features of a social world; that is, its specific and distinctive way of being temporal and spatial. The *time* of a social world is the distinctive way the corporate memory and institutions preside over the movement from one generation to another.[12] Traditions, formative events, revered leaders, predecessors of all sorts are part of a corporate memory to which social functions of the present refer for guidance. Apart from corporate memory, there can be no culture, no enduring values or criteria, laws, or customs. Social time is not just the inner time, the flow of time, of individuals, but the way in which the group as a whole endures through time. Social space has to do with both place and space. Part of a social world is a people's shared way of understanding

11. For a succinct treatment of typifications, see Schutz's essay, "Common-Sense and Scientific Interpretations of Human Action," in *Collected Papers*, vol. I.

12. On the theme of corporate memory and the temporality of the social world, see Schutz, *The Phenomenology of the Social World*, chap. 4; Sorokin, *Society, Culture and Personality*, 171ff; Margaret Mead, *Continuities in Cultural Evolution* (New Haven, Conn.: Yale University Press, 1964); and Georges Gurvitch, *The Spectrum of Social Time*, trans. Myrtle Korenbaum (Dordrecht, Netherlands: D. Reidel, 1964). See also my summary account of social duration in *Ecclesial Reflection, An Anatomy of Theological Method* (Philadelphia: Fortress Press, 1982), Appendix, "The General Structure of Social Duration."

the places that are safe, the home place, the familiar in contrast to the dangerous, the alien, and the strange.[13] Space in the social world is a way physical territories are meant and typified. In social space territories are meant as possessed, perilous, valued, protected, explored, and the like. This space is neither the objective and mathematical space of astrophysics nor the here-ness of individual experience. It is the shared meaning of how the group is placed in its larger environment. A social world thus has its specific space, the lived space as meant and shared by the participants. In sum, the social world is the deepest stratum of society, the place where the interaction between agents and sedimentations takes place.

Social Systems

If Alfred Schutz and Pitrim Sorokin were two of the great thematizers of the social world, Talcott Parsons and his associates have offered one of the most complex conceptual frameworks for the understanding of social systems.[14] Like Max Weber, Émile Durkheim, and G. H. Mead, Parsons repudiates the positivist and behaviorist suppression of the agential aspect (the sphere of personality) of the social. But the focus of his analysis is on the multiple aspects and operations of social systems. In this section, I shall reformulate and simplify what is essentially Parsons's analysis.

First, let us recall that a society is the inclusive self-sufficient social unit in which exist smaller social units and subsystems. Agents engaged in the construction of the shared social world constitute the basic stratum of any society and the basis of the operations of its social systems. As systems of social interaction, societies are constituted by three interpenetrating elements: face-to-face communities, a variety of functioning subsystems, and culture. Modern societies are usually so large and dispersed that they are not themselves communities. But their actual workings are carried on in communities, that is, in social groupings where common aims are negotiated in face-to-face

13. On the theme of social space as "the world within my reach," see Schutz, *Collected Papers*, vol. I, *The Problem of Social Reality* (The Hague, Netherlands: Nijhoff, 1967), 306–11, 326ff. For social space, see Sorokin, *Sociocultural Causality, Space and Time* (Durham, N.C.: Duke University Press, 1943), chap. 3.

14. The fullest and most important expression of Parsons's conceptual framework is *The Social System*, 1951. He has also written two succinct summaries of this framework. See *Social Systems and the Evolution of Action Theory* (New York: The Free Press, 1977), and *Theories of Society: Foundations of Modern Sociological Theory* (New York: Free Press of Glencoe, 1961), 1, Part 2, "An Outline of the Social System." For expositions of Parsons's theory, see Larry Brownstein, *Talcott Parsons' General Action Scheme* (Cambridge, Mass.: Schenkman, 1982); and Francois Bourrieaud, *The Sociology of Talcott Parsons*, trans. A. Goldhammer (Chicago: University of Chicago Press, 1981).

relations.[15] Not all face-to-face relations are communities. Communities are regional and enduring groupings which provide resources for their members for handling major life situations.[16] These resources are communicated in face-to-face activities and in a solidarity which is to some degree self-conscious. Communities can be religious groups, utopian groups, neighborhoods, tribes, towns, and villages. Throughout most human history, communities are the primary groups of societies. The *polis* was the primary community of ancient Greek society. The nuclear family is like a community, but it tends also to be a sub-community within larger communities. However, the brave new world of advanced industrial society seems to be producing sub-groupings whose interactions do not have the character of communities. In these groupings, something comprehensive and anonymous rather than face-to-face solidarity delivers the resources for living.

Second, all societies have subsystems of human interaction which have specific functions but which are not discrete communities.[17] Many of these functions build on but go far beyond human needs of survival and well-being. The general function of a society, the comprehensive and relatively self-sufficient social system, is to organize the resources and activities of its members for certain benefits, for instance, defense, mutual assistance, and the ordering of social life. Hence, all societies have over-all aims and sponsor subsystems whose function is to help realize those aims. The *political* subsystem is organized to maintain the society as a whole, and thus functions to secure the society against both external (war, defense) and internal (law-enforcement systems) threats. The *eco-*

15. It is important not to confuse face-to-face relations with Levinas's concept of the face. Face-to-face relations are enduring and more or less immediate interactions between persons. The face is the summons to compassionate obligation that a specific face-to-face relation may ignore, exploit in the form of cruelty, or realize in acts of kindness and concern. For detailed studies of face-to-face relations, see Erving Goffman, *Encounters: Two Studies in the Sociology of Interaction* (Indianapolis, Ind.: Bobbs-Merrill, 1961), and, *The Presentation of the Self in Everyday Life* (Garden City, N.Y.: Anchor Books, 1959). In this second work, Goffman defines face-to-face interaction as "the reciprocal influence of individuals upon one another's actions when in one another's immediate presence," 15.

16. This description of communities is within the line of Ferdinand Tönnies's distinction between two kinds of human association, communities (*Gemeinschaften*) and societies (*Gesellschaften*). Communities reflect what he calls the natural will, that is, human life as it takes place in primary emotions and actions. House, village, and town are his primary examples of communities, and these contrast to the city and units of national life that serve human planning and fabrication. See Ferdinand Tönnies, *Community and Association*, trans. C. Loomis (London: Routledge and Kegan Paul, 1955), 17.

17. For the concept, subsystems, see Parsons, *The Social System*, chap. 3. In addition see Émile Durkheim, *On the Division of Labor in Society*, trans. G. Simpson (New York: Free Press of Glencoe, 1933). For a description of the progressive differentiation of a society into subsystems, see also Wolfhart Pannenberg, *Anthropology in Theological Perspective*, trans. M. J. O'Connell (Philadelphia: Westminster Press, 1985), 414, n. 20.

nomic subsystem is concerned with the procurement and allocation of food and other life-benefiting resources. Examples of this subsystem range from the hunting, gathering, and farming of preindustrial societies to the production, marketing, and money exchange of modern societies. The *reproductive* subsystem creates a variety of patterns (e.g., the nuclear or extended family, gender relations, and roles) which order sexuality, birth, infant growth, and youth maturation. And each of these subsystems generates hierarchies of leaders and a multiplicity of designated roles and tasks. Each of them functions both to maintain the society's equilibrium and to help it adapt to internal change and external challenge.

Third, every society has a system of culture.[18] In popular parlance, the term, *culture,* is sometimes used for a societal entity. But social scientists are more or less agreed that culture describes that aspect of a social system or society which gives it its sense of direction, which carries its values through a deposit of symbols. Culture, in other words, describes the traditions that govern beliefs and behavior, the "shared ways of believing, doing, evaluating."[19] Culture, too, is borne by subsystems and institutional vehicles whose function is to legitimate, maintain, and transmit the traditions involved. Thus, religion, education, and the arts are major spheres and vehicles of culture. These institutions sediment society's deepest values and convictions about what is real, true, important, good, experienceable, beautiful, and knowable. Carrying these sedimentations are the society's comprehensive myths, stories, heroic legends, and primary symbols. Communities, functioning subsystems, and culture have both structural and dynamic aspects. That is to say, they are both persisting patterns that organize and regulate human life and processes that are constantly changing, adapting, and responding.

SOCIAL VULNERABILITY

Distinctive ways human beings are vulnerable arise in each of the spheres of human reality. Agents are vulnerable to physical injury, disease, death, and to humiliation and insult. Interhuman relations are vulnerable to demise, change, and wounding. The social, too, carries with it a distinctive vulnerability. The social world and social systems introduce

18. Definitions of culture vary widely in sociology and cultural anthropology. There does appear to be a consensus that the term, culture, should not be used as another term for society. Instead of designating social units, it is more a term for the guiding ideas, values, and belief-systems of a society. In Parsons's view, culture is the normative aspect of a social system, the definer and bearer of roles, values, beliefs, and the like. For an extensive listing and study of the many definitions of culture, see A. L. Kroeber and C. Kluckohn, *Culture: A Critical Review of Concepts and Definitions* (Millwood, N.Y.: Kraus Reprint Co., 1978).

19. Marc J. Swartz and David K. Jordan, *Anthropology: Perspective on Humanity* (New York: Wiley, 1976), 3.

into human life a vast complex of possibilities, situations, and incompatibilities. Vulnerability itself means an entity's capacity of being damaged, distorted, or even eliminated. Its realization is always some kind of suffering. The absolute vulnerability of any living thing is the vulnerability to death. Two types of vulnerability arise in connection with the social: social incompatibility, and, social suffering.

Social Incompatibility

Social incompatibility, not to be confused with evil and oppression, names the intrinsic conflicts and tensions that constitute the very reality of the social. It has two basic forms. The first form is the structural incompatibility between the social itself and its participating agents. Sigmund Freud has provided us with the classic account of this incompatibility and continental philosophers such as Sartre, Heidegger, Marcel, and Buber have offered a variety of emendations. This incompatibility is the alienation between the social and self-presencing, autonomous individuals. This alienation is not between individuals nor between groups but between individual agents and their own external social facticity. We recall that the social is a sedimented world of patterns, symbols, and processes that endures through time. As something always already there, it functions to shape, limit, regulate, and sometimes threaten the individual. It makes external and heteronomous claims on the individual from the day of birth and throughout life. Its demand and claim is not presented in the personalized form of the face (evoking compassionate obligation) but as something which does not take into account the individual's open-ended and self-initiating being.

In Freud's version, this alienation occurs as a conflict between the repressive requirements of the social and biologically originated instincts and desires.[20] Instincts and desires are the raw materials of the human infant which the social must tame in order to incorporate it into the family and society. In this taming, instincts and desires are forced to adapt to external regulations which cripple "the ego's theoretically limitless organizational expansion from the very beginning of the child's experience."[21] The very existence of the social effects repression in

20. Freud's theory of alienation in the form of the repressive effect of society on instincts can be found in *The Future of an Illusion,* trans. W. D. Robson-Scott (New York: Liveright, 1953), and *Civilization and Its Discontents,* trans. J. Strachey (New York: W. W. Norton, 1962). For an exposition of the Freudian view, see Ernst Becker, *The Birth and Death of Meaning: Perspective in Psychiatry and Anthropology* (New York: Free Press of Glencoe, 1962), chap. 6; Herbert Marcuse, *Eros and Civilization: A Philosophical Inquiry into Freud* (Boston: Beacon Press, 1955); and Jeffrey Abramson, *Liberation and Its Limits: The Moral and Political Thought of Sigmund Freud* (New York: The Free Press, 1984).

21. Becker, *The Birth and Death of Meaning,* 56.

instinct-driven agents and the result is neurosis. Neurosis is the price human beings pay for the ordering benefits of society.

Continental philosophies of the personal, the existential, and the dialogal do not begin with the biology of instincts and desires but with the irreducible mystery of the individual person and the interpersonal. Here occurs a chasm between the self-determining and open-ended subject or subjects together in relation and the impersonal world of collectivity. These philosophers describe this chasm in a rhetoric of oppositions: subjective existence and the crowd (Kierkegaard), the for-itself and the practico-inert (Sartre), *Dasein* and the "they" (Heidegger), human spirit and the "they" (Nicolas Berdyaev), togetherness and socialization (Marcel). This alienation is not just the effect of the repression of desires by the social-external but an incompatibility of spheres and the luring of the personal away from itself into the sphere of anonymity and the impersonal. What the Freudian and the continental philosophical versions of alienation have in common is an insight into the incompatibility between the life and agendas of the individual and the requirements of the social.

The second form of social incompatibility is not between agents and the social but pertains to the incompatibilities and competitions unavoidable to the workings of social systems. Let us recall that the interhuman is structured by benign alienations and antipathies. In actual situations, these benign alienations become sedimented into enduring social structures, are symbolized in culture, and are carried by institutions. Incompatibilities and conflicts abound in the sphere of the social which are not just between the aims and agendas of individuals but between the groups which individuals form. As a relatively self-sufficient and comprehensive entity, a society tries to harmonize the aims and functions of its subgroups. In some sense, religious communities, industries, and book clubs may help stabilize and enrich their society. However, none of these things can make these contributions without being granted some autonomy and the result is that the groups, communities, and subsystems of a society take on a life of their own. This means that each group presses agendas that compete with the agendas of other groups. Each relatively autonomous group works on behalf of its own survival, efficacy, and well-being. It works to perpetuate the conditions of its own growth and to expand the scope of its influence. Accordingly, in our society, schools, churches, governmental agencies, sports, and environment groups all compete for the society's distribution of resources.

A society thus is made up of groups whose aims and competitive striving are incompatible. Incompatibilities and competitions between groups (e.g., families, tribes, genders) occur in the preindustrial peoples.

They are vastly extended in advanced industrial societies which must find ways to distribute limited resources, assign tasks for the maintenance and betterment of its quality of life, arrive at processes of governance, and adjudicate levels of privilege which the range of human talents produces. Some societal tasks are relatively easy and require less skill and ability than others, hence, the distribution of tasks produces levels of status and with that levels of privilege. These tasks include systems of defense, internal systems of protection against crime, and systems of production and education, all of which need designated leaders with their respective status and privileges. The result is the stratification of society into self-conscious groups in competition with each other: proletariat, bourgeoisie, and aristocracy; or blue-collar workers and professionals; or law enforcement people, government bureaucrats, military personnel, and clergy; or recent migrants and non-migrants; or adolescents, the middle-aged, and the elderly.[22] Each quasi-autonomous and self-conscious constituency develops a rationale for receiving its part of the society's offerings, but the society cannot respond equally to all of these appeals. It can only partially adjudicate and harmonize these claims. No society can allocate 50% of its resources to defense, 50% to education, 50% to cultural and aesthetic subsystems, and 50% to waste management and the saving of the environment. But the quasi-autonomous subsystems pursue their quite legitimate aims and become hungry maws with insatiable appetites. And although antipathies and resentments inevitably attend these conflicts arising from social incompatibility, social incompatibility as such is not evil. Rather, it bespeaks the intrinsic finitude and tragic structure of the social.

Suffering and the Social

Each of the spheres of human reality is the occasion for distinctive kinds of suffering. Human agents suffer bodily pain, psychological anguish, and interpersonal griefs. In human individuals, suffering is never a mere neurological stimulation but an interpretive response to the assaults and frustrations of life situations. The memories and anticipations of agents add a whole dimension to suffering, bringing it forward from the past as something to dread in the future. The social sphere takes

22. I do not intend to revive the old *laissez faire* theory that society is fatefully and essentially structured by the range of individual giftedness implying that the role of governance is to maintain that natural structure. My point is that differentiations of roles and tasks which differ from each other in complexity, danger, or challenge cannot occur without some attending differentiation of status and privilege. Status, thus, is inevitable to a segmented and differentiated society. This in no way implies that distributions of roles and status are a freezing of individuals into strata or a freezing of the strata themselves.

suffering onto a new plane in at least four ways: thematic sedimentation, expansion of the occasions of suffering, social alienation, and social evil. Further, it is the sphere of the social where human suffering is thematized in the ethos, world-views, and symbols of society.

First, the social institutionalizes human experience into available deposits of values, roles, and the like. Accordingly, our various types of suffering are sedimented in the society's corporate memory. Suffering finds enduring expression in basic metaphors. Through the centuries, leprosy, tuberculosis, and cancer have become complex symbols for both social status and our mortal condition.[23] Thus, in human social worlds of shared meanings, suffering can be heroic, trivial, meaningless, or repressed. It can also be an instrument of political exploitation and interrelational manipulation. Thus, in the sphere of the social, suffering becomes reified, thematized, and symbolized into the corporate memory and as such is passed from generation to generation.

Second, the social introduces levels of human experience that carry with them their own specific vulnerabilities to suffering. The social, we recall, includes both the social world and social systems. It is the sphere of shared meaning, group convictions, home-worlds, typifications, and roles. It is through these things that human agents take on complex and nuanced identities that reflect their various group participations. Group participation also evokes passionate loyalties to causes, people, and groups. And with these nuanced identities and passionate attachments come new possibilities of suffering. For in the clash of social incompatibilities, identities are threatened and loyalties go unrewarded. Further, as institutions fail or decline and as symbol systems are discredited or change, human beings suffer to the degree that they have been defined by them.

Third, social incompatibility expands the field of suffering. To participate in a social group is to be part of its incompatibilities and competitions. And most human beings participate in a variety of groups and social systems. Caught in the clashes and competitions of groups, we suffer by experiencing various antipathies directed toward us. Finally, social evil introduces the most intense and utterly dehumanizing suffering which history has known. Subjugation or oppression is the distinctive form of social evil and the suffering it promotes are forms of victimization. This suffering includes but does not stop with physical injury, confinement, and death. The victims of subjugation experience deprivations of humanness, rights, and the face. Because subjugation nihilates the human agent in all its dimensions, it perpetrates the deepest and most extensive kind of human suffering.

23. Cancer as a metaphor is the theme of Susan Sontag's book, *Illness as Metaphor* (New York: Farrar, Straus and Giroux, 1978).

A CRITIQUE OF SOCIAL MANICHEANISM

I have argued in this chapter that distinctive vulnerabilities to suffering arise with the sphere of the social because of intrinsic social incompatibilities and social oppression. Accordingly, it is tempting to adopt the Manichean notion that the social is itself the Fall. *Manicheanism,* the view that what makes a mundane entity real is also what makes it evil, has been a recurring tendency in philosophy and religion. A biological Manicheanism traces the origin of evil to our phylogenetic heritage, our primate instincts. For ego-self Manicheanism, evil is the very fact and act of individual consciousness. There is even a gender Manicheanism which suspects that evil originated in that distant turn of evolution that brought males into existence. For social Manicheanism, the very fact and existence of social sedimentation and institutionalization is evil. The social and oppression are identical concepts. Few writers explicitly argue that the social is evil or the origin of evil. But many show tendencies toward social Manichean ways of thinking about the social. Romanticism's critical response to the new industrialism set the tone. Jean Jacques Rousseau's idealization of the primitive state suggests that the social itself is the evil that plagues us. Some Christian pieties locate the good and the salvific in the human heart and thus evil in the collective and the institutional. And we can discern social Manichean tendencies in twentieth-century Continental philosophy, which is not unrelated to the Romantic tradition. Some passages in the writings of Kierkegaard, Buber, Berdyaev, Heidegger, Sartre, Marcel, and Levinas make the social into something that lures the human being away from true reality into conformity, impersonality, and anonymity.[24]

It seems evident that a consistent social Manicheanism is as difficult as a consistent biological or psychological Manicheanism. It retains the incoherence that structures all Manicheanisms, the need to assume as necessary and good the very thing one regards as evil or the origin of evil. All of the goods (pleasures, satisfactions, creativities, joys, dialogues, etc.) that serve as criteria for identifying and defining evil require and presuppose the operations of all the spheres of human reality. Because it orders human life through sedimentations and institutionalizations, the social is as much the origin and condition of human goods as it is the apparatus for human evil. Why is it not itself evil? If evil means anything which evokes a painful or negative experience, then the social as a sphere of intrinsic

24. In Sartre's late writings, the social is a sphere of the practico-inert, an externality which effaces the individual's praxis and invites it to live its reality as a being-outside-in-the-thing. See his *Critique of Dialectical Reason; Theory of Practical Ensembles,* trans. Alan Sheridan-Smith (London: NLB, 1976), 28.

incompatibilities is evil. However, since anything real can be the cause and occasion of pain, such a notion of evil would also have to identify evil with whatever is actual, a move that removes the basis for distinguishing between evil and good. On the other hand, if we distinguish evil from suffering and benign alienation, it becomes very difficult to establish that the social as such is evil. To make the case, we would have to show that there is something intrinsically evil about the mere fact of sedimentations and institutionalizations, about the shared world of human meanings, and vehicles of corporate memory. But it is evident that the mere fact or process of sedimentations, shared meanings, and institutions is not a fact or process of subjugation. Subjugation needs these things for its workings, but it is itself not these things. This inability to identify the constitutive reality of the social with evil is repeated in biological Manicheanism when it fails to discover the dynamics of evil simply in the operations of the brain or the organically-based drives. However oppressive are the actual social powers of human history, the essential function of corporate memory, institutions, and social subsystems is not to oppress.

Human history attests to the stubborn and pervasive facticity of evil. It also attests that evil is not a mere fate, an ontological necessity, or an incurable disease. The fatefulness of evil is a myth which contributes to and legitimates the entrenchment of social evil and discourages resistance to it. The challenge and even reversal of social evil is possible only because the social is not evil in itself but is always that which evil appropriates and corrupts. Thus, the sphere of the social is not simply a sphere of vulnerability to suffering and evil. It is also the sphere that delivers to human beings their past. And because it does this, it makes possible the enriched worlds of aesthetics, of scientific and cognitive accomplishments. It is because of the social that we human beings experience the world in its complexity, beauty, mystery, and resourcefulness. This is why Maurice Blondel argues that there is an aspiration for the social. Collaborations and co-actions are necessary if we are to have adequate nourishment, safety, medical treatments, and symphony orchestras.[25] Thus, if evil is an appropriation of the apparatus of the social, redemption is never from but always within the social. Redemption, in other words, is as much political as it is personal and interhuman.

25. See Maurice Blondel, *Action* (1893): *Essay on a Critique of Life and a Science of Practice*, trans. O. Blanchette (Notre Dame, Ind.: University of Notre Dame Press, 1984), Part III, Stage Four, chap. 2.

3

THE PERSONAL SPHERE

> Personality is like nothing else in the world, there is nothing with which it can be compared, nothing which can be placed on a level with it. When a person enters the world, a unique and unrepeatable personality, then the world process is broken into and compelled to change its course, in spite of the fact that outwardly there is no sign of this.[1]
>
> *Nicolas Berdyaev*

The third sphere of human reality is the sphere of embodied, impassioned, and self-transcending individual agents. Human agents have their distinctive complexity and I shall use the metaphor of dimensions to express several very important aspects of this complexity. Personal being (subjectivity, historicity) is no more necessary or intrinsic to human agency than embodiment or elementary passions. However, anthropologies that suppress the personal dimension tend to distort the way the other dimensions and human reality as a whole are understood. I shall, accordingly, begin this exploration of human agency with the dimension of the personal.[2]

THE SELF-PRESENCING CHARACTER OF PERSONAL BEING

We human beings never experience ourselves as initially worldless so that we must search for an environment to occupy or demonstrate that there is a world around us. We experience ourselves from the beginning as part of mundane and interhuman situations. This is why human self-knowledge is always a knowledge of a condition rather than simply of an individual and isolated entity. Yet, we do experience ourselves in our worldly and interhuman environment as personal

1. Nicolas Berdyaev, *Slavery and Freedom*, trans. R. M. French (New York: Charles Scribner's Sons, 1944), 21.

2. The sources for this chapter are too many to list. I am most dependent on the philosophical anthropologies that arose in the wake of Kierkegaard. Major figures in this line are Blondel, Husserl, Max Scheler, Heidegger, Marcel, Sartre, Buber, Michael Polanyi, Ricoeur, Miguel de Unamuno, Merleau-Ponty, and Rahner. Needless to say, these explorations have been conducted under many different rubrics and have promoted a variety of terms. Thus, the personal is articulated as Spirit (*Geist*), subjectivity, Existenz, the for-itself (*pour-soi*), Being-there (*Dasein*), the will, and self-consciousness.

beings. Nor is it the case that our being as personal remains in hiding until it is discovered by a deliberate, reflective philosophical reflection. We human beings are aware of ourselves as personal in the very course of our existence. Turning to this primary self-understanding, we can obtain a preliminary and commonsense meaning of personal being.

First, the human experience of anything has a certain strangeness about it. It is strange because to experience what is over against us may evoke such emotions that we are drawn out of ourselves. But this does not happen in such a way that there is no awareness of those emotions, of being drawn out of the self, of, in other words, the quality of the experiencing. This unfocused, background experience doubled back on itself is what enables us to recall not only the object of our experiences but the pleasure, pain, intensity, significance, in short, the quality of our experiences. In other words, a self-presencing accompanies all of our experiences of what is other.[3] This self-presencing should not be confused with acts which reflect back on and objectify our emotions or responses. Acts of this sort tend to interrupt the normal course of experience by turning the attention from what is other to the quality of experience itself. When we say that we know ourselves as personal, we mean that we are aware of this self-presencing aspect of its experience. Self-presencing is not produced by reflection but is the starting point for any reflective interrogation of personal being.

THE ELUSIVE CHARACTER OF PERSONAL BEING

In spite of this indirect awareness of the quality of our experiencings, our personal being is not readily available to inquiry. Because it is the self-presencing element in all worldly presentations, personal being is not an ordinary worldly reality present to perception and available for demonstration and experimentation. To regard it as an external entity is to abolish it from the start. On the other hand, because of our self-awareness, personal being is not merely an implied or logically derived reality, something utterly outside of experience about which we speculate. Personal being has neither the immediacy of something external nor the mediacy of the implied. In fact it eludes us because it is too immediate. I mean by this that the personal or self-presencing must ignore itself, surpass itself, in order to engage in ordinary world relations. We human beings do not attend

3. Compare the concept of the self-presencing of the agent to Helmuth Plessner's notion of the "exocentric" stance, that is, its capacity to adopt a position toward itself and exist in a self-reflection attitude. *Die Stufen des Organischen und der Mensch: Einleitung in die philosophische Anthropologie* (Berlin: Walter de Gruyter, 1965). Pannenberg draws on Plessner to make the same point; see *Anthropology in Theological Perspective* (Philadelphia: Westminster Press, 1985), 37, 61.

equally to the painting before us and to our own act of enjoying the painting. The awareness is focused on the painting and the enjoying is the quality of that awareness. As such the enjoying is in the background as something there but not attended to. Thus the personal tends to elude sciences whose objects are given to them in acts of focused perception. It calls, instead, for a distinctive kind of reflection aware of and adapted to this elusiveness.[4] This reflection must find a way to consider what our ordinary everyday apprehensions press into the background.

Personal being is also elusive because it does not lend itself to definitions and to the discourse of ideal essences. Personal being does have features that permit description but these features are not timeless predicates shared in an identical way by all actual persons.[5] The features of personal being are modes of existence that occur in degrees. Thus, these features can be reduced, transformed, distorted, strengthened, and disciplined. They are not so much timeless essences as powers of agential action. These powers are formed in biological and social contexts and in the dynamics of self formation. They can be affected by the causalities of history, genetics, oppression, and liberation, yet as features of self-presencing, they are not the mere products of these external causalities. It is because they are variable powers of existence that they have been interpreted throughout history in both descriptive and ideal ways. Philosophical anthropology from Plato to the present contains descriptions of personal being as will, reason, consciousness, memory, and feeling But with only a slight change of agenda, these concepts take on an ideal and normative character. They posit what the human being ought to be when it fulfills itself. When human being is genuinely personal, it is rational, perceptive, sensitive in feeling, not merely subject to its remembered past, and so forth. Thus, the features of personal being describe not just a structure but a task. They take on this ideal or task character because personal being takes shape in the interhuman and worldly activities of everyday life. Tasks are assigned to these powers with their very forming.

THE STRANGE TEMPORALITY OF PERSONAL BEING

We human beings are aware of ourselves as personal in the course of our everyday lives. Yet, we can be aware of perceiving something, for

4. Owen Barfield's *Saving the Appearances* (London: Faber and Faber, 1957) is an example of this kind of reflection.

5. Martin Heidegger struggled with this problem created by the desire to philosophically describe the being of *Dasein* but with the conviction that the contents described are not mere essences or attributes. Under his axiom that the essence of *Dasein* was to exist, he proposed that the features of this existence were not essences but *existentials;* see *Being and Time,* trans. J. Macquarrie and J. Robinson (London: SCM Press, Ltd., 1962), 70–71.

instance, a sofa in our living room, without being aware of the many features of sense perception itself. Awareness of perceiving can evoke further reflections or even physiological investigations. Likewise, self-presencing, the initial way we experience ourselves as personal, invites further reflection. What precisely is this self-awareness that constitutes personal being? What is this strange convergence of focused awareness on what is other and indirect self-awareness?

When reflection turns back to self-awareness itself, it finds first of all something we human beings take for granted. We conduct our everyday activities in the world through quite deliberate ways of attending to or focusing on things. Cooking a meal is comprised of multiple acts of interpretive focusing: retrieving a utensil, deciding about an ingredient, reading a recipe. These specific focusings have the character of "apprehending (x) as"; thus, as skillet, stove, or recipe. Some specific meaning is the content of the "as." This content originates neither solely in the person's subjectivity nor solely in the entity. It is the way the entity occurs as that entity in the specific situation of experiencing it. And this meaning content includes sense features, placement in a setting, functions, pleasurable or displeasurable aspects, and degrees of importance. Is self-presencing, then, this self-aware experiencing of things as meanings? At this point we realize that very few of our experiences of things as meanings or as meaningful result from deliberate acts of trying to mean. Turning to a page in a recipe book appears to be a deliberate act, but that simple act involves a multiplicity of recognitions which are not deliberately or effortfully set in motion. We recognize the book as book, pages as pages, numbers on the pages as numbers, sentences as sentences, etc. without having to initiate a series of deliberate acts for each recognition. A walk through a shopping mall involves an enormous number of passive recognitions of things "as," of people, cars, sales signs, buildings, even if our focused attention is preoccupied with a daydream or by a deliberation on what store to visit next. Human beings, thus, experience the world in the mode of "apprehending (x) as" not just through deliberate effort but through a constant flow of passive recognition. Of what does this passive recognition of meaning consist?

We can recognize only what we have experienced already. Recognition, in other words, requires some retention of past experience. The experience of a thing (x) as a content or meaning has a temporal component. In fact, this experience is itself a kind of temporality or way of being temporal. This being temporal is not the experience "of" time, that is, the duration measured by clocks. It is not, in other words, the experience of things as they change, degenerate, terminate, or become renewed. Neither is it the experience of one's self as engaged in acts of remembering the past or anticipating the future. These deliberate or semi-deliberate acts occur in conjunction with decisions, plannings, interhuman communications, and other ways we are active in the everyday world. Important as they are, the specific acts of remembering and anticipating require a more primordial temporality. Nor is this more primordial temporality the mere succession of contents in a stream of consciousness. What then is it?

In the passive recognition of things as this or that set of contents, both the past and the future come together. In objective time, the time of measured change, future always remains future and past always remains past. But in the strange act of meaning something as, past contents must be retained, brought forward so to speak, to provide the contents or meanings. To experience an entity as this or that is to experience both likeness and unlikeness. It is an unlikeness because to passively recognize a car as a car is not to assert an identity between the recognized car and the various cars of the remembered past. It is a likeness because what makes the as possible is the retained car. In addition, all passive recognition of something as experiences that something not just by remembering former meanings but by retaining or bringing forward into the present what has transpired in past experience, especially the recent and vivid past. Thus the various passive recognitions that accompany stirring a pot of stew are also retentions of having put certain ingredients in the stew, of having put it on the stove, and so forth. The retained past, then, is an aspect of present passive recognition and of deliberate, effortful acts.

But the passive recognition of things as this or that is at the same time an orientation to the future. It is clear that when someone stirs a simmering stew, that person is anticipating a future outcome, the meal to be served, the time when the stew is cooked. Further, the passive recognitions at work when we apprehend the kitchen, the stove, and the people standing by also carry future expectations. For one aspect of the contents or meanings of what is recognized is how they are expected to continue in the future as things which wear out, break, continue as available for use, or available for admiration by others, and so forth. Thus, to use Edmund Husserl's language, to mean things as this or that is also to engage in *protentions* of the future. Note, however, that like the retentions, the protentions or anticipations take place in the present. The present of personal being is, of course, a moving present. But its strangeness is due to the simultaneous coming together of the retained past and the protended future and this happens not as the result of effort but in the passive experience of things as meaningful.[6] And this is

6. The first analysis of this simultaneous convergence of the passively retained past and protended future into a moving presence is probably that of Edmund Husserl's lectures on internal time-consciousness edited and published by Heidegger in 1928. See Edmund Husserl, *The Phenomenology of Internal Time-Consciousness*, trans. James Churchill (Bloomington, Ind.: Indiana University Press, 1964).

what reflection discloses as personal being or self-presencing in its most formal sense. To summarize, self-awareness is the strange conjunction of retention and protention in present passive recognitions of the meanings of things.

DETERMINACY AND TRANSCENDENCE

The simultaneous convergence of retention and protention into the ever-moving present is the most formal meaning of human temporality. And it is this temporality which provides the basis for some things we human beings treasure the most about ourselves, our determinacy and our transcendence.

Determinacy

The theme of determinacy moves the description of personal being or self-awareness in the direction of the concrete. Meaning things *as* and the synthesis of past and future in the present are themes in a very formal account of personal being. When we move toward a more concrete description, we discover that self-awareness is a paradoxical combination of determinacy and transcendence. To say that the human present is a flow of past retentions and future anticipations is a very abstract statement. The passive recognitions and acts of meaning which constitute this flow do not simply succeed each other. They shape and structure what we human beings are as selves or persons. Like the experiencings of all living things, human experience has the character of a shaping or forming of being. Through it our being takes on more and more content. As our experiences accumulate over time, we become more and more enriched, complex, and determinate. The passive recognitions, acts of meaning, memorable experiences, and varieties of influences become sedimented, not just as items stored in the memory, but as the self shaped in a determinate way.

The determinacy of personal being is its *being as* or *I-as*. We human beings experience ourselves not simply as abstract receptacles into which the past is poured but *as* man or woman, Asian or African, child or adult, religious or non-religious, and so forth. There is always a specificity to personal being or self-awareness and that which specifies is a shaping over time, an accumulation of personal tastes, technical prowess, everyday life wisdom, traumas, disappointments, and accomplishments. As personal beings we are always the ones who did this, experienced that, feel a certain way about this, are opposed to that. Even if we regret some past act and think of ourselves as no longer like that, we nevertheless remain the ones in whose past that event occurred. Our determinateness or specificity includes our repudiated past. And while most specific events of life may so recede into the background as to be unavailable to recollection, they nevertheless play a part in the accumulative shaping of the human being. The myriad events of childhood accumulate into a specific kind of adolescence. Furthermore, we human beings are not related to our own specificity or I-as in an utterly neutral or indifferent way. We may, of course, repudiate or disvalue certain aspects of what we have become, for instance, being male rather than female or having poor health or insufficient education. But these disvaluings themselves reflect the shaped self, the I-as, the one who, because it is that who, can envision and value different future specificities.

Transcendence

Because human determinacy is a way we human beings are temporal, it is not a mere succession of contents like the changes that occur in the rise and erosion of a mountain range. Our determinacy, our being as this or that, is something we are aware of, and this is a way we mean ourselves and are present to ourselves. But being able to mean ourselves presupposes another feature of our temporality. Our retentions of the past and protentions of the future converge in our living present in the form of meanings. Only by an act of retaining the meaning of a jet airplane coupled with a projection of its typical possible behavior are we able to mean the entity we perceive as a jet airplane. For the most part this act of meaning a thing as x or y occurs spontaneously and does not require deliberation. However, it shows that we do not experience things as mere stimuli but as specifically meant x's or y's. Further, we are aware of this experience or meaning of things as. We are aware that something is x, or possesses or lacks the feature of y. In short, our temporality includes the grasp of elements of possibility in things and situations. And the grasping of the possible brings with it a variety of acts which wrench us loose from preprogrammed responses; acts of deliberation, planning, projections of outcomes, and decisions. We are now ready to describe the second feature of human temporality. Because of our apprehension of possibilities, we can project what is possible for ourselves. And this is an aspect of our awareness of ourselves or self-presencing. We can apprehend features of ourselves, reflect on our own desires, failures, and accomplishments, and weigh the outcomes of our actions. Human transcendence then is this capacity to exist self-consciously in the face of discerned possibilities and to respond to situations in the light of what is discerned. Transcendence is the heart and very possibility of human action and is what makes us moral, cognitive, and aesthetic agents.

Negatively, transcendence means the irreducibility of human beings to any fixed contents or set of essences. This is why Heidegger contended that our *essentia* was to exist, why Sartre argued against the concept of a fixed human nature, and why Marcel depicted the human being as *homo viator,* ever on the way. Transcendence as irreducibility also means that we cannot be reduced to our determinacy, our I-as. In fact without transcendence, there is no I-as since the I-as requires a transcending self-awareness of one's determinacy. It also requires transcending because the I-as forms or accumulates only through a continual surpassing of whatever content or shape one has at any given time. This temporal enrichment is not just an adding of ingredients to a recipe but something that happens through our respondings in the face of discerned possibilities. But because of our constant projection of our own being and situations into the future, no specific determinacy exhausts what we are. Possibilities for a different I-as are ever before us.

Positively, human transcendence describes the self-initiating aspects of self-presencing. This is what St. Augustine and other Western philosophers call the will (*voluntas*), what Nicolas Berdyaev calls true freedom and creativity, and what philosophers from Samuel Taylor Coleridge to Ray L. Hart call the imagination.[7] Self-making, the Dionysian side of personal being, is not just an act which fits our action to anticipated outcomes, a calculation of benefits and perils. It is actually a bringing about of one's being, a subjecting of our being to novelty. Aesthetic experiences and activities are better clues to the self-making aspect of transcendence than cognitive attempts to locate causes. Because transcendence is itself an existential and not a fixed essence, it occurs in degrees and can be repressed, distorted, or promoted. Yet, it is difficult to imagine a being as human which has no element of transcendence whatever. Even such things as masochism, giving up, despair, and catatonia are responses of human self-making and as such ciphers of transcendence.

Space, Body, and Language

As personal or self-presencing beings, we have a distinctive temporality in which the past, present, and future so converge that we experience the world through meanings and possibilities. And this temporality makes possible both our determinacy and our irreducible and self-making transcendence. These notions are not predicates of individual entities but descriptions of the distinctive ways human agents exist in the world and even "have" a world. This is why personal agency is at work in the behaviors, relations, and features studied by

7. The most extended and profound historical and philosophical analysis of the imagination in modern times is surely Ray L. Hart's *Unfinished Man and the Imagination: Toward an Ontology and a Rhetoric of Revelation* (New York: Herder and Herder, 1968).

various sciences. Thus, the personal dimension influences the sense in which we are social, embodied, linguistic, historical, economic, gender-related, political, playful, and religious. I submit three examples of the way personal agency enters into the subject matters of the sciences of human being: space, body, and language.

As self-presencing (temporal, determinate, transcendent), we exist in space not simply as located physical objects but in and through ways of meaning and evaluating our locations. Unlike mathematical space, our lived space has a center, namely our embodied selves.[8] My bodily location establishes the difference between "here" and "there," and the familiar social space of my family, tribe, or village establishes the difference between the world of "home" and the alien or strange world. And "here" and "there" bestow a certain meaning on the way I act in my environment; thus, coming home, emigrating to another country, getting lost in a strange neighborhood, exploring new territories, going underground.

Because we are personal agents, we are neither bodies nor do we possess bodies. To say we are bodies reduces our transcendence to physical operations. To say we possess bodies suggests that we are some sort of nonphysical substance which operates our bodies as if they were machines. Perhaps more than any other philosopher, Maurice Merleau-Ponty has explored the strange and distinctive way human beings are embodied beings.[9] Whatever we say about our transcendence, it is an embodied transcendence that exists in the world in bodily relations and activities. The lived-body of embodiment is not an external physical object which we perceive or experiment on, but rather is a field of initiating activity whose operations are our way of experiencing and relating to the world.

This last two-thirds of the 20th century is, philosophically speaking, the era of language. Fascination with language organizes the agendas of both Anglo-American and hermeneutic philosophies as well as structuralism and deconstruction. Our relation to language resembles our relation to our bodies; it is not merely an instrumental relation. For it is language that is operative in the retentions and protentions which effect

8. Among the many studies of human or lived space, see the following: Gaston Bachelard, *The Poetics of Space*, trans. M. Jolas (New York: Orion, 1964); Otto F. Bollnow, *Mensch und Raum* (Stuttgart, W. Ger.: W. Kohlhammer, 1963); Alfred Schutz, "The Stranger: An Essay in Social Psychology"; and "The Homecoming," in *Collected Papers*, 3 vols., ed. M. Natanson, (The Hague, Netherlands: M. Nijhoff, 1962–66), vol. 2; "Some Structure of the Life-World," in *Collected Papers*, vol. 3; and "Symbol, Reality and Society," #3 in *Collected Papers*, vol. 1.

9. See Maurice Merleau-Ponty, *The Phenomenology of Perception*, trans. C. Smith (New York: Humanities Press, 1974), Part One. For a survey of the motif of embodiment in the early phenomenological movement, see Richard Zaner, *The Problem of Embodiment: Some Contributions to a Phenomenology of the Body* (The Hague, Netherlands: M. Nijhoff, 1964).

transcendence. Through language we envision possibilities, experience the world in felt aesthetic ways, and bring the evaluated past to bear on the present. Language, thus, is not just an available deposit of agreed-upon signs we use to communicate. It is part of our very being as personal, irreducible, and creative.[10] Our being as personal is at the same time linguistic.

The synthesis of determinacy (social and historical location in space and time) and transcendence is the human agent's proper autonomy. Put negatively, there is nothing improper, corrupt, or evil about finite location, being the perspectival center of one's world, or being irreducibly personal.

THE VULNERABILITY OF PERSONAL BEING

All living things exist amidst a variety of perils. This situation is their vulnerability. More precisely, vulnerability is that about a living being which makes it able to be harmed and able to experience that harm in some form of suffering. The vulnerability of human agents is complex because they are multi-dimensional beings. As organic beings we are vulnerable to physical injury, disease, pain, and death. As social beings we are vulnerable to social incompatibility, social suffering, and oppressive social systems. And we are vulnerable in a very distinctive way because we are personal or self-presencing beings. That which we are vulnerable to has both objective and experiential aspects. In the objective sense we are vulnerable to what alters our being in a destructive or harmful way. For instance, we are vulnerable to strokes whose effect on the central nervous system causes blindness or paralysis. The experiential aspect is our actual experience of this alteration and this is usually some form of suffering. Suffering is the interruption of some rather self-conscious state of satisfaction (organic, psychological, etc.). The experiential aspect of vulnerability is a vulnerability to this interruption, that is, to suffering. Thus, we experience a stroke and its effects as suffering. What we are vulnerable to then is the experience (suffering) of an objectively harmful alteration of our being. Personal vulnerability is a distinctive way of experiencing suffering and to a distinctive way the agents can be harmed or under distortion.

10. A few of the seminal philosophical works on the theme of language in this century are the following: Ernst Cassirer, *The Philosophy of Symbolic Forms,* vol. 1, *Language,* trans. R. Mannheim (New Haven, Conn.: Yale University Press, 1953); Martin Heidegger, *On the Way to Language*, trans. P. D. Hertz (New York: Harper and Row, 1971); Walter Ong, *The Presence of the Word: Some Prolegomena for Cultural and Religious History* (New York: Simon and Schuster, 1967); and Jacques Derrida, *Of Grammatology,* trans. G. Chakravorty Spivak (Baltimore: Johns Hopkins University Press, 1974).

If suffering means the interruption of some state of experienced satisfaction, presumably all living things capable of experiencing are able to suffer. But with self-presencing comes a very distinctive suffering. The root of this suffering is our strange temporality and its concomitants of lived space, embodiment, and language. Temporality paradoxically lifts us above time. For the convergence of the past and the future in the passive flow of consciousness makes it possible for us to be self-consciously aware of the past and future through acts of remembering and anticipating. And both the immanent (undeliberate) retention and protention and the self-consciously or reflected past and future are carried in linguistic expressions of symbols and metaphors which are weighted already with valuations of all sorts. We remember a past event as painful, delightful, or trivial; a certain person as boring, interesting, or dangerous. And through these weighted evaluations, we anticipate recurrences of these events or future meetings with the person. Because of this existence above time as well as in time, we experience interruptions of our states of satisfactions (suffering) in grades of significance. Pain itself is subject to gradations of intensity that depend in part on the way pain is meant, symbolized, and given importance. To experience a broken finger is to experience physical pain. But prior to this experience, we already have attitudes and ways of valuing and symbolizing our bodies and parts of our bodies. The concert pianist experiences a serious injury to a hand or finger through attitudes which have assigned crucial importance to the hands. People whose attitudes toward their bodies are dominated by neurotic shame or guilt will experience bodily disablement in connection with that guilt. The physical suffering of the body has provided these examples, a topic I shall elaborate in chapter 4. But the point holds true for all human suffering. We suffer the interruptions of our states of satisfactions in gradations of intensity that depend on meanings and valuations because these states are themselves ways we meaningfully exist in the world. This is why we human beings can suffer disappointments, frustrations, boredom, depression, worry, and the like. All of these sufferings bespeak our power to remember and anticipate, our capacity to entertain meanings and significances, and the symbolization of our experience in language.

Personal being is also distinctively vulnerable because of its determinacy (its I-as) and its transcendence. *Determinacy* refers to the fact that the flow of temporality and experience accumulatively shapes or specifies us. The human agent is the one who grew up in this family, is of this gender, and has such and such a career. When we say the word "I," we do not mean an empty or contentless self or will but rather the "I" of these contents. The "I" as black, female, Nigerian, student, or professional

professional calls for acknowledgement and to be taken seriously. It is just this shaped I-as that constitutes a distinctive vulnerability. If the human agent is not just bones and tissue but the shaped, determinate, and embodied "I," then its very determinacy is vulnerable to assault and distortion. For the I-as exists always as a claim on behalf of itself, and this makes it vulnerable to whatever would deny that claim or assault the conditions of its specific I-as. Personal being as determinate can be refused acknowledgement, falsely universalized, and negatively stereotyped.

Transcendence refers to the irreducibility and the self-making of human agents. It, too, carries a distinctive vulnerability. Irreducibility means that our reality always surpasses any named content, structure, or set of attributes, and this includes the determinate or I-as aspect of our being. As irreducible our reality is never that of a thing, object, or content. Thus, our very reality asks to be dealt with not simply as a thing or an object subject to external control. But because we are so constituted, we are deprived of our being when our transcendence is not acknowledged. Because the harm or health of personal agents is tied up with acknowledgement, a full treatment of their vulnerability is not possible without introducing the interhuman. For it is the other who can refuse to acknowledge transcendence or who can assault the personal in the form of insult, humiliation, control, and objectification.

But personal being possesses a deeper vulnerability yet, a vulnerability especially discerned by Freud and present in Ernst Becker's expanded version of the Oedipus Complex.[11] There is in personal being a structural alienation precisely because of its combination of determinacy and transcendence. Objectifying and quantifying social sciences see only the determinacy aspect. Or at least they study human beings as they are constituted by their historical, social, and cultural contents. Some approaches see only transcendence; the willing, deciding, meaning individual. But there is no real human being who is not experientially and historically determinate and who lacks transcendence. Furthermore, there is never a mere harmony between the two. To survive and experience satisfactions, human beings need societies with their traditions, norms, and regulations of life. But these things are not designed for transcendence. The norms are not adapted to the specific tastes and agendas of each individual. They deal with transcendence through socialization, control, and punishment. And they both create and ignore the specifically shaped determinacy of individuals. Thus we

11. Ernst Becker, *The Birth and Death of Meaning: A Perspective in Psychiatry* (New York: The Free Press of Glencoe, 1962), chap. 6.

human beings resist the societal and familial realities on which we depend for survival and definition. Like the interhuman, personal being also has its own structural alienation. It is a benign alienation because its dynamics are those of tragic choices rather than evil. The alienation is between the irreducible self-making of transcendence and the contentful I-as of determinacy. This, too, is a type of suffering, and it is the most formal feature of the tragic structure of the sphere of agency.

4
THE BIOLOGICAL ASPECT OF PERSONAL BEING

> There is a wolf in me . . . fangs pointed for tearing gashes . . . a red tongue for raw meat . . . and the hot lapping of blood—I keep this wolf because the wilderness gave it to me and this wilderness will not let it go.[1]
>
> *Carl Sandburg*

When we human beings try to understand ourselves, what fascinates us are those traits that distinguish us from nature and other living things. This fascination has dominated Western thought from Plato to existentialism and philosophies of mind.[2] From Charles Darwin to the present, another fascination has turned our attempts to understand ourselves to various networks of causality and to our continuities with nature. The outcome of the two fascinations and parallel lines of study is a new dualism that overlays the old dualism of body and soul.[3] According to this dualism, human agents are a convergence of phylogenetic and social causalities and personal existence. Some interpretations of human agency simply choose one of the two poles as the real human being. It is not, however, the case that the sciences reduce the human being to causal systems and the nonsciences defend human transcendence. Reductionism is a philosophical, not a natural

1. Carl Sandburg, from "Wilderness," in *Cornhuskers* (New York: Holt, Rinehart & Winston, 1918, 1946).

2. Several recent monographs in the philosophy of human being do focus on biology and are exceptions to the prevailing tradition. The most comprehensive work of philosophical anthropology that gives biology a central place is probably Susanne Langer's *Mind: An Essay on Human Feeling,* 3 vols. (Baltimore: Johns Hopkins University Press, 1967). See esp. vol. 2. In addition, see Hans Jonas, *The Phenomenon of Life: Toward a Philosophical Biology* (New York: Harper and Row, 1966); and Mary Midgley, *Beast and Man: The Roots of Human Nature* (Ithaca, N.Y.: Cornell University Press, 1978). Arnold Gehlen has written a comprehensive account of human reality from a biological perspective, *Man: His Nature and Place in the World,* trans. C. McMillan and K. Pillemer (New York: Columbia University Press, 1988). A brief but important work from an earlier generation is Max Scheler's *Man's Place in Nature* (Boston: Beacon Press, 1961). It appeared originally in 1928 under the title *Die Stellung des Menschen im Kosmos.*

3. For an account of how Darwinism and the natural sciences helped promote a new dualism, see Jonas's essay, "Philosophical Aspects of Darwinism," in Jonas, *The Phenomenon of Life.*

or social scientific issue, and it is defended or opposed by both scientists and philosophers.[4]

We should not confuse the data and conclusions of specific research projects (e.g., physiology of brain circuitry) with general paradigms of human reality, human condition, or even human agency. Paradigms are not absent in research projects but their function is to guide the selection of pertinent data and methods. Philosophical anthropologies use paradigms to understand acting dimensions of human agency. I began this exploration of human agency with the personal not to foster another dualism between human self-transcendence and human causal systems but to establish what is being considered in the first place, human agents. An initial attention to personal being helps us to avoid the subtle domination of a reductionist paradigm. Whatever the human being is in its various spheres of causality, it is personal and self-presencing. Reflection on personal being lends itself to insights into the complex multidimensionality of human agents which when ignored invites notions of human beings as aggregates of data.

Reductionism to spheres of causality has not, however, been the characteristic temptation of either ancient or modern theological anthropologies. The ghost of Mani has always haunted Christian theology with the result that theology interpreted the distinctiveness of human agents as something floating above nature and the body. Christian theology used Platonic, Cartesian, transcendental, and mind philosophies to distinguish the *imago Dei* as will or reason and to assign networks of natural causality to the margins of the human condition. Mechanism as the dominant model for understanding nature brought with it the dualism we associate with the Cartesian tradition. And when theology appropriated this scheme, it assigned sin, piety, virtue, and salvation to the realm of consciousness or the subject. The era shaped by Immanuel Kant sealed this approach by an *apologia* that placed religion (faith, revelation) in a region unreachable by mundane

4. The term *reductionism* occurs frequently in this essay. What makes biological reductionism reductionistic is the reducing of the complexity and totality of the human being to that aspect which its focused research investigates in such a way as to deny the complexity. Complexity is acknowledged but it is defined by the perimeters of the focused research. Thus the full reality is identified with the data yielded by the ever-changing focused research. Human being is the physiological operations of the brain. More specifically, biological reductionism tends to suppress one whole aspect of the living entity with which it deals, the most general feature of its livingness, namely, its self-initiation. The being of the entity is thus a set of externally perceived and quantified operating systems. Both general and specific aspects of reductionism are metaphysical in character. That is, the claim that the research exhausts the reality (if not complexity) of human being presupposes a concept of what reality as such is, thus, as physical, mundane, functional, etc.

sciences. This freed theology to formulate its revelational or Scriptural version of human good and evil as if they had no relation whatever to the awesome realities being studied by neurophysiology, microbiology, and sociobiology.[5]

This isolation does protect the region of faith: it also fosters some unfortunate choices. One option is that the human being described by the sciences is the real human being. Hence, aggression (intra-species fighting behavior) is the nonmythological and scientifically demonstrated depiction of what the religious tradition has rather vaguely called sin. According to this Comptean option, the true (scientific) account of human reality has already replaced the religious account. A second option is that theology describes the real human condition and what the sciences are studying and discovering has little or no bearing on the issue. Here, the real human being is something spiritual or mental that flies above earth, body, and causality. The third option, dualism, asserts that the causal networks studied by the sciences and the realities attested by faith are both real but have nothing to do with each other.[6] But when theologians take the dualist course, they find it difficult not to fall back into the second option, giving only lip service to the biological and the empirical. This is because of faith's claim that its primary symbols express the central reality of human agency and its condition. Here theology resembles those views that acknowledge our biological and evolutionary aspects but argue

5. Two contemporary movements in theology have given some attention to what Melvin Konner calls "the biological constraints on the human spirit." See *Tangled Wing: Biological Constraints on the Human Spirit* (New York: Holt, Rinehart and Winston, 1982). Process theology's conceptual framework reflects an organismic way of thinking and its agenda to relate theology and the sciences has resulted in specific monographs on biology. See esp. Charles Birch and John B. Cobb, Jr., *The Liberation of Life: From the Cell to the Community* (Cambridge, Eng. and New York: Cambridge University Press, 1981). Second, feminist theology has incorporated biological as well as political themes in the theological analysis of gender and the human condition. Besides these two movements, the most prominent twentieth-century philosopher of religion whose framework was biological is Teilhard de Chardin, a paleontologist and geologist who offered a very popular and influential monograph on human beings called *The Phenomenon of Man,* trans. B. Wall (New York: Harper, 1959). See also the papers collected in a conference in England edited by I. T. Ramsey, *Biology and Personality: Frontier Problems in Science, Philosophy, and Religion* (New York: Barnes and Noble, 1966).

6. The Cartesian tradition of two separate spheres and the post-Kantian tradition which assigns religion to its own distinctive sphere continues in the Karl Barth school. And one can not but think that the Barth school's appropriation of selected Wittgensteinian concepts (form of life, language games) is yet again one more version of theology's self-immunization against any possible critique from perspectives and frameworks other than its own. Thus immunized, theology is exempted from obligations to relate the reality claims of faith to the mundane descriptions of the sciences. In this view genetics, evolution, and the physiological bases of the emotions have little to contribute to the understanding of human sin, (theological) freedom, or (theologically described) human goods. Cartesianism, it seems, wins another round. There is no little irony in the fact that this approach sometimes describes itself as "postmodern."

that we have developed so far beyond the instinctual toward something unique that we have virtually no biological nature at all. Theological dualism promotes this notion insofar as it interprets human agency as whatever transcends the biological; thus, culture, language, freedom, history, and the personal. The human agent is thus a mere plasticity, a kind of blank page on which culture, self-determination, or faith inscribe themselves.[7] It should be clear that such an approach has difficulty introducing nature (the larger environment of life process) into its understanding of human reality. Gnosticism thus may not be as dead as it seems. The dualist option simply continues the Cartesian tradition, and may be a modern version of the old distinction between the natural and the supernatural. All three options show that theology pays a high price for its protection against scientific muggers.

THE BIOLOGICAL AS A DIMENSION OF HUMAN AGENCY

The thesis of this chapter is a modest one. The condition of human agents, whatever else it is, is the condition of living animals. The features that constitute life, animality, and being a mammal and a primate are not eliminated or left behind by whatever constitutes human agency. While it is the case that ciphers of transcendence such as self-presencing, love, and evil are not simply terms for physiological states, it is important to remember that these things occur in conjunction with a living organism. We have no idea what these things would be (if they could occur at all) in something non-living, in a plant, or in an invertebrate animal. The organic and the phylogenetic are not just possibilities or theoretical hypotheses about our condition. They constitute an aspect of that condition itself. Accordingly, the biological is a certain facticity of human reality along with the facticities of the interhuman and the societal. Furthermore, the biological dimension of agents does not occur prior to or even alongside of these other facticities but pervades and influences them. None of them would be what they are if human being was not a biological being.

What constitutes this biological facticity? In the most general sense, it means that human beings are biological beings. As a specific form of organic life, our being has arisen among other life-forms as the result of evolutionary process and natural selection, and the individuals of our species obtain existence by means of reproduction and by cell replications

7. Mary Midgley makes this point in an eloquent way. See *Beast and Man*, 19–24. It is important to note that controversy over the human being as an instinctless, cultural being without any biological nature at all is not simply between biologists and philosophers and theologians. It has also been disputed between biologists and social scientists who think that cultural and historical comparisons are sufficient accounts of the human condition.

governed by genetic codes. As biologically specific, we human beings occupy a niche in the hundreds of thousands of species of living things on this planet. We have the features of living rather than nonliving things. As animals rather than plants, we are mobile and perceptual and share with all animals the standard twenty amino acids. As vertebrates distinguished from nonvertebrates, we have a back-bone and other features of vertebrate life-forms. As mammals in distinction from bacteria, insects, and most reptiles, we are warm-blooded, live-bearing (some reptiles have this feature and a few mammals are egg-laying), and nurse our young. In contrast to marsupials and felines, we share many physiological and even behavioral features with primates. As the one remaining hominid on the planet, we have erect posture and are bipedal.[8] All these taxonomical observations add up to the fact that human specificity is the specificity of a species.[9]

Because we are a species of animal, we can be studied by sciences of taxonomy (biological classification), comparative physiology, and ethology (comparative study of animal behavior).[10] Comparative studies need not reduce the human agent to an identity with its biological ancestors or to other primates. All such reductions are transempirical interpretations whose warrants are not specific physiological, ethological, or taxonomical evidences. Further, these comparative studies yield both similar and distinctive features of the human biological condition.[11] Some similarities

8. The hominids include homo sapiens and their ancestors after divergence from the line which leads to the African great apes. At one time there were at least two hominids; homo including types preceding homo sapiens and the southern ape, australopithecus who lived between 6 million to 1 million years ago. See Bernard G. Campbell, *Emerging Humankind,* 5th ed. (Los Angeles, Calif.: University of California, 1988), 42–46.

9. On the concept of species, see E. Mayr, *Animal Species and Evolution* (Cambridge, Mass.: Harvard University Press, 1963). Criticisms directed at Carolus Linnaeus and taxonomy have called into question the concept of species since it seems to depend on a pre-evolutionary notion of distinct essences. However, species can be a functional category rather than unhistorical essence. For instance, a species can mean a population of animal life able to mate and reproduce its kind and unable to mate with and reproduce with any other population. For a defense of species along these lines, see Steven J. Gould, *The Panda's Thumb: More Reflections in Natural History* (New York: W. W. Norton, 1982), chap. 20.

10. A partial list of physiological features which human beings possess as living, mammalian, and primate are the following: the internalization of key organs of breathing, digestion, and elimination; a certain ratio of external surface to internal surface thus a certain proportion of size to weight; a weight significant enough to be subject to gravity; air breathing; warm-bloodedness; frontal vision; highly developed visual and auditory powers but less developed senses of taste and smell; opposable thumb; highly developed coordination between hands and eyes; upright posture; flattened feet and bipedalism; absence of predator-type teeth and claws; terrestriality; developed cerebral cortex; bisexual and diploidal reproduction; lengthy period of prenatal development and lengthy period of postnatal infant helplessness; the breast feeding of infants; pair bonding; and permanent family units.

11. Some of the distinctive physiological features of homo sapiens are as follows. A highly developed size of the cerebral cortex in relation to body weight. (In absolute terms, an elephant's brain is four times heavier than a human brain.) The human being is

are homologies, that is, traits which we share with other species due to a common phylogenetic ancestry. But these similarities themselves contain features that distinguish human beings as biological beings. It is important to note, however, that distinctive features are exemplifications of our biological condition, not evidences of its surpassing. Even with our outsized cerebral cortex, our long life (in relation to our size and weight), and our complex facial expressiveness, we are still organic, living animals.

How do species come about? They originate through millions of years of natural selection. In our case, we originated in the specific evolutionary line which led to the primates. Accordingly, we have prehuman biological ancestors.[12] How does a species survive over time? In the case of mammalian primates, it is by sexual mating and reproduction in which the genetic code carried by the DNA of individuals is transferred (with its mutations and recombinations) from the adult to a new and finally independent individual. Thus, our genetic heritage is at work in everything we are and do and makes possible the features which we think distinguish us from everything else. To that heritage we owe our anatomical structure, the interior bodily conditions of our survival as individuals, our phases of growth from infancy to adult, and even traits of personality and behavior.

The biological, then, is a factical dimension of our agential reality. We express our biological condition when we say that the new baby looks like her grandmother or that tallness runs in the family. Biological reductionism (biologism) is a nonempirical identification of the agent's condition with its biological condition. Opposite to biologism is a weak or trivializing version of the facticity of the biological. According to this weak view, genetic factors are limited to anatomical features, including the complex structures of the brain, but do not apply to the distinctive features of human nature. The weak view thus sees the biological as the necessary condition, the sine qua non for distinctive human powers. The evolutionarily developed body is a background and bearer of human

exceptionally long-lived, again measured by its size and weight. In contrast to living primates, human beings have upright postures, are hairless, bipedal, and have a flattened face. Further, the human face is expressive in very complex ways. Sexually, human beings lack an estrus period. (In primates there is some remnant of a monthly sexual cycle.) For a fuller treatment see G. G. Simpson, *Biology and Man* (New York: Harcourt, Brace and World, 1969).

12. Assembling the fossil record of prehuman primates has been virtually a mid-twentieth-century accomplishment which began with Raymond Dart in the 1930s and continued through the work of the Leakeys in the 1950s to the present. The consensus is that homo sapiens is very much a latecomer on the evolutionary scene (possibly as late as 60,000 years ago) and if Gould and Eldridge are correct, the appearance occurred like so many species in a fairly sudden eruption rather than a gradual emergence of millions of years. See Steven Jay Gould and W. Eldridge, "Punctuated Equilibria: The Tempo and Mode of Evolution Reconsidered," in *Paleobiology,* 3/2 (Spring 1977): 115–51, and also Gould, *The Panda's Thumb,* chap. 17.

nature, the ashes from which the phoenix of our distinctive being arises. Body and brain are things we use to experience and act as we do. We cannot listen to symphonies or fall in love without them, but what constitutes our distinctive condition are the aesthetic and intellectual activities which bodies and brains make possible.

We should not let the excesses of popular works on "the naked ape" and territorial aggression blind us to the deficiencies of the weak view. Even the ancient Platonic description of the "lower powers of the soul" and the traditional theological notion of concupiscence go beyond the view of the biological as a mere sine qua non. The weak view simply cannot survive in the face of recent decades of genetics, neurophysiology, and sociobiology.[13] Instead of being an available instrument employed by a transcending person or mind, the body and the biological describe powerful needs and tendencies that motivate human actions. Studies of biological elements in human pathology also add to the discreditation of the weak view. Pathology refers to more than simply cancer or sickle-cell anemia. Biochemical elements are at work in mental retardation, in various behavioral disorders, and in tendencies toward depression and mental illness.

The biological dimension of our human condition is not restricted, then, to the inheritance of gross anatomical structures and to bodily vulnerabilities. A stronger view would understand how genetic factors and thus the whole biochemical internal environment of human physiology are at work in needs, tendencies, emotions, reflex-type responses, slow-building hormonal influences, and even behaviors. The strong view of the biological element in the human condition falls between the weak view and biological reductionism. It is the nonreductionist affirmation that human being is constituted by powerful phylogenetic influences that are more than mere possibilities or fields to be manipulated by the will. The strong view is, however, only a general approach to our biological condition. It does not constitute a specific solution to the way biological and personal dimensions are related to each other, or, more specifically, how consciousness and the brain are interrelated.[14]

13. For a summary of recent research on the biology of human beings, see Konner, *Tangled Wing*, esp. Part One.

14. The most eminent neurophysiologist who has devoted many writings to the philosophical problem of the brain and consciousness is John C. Eccles. See his *Facing Reality: Philosophical Adventures by a Brain Scientist* (New York: Springer-Verlag, 1970), and his Gifford Lectures published as *The Human Mystery*, 2 vols. (New York: Springer Verlag, 1979). See also Karl Popper and John C. Eccles, *The Self and the Brain* (New York: Springer International, 1977). Other major works on the subject include J. N. Findlay, *Psyche and Cerebrum* (Milwaukee: Marquette University Press, 1972); and G. G. Globus, et al., *Consciousness and the Brain: A Scientific and Philosophical Inquiry* (New York: Plenum, 1976).

BASIC ELEMENTS OF THE HUMAN BIOLOGICAL CONDITION

Biology is a dimension of our human condition.[15] The strong version of this thesis discovers phylogenetic needs and tendencies at work in our struggles to survive and reproduce, and in our fears, emotions, and behaviors. These needs and tendencies are not simply hidden processes such as the transference of nerve impulses along the axons of the brain. Some of them are elemental features of our biological condition. Any account of the biological dimension of human agency sets the tasks of identifying and describing these elements. I shall expound five of these elements without any consideration of their relative importance or their interrelation.

Maturation

One feature human beings share with all living things is an organically set life-span, a growth process that begins at birth and continues through infancy, maturation, decline, and death. Human maturation resembles the life-cycle of all primates although it has species-specific features. The human life-cycle begins with a long, prenatal period in which the brain and upper body undergo more development than the lower body. This development continues through a very long infancy and juvenile period in which the child is initially helpless in its environment and dependent on the adults for nourishment and protection. Hormonal and bodily changes in puberty and adolescence mark its transition to adulthood and to the physiological maturation of gender characteristics. Changes continue in the adult period that, unless interrupted, end with physical deterioration in old age and death. This genetically determinate life-cycle is not simply something hidden to human awareness. The life-cycle is the way human agents experience themselves as biologically temporal. In development through infancy to old age, we experience a constraint on the way we exist in the world. In other words, physical maturation and decline are connected with our human experience of limitation, particularity, vulnerability, and mortality.

Reproduction

Human agents are brought into being through reproductive processes and their physiological makeup includes the reproductively oriented

15. The biology of human being is not a single science but a gathering of sciences; thus, paleoanthropology, evolutionary biology, genetics, neurophysiology and research on the central nervous system, sociobiology (itself a synthesis of disciplines), primatology, ethology (the comparative study of animal behavior), and many others. A good survey of the research is Konner's *Tangled Wing.* In this chapter I have made special use of this work, Midgley's *Beast and Man,* various collections of the essays of Steven Jay Gould, and Campbell's *Emerging Humankind.*

features of gender and sexuality. Because gender and sexuality reflect personal, intersubjective, and cultural dimensions, any comprehensive interpretation of these things would require psychological, cultural, and phenomenological explorations. Important as these psychological, cultural, and phenomenological aspects are, they do not displace the biological dimension. Gender itself is a genetically based twofold division within the human species, the function of which (considered in evolutionary perspective) is reproduction.[16] Contingencies of course abound. Actual mating and reproducing thus vary with all sorts of personal, institutional, and even medical conditions. Thus, gender does not impress a simple, unambiguous, and universal destiny or even standard of behavior on all human beings. These contingencies do not remove but rather build on chromosomal, endocrinal, and other physiological processes at work in gender differences.[17]

In addition to being structured by a two-fold gender, the human biological condition is a sexual condition. Sexuality itself is of course a matter of gender experience however much the experience of gender is transcended, but it also has to do with strong physiologically prompted dispositions which vary in the course of human maturation and decline. Like most biologically based needs, sexual needs can be repressed, sublimated, morally regulated, and aesthetically celebrated. But these personal and social acts refer back to something biologically given that plays a powerful role in human motivation.

The Biological Unconscious

Most biologists now reject René Descartes's view that animals (and bodies) are automata. This does not necessarily carry with it an affirmation of free will in animals, but it does assert self-mobilization and responsiveness in animals. However, there is a bit of truth in Descartes's view. Descartes knew that the vast majority of bodily processes do not depend on the will for their operations and when we consider the mechanistic model for all world causalities that prevailed in his day, we should not be surprised that he thought as he did. In fact present-day physiologists continue to use the metaphor of mechanism

16. On the subject of gender, see Konner, *Tangled Wing,* chap. 6.

17. There appears to be some tension on the subject of gender in the feminist movement. Such tension is inevitable and even productive in vigorous social movements. One wing of the movement sees gender as the basis for distinctive ways of experiencing the world and argues that woman's body and nurturing functions make possible important ways women can contribute to society. Another wing senses possible stereotyping and exploitation from such an emphasis. For a strong criticism of sociobiology and the whole literature of gender research in general, see Anne Fausto-Stirling's *Myths of Gender: Biological Theories about Women and Men* (New York: Basic Books, 1985).

to describe bodily processes. Whatever our metaphor and whatever our view of transcendence and freedom, it is clear that the hundreds of millions of neural and other events necessary to our ongoing life take place outside conscious awareness and deliberation.[18] Even the ever so brief blink of an eye occurs in conjunctions with operations in the brain so complex and so rapid that they cannot be completely traced. More complex acts such as flexing the fingers of a hand, reading a sentence in a book, eating a meal, or recognizing a familiar melody occur in conjunction with an immeasurable array of neural (that is, both electrical and chemical) events in the central nervous system. Following Melvin Konner, let us call this pre-aware system of bodily processes the biological unconscious.[19]

The *biological unconscious* is not just a term for physiological events that are mobilized by human actions. In part it describes the continuing firing of nerve cells (neurones) in the brain, a constant neurological monitoring and regulating of the total organism. Firing occurs whether we are awake or asleep. But the biological unconscious should not be thought of simply as the flow of neural impulses. It includes what P. D. Maclean calls the reptilian brain and the old mammalian brain.[20] These are the parts of the brain (the brain stem, the limbic system) that store and control instinctual behavior and that bestow emotional tones on experience. The biological unconscious also includes the physiological processes necessary to learning, the storing of experience in the form of habits, and the quick automatic, almost reflexive responses of the athlete. The biological unconscious is neither something external to our being that causes our seeing, hearing, or thinking nor an available instrument that we draw on when we need it. It rather constitutes what we are as biological beings. To summarize, the biological unconscious refers to those pre-aware physiological operations that constitute ongoing life processes, make possible all human acts and sensations including thinking and feeling, dispose human beings in certain directions of mood and feeling, and assist the habituation of behavior.

18. "Millions of processes—the whole dynamic of metabolism, digestion, circulation and endocrine action—are normally not felt." "It is this transiency and general lability of the psychical phase that accounts for the importance of preconscious processes in the construction of such elaborate phenomena as ideas, intentions, images and fantasies, and makes it not only reasonable but obvious that they are rooted in the fabric of totally unfelt activities which Freud reified with the substantive term, the 'Unconscious.'" Susanne K. Langer, *Mind: An Essay on Human Feeling,* vol. 1, 22.

19. Konner's term is simply the unconscious. Because of the long history and rich connotations of this term, I have selected the term, biological unconscious, for the biological aspect of the unconscious. See Konner, *Tangled Wing,* chap. 9.

20. See Konner, *Tangled Wing,* chap. 7 and D. P. Maclean, *The Triune Brain in Evolution: Role in Paleocerebral Functions* (New York: Plenum Press, 1990).

Flexibility

The very fact of evolution, the emergence and dying out of hundreds of thousands of species on this planet, attests to the flexibility of our biological condition. If reproduction were simply the cloning of new individuals after old ones, a species would never originate. If we posit its existence, it would not last long because of its inability to adapt to a changing environment. And it could certainly not evolve into a new species. Biological flexibility is just this capacity to adapt to change and to undergo, conditions permitting, species evolution. The basis of biological flexibility is the many genetic variations within a species at any given time, some of which might survive and be passed on in reproduction if they are adaptive. It also requires the presence of mutations in a gene pool of a species which supplies the traits that enable the species to adapt and which endure through the genetic combinations of reproduction. Flexibility should not be identified with natural selection since the only thing natural selection does is weed out maladaptive traits or behaviors among those already present in the species.

A second sense of flexibility is the range of adaptive behavior present in a species or individuals within a species.[21] The overspecialized eating habits of the everglades kite show an exceedingly narrow adaptability and therefore a delicate vulnerability to survive as a species. This species of hawk eats only a particular genus of snails and its survival is tied to the fate of that snail. On the opposite end of the spectrum, human beings are enormously adaptive to diverse conditions of food resources, weather extremes, and complex cultural situations. Behind this flexibility is the complex, interspherical character of human reality and the dimensions of human agents. But this flexibility is not simply psychological and cultural. In the narrow sense of flexibility, the presence of mutations and gene combinations, there is enormous flexibility due to the vast complexity of the nervous system, particularly the cerebral cortex. This same cerebral cortex is also the basis of memory, language, and flights of imagination that are the grounds of personhood and culture. Flexibility in the broad sense is the transcending way in which human beings are instinctual, that is, motivated by strong, genetically based tendencies. Most of these tendencies are what Mary Midgley calls open instincts, tendencies that must be filled in by experience and learning because they are not stereotyped behaviors.[22] Sexuality is an example

21. Arnold Gehlen contends for a distinctive kind of flexibility that comes with human beings. He points out that because of language, human reality transcends the specializations of most animal species and is world-open. See *Man: His Nature and Place in the World,* 40, 232, 336.

22. Midgley, *Beast and Man,* chap. 3.

because it is open to enormous variations of individual creativity and cultural expression. Flexibility then in both its narrow and broad senses is one of the basic elements in the human biological situation. It too describes something, the absence of which would be a serious deprivation of the human agent.

Kinship

The theme of kinship[23] places us in the middle of an intense and ongoing controversy in biological anthropology.[24] Prior to this controversy and according to the usual division of labor, the biological element of human beings was limited to the anatomy and physiology of individuals (studied by biological sciences) while the social element of human beings as trans-biological was handled by sociology and cultural anthropology. This implied that the effects of biology stop with the individual and have no location in the social. Human beings in groups display the cultural supplementation of biological. In recent years an opposing view has challenged this restriction of the biological to individual organisms. Konrad Lorenz and ethology popularized by Robert Ardrey and Desmond Morris contended that human social behavior (everything from parenting to warfare) is biologically explainable. E. O. Wilson carried this line into a synthesis of biology and social sciences (sociobiology) whose thesis was that biological (genetic) factors are at work in a very large group of human

23. I have reserved the terms *social* and *sociality* for a dimension of the human condition which gathers up the other dimensions. Hence, I am using the term *kinship* in a broader way than it is used in biology. Here, it simply refers to the biological aspect of the social.

24. Although its roots had been forming for decades, sociobiology appeared rather suddenly on the scene with Edward O. Wilson's promotion of a synthesis of biological sciences into a new discipline of the biological roots of animal (and therefore also human) behavior. *Sociobiology: The New Synthesis* (Cambridge, Mass.: Belknap Press of Harvard University, 1975). For a less technical account of the major argument, see Wilson's *On Human Nature* (Cambridge, Mass.: Harvard University Press, 1978). An excellent summary is David Barash's "Evolution as a Paradigm of Behavior," in Arthur L. Caplan, *The Sociobiology Debate: Readings in Ethical and Scientific Issues* (New York: Harper, Colophon Books, 1978). Wilson's monograph evoked an almost immediate convergence of biologists who had been working along similar lines so that it became, if not a science, at least a movement and a school in the biological study of human beings. A more qualified and guarded version of the main thesis can be found in the writings of David Barash. See, for instance, his *Sociobiology and Human Behavior* (New York: Elsevier, 1977). The major articles which reflect the early movement are collected in T. Clutton-Brock and Harvey, eds., *Readings in Sociobiology* (San Francisco: W. H. Freeman, 1978). In addition, see Georg Breuer's *Sociobiology and the Human Dimension* (Cambridge, Eng.: University of Cambridge, 1982) and John and Mary Gribbin, *The One Percent Advantage: The Sociobiology of Being Human* (Oxford: B. Blackwell, 1988).

Forming as rapidly as the movement was a severely critical response to sociobiology. Many perceived reductionism, biological imperialism, and oppressive politics in Wilson and his disciples. See Arthur L. Caplan, *The Sociobiology Debate.* A good summary of the major criticisms is Stephen Jay Gould's "Cardboard Darwinism," *The New York Times Book Review,* 33/14 (Sept. 25, 1986), 47ff.

social behaviors. The texts of both literatures contain simplistic and reductionist passages that have evoked severe criticisms.[25] The controversy goes on, but two extreme positions do seem inadequate: the claim that detailed human social behavior is explainable genetically, and, the claim that human social behavior has no biological basis whatsoever. The first extreme is vulnerable both to the charge of reductionism and to the charge of lack of evidence. As a reductionism, it ignores the spheres and dimensions of human reality. As a case, it fails to trace the causal lines from genetic codes to behaviors.

Yet there seems to be enough evidence to falsify the second claim. If a phylogenetic heritage shapes the experiences, needs, and behaviors of human individuals, how could this *not* affect the way human individuals are together in groups? For example, if the whole phenomenon of gender and sexuality has a powerful genetic element, how could there not be some genetic element at work in human mores and institutions that have to do with reproduction? It would seem that the long period of infant helplessness would have some affect on the way parenting occurs in the human species, perhaps even calling forth the permanent family unit. This is confirmed by the fact that most primates have such units. (This is not to say that primate families are necessarily monogamous.) Needless to say, the evidence assembled by sociobiology from a variety of disciplines backs up more specific claims than these generalities. From cultural anthropology, sociobiology assembles evidence for a number of human social behaviors present in some form in all human societies. It contends that because these social behaviors pertain to the control of population and reproduction, they are contributive to the survival of the species. The evidence cited does not demonstrate a causal relation between specific genes and specific social behaviors, and hence does not explain the behaviors. It does point to genetic influences at work in such things as communication, territoriality, and even social flexibility.

25. Erich Fromm has subjected what he calls "neo-instinctivists" (Freud, Lorenz, Ardry, and others) to a withering criticism. See *The Anatomy of Human Destructiveness* (New York: Holt, Rinehart and Winston, 1973), Part Two. For specific criticisms of both the Lorenz school and sociobiology, see John Klama (a pseudonym for three authors), *Aggression: The Myth of the Beast Within* (New York: Wiley, 1988). Works directed especially against sociobiology or at least its more reductionist expression are Philip Kitcher, *Vaulting Ambition: Sociobiology and the Quest for Human Nature* (Cambridge, Mass.: MIT Press, 1985); R. C. Lewontin, S. Rose, and L. Kamin, *Not in Our Genes: Biology, Ideology, and Human Nature* (New York: Pantheon Books, 1984); John D. and Janice I. Baldwin, *Beyond Sociobiology* (New York: Elsevier, 1981); and Joseph W. Smith, *Reductionism and Cultural Being: A Philosophical Critique of Sociobiological Reductionism* (The Hague, Netherlands: Nijhoff, 1984). Mary Midgley offers an appreciative but sharply critical analysis of Wilson throughout her work, *Beast and Man*.

STRIVING AS THE UNITY OF THE HUMAN BIOLOGICAL CONDITION

No comprehensive account of the human biological condition can avoid the themes of maturation, the biological unconscious, reproduction, flexibility, and kinship. However, even when taken together, these themes do not describe the general biological trait in all of these elements. Generally speaking, the role or function of all of these elements has something to do with the survival of the individual or species. They point to and converge in individuals striving to survive in a rather perilous environment and in pursuit of various conditions of their well-being and in opposition to whatever withholds those conditions. Thus, as a single dynamic, the biological condition of human agents is marked by a striving in an environment that is both supportive and threatening.

No living thing can exist apart from the set of conditions to which its type is adapted and on which it depends. Human beings are finely tuned to a more or less stable environment of a very specific type, and one meaning of their finitude is their dependence on their environment. With the assistance of technology, we can extend these conditions to other environments, under water, for instance, but we cannot cancel the conditions. Furthermore, our empathetic imagination can only slightly help us to enter the environments of other living things. We really have no idea what it would be like to swim weightlessly in the viscous environment of a bacterium. Limitation, then, is part of what it means to adapt to and depend on a specific environment.

Limitation also means living in an environment that is both indifferent and dangerous. Environments of living things are not automatic dispensers of the conditions of life. They do not initiate, promote, or secure the life or well-being of any individual or species. They also contain all sorts of things that constantly threaten the conditions of life and the well-being of their occupants. In the human environment are external perils of famines and floods and internal perils of viruses and bacteria. Thus, from the perspective of the living thing itself, the environment is not just indifferent to its existence; it is full of dangers. Because of this indifference, all life forms must actively wrest the conditions of life from the environment. Because of the dangers of the environment, they must constantly avoid what would prey on them, harm them, and compete with them for nourishment and space. This is why striving is the most general feature of the human biological condition. All life forms strive and human beings are no exception. Because the environment is indifferent and dangerous, it demands a striving that is both a seeking and an opposing. What we strive for is whatever promotes the conditions of life and well-being, and the object of this seeking correlates with elemental human needs and tendencies. What we strive against is whatever interferes with these conditions or withholds what is needed. And it is clear that human agents are equipped for both aspects, that is, for both procurements and for resistance and attack. If we were not, we would have disappeared long ago as a specific life-form.

Genetically Rooted Needs and Tendencies

That for which we strive and the equipment we possess for striving have phylogenetic and not just cultural roots. The motivations behind many human actions reflect fundamental needs and tendencies that are part of our genetic code. Again, we need to avoid the extremes of biologism and environmentalism. Reductive biologism sees human beings as little more than automata pushed around by their genetic codes whose behaviors are the output of stereotyped instincts. Environmentalism argues that human beings are so remarkably free from instinctually prompted stereotypical behaviors that human culture and personhood have more or less left instinctuality behind.[26] But if the human condition has a biological dimension, then human culture and transcendence have not simply obliterated striving nor have they suppressed the genetic element in this striving. Instinctuality, in other words, does play a part in human action and motivation. Human action shows its rootage in instincts in at least two ways: the presence of survival-oriented needs, and, the presence of genetically rooted tendencies.

Survival-oriented needs are not absent from the striving that attends human life.[27] Some of these needs do resemble instincts in the narrow sense of preprogrammed, stereotypical behaviors; for instance, reflexive responses of pain or panic to the immediate removal of the conditions of life. We choke when our breathing is cut off and cough when our lungs or esophagus are irritated. We flinch from painful stimulation and make efforts to avoid its recurrence. In addition to immediate, reflexive type responses, are survival-oriented needs which prompt long-term actions. We do whatever is called for to avoid thirst, hunger, or freezing cold. We search out specific environments of safety against all sorts of dangers.

26. The classic study of instincts is Niko Tinbergen, *The Study of Instinct* (Oxford, Eng.: Clarendon, 1951). For two excellent philosophical discussions of instinct, see Mary Midgley, *Beast and Man*, chap. 3, and Susanne K. Langer, *Mind: An Essay on Human Feeling*, vol. 2, chap. 12.

27. A helpful summary of basic survival-oriented needs can be found in Bronislaw Malinowski's *A Scientific Theory of Culture and Other Essays* (Chapel Hill, N.C.: University of North Carolina Press, 1944), 85. He lists safety, bodily comfort, growth, movement, health, and metabolism.

These reflexive and long-term responses depend on specific physiological features such as lungs oriented to a rather narrowly defined formula of air.

Human actions are also motivated by genetically rooted tendencies or dispositions which are broader than the needs to preserve the conditions of life. Mere survival is not identical with well-being. But our tendencies toward well-being and satisfaction have a biological as well as a cultural origin. These tendencies are not easy to describe since we know them only through the complex wrappings of culture and its symbols and the idiosyncrasies of individual preferences. Thus, the only sexuality we know is never a purely physiological event or need unmarked by acculturation and the personal. Yet, few would promote the view that human sexuality has no phylogenetic or hormonal aspects whatsoever. Since it pertains to reproduction and survival of the species, we cannot totally separate sexuality from survival-oriented needs. Yet, sexuality clearly pertains to broader satisfactions than simply physical survival. Other needs born of the human physical organism include the need for excitement and stimulation, for physical activity in the environment, and for social and communicative expression. Some suspect that there may be a genetic element at work in the need for play, companionship, and aesthetic enjoyment. To repeat an aforementioned point, genetically rooted needs and tendencies do not demonstrate some direct causal relation between the genetic code and specific individual and social behaviors. They do show that the striving of the human biological condition arises from needs and tendencies that reflect the human phylogenetic heritage.

Aggression

The underside of striving is the resistance to what threatens the conditions of well-being. To have survival-oriented needs and basic tendencies is also to resist and oppose. Animals deal with dangerous predators by flight, threatening behaviors, and physical self-defense. Animals are equipped to resist predation, assaults on the brood and the young, and attacks from other species' members. They are also equipped to threaten and fight with members of their species over disputed territories, group rank, and mating. In its most general sense, aggression is the capacity of an animal to mobilize itself against other threatening life-forms.[28]

28. In zoology and ethology, *aggression* means injury-oriented behavior of animals toward their own species. Some biologists have now expanded the term, other disciplines have adopted the expansion, and a popular literature has dramatized it thus laying on the term a number of ambiguities. One ambiguity is perpetrated by those who fail to distinguish between the predatory behavior of carnivores (almost always directed toward members of

As living animals who strive for life and satisfaction, human beings are physiologically equipped for aggression toward other living things which threaten them. Once human beings discovered weaponry, their primary threat was not from nonhuman competitors but from other human beings. It is true that as species go, we morphologically are not well-equipped to protect ourselves against large predatory animals. We lack the teeth of wolves and the claws of cougars. However, our enlarged cerebral cortex, highly coordinated hand-to-eye coordination, and opposable thumbs equip us with subtle capacities for weaponry and for complex plans for defense and attack. Our equipment for aggression also includes something we share with our primate cousins, the biochemically rooted capacity for fear and what Konner calls rage.[29] While fear pertains generally to any threatening situation, rage or anger tends to be limited to situations of conflict with other human beings. Our omnivorous predation of other species requires no anger. Our attacks on each other do. And this distinction between nonangry predation and angry agonistic (intraspecies fighting) behavior holds for other animal species. Like other animal species, we human beings have the capacity to attack and harm each other from motives other than simply predation, that is, in various situations of competition and conflict. We are biochemically or hormonally prepared to defend the brood and the young, to fight over

other species) and the fighting behavior, especially among males, between members of the same species. When the term is applied to human beings without this distinction, it seems to summon evidence that human beings are aggressive because of their carnivorous prehominid ancestors. Ethologists like Konrad Lorenz are careful to limit aggression to intra-species behavior. Lorenz is especially helpful in distinguishing several aggressive behaviors which occur within species (defending the brood, resisting a predator, and fighting over territories, social position, or mating) and in showing the adaptive or survival value of aggression. See *On Aggression* (New York: Harcourt, Brace, and World, 1966), chap. 3. Lorenz's classic work is marred when he forgets his own careful and precise delineations of types of animal aggression and expands aggression to cover human evil. This move promotes the second ambiguity of the term. Thus aggression comes to mean a general term for intra-species fighting (agonistic behavior) and an inclusive term for all human hostile and destructive behavior from war to violent crime. Such an identification is reductionistic because it assumes that general behavioral analogies (for instance, between a human being attacking an enemy in war and a bird attacking another bird which is testing its territory) are homologies (traits owed to an inherited and common phylogenetic heritage) and the dynamics of animal behavior coincide with those of human culture and personality. Criticisms of this "neo-instinctivist" view of aggression are widespread. See Fromm, *The Anatomy of Human Destructiveness*, chap. 9. Fromm is one of those who uses the term *aggression* in an inclusive way, but he is careful to distinguish between benign and malignant aggression and to argue that the dynamics of the two are very different. For other criticisms of the Lorenz school or its popularizations, see Klama, *Aggression: The Myth of the Beast Within*; Ashley Montague, *Man and Aggression* (New York: Oxford University Press, 1968); Ernst Becker, *The Birth and Death of Meaning*, 164–74; and Pannenberg, *Anthropology in Theological Perspective*, trans. M. J. O'Connell (Philadelphia, Pa.: Westminster Press, 1985), 142–52.

29. Konner, *Tangled Wing*, chap. 9.

social position, possessions, and disputed territories.[30] Whether research has broken down the capacity for aggression into gender differences is under dispute.[31] What is established, at least in other animal species, is some relation between the capacity and disposition to attack and chemicals such as adrenalin and testosterone.

Is this aggressive underside of striving for survival and well-being an instinct? Again, the ambiguity of the term *instinct* shows itself. If instincts mean specific, genetically programmed, unlearned behaviors such as the fishing techniques of the angler fish, there is no human instinct for aggression. There is no specific predetermined fighting behavior universal in the human species. The popular literature on aggression propounds this highly misleading view.[32] Its case is made only through premises and arguments that lack empirical demonstration. The case for instinctual aggressive behavior begins by construing complex cultural phenomena like warfare or criminality as discrete behaviors. It proceeds then to posit an analogy (not homology) between these behaviors and the intraspecies conflicts of animals. It regards this analogy as evidence that human conflicts arise from genetically coded behavior. Thus, human conflicts of all sorts are genetically and instinctually explained. Human beings are said to show aggressive behavior because of their evolutionary derivation from "killer apes." The primary fallacy here is the notion of a direct or proximate one-way causality between genes and behavior that ignores flexibility, transcendence, and acculturation, in short, the spheres and dimensions at work in the actions of human agents.

Another popular notion of aggression, sometimes connected with the killer instinct view, promotes this hydraulic metaphor as pure science. In this view, the biochemistry of human beings produces an urgent need for assault on others which, like hunger and elimination, must be satisfied. This hydraulic theory of aggression combining Konrad Lorenz and popular Freudianism has become a widespread paradigm in popular culture and among therapeutic professionals. One can only speculate on the reason for its popularity. As a metaphor (the steam kettle or steam engine), it is easy to understand and it appeals to specific and characteristic human experiences such as detumescence (the orgasmic release of sexual tension), the momentary satisfaction obtained by expressing held-back

30. See Bronson and Desjardins, "Steroid Hormones and Aggressive Behavior in Animals," in Basil E. Eleftheriou and Paul Scott, eds., *The Physiology of Aggression and Defeat* (New York: Plenum Press, 1971).

31. See Fausto-Stirling, *Myths of Gender*, 132.

32. The writings of both Desmond Morris and Robert Ardrey promote this view. See Morris, *The Naked Ape* (New York: Dell Publishing Co., 1969), and Ardrey, *African Genesis: A Personal Investigation into the Animal Origins and Nature of Man* (New York: Dell Publishing Co., 1961).

feelings, and having anger defused by violence. The fallacy of the view is that it extends the dynamics of these very specific experiences to a comprehensive interhuman, personal, and cultural phenomenon, that is, to all human conflictual and agonistic behavior. Further, if aggression in the biological sense is not an instinct-driven behavior but a biochemically rooted emotional capacity to react in certain situations, it is not simply a constant pressure of something to be released.[33]

Are we saying then that aggression is limited to nonhuman animal species? Have culture and transcendence totally transported human beings beyond what disposes animals to fight among themselves? It seems clear that part of the human biological condition is what Erich Fromm calls benign aggression, a biologically adaptive capacity for self-assertiveness which can result in attacks on others.[34] *Benign aggression* is neither a genetically caused specific behavior nor a universal urge to violence which is frustrated when not expressed. Nor is it a term for all injurious human competition and conflict. Like all human phenomena, human conflicts are intersphericaly complex and do not lend themselves to reductive explanations. One option is to adopt Fromm's nomenclature and use the term *aggression* as the comprehensive term for human destructiveness but distinguish between benign and malignant aggression. In this usage malignant aggression expresses the complex reality of human evil. I prefer to use the term *human evil* for that reality, and reserve the term *aggression* for the genetically and biochemically rooted capacity to resist, defend, and attack. Only in specific situations does this capacity become a positive tendency or inclination. Accordingly, because human evil is a more comprehensive phenomenon with its own dynamics, it should not be reduced to or confused with this genetically inherited capacity. On the other hand, because the capacity for aggression plays a role in the dynamics of human evil (see chap. 12), we cannot conclude that destructive conflicts between human beings have no relation at all to the way they

33. The term *drive* suggests the hydraulic metaphor. Konner sees the concept of drives which has dominated twentieth-century psychology as now discredited. (Konner, *Tangled Wing*, chap. 5.) J. P. Scott argues that fighting behavior is not evoked by some spontaneously arising internal energy triggered by an external stimulus and thereby released but is a continual adapting to situations as they arise. See "Theoretical Issues Concerning the Origin and Cause of Fighting," in Eleftheriou and Scott, *The Physiology of Aggression and Defeat*.

34. "Capacity for aggression" refers to everything which has equipped human beings to resist or attack in situations in which their aims or needs are threatened by other human beings. This equipping is not a single faculty but a multiplicity of things. Here Konner is helpful when he lists such things as the physical (neural circuitry), slow-acting physiological determinants such as hormone levels, gene coding and embryonic development, the phylogenetic history of the species, and the adaptive function aggression might serve. (Konner, *Tangled Wing*, chap. 9.)

are biologically equipped. As a capacity to oppose and resist, aggression is not so much a need to be satisfied as the negative underside of such needs. As such, it is an elemental aspect of the striving that marks the human biological condition.[35]

To summarize, in its biological sense, the human agent is a living animal who strives to maintain the conditions of its existence and to obtain its organically rooted satisfactions in an indifferent and dangerous world. Accordingly, it is biochemically and morphologically equipped to oppose, fight back, and attack. Our biology, in other words, disposes us toward a range of satisfactions and equips us to oppose whatever threatens to remove them.

Three concluding comments are in order. First, if there is a characteristically modern, that is, postclassical, consensus about human agency, it is the conviction that nonrational or appetitive traits (affections, will, desire, and interest) are primary in our psychological makeup. This consensus contains only a faint hint of the older hierarchical view in which reason is called to govern the wild horses of emotion and desire. This ascent of the appetitive soul to prominence is argued by such moderns as Jonathan Edwards (the affections), Arthur Schopenhauer (the will), Freud (desire, instincts), and Jürgen Habermas (interests). It prevails in Marxist, existentialist, personalist, feminist, and pragmatic approaches to the human condition. It is also confirmed in the biology of the human being. In biological perspective, what is central and primary is what the human being needs in the struggle for life and well-being. In this view the human being is a living animal oriented to its environment by way of sense perception, disposed emotionally toward certain organic satisfactions, and able to be mobilized against what opposes it.

The second comment anticipates Part Two of this work since it is about the relation of aggression to human good and evil. If the biological dimension of agency is not separate from the other dimensions, then the tendencies and oppositions of striving are at work when the agent goes wrong and experiences freedom. A risk attends this acknowledgement. Widespread is the tendency to reduce human action and especially human evil to external causalities. Ancients and moderns have traced evil to the beast within. I only note that straightforward biological analysis of human propensities yields no such thing. No inexorable causality marks the journey from the hypothalamus and the hormones to human evil. Abstracted

35. J. Z. Young states the point succinctly: "The capacity for rage when appropriately aroused is undoubtedly a 'physiological' response, including activation of specific hypothalamic and other centres and is a 'defence' instinct. It is less clear that there is in man an inborn 'need' for aggression or cruel behavior." *The Study of Man* (Oxford, Eng.: Clarendon, 1971), 629.

into itself, the human biological condition is neither good nor evil but a set of capacities and tendencies which are the root of but also gathered up into the distinctive experiencing life of human beings, thus into language, embodiment, and ways of being spatial, social, and temporal.

Finally, even as we must distinguish the phylogenetically based but situationally evoked aggression and human evil, so we must distinguish the limitation and danger of the human biological condition from the more inclusive category of tragic existence. Tragic existence means a necessary or inescapable interdependence between suffering and satisfaction, between goods obtained and prices paid. The tragic is foreshadowed by the biological in that the heritage of human phylogeny makes possible everything from language to personhood and carries with it the possibility of extreme suffering. But at the abstracted level of the biological condition, all we can speak of is the vulnerability of the individual or species in a limiting and dangerous environment. To call these things tragic requires the personal, in other words, transcendence. But the tragic so experienced is not disconnected from the perils and vulnerabilities of organic life.

5
ELEMENTAL PASSIONS OF PERSONAL BEING

But all subsists by elemental strife;
And Passions are the elements of life.[1]
Alexander Pope

Half-conscious of his frenzied, crazed unrest,
The fairest stars from Heaven he requireth,
From Earth the highest raptures and the best,
And all the near and far that he desireth
Fails to subdue the tumult of his breast.[2]
J. W. Goethe

AGENTS AS EMBODIED PASSIONS

I continue to explore the third sphere of human reality, the sphere of human agency. So far I have offered brief accounts of the personal and biological dimensions of human agents. It is important not to forget that what is under consideration is a living, acting individual. And living individuals are ever active in actual situations. To live is to act. And to act means to exist in situations that offer resistance and that call forth efforts. Situations present us with what must be picked, gathered, cooked, shaped into a tool or weapon, built, avoided, thought about, escaped, learned, climbed, uncovered, composed, tracked down, and hidden. What prompts us to engage in these multiple efforts of everyday life? Effortful action is never a mere passivity, a posture of indifference. It is motivated. It serves short-term and long-term aims that guide what we value, choose, and attempt. And engendering these aims are all sorts of interests, needs, desires, wishes, and even phylogenetically rooted tendencies which determine what we value, choose, and attempt. In short, the human agent lives in situations through effortful activities fueled by desires. Let us recall that personal being has a unique temporality in which retention and anticipation are conjoined in an ever-present flow of experience. But this is only the most formal meaning of human temporality. In our actual situations, the temporality of agents is never a

1. Alexander Pope, *Essay on Man,* Epistle 1, 5, 169–70.
2. J. W. Goethe, *Faust,* trans. B. Taylor (New York: Washington Square Press, 1964), Prologue in Heaven.

flow of experience, a directional movement from the past to the future, or even the experience of external changes. Agents are temporal as interests and passions orient them toward discerned future possibilities. We human agents are temporal in and through our desires.

Desire (*epithumia, eros, appetitus*) is a recurring theme in the anthropologies of ancient Greece and early Christianity.[3] Suspecting that desire was the culprit behind life's troubles, ancient anthropologies explored ways in which it could be tamed. The Christian-Platonic tradition proposed that desire should adapt itself to the way things are. But desire as such does not discern the way things are. Thus, desire needs the guidance of the faculty that apprehends reality, namely reason (*nous, ratio*). But in recent centuries of Western thought, there have arisen anthropologies that challenge reason's hegemony over desire. Goethe, Kierkegaard, Jonathan Edwards, Charles Fourier, Marx, Freud, Maurice Blondel, and Buber are only a few who have contributed to this reversal. In their view, the passions are not just more powerful than reason: they are needed to properly orient reason's function. Things like justice, loyalty, and loving-kindness are engendered not by reason but from interests and desires. When reason loses its connection with these things, it loses what makes it important and useful. Further, it loses its proper norms and degenerates into a destructive and manipulative instrument. This modern anthropology of desire sometimes effects another reversal that ends, paradoxically, in a new rationalism. Narrow or reductionist types of empiricism reduce desire to the need system we share with other primates or to the complex of interests that constitute advanced industrial societies. Society's regulations help order the genetically rooted needs. Political and economic institutions take charge of the interests they themselves create. Desire is again subjugated to reason, namely, a pragmatic and technological reason cut loose from all connection with the normative passions that humanize human life.

Advanced industrial societies foster cynical versions of both desire and reason by reducing desire to a visible and manipulable phenomenon of the marketplace. Their sciences offer the research tools for understanding this visible and marketable desire. But even the so-called rationalism of premodern philosophies knew a deeper desire, something residing in what Edwards called the heart. I have no inclination to discredit the

3. In classical Greek philosophy, *epithumia* is the desire for the pleasant, an appetite for what we discern to be a fulfillment good. For different ways Plato, Aristotle, and the Stoics interpreted it, see F. F. Peters, *Greek Philosophical Terms: A Historical Lexicon* (New York: New York University Press, 1967), "Epithumia." For a history of passion in Western thought, see Denis de Rougement, *Love in the Western World*, trans. M. Belgion (New York: Harcourt, Brace and Co., 1940).

empirist's concern with society-based interests and genetically rooted needs. These studies help uncover the multitude of fears, wishes, hopes, interests, and even phobias and manias that attend human life. However, we must ask whether there are more elemental desires behind this plethora of felt yearnings. Few would deny that biologically rooted desires and needs related to survival, comfort, and reproduction have a fundamental character. They are not just passing fads of societal subsystems and epochs. But only a biological reductionism that represses the personal dimension and interhuman sphere would contend that biological needs are the only basic desires.

THREE ELEMENTAL PASSIONS

The various dimensions of human agents all show agency as a desiring existence. Our temporality is not just a flow through time but a telic orientation to things needed and sought. Our participation in our interpersonal relations and social institutions is not indifferent but interested. But agents exist in the world not simply as miscellaneous aggregates of interests. Some things concern us more than others. Many aims and even long-term agendas are set by deep and comprehensive desires that appear to structure the very way we exist in the world and move through time. I shall call these deep desires *elemental passions.* Passions are elemental when they are directed toward the spheres of human reality, are found in some form throughout human history, and are at the root of more specific motivations and behaviors. They are basic hungers that point the actions of agents in certain directions. In spite of the great variety of social systems, we would not recognize a society as human whose agents totally lacked these passions.

Without pretending to an exhaustive analysis, I shall explore three of these passions. One of them occurs in conjunction with personal being itself. It is the passion of the agent for its survival and the well-being of its own agency, its very reality. A second takes place in connection with the way agents experience the sphere of the interhuman. While the interhuman is a sphere of human reality irreducible to agents, it also impinges on agents in such a way as to evoke their deepest passions. In other words, agency itself is structured by a passion for interhuman confirmation and fulfillment. I also contend that the passion for the interhuman carries with it a need for the social. The third passion does not arise in connection with any of the spheres. It may be that it has some rootage in the biological dimension of our being. It arises in connection with our world negotiations, and is the passion for reality. It is my conviction that the character and workings of both human evil and redemption elude us as long as we fail to apprehend these deep passions of human agency.

All of the elemental passions embody the following four features. First, the very fact that they are passions means that they are never terminated. Their drive is ever beyond their present realizations. Thus, their imagined objects or references are always penultimate. Second, these passions are not so much for discrete entities or objects as states of affairs. Even the passion to possess a specific object is a passion for a state of affairs of having, enjoying, and the like. And even when the reference of the passion is something specific, the passion desires at the same time whatever conditions are necessary for the existence and maintenance of that thing. To desire justice, affection, or security is to desire a very broad and complex set of conditions.[4] Third, because they are passions for, they are at the same time and in an intrinsic way, negations. They negate or oppose what stands in their way. They resist and try to overcome conditions that frustrate them or compete with their penultimate fulfillments. Finally, the passions manifest the natural egocentrism of human agents. This is not to say that they are corrupt or evil.[5] But as passions they are desires on

4. Aspiration or desire is the unifying theme of Maurice Blondel's remarkable piece of reflective philosophy, *L'Action* (1893). Looked at in one way, this philosophical anthropology is a multi-strata description of human life. But what ties the strata together is a dialectic of desire. Blondel thus corrects the abstraction which one stratum perpetuates by uncovering a desire past that stratum, thus from intentions to and past the organic body, from individual to social action, etc.

5. A contemporary theologian who argues the opposite position is Wolfhart Pannenberg. According to Pannenberg, natural human egocentrism is itself sin. He speaks of the classical tradition's inability to see sin's "rootedness" in "the natural conditions of human existence." *Anthropology in Theological Perspective*, trans. M. J. O'Connell (Philadelphia: Westminster, 1985), 108. With this statement I have no disagreement, since to say that sin is rooted in such conditions is not to identify them with sin, nor is it necessarily to say that that rootedness is a cause of sin. But Pannenberg also says, "Why, then, is the egocentricity of human beings regarded as sin but not the analogous forms of centrally guided behavior that are found in animals?" (109). And he accepts the implications of this position when he says that "the natural conditions of their existence, and therefore that which they are by nature, that human beings must overcome and cancel out if they are to live their lives in a way befitting their 'nature' as human beings" (108). Another implication is that *Angst* or dread, "the feeling of dizziness when freedom is left to its own resources," presupposes sin (102). Thus, he rejects Kierkegaard's notion of a constitutive ontological anxiety that is the presupposition of sin and argues instead that it is the effect of sin (104).

I find this little passage resembling ancient Manicheanism quite puzzling in an otherwise excellent interpretation of sin. One of his grounds for identifying natural egocentrism and sin is his distinction between the natural condition of human beings and their essence, which is a task and a destiny. If the distinction is really meant chronologically, thus, identifying stages of human racial development which we are meant to transcend, the distinction is one between primitive states and maturation, not sin and non-sin. Schleiermacher saw this point clearly. If, however, it is an ontological distinction, it posits something about human beings which they may transcend, but which they are never without. It is surely proper to say that as self-transcending and personal, human beings transcend their embodiment, their organic needs, etc. But this is not to say that embodiment, needs, and the like are ever canceled, nor does it show they are necessarily sinful. If natural egocentrism is really sinful, then the effect of redemption and the presence of the sacred will be to eliminate it, and the final and eschatological projection of redemption will have human beings as utterly lacking of natural egocentrism. But to be a finite creature at all, distinguished from God,

behalf of the desirer. They yearn for fulfillments that pertain to the one who yearns, even if those fulfillments have to do with goods of others or a broad system of living things.

The Passion of Subjectivity

The passion of subjectivity is both something familiar and elusive. It eludes us because the focus of our everyday actions is not directly on our subjectivity itself but on things at hand. It is familiar because it sounds the tone, sets the prevailing attitude of all of our actions. We ask: Is it dangerous? Will I like it? Is it satisfying? Matters of life or death are not usually the subject of our everyday world preoccupations but they are never very far removed. Hence, our panicked response to a near fall over a cliff or to learning that a trivial symptom may be the signal of our impending death. What prompts the panic is a qualitatively different kind of prospect, the prospect of our very nonexistence, removal of the absolute condition of all other prospects. Biological anthropologists will be quick to remind us that evolution builds the urge and even the skills to survive into every individual of every species, and we human beings are no exception. But this phylogenetic heritage is only one element in the passion of subjectivity. The biologically rooted urge to survive continues but in a transformed way in personal or self-presencing agents. The very meaning of survival broadens. The question, How did you survive that terrible job? does not mean, Why are you not dead? It rather means, How did you bear up under immense pressures and how did you manage to keep your poise and integrity in the face of the job's challenge to your person? The passion of subjectivity is, thus, the way a self-presencing being exists.[6] It is self-presencing as itself a passion.

Why is self-presencing a passion? Personal being is a distinctive way of being temporal in which the remembered past and the anticipated future converge in the flow of the present. This time above time makes

means self-direction. This would be as true for angels as for animals. Pannenberg has fostered this problem because he fails to identify what constitutes natural egocentrism, namely, the embodied centeredness of the individuals lived-space and lived-time, desires for well-being, and needs originating from our biological condition.

A second and perhaps major ground for Pannenberg's is the argument that to be naturally egocentric and thus to be anxious for one's own condition is the opposite of believing in God or being God-centered. Thus he can argue that even the ontological anxiety we have as finite and limited is sinful and a sign of sin. But such anxiety is simply the affective and experiential mark of being creaturely vulnerable. I cannot see how Pannenberg can say this is a sign of sin without saying sin is finitude itself. This is why his view perpetuates a bit of ancient Manicheanism.

6. The theme of the passion of subjectivity can be found in many philosophers. Its seminal and perhaps definitive expression is to be found in the works of Søren Kierkegaard, especially his *Concluding Unscientific Postscript,* trans. David Swenson (Princeton, N.J.: Princeton University Press, 1941), Part Two, chaps. 1–3.

possible our way of relating to things in acts of meaning. We are *homo poeta*.[7] Through bearers of meaning (gestures, images, words), we perceive things, disregard, delight in, and weigh evidences. And once we invest future possibilities with meanings, we can consider those possibilities abstractly. We can project ourselves and even our vulnerabilities onto the future and thus reflect on them. In such reflection, we become thematically aware of ourselves and our situations. And with thematic self-awareness come transcendence, irreducibility, and self-making. It would be misleading, however, to think that these marks of personal being are attributes of an object (the self) about which we are passionately concerned. They describe instead a passionate way of existing, an embodied, self-presencing "I" impassioned to be itself. Thus, the passion of subjectivity is the passion of the self for itself, not as a *Doppelgänger*, a replicated self-as-object, but as a passion to exist as itself.

The passion of subjectivity for itself is also a passion of resistance.[8] We resist what threatens to annihilate, reduce, or challenge our being as self-presencing. We resist challenges to our autonomy and misinterpretations of our determinate or specified being, our I-as. But these challenges are only emissaries of a final challenge.[9] Because we are able to thematize future possibilities as possibilities, we develop an acute sense of the contingency of events. The future we need and hope for may not come about. Our specific aims and agendas do not roll forth from a predetermined cosmic scheme. And we sense with this the contingency of our own being, our being as this and that, and our very transcendence and self-making. It is under this shadow of contingency that the passion of subjectivity conducts its resistances. Poets throughout human history have sung this sense of mortality, a sense that arises because a sure knowledge of a fulfilling destiny is not a constitutive aspect of our subjectivity. This absence is not a metaphysical fact, a basis for the cognitive certainty that there is no such destiny.[10] It is simply the passion of subjectivity for itself projected into an uncertain future.

7. *Homo poeta* is Ernst Becker's term to describe human beings as creators of meaning. For an extended treatment of this theme, see Becker, *The Structure of Evil*, 169–210.

8. Alexandre Kohève's brilliant study of Hegel's *Phenomenology of Spirit* begins with the contention that the "I" of human beings emerges not with simply animal-type desires but with a negating type of desire which moves to action. This negating action is what gives the "I" its content. See *Introduction to the Reading of Hegel: Lectures on the Phenomenology of Spirit*, trans. James H. Nichols, Jr. (New York: Basic Books, 1969), 3–9.

9. One of the most eloquent and passionate statements of the resistance of personal being especially to the ultimate threat of death is Miguel de Unamuno's *The Tragic Sense of Life in Men and Peoples*, trans. J. E. Crawford Flitch (London: Macmillan, 1921).

10. Nothing is being said here one way or the other about teleology and the objective issue of human destiny. The symbolic world of religious faiths, their theologies, or even certain metaphysics offer versions of this issue. The only point being made here is that we

The passion of subjectivity for itself is at the same time a passion for something other than the agent itself. Even the biologically rooted struggle for life and well-being is a struggle for the environmental conditions of life and is therefore directed beyond that on behalf of which the struggle takes place. This double orientation also structures the passion of subjectivity. The agent's passion for its own transcending specificity is necessarily a passion for the conditions that maintain such a reality. The resisting side of the passion shows this. The agent is up against something (death) that will remove it from the world and something (the world) whose operations do not conspire to prevent this or even affirm the importance of the agent's well-being. The passion of subjectivity is thus directed beyond subjectivity itself to whatever realities, world system, or transworldly powers that could maintain its distinctive subjectivity.

The Passion of the Interhuman

Few human beings are so hermit-like or misanthropic that they deny their need for other human beings. Silas Marner types need others from whom to separate themselves and misanthropes need others against whom to direct their rancor. All sorts of social needs and dependencies attend the families, friendships, leisure activities, and work of everyday life. A reductionist method would leave the matter there. It is content to observe that human social needs originate in biologically rooted tendencies toward survival, reproduction, and the life of societies. For a dimensional anthropology, no human phenomenon is reducible to the causal workings of organisms and societies. And any method that avoids the dimensions will also miss the elemental passions.

A second deep passion constitutive of the life of agents is a passion for the interhuman. Let us recall that in interpersonal relation unmergible selves (alterity) that are already social selves (intersubjectivity) exist toward each other in face-to-face relation. Why does the interhuman evoke a passion? Why is the very being of agents constituted by the desire for interpersonal or face-to-face relation? An initial proposition may assist us. The passion of the interhuman is a passion for reciprocal relations characterized by compassionate obligation and for the social as the sedimented condition that protects and supports those reciprocal relations. Three themes reside in this proposition: the aspiration of the subject for the other's acknowledgement; the aspiration of the subject for others to acknowledge; and the aspiration for community.

human beings do not have some sort of cognitive certainty about our destiny built into our experience or into the dimensions of our being. The only things built into our being are aspirations.

1. In chapter 2 I described the shared world coming forth from ongoing cognitive reinforcements. We agree together that an event really happened, that a certain object is there before us, and that it has certain features. In these agreements, the actors mutually acknowledge one another's perspectives and experiences. They confirm, validate, and cognitively negotiate with each other. Behind these acknowledgements of the interhuman is a deep passion. We are rightly suspicious of the cognitive status of claims that have no possible intersubjective verification. The agent's aspiration to know, to sort out what is real (the third elemental passion), carries with it the need for the reality confirmation of the interhuman.

Mutual acknowledgements needed by our cognitive life are behind our need and desire for the interhuman. But cognitive attitudes are only one way human agents exist in the world. The passion of subjectivity is the agent's passion to exist as its own autonomous and self-making self. But the agent also discerns and experiences that it cannot bestow these things on itself by its own act. It thus aspires to an acknowledgement by a genuine other not just of its cognitive perspective but of its own subjectivity. We human beings desire confirmation from the other of our integrity and reality. We aspire to approval, respect, and love. And we bitterly resent the other who withholds these acknowledgements and deals with us as if we were not real agents.[11] To use Emmanuel Levinas's concept, we want genuine others to discern in us the face, which is to say, something that evokes from that other a response of compassionate responsibility. This desire is not just for cognitive collaboration but for empathetic and emotional appreciation. It is the aspiration for the affection, empathy, even love of the other. It desires an other who will respond aesthetically and emotionally to the mystery, uniqueness, creativity, and even beauty of the face. This aspiration is for recognition in its fullest sense, a recognition that has the character of felt emotion and carries with it affection and love. In sum, because the interhuman is an interpersonal relation of the face, human agents are not indifferent to whether the other acknowledges their subjectivity in compassionate obligation.

2. If the passion for the interhuman meant merely the need for the other's empathetic acknowledgement, it would be incorrigibly narcissistic, dominated by the passion of subjectivity. But, the passion of the interhuman has another side. In the interhuman as interpersonal relation, the agent is already drawn beyond itself in acts that recognize and empathize

11. Kohève expounds this motif as a desire for the desire of the other and this means the desire to be recognized by the other as the value that I am. See Kohève, *Introduction to the Reading of Hegel*, 7.

with genuine others. Lured by the vulnerable beauty and mystery of the other, the agent aspires for relation itself and is impoverished when it has no others to feelingly acknowledge.[12] According to some interpretations of human needs and aspirations, this desire for relation is only a disguised form of the passion of subjectivity. Thus, the need for others to acknowledge and love is a utility to biologically and societally formed ego needs. In such a view, human interrelation has no face, and there is nothing about the other that evokes the agent's gift of compassion. But given the fact and reality of the face, the passion of the interhuman is also a desire for others on whom to bestow the gifts of empathy. This is not a need for affection that we bring to the interhuman and the face. The face itself engenders the self-transcending need for the interhuman. And human agents are deeply impoverished when they are deprived of others on whom to bestow their acknowledgements and affections.

It is somewhat ambiguous to say that love, respect, affection, and empathy are themselves the objects or referents of the passion of the interhuman. These terms describe the emotional postures of agents, and to aspire for these things is not yet to aspire for the interhuman. But the passion of the interhuman is not for emotional postures either of the desiring agent or the other. On the other hand, if these terms describe situations in the interhuman itself, then the passion for the interhuman is also a passion for these relations.

I have described two sides of the passion of the interhuman, an aspiration for acknowledgement and for others to acknowledge. These are not, however, two passions. The passion of the interhuman is neither merely a passion for the self's confirmation by the other nor a self-transcending passion for an object of affection. Located in interpersonal relation and under the lure of the face, these movements are part of one passion, a passion for human face-to-face reciprocity and intimacy.

3. Even as the passion of subjectivity carries with it aspirations directed at the conditions of subjectivity, so the passion of the interhuman reaches past its target of reciprocity to the conditions of reciprocity. This is why the passion of the interhuman is at the same time a passion for the social. The sedimentations and institutionalizations of social systems are the contexts and carriers of all specific human interactions. It is social systems that make available to interrelating human beings the stuff of the interrelation: language, symbols, norms, culture, typifications, social aims, and corporate memory. Apart from these things, there can be no

12. "The primordial drive of the self is not only an impulse toward the other and toward the value of the other, as Scheler so admirably showed; it is also an efficient energy that wants to contribute to the existence and development of the other," Maurice Nedoncelle, *Love and the Person*, trans. Sr. Ruth Adelaide (New York: Sheed and Ward, 1966), 10.

reciprocal acts of the face, no mutual acknowledgement, respect, empathy, affection, or understanding. History teaches us that oppressive societies can impoverish the interpersonal, deface the face, and replace intimacy with social relations of anonymity and deprivation. Oppression can produce forms of social consciousness dominated by resentments and anger that distort the capacity to grant to the other the gifts for which it asks. Accordingly, the aspiration of the interhuman for the social is not just for the bare fact of institutional ordering but for the kind of sociality that can serve as an environment of reciprocal intimacy. It is not really imaginable that human agents are constituted by a desire to live in Tolkein's Mordor or Huxley's Brave New World. The social horizon of the interhuman is a society whose aims and normative culture function to protect and enhance the face and its reciprocities.[13]

The Passion for Reality

We human beings are not merely personal and interhuman; we are living organisms, which is to say, we exist in the environment we call nature. The content of our experiences is the mundane content of the entities and events of our surrounding world. Rarely is our attention turned directly to our own agency. World occurrences are what get our attention. Nor do we live in our environment in the mode of indifference. Like the animals, especially the mammalian vertebrates and higher primates, we are constantly alert to the dangers and possibilities of our environment. It is important that we not confuse water with sand, that we know where there are food resources, and that we distinguish one kind of living thing from another. These things have been of paramount importance from the time of *homo habilis* and the Cro-Magnon peoples to the present. In other words, the orientation to survival and well-being we share with all living things requires us to interpret the happenings of everyday life with a fair amount of accuracy. The perils and satisfactions of life orient us to what is so and what is not so, to what is real and what is only apparent. Orientation toward reality thus arises in conjunction with our efforts to exist in our situations. The character of this orientation is primarily practical and pragmatic. The ever-changing situations of everyday life require us to adapt, to apprehend, and act on what is so. And this includes getting along in the social system. Such is the orientation to reality pressed on us by the challenges of our worldly environment.

13. In Robert O. Johann's study of love in the context of intersubjectivity, we find a version of this theme. According to Johann love as an aspiration cannot help but also be a desire for a community. See *The Meaning of Love: An Essay Towards a Metaphysics of Intersubjectivity* (Glen Rock, N.J.: Paulist, 1954), chaps. 2, 3.

This description of the biological and pragmatic root of reality orientation is abstract and thin. Structured by personal and social dimensions, our orientation toward reality takes on depth and complexity. With the interhuman comes a shared world and a new meaning of reality. What is so and not so is what is intersubjectively sharable, what is available to cognitive agreement. With personal being comes temporality (retention and anticipation carried by language) and thus the experience of the world in the form of meanings. In one simultaneous act we can synthesize various aspects of a thing into one thing. We can mean a thing in relation to its environment, locate its type, consider the conditions of its existence, and grasp its characteristic behaviors. We can isolate aspects of things to reflect on or experiment with. We can track the ways in which a thing undergoes changes through time. With meaning, then, comes self-aware perspective, interpretation, relativity, knowledge as a process, classifications, and many other notions that express our cognitive transactions with the world.

The advent of meaning changes reality in another respect. When things are apprehended in acts of meaning, their reality is never just that of sheer presence but a presenting-eluding that calls forth a process of inquiry. Because we can mean things as this or that, we probe hidden contents, explore conditions and causes and compare things. The experience and knowledge of something turns out to be a journey of perspectives, a movement among a multiplicity of facades. Each facade (aspect, dimension, causal lineage) calls for distinctive perspectives, methods, and discourses. Meant reality always has a surplus, a more. And this surplus draws the biologically rooted orientation to reality past the sheer presentation into explorations that have no set limits.

This multifaceted way we experience real things awakens in human agents attitudes of curiosity and perplexity whose orientation is not simply everyday world usefulness. Awakened by meanings and mystery, we human beings push beyond our pragmatic and biological bases of reality orientation. And once awakened, curiosity has no assigned stopping place. It can be drawn from the thing to its relation, its context, or to the context of all contexts, even to the puzzling facticity of being itself. Curiosity can be pragmatically but not absolutely satisfied. It can find out enough to make the machine work but it never tracks any reality out to a place where the questions end. Thus, even the most discrete puzzles contain an element of mystery, an element which explanation does not reach or exhaust.

Meaning and language have a second effect on our relation to reality. They make possible a distinctive kind of satisfaction. Because we experience through meanings, we experience things as meaningful, true, recurring, surprising, similar, and significant. Experiencing the world through meanings, we apprehend contrasts, colors, varieties, patterns, harmonies, and sounds. And there are satisfactions intrinsic to these experiences. Meanings enable us to experience reality not just as useful but as beautiful. It can be argued, of course, that beauty itself is a kind of utility. But if that is so, it is nevertheless a utility that stops with itself, that is sought not for the sake of something else. Nor can human agents be utterly indifferent to this aesthetic richness of reality. It does make a difference whether the world is a single, colorless, shapeless, changeless entity, or whether it presents seasons, variable terrains, colors, surprises, life-forms, familiarities. We would need to develop a philosophical aesthetics to explore what is involved in the experience of beauty and the world as beautiful. I am only contending that meaning introduces an aesthetic dimension into our experience of reality. Thus, through meaning the passion for what is so, born amidst the pragmatic needs of life, lures us toward the mystery and beauty of the world. This is the agent's passion for reality. It is the desire to understand the mundane realities about us, a desire that finds satisfaction in their illumination and in their beauty.[14]

Linear methods of analysis move from one thing to another as if each item had a separate existence. When applied to the elemental passions, this procedure tends to obscure their intrinsic interdependence. Biologically rooted tendencies to survive and seek the conditions of well-being are part of the passion of subjectivity. Biologically rooted needs for survival, the shared world of the interhuman, and the linguistic and meaning components of personal being converge in the passion for reality. And without the passion of subjectivity for itself and the passion for reality, there would be no genuine others and thus no passion for the interhuman. The elemental passions, then, are interdependent. Furthermore, these passions have a role in determining what is appropriate for and what violates human reality. Acts, policies, social systems, and symbols that would abolish or repress any one of these passions properly evoke our resistance. But, the interdependence itself is also normative.[15]

14. Charles Fourier described twelve passions of human beings which should be considered in thinking about human society. Three of these are basic passions and one of them, the "cabalistic" passion, is the passion for mystery and rich experience. For an exposition of the three basic passions, see Becker, *The Structure of Evil,* 131–32. Fourier's philosophy of the passions can be found in *The Passions of the Soul and Their Influence on Society and Civilization,* trans. H. Doherty (London: H. Baillieve, 1851), 2 vols.

15. The notion of interdependence and appropriate harmony or integration between the dimensions of the human being is an ancient one, classically formulated in the philosophical anthropology of Augustine. In his analysis, the three aspects of the soul (the animating power of the human being) are mind, will, and the emotions. Various relations of dependence mark the unity of the ensouled body so that some aspects depend on others for their operation. For instance, the senses depend on the mind for their intention. Will (*voluntas*) as

For instance, when the passion for reality loses its connection with the interhuman, and thus becomes indifferent to the shared world, the result is a subjectivizing of what is so and not so. The question of reality is reduced to the question, What is real for me? When the passion for the interhuman and the social loses its connection with the passion of subjectivity, its agenda becomes the external manipulation and control of human reality.

With these elemental passions comes another aspect of agential vulnerability. Passion is itself a vulnerability because it is constituted by a lack, a hunger for, an emptiness that would be filled. In its most formal sense, the vulnerability of passions is this ever-present nonfulfillment. There is a stronger sense in which these elemental passions are vulnerable. These basic aspirations are not mathematical or formal predicates but marks of existence. As such they exist in degrees and are subject to the biological, historical, social, and even subjective influences. A certain kind of society can have a repressive effect on the passion for reality. A type of child socialization can introduce pathological elements into the passion of the interhuman and the desire for the other as source and object of affection. Likewise, a vulnerability attends the interdependence of the passions. This interdependence is not a fixed essence but is a rather fragile condition that can undergo alteration, decline, and distortion. The *harmonia,* to use the ancient term, of the elemental passions is itself fragile and requires its own conditions.

THE TRAGIC STRUCTURE OF THE ELEMENTAL PASSIONS

The very thing that makes the elemental passions elemental also gives them their tragic character. This is the always unclosable gulf between desiring and desired that constitutes a passion. To say that the elemental passions are never fulfilled is not to say that they yearn for a contentless infinity. Subjectivity, the interhuman, and reality are not utterly general and contentless notions. For instance, the passion of subjectivity inclines toward all the contents and conditions that have to do with securing, confirming, and protecting the determinate self. This is why these aspirations do in fact have a kind of fulfillment. Agential subjectivity finds fulfillments when it is bodily nourished, physically safe, when injuries and diseases find resources for healing, and when it is secured against the depredations of others. Fulfillments of the passion

a desire unites all these aspects but for harmony to be preserved, there must be a structure of governance. Since the *ratio* of the mind is what grasps goods, truths, conditions of happiness, it is the faculty which brings the desire for the good in relation to reality. *Sapientia* or wisdom is the state of having apprehended the good by reason.

of the interhuman arise in connection with the caring nurture of infants and mature relations of friendship, cooperation, and loyalty. The passion for reality is constantly enriched by the accumulating experiences of a complex and beautiful world.

Yet it is clear that these are fulfillments that do not fulfill. The specific wishes of everyday life are sometimes realized in an unqualified way. Our wish for rain, a new car, or a birthday gift can come true. Physical needs like hunger can be momentarily satiated. But the elemental passions are never brought to an end even when momentarily fulfilled. This is because of the ever-present gulf between their projected referent and their actual realization, satisfaction. Consider the passion of subjectivity. We aspire to a secured and meaningful existence in the face of all things that imperil us. We resist the status of momentary entities originating from and destined for chaos. We want some other destiny than annihilation, and some other total environment or world-scheme than the arbitrary clash of subatomic particles. The subjectivity we seek is an invulnerable subjectivity, our agential being as invulnerable. But there is nothing about the agent that possesses and secures this invulnerability. The only agent who looks back at us in the mirror is an imperiled agent. Its very passion shows its constitutive vulnerability. Nor is there anything about the agent's environment by way of conditions of safety, comfort, or meaning that promises invulnerability. Thus, an abyss yawns between what the passion seeks and what it gets in its everyday life fulfillments.

The passion of the interhuman stretches over the same gulf. This passion is for an unqualified intimate reciprocity, a relation of mutual acknowledgement that preserves genuine otherness yet has the character of total empathetic understanding and affection. Desired is a co-relation of unqualified understanding, confirmation, respect, and love. We want others who are genuine others and who therefore relate to us from their perspective and autonomy but who can so penetrate our own otherness as to absolutely understand and promote our being. What we actually experience are relations darkened by misunderstanding, ego-oriented intentions, and incompatible agendas with their attending antipathies. The empathy and insight we experience from the other and offer to the other are always mixed with misunderstanding, reservation, and benign alienation. Because of human evil, it is also mixed with violation and subjugation. When this passion reviews the social systems it needs, it experiences a similar gulf. The social that we want is an ideal, a utopia. The social that we have is at best a restrictive and compromising community and at worst a dehumanizing oppressive system.

The passion for reality is a passion to understand and experience the mystery of things in their full reality and beauty. Its referent is the totality of things, the events, processes, and contents of what we call the world. This passion has carried human history to astonishing levels of pragmatic and theoretical knowledge and to heights of aesthetic accomplishment. Yet neither the mass of theoretical knowledge nor theories about the world's origin and meaning end the reality pilgrimage. Familiar is the metascientific attitude that claims that this or that method or discovery is the pot of gold at the end of the cognitive rainbow. These attitudes repress the passion for reality by their claim to a final or definitive realization. Thus, the mystery of the world is resolved into a big-bang theory of the origin of the cosmos. Or it is eliminated by methods which discredit by fiat and in an a priori way knowledge itself. Or it is ended by discrediting all cognitive undertakings but criticism itself. However, since explanation must always concern the relation between one apprehended or posited state of affairs and another, the most advanced theories of the origin of the cosmos remain theories of transition from a posited instability to a discerned cosmos. The apprehending or positing must occur before the explanation begins. Cosmogonical theories do not directly apprehend or explain that which is initially posited, the facticity of the precosmic. In the presence of this facticity, there continues an awe and perplexity about the very existence of things. Here too the gulf between the referent and realization of the elementary passion remains unbridged.

It should be clear why elemental passions are tragic in character. These passions propel us human beings into action. They are our deepest motivating inclinations. Yet they cannot be fulfilled. They must ever remain hungry and thirsty. Yet they are not empty wishes, idle fancies. They do obtain realizations of all sorts in everyday life, but realizations are always disproportionate to the passions themselves.[16] This interdependence between passion and referent is tragic because we cannot have the fulfillments without the passion and the very existence of the passion requires some fulfillments.

ETERNAL HORIZON

I have argued that a gulf yawns between the elementary passions and their references. However much they find fulfillment, the flame of desire still burns. Something about these provisional realizations disqualifies them as the real and final referent of the passions. The agent passionately yearns for whatever would secure and guarantee its own existence and meaning. It finds in its social system resources for safety and health and a symbolic framework that assigns it its place in the world. But the social

16. For an analysis of intrinsic disproportions that constitute the fragility of human existence, see Paul Ricoeur, *Fallible Man*, trans. C. Kelbley (Chicago, Ill.: H. Regnery, 1950).

system itself is fragile and corruptible. It is not invulnerable against the perils of nature and history and against internal cataclysm. It cannot, therefore, be that which fulfills the agent's passion for itself. We passionately desire a community of intimacy that can bestow and receive unqualified love and understanding. But the limitations of our knowledge in the face of otherness and the benign alienations of the interpersonal prevent any specific individual or community from being this absolute fulfillment. We would understand the things, even the worlds, that swim into our presence out of micro and macro facticities but our actual discoveries and insights altogether do not dispel the mystery of that facticity. Thus, the realizations and satisfactions that our passions do obtain are always only penultimate referents. Our elemental passions ever desire through and past these things. They strive through what they actually experience, what is presented to them, and what momentarily fulfills them.

Because the passions desire through the relative realizations at hand in the world, the referent of the passions is not an entity in the world system but the horizon of entities and resources. Because no finite resource fulfills the passions, their referent is an infinite resource, an eternal horizon. As such this referent cannot coincide with any finite entity of the world system or the world system as a whole. Does this nonspecific eternal horizon of the passions evoke a fourth passion, a single eros for the eternal? The most we can say is that the elemental passions do not point to three separate referents. However, to say that there is a single, concrete passion for the eternal suggests there is a discrete referent or object. This is just what the eternal horizon is not. Nor does passion's relation to that horizon have the character of belief-in, thematization-of, or argument-for. We are familiar with these activities of reflection present in the everyday world and in philosophies and religions. But a passion and its referent is not a cognizing, thematic activity. It is simply how agents exist in the world.

Only now are we ready to ask whether God is the referent of the elemental passions. We recall that while the referent of the elemental passions has content, it is unspecified as an existing entity. The passions themselves make no claim, utter no belief. They can and do reside in passionate atheism and passionate theism. Insofar as God is not an empty but a determinate symbol, a symbol that both has content and specifies a reality, God does not seem to be the referent of the passions. Thus, eternal horizon is no more a term for God than terms like absolute, ultimate, or infinite. And no bridge of deductions can be built from the fact of the passions and their referent to an existing God. It is equally important to note that no bridge of deductions can be constructed from the projective nature of the eternal horizon to the metaphysical conclusion that there is no God. The fact that human reality includes a passion whose referent is an eternal horizon may seem to support Feuerbachian projective theories of religion. But this support is not that of a metaphysical conclusion about a nonexistent. The fact of passion and its referent provides no more basis for a conclusion about the nonexistence of the referent than the existence.

On the other hand, this anthropological structure is not utterly unrelated to the question of God.[17] The eternal horizon of the passions is not simply a nothingness but is whatever would fulfill the passions. Thus, it is whatever would ground the self and constitute the mystery of things. This being the case, the human passion for the eternal is that feature of the human agent apart from which there could be no question of God. If we human beings were not so constituted, the only God we could possibly entertain and relate to would be either an entity at hand in the world or an utter heteronomy, something which had no relation to our desire for an unqualified acknowledgement, understanding, and being oneself. It is only because we are able to passionately desire through our penultimate satisfactions that the very notion of God is meaningful.[18]

17. From Schleiermacher through Pannenberg, theologians have tried to understand why the act or posture of religion or piety has a universal referent. In the theology of Paul Tillich this theme is explored in the notion of an unqualified or ultimate concern. In the theology of Karl Rahner, it is present as "the ultimate horizon which he himself is and which he alone forms." See *Foundations of Christian Faith: An Introduction to the Idea of Christianity,* trans. W. V. Dych (New York: The Seabury Press, 1978). It is also expressed as the "luminosity of being." See *Hearers of the Word,* trans. M. Richards (New York: Herder and Herder, 1969), chap. 33. Among recent theologians see Langdon Gilkey, *Naming the Whirlwind: The Renewal of God-language* (Indianapolis: Bobbs-Merrill, 1969), and Pannenberg, *Anthropology,* 473–74.

18. Beginning with the work of his youth, *Speeches on Religion to its Cultured Despisers* and continuing through his *Glaubenslehre,* entitled in English, *The Christian Faith,* Friedrich Schleiermacher formulated a fundamental ontological basis for piety (*Frommigkeit*) as absolute or utter dependence on an undesignated Whence. In *The Christian Faith* he contended that piety was located in *Gefühl* or immediate self-consciousness, that its essential character was a structure of utter or absolute dependence, and that the basis or origin of this structure was an element in the constitutive reciprocity human beings had with the world. That about ourselves which is utterly dependent is our freedom, our self-initiation. This freedom does not arise in connection with any mundane causality or interchange nor is it *causa sui.* The description of the agent's desire through penultimate mundane referents under an eternal horizon is part of this Schleiermacher lineage. It is, one might say, a Blondelian modification of Schleiermacher. In my formulation the eternal horizon or Whence is present not in connection with sheer nonexplainability or the experience of sheer givenness in human self-initiation but with the telic or existential desiring orientation of the agent. The theme of dependence has not completely disappeared because the eternal horizon as desired is that on which the fulfillments of the passions would depend. But the nature of the relation to that horizon is more desire or passion, than dependence. In my judgment, dependence becomes an explicit theme when the eternal horizon ceases to be a mere horizon and is manifest as the sacred, that which in some way does ground and fulfill the passions.

PART TWO

A PARADIGM OF GOOD AND EVIL

The chapters of Part One constituted a philosophy of human reality but not a theology of human condition. Their resources were various sciences and philosophies, not the primary symbols and traditions of a religious faith. I turn now to what was set aside, a specific religious tradition's paradigm of the human condition. I do this aware that the Enlightenment has fostered many offspring who think that together, sciences and philosophies exhaust the resources for illumining the human condition. Thus, they see religious faiths and the interpretations of reality they spawn as cognitively barren and incapable of contributing anything to ongoing explorations of the human mystery. But these offspring have strayed from their parent, the Enlightenment. For it was the Enlightenment's criticism of superstition and authority that uncovered the historicality and contextuality of human beings and with that the historical and contextual nature of truth itself. Specific historical times and movements may embody enduring insights into evil, hope, suffering, and freedom. Thus we continue to consult the religions and philosophies of ancient Greece, the Roman way, the stories of preindustrial hunters and gatherers, and the early Buddhist criticisms of Hinduism. Harder to believe, truths about our condition may even shine through the follies and pretentions of advanced industrial societies.

This move to a theological analysis does not, however, require precritical modes of thought, supernatural cosmologies, or appeals to ancient authorities. It is a move into the determinate experience of a religious faith as it has come to expression in an enduring system of symbols. There is nothing about this move that absolutely prohibits consulting and making use of the determinate experience of various religious faiths, thus approaching the human condition through what W. C. Smith calls a world theology. Although I am intrigued by this approach and am convinced of its importance, I have opted for the more traditional way. I shall primarily attend to the historical experience, tradition, and symbol system of one rather comprehensive religious tradition, the Hebraic tradition, and especially its successor, Christianity. This is, in other words, an exercise in Christian theology. This exercise proceeds from the question: Does this particular lineage of historical experience contain or disclose truth about the human condition? Do stories, symbols, and doctrines of Adam and Eve, the Psalmist's personal guilt before God, prophetic denunciations, the Fall, justification, and freedom come together in an overarching paradigm about human evil and its overcoming? The explorations which follow are guided by the conviction that a paradigm did arise with the historical experience of the Hebraic peoples and their religious ancestors.

Some readers may regret that a certain step or beginning point is absent from the analysis. With certain exceptions, theological treatments of major themes begin with a historical retrieval of their subject from Scripture and tradition. They do so because Scripture and tradition are the deposits of the paradigm they would interpret and because the authority of these deposits gives the paradigm its cognitive status. In more conservative versions of this procedure, the retrieval (the exegesis, the interpretation) itself sufficiently displays the truth and reality of the subject matter. What happens after the retrieval can only be setting forth the coherence between textually established truths or applying the truths to situations. Less conservative versions begin with hermeneutic retrievals aided by critical scholarship and proceed to various forms of literary, experiential, or praxis-oriented ways of ascertaining the truth of the texts. This step of textual retrieval of the subject is largely absent in these explorations. I shall not be attempting to ground claims about features of human evil or freedom by citing Pauline or prophetic texts, expounding major confessional documents, tracing the history of controversies, or surveying the landscape of contemporary religious thought. Extensive are the literatures that contain these things, and my explorations would not have been possible without them. These literatures have helped me to identify in these texts a comprehensive paradigm of the human condition. I shall explore elements of that paradigm but shall not repeat the textual work of the biblical and historical disciplines.

This analysis begins, then, with where the text expositor leaves off. Its interrogation is guided by a different question than historical scholarship poses: In what way does the Hebraic and Christian paradigm of the human condition express the truth of things? Does that paradigm have anything to do with the way we experience ourselves and our world? The term, *experience,* especially when used in connection with theology, invites serious confusions. It can evoke the picture of a discrete experience grounding each and every theological claim or surmise. But experience need not mean autobiographically significant discrete experiences. A great deal if not most of our experience occurs tacitly and has an enduring, not just a momentary, character. Memories, temporality, deep convictions, repressed guilt, and enduring relations such as loyalties or affections are all part of human experience but are not simply experiences. In this broader and deeper sense of experience, these explorations exemplify experiential theology. And if there is no connection whatever between elements in the Hebraic and Christian paradigm and the way we experience ourselves and our world, that paradigm is surely cognitively vacuous.

Part Two presents a theology of the human condition as historical freedom. As historical, it is concerned with the sphere of actual events and relations, the realm of everyday action. Because of this focus on the historical, one whole aspect of the paradigm of freedom is absent from the analysis, the motif of transhistorical apotheosis of human individuals or transhistorical completion of history itself. *Freedom* is the term I am using to gather up and unify the vocabulary of salvation in Hebraic and Christian symbolism. This term is rich in meaning, having to do with all of the senses in which the power of human evil is broken and new possibilities and actualizations of good arise.

The Introduction to Part One summarized the contents of the philosophy of human reality in major propositions. The following nine propositions summarize the contents of Part Two.

1. *Human evil and historical freedom occur together in three distinguishable spheres, which reflect three of the dimensions of the human condition: the spheres of the individual, the interhuman, and the social.* Human evil and good appear in these three spheres as idolatry and being-founded (chapters 7 through 12), alienation and communion (chapter 13), and subjugation and theonomous sociality (chapters 14 and 15). This proposition negates ways of understanding evil and freedom that posit exclusions or oppositions between the social and the individual, ontology and praxis, politics and virtue, etc.

2. *Human evil as an individual response is constituted by a distinctive dynamics, and as such is to be differentiated from tragic existence and its vulnerabilities as well as from the dynamics of pathology.* Correlative to this, historical freedom is to be distinguished from therapeutic displacements of pathologies and the solace-oriented and distractive flight from tragic existence.

3. *Because individual, interhuman, and social dimensions are mutually interpenetrating and multi-layered and because their realities at any given time remain hidden, evil and freedom do not occur merely as momentary incidents on the surface of experience but pervade and transform the topography of these spheres.* Thus, the exploration of historical freedom is an archaeological reflection, a tracing or uncovering of the ways in which evil and freedom

transform the various dimensions of personal being (its determinacy, temporality), biological being (its needs and aggressions), the interhuman (face, and obligation), and the social (power and institutionality).

4. *The intrinsic vulnerability and tragic character of the human condition are the background and origin of the dynamics of evil in individuals.* Correlative to this, historical freedom is not a release from vulnerability and the tragic but a way of existing as vulnerable and as tragic. This proposition excludes assertions that vulnerability (including mortality) and suffering are punishing outcomes of evil or that freedom (piety, righteousness, sanctification, etc.) is life without suffering and vulnerability.

5. *The content of historical freedom is not strictly correlated with human evil as the mere correction of a distortion. If that were so, the content of historical freedom would be contained in a generic description of human reality (Part One) minus evil. Something occurs in connection with the breaking of the powers of evil that introduces a new set of possibilities of good in human individuals and communities.*

6. *Because evil arises in connection with the passion for the eternal and because historical freedom (salvation) can occur only when this passion finds its referent, freedom has an intrinsically theonomous character.*

7. *Evil and redemption are interspherical.* Their operations in each sphere of human reality influence their operations in the other spheres. Thus, no account of human evil and redemption is adequate that restricts itself to one or even two of these spheres.

8. *Human reality is redeemable, transformable toward the good, because the dynamics of evil at work in each sphere have no necessary status in that sphere.* Evil, in other words, is not merely another word for biological, social, or psychological dynamics, or for the tragic structure of existence.

9. *While all the spheres are primary in their own order, the workings of redemption require a primacy of the interhuman as a primary condition of redemption in communities of the face.*

6
IDOLATRY

> The present only toucheth thee.
> But, och! I backward cast my ee
> on prospects drear!
> And forward, though I canna see,
> I guess and fear.[1]
>
> *Robert Burns*

> Idolatry is the chief crime of mankind, the supreme guilt of the world, the entire case put before judgement. For even if every sin retains its own identity and even if each is destined for judgement under its own name, each is still committed within idolatry.[2]
>
> *Tertullian*

I begin this study of human good and evil with the sphere of individual agents. Since agents only exist in interdependence with the interhuman and the social, this beginning is also an abstraction. It is, nevertheless, a useful abstraction. Anatomy and physiology, too, focus on abstract aspects of a more comprehensive and complex entity. Human bodies and organs do exist and so do human agents.[3] Individual agents, not nations, groups, or social systems, experience the world. Theologies and philosophies that ignore agents and the dimension of personal being incline toward reductionist interpretations of

1. Robert Burns, "To a Mouse," in *The Poetical Works of Robert Burns* (New York: Hurst and Co., n.d.), 44.

2. Tertullian, *De Idolatria,* trans. J. H. Waszink and J. C. M. Van Winden (Leiden, Netherlands: E. J. Brill, 1987), 23.

3. Reflection on individuals and their problems and dimensions need not entail individualism. Individualism is a way of either experiencing or interpreting the human condition as if the interhuman and the social were nonexistent or unimportant. For a fuller analysis of individualism as the primary world conviction of North American culture, see my essay, "Praxis and Piety: Hermeneutics Beyond the New Dualism," in Peter J. Paris and Douglas A. Knight, eds., *Justice and the Holy: Essays in Honor of Walter Harrelson* (Atlanta, Ga.: Scholars Press, 1989). For a criticism of the false antithesis between the individual and the corporate, see Mary Midgley, *Wickedness: A Philosophical Essay* (London, Eng.: Ark Paperbacks, 1984), 51–52. For the importance if not primacy of the individual, see Wolfhart Pannenberg's criticism of John C. Cobb in *Anthropology in Theological Perspective,* trans. M. J. O'Connell (Philadelphia: Westminster Press, 1985), 399–409.

interpretations of social evil and liberation. Political revolutions that are indifferent to individuals tend to be de-humanizing revolutions.[4] Concern for the individual is not the invention of romanticism or modern individualism. The Psalmist's deep remorse over her or his sins, Jesus' words "You are of more value than many sparrows," and the poignant cry of Paul, "Who will set me free from the body of this death?" express intense awareness of and even compassion for individuals. I begin then with an examination of the dynamics of individual evil or what Martin Luther called the bondage of the will. Conventional wisdom perceives an irreducible difference between suffering and (moral) evil. There is something qualitatively different between experiencing an injury and an act of cruelty, between the bubonic plague and the holocaust. Theologies of the Hebraic religions (Judaism, Christianity, Islam) use the term, *sin,* to make this differentiation. Sin, a Hebrew term which has found translation into Greek (*hamartia*), Latin (*peccatum*), and many other languages ancient and modern, is not a reality term in advanced industrial and therapeutic societies. Its connection with experience having become tenuous, it is less and less a term we use to interpret things like apartheid, rape, or malice. Familiar is the therapeutic language which has replaced this "god-term" (Phillip Rieff); not having oneself together, having anxiety attacks, lacking wholeness, stress, aggression, being out of touch with one's feelings, being hostile, dysfunctional, passive-aggressive, and defensive. This is, of course, the professionalized and now even popular language a therapeutic culture uses to account for why we are cruel, malicious, and bigoted. This language is not utterly vacuous or empty of reality. One reason it is a functional discourse is not just its individualism and narcissism but its power to voice things we do in fact experience. Therapeutic discourse has an experiential reference: sin does not. When modern teenagers sing in church, "my sinful self my only shame," virtually nothing comes to mind that has anything to do with the way they experience themselves, their peers, or their social world.

Given this situation, a contemporary theology of individual evil (sin) that would explore the connection between this ancient Hebraic symbolic term for evil and reality faces at least three formidable tasks. First, it must discover what makes the actual inclinations of sin different from our sufferings and vulnerabilities. Responding to this issue, the present chapter

4. The reduction or objectification of the individual is Ernst Becker's primary criticism of the later Karl Marx and of twentieth-century developments in the social sciences. Thus, "in Marx's later work man turned out to be an objective thing, offered up passively to the forces of society and history. . . . The problem of the whole, thinking, feeling, acting man was sacrificed to an ideology." See Karl Marx, *The Structure of Evil: An Essay on the Unification of the Science of Man* (New York: G. Braziller, 1968), 67.

analyzes sin as a distinctive dynamic. In a sense, to discern this dynamic is to discern sin's origin. But to grasp sin's origin does not mean discovering some cause of our concrete acts of sin. Origin has to do with the situation or environment that evokes the response of sin and with features of human agency that make this strange self-enslaving act possible. Even if sin is not simply externally caused, it is not a human act if it has no motivation whatsoever. I shall contend that the tragic character of our condition is the primary motivating background of sin's origin.

Second, a theology of sin must trace the way sin reaches and alters the structures and operations of the human agent; our ways of being spatial, temporal, determinate, aggressive, biologically needy, and guided by elemental passions. Only through such explorations can we understand how the reality of sin resides not just in momentary acts but in tacit and even unconscious dispositions (chapters 8 through 12). Third, it must show how the first two things illumine actual events and realities of present-day history. These are the tasks that constitute a theology of the bondage of the will.

TRAGIC EXISTENCE

Everyday experience confirms the legacy of corporate wisdom in the conviction that human life is a mixture of satisfactions and sufferings. Religions, literary traditions, philosophies, and world-views differ from each other in their emphasis on either the satisfactions or the sufferings. But the mixture is undeniable. Human life is not pure suffering. Satisfactions range from minor or intense physical pleasures to the joys of relation and creativity. Much of our everyday-life talk is preoccupied with these satisfactions. And no actual human society in history has been utterly bereft of satisfactions. The way societies in history interpret and record their sufferings indicates types and levels of satisfaction. Suffering is the other side of the mixture. In its experiential sense suffering is that quality or tone of experience that interrupts a state of satisfaction. Physical pain is a suffering insofar as we experience the interruption of an organic state of satisfaction. An insult causes us to suffer if it interrupts a state of self-satisfaction characterized by self-esteem. We suffer from the loss of the loved other because the loss interrupts a satisfying and valued relation. In its more objective sense, suffering is something that works actual harm to our well-being, and this includes deprivations that prevent developments toward well-being.[5]

5. Well-being need not mean simply a static structure. The well-being of personal agents can concern everything from minimal conditions of life to what enables or promotes their world openness, their transcending creativity.

Human suffering clearly involves more than physical pain.[6] Like all human experiences, it is multi-dimensional, a convergence of the biological, the passionate, and the personal. This does not mean that some sufferings are biological and others are personal. Since these things are dimensions and as such constitutive of everything the agent is and does, they will enter into all sufferings. On the other hand, human agents do experience fundamentally different types of suffering. Altogether, these sufferings constitute the tragic condition of human agents, an intolerable condition that opens them to the dynamics of evil.

The Suffering of Vulnerability

Each of the dimensions of the human agent carries with them a distinctive vulnerability. Because of the temporality, autonomy, and continuity of our being as persons, we are subject to assaults on our self-esteem that range from minor rebuffs and insults to programmed de-humanizations. As organic beings and higher primates, we are subject to a wide range of injuries and diseases and to very high degrees of pain. Our interhuman reality and the reciprocal intimacies of the face make us vulnerable to the losses and sufferings of relation. As social worlds form our continuities and specific identities, we are vulnerable on two fronts: the fragility of the social worlds themselves and the assault on identity when social worlds change. Nor do these vulnerabilities remain separate from each other. The self's capacity to transcend the present toward the past and future carries with it an awareness, even a symbolization, of all the other vulnerabilities, especially the vulnerability to death. In its narrow and precise sense, vulnerability means the possibility of assaults, declines, and injurious incidents. But since all physical organisms do in fact decline and die, all embodied agents experience challenges to their self-esteem, and all interhuman beings experience loss, vulnerability also names a condition of actual suffering.

The Suffering of Benign Alienation

Incompatibility and competition are present in the relations of all living things. Human autonomy greatly exacerbates this feature because the aims and agendas of its very reality do not coincide with those of others. Agents suffer this disharmony in two ways. First,

6. Louis Lavelle distinguishes between pain and suffering arguing that pain is a passive experience restricted to the body while suffering is an interpersonal experience in which imagery and activity are involved. See Louis Lavelle, *Evil and Suffering* (New York: Macmillan, 1963), vol. 2, chaps. 2 and 3. While I do not dispute the distinction he is trying to make, I think Lavelle has not been successful in his way of distinguishing physical and other types of suffering. The reason is that the things he attributes to suffering (activity, interpersonal relations, imagery, etc.) also function in and shape the human experience of physical pain.

because of these incompatibilities and competitions, the aims and acts of the human world are always undergoing challenge, limitation, and displacement. And because agents are committed to their aims and agendas, they suffer when these things are challenged and when they fail. Second, since we human beings do not pursue our causes in modes of indifference, these challenges and displacement evoke emotional antipathies directed at other persons. And antipathy, too, is a suffering because it interrupts states of satisfaction.

The Suffering of Ontological Alienation

Human existence stretched across the gulf between elemental passions and their fulfillments is a suffering existence. This gulf is not so much an eventful interruption of a specific satisfaction as a structural interruption of a perpetual state. The deepest alienation of the life of agents is this structural disproportion between referents and realizations of the elemental passions. It is a form of suffering because this gulf is also an experience of desire that ever exceeds its fulfillment. Elemental passions are themselves sufferings because they are a kind of hunger. This suffering has the character of alienation because it is an experience of the world, of things at hand, both as offering and as withholding what we need. Effort, not isolation, dominates our relation to our environment. In effort we make use of, fashion, control, know, relate to, or create. But even the penultimate fulfillments of our efforts both offer and withhold, satisfy and frustrate, promise and betray. Hence, our relation to the resources of our well-being and satisfactions is not a harmonious unity but an alienation. Because this alienation is an immanent aspect of the very structure of our passionate existence, it is an ontological alienation, an alienation at the heart of our way of being in the world.

The Timbre of Discontent

It is because of the spheres of human reality and the dimensions of human agency that human suffering varies in type and intensity. Our temporality and our orientation to meaning introduce anticipations, fears, metaphors, and even guilt into our experience of physical pain. The face-to-face relations of the interhuman enable us to experience political and economic oppression as dehumanizing deprivations.

But our multi-dimensionality does more than simply make suffering intense and pathetic. The passions and the vulnerabilities of human agents combine to bestow on actual lived experience a tone or timbre of discontent. We should not confuse this pervasive tone of discontent with a claim that human beings are basically unhappy, cynical, and in despair. This is not to argue for or against pessimism or optimism. Discontent is simply the emotional tone life takes on when it is a mixture of satisfaction and suffering. Henry David Thoreau's remark that we all live lives of quiet desperation is a rather exaggerated way to describe the tone of discontent. This discontent varies, of course, from society to society and epoch to epoch. To the degree that modern industrial societies have displaced primary symbols with marketplace discourse, meaning-mediating primary communities with bureaucracies, and moral traditions with legal precedents, they effect distinctive kinds of discontent; in some cases virtually a resentful and nihilistic savagery. The tone of discontent seems to be less intense and visible in pre-industrial, tribal societies where traditions, primary symbols, and communities survive. Yet, no human society so manages the conditions of life and well-being that it renders its members invulnerable. All human societies take for granted the persistence and inescapability of suffering. The result is that no human being lives outside of or above the tragic interdependence of suffering and satisfaction. Hence, no human being totally avoids the timbre of felt discontent.

A philosophical lineage that begins with Søren Kierkegaard interprets this discontent as *anxiety*.[7] The term does not describe a momentary psychological incident or a fearful anticipation of a specific future peril but the mood that attends the agent's awareness of its own non-necessity. The mood results from the agent's inability to be indifferent about the imperilment of its own subjectivity. Accordingly, anxiety is specifically correlated with the passion of subjectivity. But the Kierkegaardian insight needs to be expanded beyond this correlation because the timbre of anxiety is evoked by the agent's total fragility. Human life structured by vulnerability and suffering is what effects discontent and anxiety. And what gives this tone of discontent to our ongoing existence is our awareness of our general and unavoidably imperiled future. Our various satisfactions may distract us but they never remove this awareness. Even interpretations of suffering as an emissary of punishment or as a temporary holding point on the way to some final victory do not remove anxiety's deep conviction that suffering is a kind of destiny.

THE CLASSICAL VISION OF HUMAN EVIL

Unlike Christology and the doctrine of the Trinity, sin never obtained a technical and detailed creedal expression in early Christianity. There is, however, a classical theology of sin which emerged from the

7. See Søren Kierkegaard, *The Concept of Anxiety*, trans. R. Thomte and A. B. Anderson (Princeton, N.J.: Princeton University Press, 1980). Two twentieth-century appropriations of Kierkegaard's concept are Reinhold Niebuhr, *The Nature and Destiny of Man: A Christian Interpretation* (London, Eng.: Nisbet and Co., 1941), vol. 1, 195–206, 266–68; and Paul Tillich, *The Courage to Be* (New Haven, Conn.: Yale University Press, 1952), 40–63.

repudiation of both Pelagianism and Manicheanism in the patristic period, the primary architect of which was Augustine of Hippo. And his theology of sin became a part of both Catholic and Protestant orthodoxies. Classical Protestant theologies of sin remain Augustinian even when they displace the Augustinian psychology with the Pauline discourse and framework. This classical theology of sin has seven general features.[8] Three of these features can be extracted from their ancient conceptual frameworks and reformulated. In my judgment two of them are essentially precritical, that is, they contain cosmological elements that cannot survive the impact of modern sciences and modes of thought. Two others are also problematic because of their inherent theological content.

The three retrievable features of the classical view are the differentiation of sin from suffering and tragic finitude, the view of sin as distortion of (human) reality, and theocentrism. Differentiating sin from the tragic is one of the seminal insights of the Hebraic tradition.[9] Without this insight, the problem that preoccupies human beings is reduced to suffering and vulnerability. This is the problem of self-aware finitude struggling to maintain the fragile conditions of life and well-being. The religious faiths of very ancient, even prehistorical, peoples interpret and ritualize the awesome powers of world process that are the conditions of life itself. Reflecting the rise of the great civilizations, Vedic faith in India and Homeric religion arose as cosmogonical and patriarchal orderings of this ancient legacy. In these faiths the ritualization of the sacred occurs in the face of a new set of problems introduced by agriculture, urbanization, and society. Quasi-philosophical movements like Brahmanism, Gnosticism, and Manicheanism pressed the logic of this legacy to its completion. The evil we are up against is the world system itself, the very existence and character of imperiled finitude, the very structure of the self and its self-presence.

This is not to say, however, that ancient and pre-industrial peoples had no experience of what Emmanuel Levinas calls the face, the mysterious presentation of vulnerability that evokes compassion and obligation. The

8. Some helpful studies of the classical theology of sin are the following: J. N. D. Kelly, *Early Christian Doctrines* (London, Eng.: A. & C. Black, 1958), chap. 13; A. Claudel, "Peché," in *Dictionnaire de theologie catholique,* ed. E. Mangenot (Paris: Letouzey et Aue, 1903–50), vol. 12; H. L. J. Heppe, *Reformed Dogmatics Set Out and Illustrated from the Sources,* rev. E. Bizer and trans. G. T. Thompson (London, Eng.: Allen & Unwin, 1950), chaps. 14, 15; H. F. F. Schmidt, *Doctrinal Theology of the Evangelical Lutheran Church,* trans. C. A. Hay and H. E. Jacobs (Minneapolis: Augsburg, 1961), Part Two.

9. The Adamic myth and the tragic myth are two of four comprehensive myths of evil in Paul Ricoeur's typology. His is the most detailed and perceptive study I know of the components and structural differences between the Adamic and tragic myths. See Paul Ricoeur, *The Symbolism of Evil,* trans. E. Buchanan (New York: Harper and Row, 1967), Part Two.

face is at work in human interrelatings in all known civilizations and peoples. In fact, pre-industrial peoples from hunter-gatherers to the early great civilizations tend to discern something like face in all living things. But this discernment did not bring with it the Hebraic (including Zoroastrian) differentiation between imperiled finitude and evil. The Hebraic peoples sensed something about the face which made possible acts of individual and social violation whose consequences accumulated in history. Furthermore, they connected the normativity of the face and the grounds for opposing interhuman violations with the sacred. And this introduced a new paradigm and symbolism for understanding the sacred which went beyond the maintenance of the world system and the support of the body politic. Because interhuman violations (evil) were not just fateful inevitabilities, they called not just for ritual protection but for resistance and change. And with this differentiation between the human tragic condition and human sin come a new sense of salvation and the notion of history itself. The human problem is, thus, not just ontological (a tragic fate) but historical (an addressable bondage).

Radical theocentrism is the second feature of the classical view of the human condition.[10] According to the typical expression of theocentrism in the ancient writings, human agents are sinful in that human beings transgress the covenant and commands of an all-powerful, personal being. Carried in a monarchical metaphor, this expression nevertheless insightfully grasps a relation between the face and the sacred. According to this insight, a certain way of construing and relating to the sacred is at work in the violations of the face and social oppression. Driving the acts of human evil is a passion gone wrong. This passion is that which shows itself when human beings attempt to relate themselves ritually and cultically to the sacred. Sin (moral corruption, oppression, interhuman violation) arises from a skewed passion for the eternal, in other words, idolatry.[11] In other words there is something about an absolutized attachment to the sacred as something at hand in the world (a nation, for instance) that is at work in such things as cruelty, hard-heartedness, and oppression. If that is the case, the dynamics of evil can be broken only by knowledge and worship of what is truly eternal. This is a theocentric way of understanding what it means to be human because apart from this worshipful obedience,

10. On the theocentric element of sin, see Paul Ricoeur, *The Symbolism of Evil,* Part One, chap. 2. H. Richard Niebuhr's notion of "radical faith" is likewise a theocentric way of understanding human evil. See H. Richard Niebuhr, *Radical Monotheism and Western Culture* (New York: Harper and Row, 1943), esp. chaps. 2 and 6.

11. On the theme of idolatry, see Wilfred Cantwell Smith, "Idolatry," in John Hick and Paul F. Knitter, eds., *The Myth of Christian Uniqueness: Toward a Pluralistic Theology of Religions* (Maryknoll, N.Y.: Orbis Books, 1987).

human agents migrate quiet desperation to desperate and cruel self-securings.

The third feature of the classical view follows closely on the first two. Sin is an alteration of the *being* of human agents. A psychological and individualistic way of expressing the insight is that sin modifies the very structures of the self. To express it negatively, sin is not located simply in observable behaviors. What does it mean to say that sin is an alteration of *being?* The being of human agents is constituted by the dimensions of self-presencing, the biological, and the passions, as well as by participation in the spheres of the interhuman and the social. To say that sin alters our being means that it distorts our temporality, our biological aggressiveness, and our passions for reality and the interhuman. From the Psalmist through St. Augustine to Jonathan Edwards, both sin and salvation affect deep dispositions, the inclinations of the heart as well as institutions of rule and barter. Thus, the classical theology interprets sin as a bondage, a universal condition, a shift that takes place at history's very beginning.

Two precritical features of the classical view are the comprehensive cosmological narrative framework and the quasi-biological explanation of sin's universality. A cosmic metaphysics was the assumed comprehensive setting for all of the classical doctrines. Most classical Christian doctrines presupposed a cosmic and narrative scheme that began with the event of creation and is to end with the eschaton. Augustine's *The City of God,* Dante's *The Divine Comedy,* and John Milton's *Paradise Lost* and *Paradise Regained* are epic portrayals of this cosmic narrative. When placed in the cosmic narrative, sin or human evil has a historical origin. It takes place in connection with an event in the life of the first human nuclear family. It also has a prehistorical origin in the corruption of transhistorical powers, the rebellion and fall of Satan.[12] The second feature, the universal spread of sin through human propagation, presupposes a historical origin of sin. Sin persists in history through a corrupted and biologically transmitted human nature.[13]

Two theologically problematic features of the classical view are the dominance of a monarchical metaphor in determining the nature of the act of sin as a prideful rebellion, and, the expulsion of the element of the tragic

12. The theme of the fall of Satan is present in both the Koran and a Jewish source, "The Life of Adam." See F. R. Tennant, *The Sources of the Doctrines of the Fall and Original Sin* (New York: Schocken Books, 1968), 199–201. A classic Christian theological expression of the doctrine is St. Anselm's "The Fall of Satan." See *Anselm of Canterbury: Truth, Freedom and Evil,* trans. J. Hopkins and H. Richardson (New York: Harper and Row, 1965).

13. For the main difficulties of this notion, see F. R. Tennant, *The Origin and Propagation of Sin* (Cambridge, Eng.: Cambridge University Press, 1906), Lectures 1 and 2.

from the origin of sin. According to the monarchical metaphor, the primary relation between human beings and God is the relation of inferior and relatively powerless subjects to a superior and commanding will. Submissive responses of honor and obedience are what this relation properly requires. The very essence of sin, then, is to fail to acknowledge the sovereign as sovereign and to repudiate the subject to master relation. In a monarchy the one response absolutely forbidden to the subject is rebellion, and this holds true for the divine monarchy as well. Formally speaking, the essential character of sin is rebellion, the assertion of the subject's autonomy against its proper authority. Whatever would prompt human beings to repudiate this proper relation? What would prompt a subject to rebel, to defy what is utterly superior to it and properly commands it? The fall of Satan literature offers a clearer example of the origin of sin than the Adam and Eve story because it describes the very first sin of any creature. In this story prideful envy of the power, authority, and superiority of the sovereign prompt Satan to rebel.[14] What monarchs fear most from subjects is the one thing that can bring the monarchy down, the prideful resistance to the power and authority of the monarch. If subjection to royal power is the root metaphor for the relation between human beings and God, then the nature of sin must be a defiance, a repudiation of that relation prompted by pride. The monarchical metaphor is theologically problematic not because superiority and command are utterly inappropriate concepts for the relation between God and human beings but because of what happens when these concepts are made central and definitive.[15]

The classical view clearly distinguishes suffering (the tragic) from sin. But this theology of sin suppresses the tragic element in the Adam and Eve story and interprets the origin of sin as a sheer act of will. This voluntarism contains both an insight and a problem. The insight is that human beings are able to depart from their own ideality, that is, from capacities and features necessary for their well-being. The insight, then, is that human evil or sin is ontologically contingent. It takes place in conjunction with human self-making. If this were not so, evil would be an externally

14. The motifs of envy and pride are especially prominent in Milton's account of Satan's rebellion in *Paradise Lost*.

15. The monarchical metaphor is under attack from different points on the theological spectrum. Charles Hartshorne has led the attack. His lifelong project of a neo-classical theism has identified the monarchical metaphor as partly responsible for the incoherences of classical theism. See Charles Hartshorne, *Omnipotence and Other Theological Mistakes* (Albany, N.Y.: SUNY, 1984). Theological feminism has also mounted a strong attack. See Rosemary Ruether, *Sexism and God-Talk: Toward a Feminist Theology* (Boston: Beacon Press, 1983), chap. 2, and Sallie McFague, *Models of God: Theology for an Ecological, Nuclear Age* (Philadelphia: Fortress Press, 1987), 63-68. See also two monographs: Anna Case-Winters, *God's Power* (Louisville, Ky.: Westminster/John Knox, 1990), and Wendy L. Farley, *Tragic Vision and Divine Compassion* (Louisville, Ky.: Westminster/John Knox, 1990).

(from society) or internally (from hormones) caused condition or act. The problem with this account of sin coming about through the will alone is its suppression of the context and motivation of this voluntary act. To make sin into a sheer act of prideful rebellion obscures its character as a response to a condition, a way of dealing with the world. Thus, what attracts human beings toward evil remains a sheer mystery. The situation of human evil is a situation of utter autonomy facing sheer possibility. The issue of the context and motivation, the issue of sin as a response to something, is not entirely absent from the old stories. The lure of the tree of knowledge hints at a response to the limitations of finite knowledge.[16] And in the fall of Satan story, envy is a motivation for rebellion. Envy implies an already present corrupted disposition that motivates Satan to rebel, hence implies a fall that precedes sin itself. Similarly, something about Adam and Eve made them seducible before they were seduced, and that something was not the formal faculty of self-making or the capacity to make choices. The serpent appeals to a discontent already present on the Edenic scene. But these themes are not emphasized in the classical Christian theologies of sin. In its interpretation, motivations for actual sin arise simply from the possibility of human self-determination. The self-determining will is itself its own motivation. Motivations, we might say, are willed into existence. Thus, voluntarism wins out and the human tragic condition is suppressed.

Voluntarism is not the deepest reason for the classical view's suppression of the tragic context of sin. Also at work is another problematic metaphor. Suffering, vulnerability, and the tragic cannot play a role in the motivation of sin because these things occur as sin's offspring. Sin brings human mortality into the world. The pangs of childbirth and the drudgery of work come with exile from the Garden of Eden. Thus, it is sin that introduces suffering and the tragic into a perfect (though incomplete) world. This concept depends only in part on the cosmic narrative and the notion of an eventful origin of sin (the Fall). Also at work is a judicial metaphor for the relation between human evil and suffering. When this metaphor reigns, suffering succeeds evil as its punishment. Accordingly, the tragic cannot be sin's context because it is its consequence. Sin thus is contextless, and its only motivation is simply its own formal possibility.

16. Martin Buber has retrieved the nonvoluntaristic elements from the Adam and Eve story. His interpretation is unusual because he sees the Adam and Eve part of the story as itself the background of sin and the Cain story as the origin of sin. The Garden and the exile thus describe human beings becoming aware of their own finitude and sensing the opposites in the world of fortune and misfortune, order and disorder. Buber thus contends that tragic existence is the background of the sin in this early Hebraic saga. See his "Images of Good and Evil," in Martin Buber, *Good and Evil* (New York: Scribner's, 1953).

Like all interpretive and historical accomplishments, the classical view is a mixture of retrievable wisdom and problematic contents and metaphors. Are the elements of insight so entangled with cosmological elements and problematic metaphors that they are inseparable? Do these entanglements simply discredit the classical theology of sin? That was more or less the response of the Enlightenment to the Hebraic paradigm of human good and evil. Against this view, I shall attempt to disentangle the classical wisdom from the problematic cosmology and metaphors and shall try to show how that wisdom illumines the condition of human agents.

THE DYNAMICS OF HUMAN EVIL

Human evil is not simply tragic vulnerability and suffering because it is a way of responding to these things, a way of existing in the world in which persisting dispositions influence the whole course of action. "Way of existing" and "dispositions affecting action" more or less constitute what I am calling the dynamics of evil. How does this dynamics come about and what are its features? I shall develop an interpretation of this dynamics in six steps.

1. According to the account of human reality in Part One, human agents are constituted by elementary passions that press past the everyday satisfactions and goods at hand. Further, our condition is one marked by vulnerabilities and tragic suffering that bestow a tone of discontent and anxiety on our lives.

2. Because we are self-presencing (temporal, imaginative, linguistic), we experience the present in connection with memories and anticipation. Accordingly, we experience things self-consciously. That is, we experience them through an awareness of what they mean; what they signify, what they resemble, and what is their importance. Experiencing things self-consciously also means that we are aware of and can even reflect on the quality and tonality of our experiencing. The thing experienced does not so dominate our consciousness that we are unable to be aware of the experiencing itself. We can in other words objectify and reflect on our own experiencing which means also the past course and future prospects of experience. This is why we can imagine things as different, project various aspects or phases of things, engage in explanations, and relate things to each other.

All of these features of personal being come together to enable an act that we so take for granted that we rarely explicitly attend to it. We are able to reflect on the meaning and nature of our total situation, the world itself. It is true that the stuff of our everyday struggles is always something specific. Specific events evoke our efforts, plannings, and fears.

But because of our self-conscious way of experiencing these things, we are able to ponder them together, to synthesize them into a total situation. We are concerned not simply about the specific meal on the table but the competence of our leader, the state of the nation, and even the character of our total environment as threatening or supportive. In other words, we are conscious about and can ponder our condition as such. And because our agential passions are for ourselves, we are unable to strike a neutral, objective, or indifferent pose about our vulnerable condition. Our condition is present to us in the modalities of passion and moods of discontent and anxiety. This self-consciousness about our condition is not, to be sure, the same thing as intellective interpretations of it which we have from poets, scientists, and philosophers and which are carried in mythologies, cosmogonies, and world-views. We human beings exist in the world self-conscious of the problem of the world (our condition) whether or not we contribute creatively to a symbolic expression of that problem.

3. Tragic vulnerability effects a tone of discontent and anxiety in the lives of human agents. Not to be confused with specific experiences of pain, worry, and grief, this pervasive existential tone is fueled by the intrinsic frustrations of the elemental passions. For instance, because the passion of subjectivity for itself and the conditions of its own securing does not find what it yearns for, it fosters a discontent with that perennial yearning, that nonfinding. This is why discontent is a tonality of our very existence in the world. Discontent, we might say, is the negative and suffering side of the elemental passions.

What happens to these persisting discontents when we become aware of them as an aspect of our very condition? These negative tonalities of the elemental passions converge into a single, intensified experience of negation. That is, intensive discontent follows on our awareness of our total condition. Subjectivity yearns for its confirmation and securing. The passion for reality reaches toward the mystery of things. The human being yearns for the understanding and compassionate other. Informed by these yearnings and their discontents, our self-awareness is constituted by the question of the world but it receives no answer. Whatever clues there might be to our place in the scheme of things, they are not built into our phylogenetic legacy, history, or everyday world transactions. They are not buried in the yearnings and discontents of existence itself. This is not to say that there is no meaning in the totality of things. It only says that such meaning is not itself contained in the act of existing. Thus, hiding at the heart of things appears to be chaos. And this is the one situation we human beings seem incapable of accepting. Because of the intensity of the passions and their discontents, we find this situation to be intolerable. What is intolerable is not the intellectual concept of ultimate chaos, in other words, one of the several alternative metaphysical speculations about the world. There are some who almost casually, even passionately, embrace that speculation. We human beings seem quite capable of accepting, even passionately arguing for, world-views in which we ourselves have no significance whatsoever. Nihilists of various sorts warmly embrace scenarios of violence and depravity. Scientists coolly contemplate our sun's final fling or the ultimate randomness of life processes. But the intolerable sneaks past world-views, methods of criticism, and metaphysical speculations. For it is human passionate existence, not the intellect, that cannot accept its own ultimate nonsignificance. And through this weakness, this incapacity to tolerate a clue-less world enters the initial act of the dynamics of evil, a double-sided act that is at the same time a refusal and an insistence.

4. What happens when we anxiously experience our vulnerability as our ultimate condition? Because the experience is intolerable, it becomes something which itself forces from us a response. And given our elemental passions, that response must be some sort of resistance. Victimized by an intolerable situation of physical and de-humanizing personal abuse, a child resists by creating and living in alternate personalities, by retreat into catatonia or by internalizing deep images of self-blame and self-deprecation. What kind of resistance is possible when the world order itself is the problem? The one course resistance can take is to remove, suppress, or defeat what makes this intolerable condition an ultimate vulnerability. The negative side of this response is a refusal or denial of the condition itself. That is, we refuse our tragic vulnerability and with that the totality of things as chaos. This denial is not so much an act of disbelief as a negative existential posture that refuses to abide by tragic vulnerability. This posture would suppress the vulnerability of the human condition and transform it from something necessary and inescapable to something accidental and contingent. And if the tragic is sporadic and accidental, it can be avoided, tamed, managed, and even defeated.

When human agents transform inescapable vulnerability into something contingent and manageable, they refuse the structure and situation of their finitude. Since the passion of subjectivity is a passion on behalf of finitude, how is this response possible? How can agents both strive for and refuse their own finite reality and condition? The contradiction is only an apparent one. What we refuse is not subjectivity itself but the necessity and inescapability of tragic vulnerability. But a deeper contradiction lurks in this refusal. The tone of discontent is the negative underside of the elemental passions. Is not the refusal of tragic existence just another expression of discontent? If passions do strive through worldly satisfactions toward an eternal horizon, is not this itself a denial of the structure of finitude? The answer is no. The reason is that the eternal is simply the undesignated horizon of the elemental passions. It is not an entity or state of affairs which, if realized, would displace the contents of these passions. The eternal as horizon is thus not a cancellation but a fulfillment of subjectivity, knowledge, and interhuman relation. Apart from this undesignated horizon, we would not experience the chaos and unavoidability of suffering as intolerable and would not develop existential postures of denial.

5. Refusal is only the negative aspect of our existential response to our tragic destiny. Its aim is to change the meaning of tragic existence from something intrinsic to something eventful, contingent, and manageable. The positive aspect of this response is a posture of insistence. Unable to abide chaos as the ultimate truth about the world and our destiny, we move to free ourselves from intolerable discontent. We insist on a secured subjectivity, a finally satisfying face, a final enrichment of knowledge and experience. Guided by the conviction that because tragic finitude as contingent can be defeated, we move to defeat it. We locate what can displace chaos at the heart of things, offer the meaning which gives our lives significance, and provide the securing conditions and final enrichment the elemental passions desire. Driven by this insistence, we thus move through our times and places alert to anything that might fill our existentially hungry maws. What is it that solves the problem? A hunger that must be fed is never choosy. It settles for anything whatever, and this means what it can in fact find and what holds some promise of solving its problem. We do not look to sources of peril and pain (disease, ugliness, enemies) to remove our vulnerability but to things that already function to satisfy our needs and desires. And the more deeply and comprehensively a good offers satisfaction, protection, meaning, and the like, the more it is a likely candidate for being the displacer of chaos. Thus, the perennial candidates for things that remove our vulnerability and provide a securing foundation are religions, sciences, nations, social movements, comprehensive interpretive schemes, methods that enable criticism of or interpret the world, value-preserving institutions, and even revolutions to procure freedom and justice. This insisting on and finding a substitute for vulnerability is not just a repetition of the passionate striving through mundane goods toward their horizon. It transforms that striving into attempts to make these goods at hand fulfill these passions and end the tone discontent.

6. This existential posture that would render tragic vulnerability contingent modifies both our relation to mundane goods and to the eternal horizon. How does it alter our relation to mundane goods, that is,

the realm of space-time entities and world processes? When goods at hand are not forced into the role of making us invulnerable, they can be experienced in more or less straightforward ways. We mean and interpret them as sources of relative satisfactions. Music and literature enrich experience with deepened insight and momentary pleasures. Governments and their armed forces maintain social stability. Religious faiths mediate resources for living by preserving past wisdom and ritualizing the present. But relative satisfactions are all these finite and historical powers can deliver. Finite and contingent as they are, their delivery of satisfaction is never a sure thing, and when it occurs, it is at best a relative fulfillment. Weakened and corrupted governments can fail to defend the peace. The symbol systems of religious faiths can become instruments of oppression. Straightforward and realistic ways of meaning these goods take these possibilities into account.

But the posture of refusal and insistence must have more. It adds a second layer of meaning and expectation onto mundane goods. Insisting that tragic vulnerability be removed and on being secured, the agent turns to goods at hand to effect this miracle. The result is a relation to mundane goods at hand that contains two expectations: one directed to their ordinary functions, the other to their supposed power to solve the human existential problem. In the second expectation, we look to the good to displace chaos, set us on the road to our true destiny, and fulfill our elemental passions. In other words we mean or relate to the mundane good as if it itself were the eternal horizon. Thus, we mean and relate to our nation (its history, symbols, tradition, Constitution, future) as the key and clue to the questions of destiny and ultimate meaning. If the nation is intact, chaos is held off, tragic existence is defeated, and vulnerability is removed. The nation may not have done this quite yet but given time, given the defeat of its internal critics and its external enemies, given certain developments, it will accomplish these things for us. The same claims can be made for any good: religion, the denomination, the parish church, our mate, family, world-view, guru, corporation, or economic system.

The desperate insistence that something, anything, remove the pain of insecured existence also changes our relation to the eternal horizon. As the horizon of penultimate satisfactions, the eternal horizon is intrinsically irreducible to those satisfactions or to the mundane goods that procure them. But once we think of those goods as able to secure us against tragic vulnerability, we collapse the horizon into these goods. We construe the non-mundane referent of desire to be the goods at hand. In other words, we mundanize the eternal horizon, the referent of the elemental passions. This mundanizing act does not actually abolish elemental passion as a striving through goods at hand nor does it eliminate the distinction between the eternal referent and the goods. It rather founds a whole new set of expectations toward the goods and with them a whole new set of fears and actions. The specific acts and postures of evil are born from these expectations and fears.

Readers familiar with the religious faiths that sprang from Hebrew religion will recognize what these six steps have just described, namely idolatry.[17] This theme is present in the texts of these faiths in connection with prophetic criticisms of false ways of representing the sacred. Because the issue seems to be one of a competition among deities, religiously surfeited moderns dismiss the notion of idolatry as quaint or ethnocentric. Some feminists discern in this theme the patriarchal exclusion of the ancient matriarchal tradition of the moon goddess. And these texts do approach idolatry in the framework of these exclusions; the one deity excluding the many, the worship of the sacred as Yahweh and only Yahweh. But these texts are also concerned with a much broader dynamics of human action. This dynamics is especially apparent in the prophetic exposure of the vast corruptions that attend absolute trust in the nation, even the sacred nation elect of God. Other deities are attacked insofar as they symbolize and legitimate the absolutizing of a nation. The Hebrew prophets sensed the connection between moral corruption and the act that substitutes a mundane good for the eternal horizon. In this deeper sense the dynamics of human evil is the dynamics of idolatry and should not be reduced to issues of cultic conflict.

THE DIMINISHING OF FREEDOM

The following chapters explore the devastating way that idolatry distorts the dimensions of human agency. In all the dimensions this distortion has one common effect, the diminishment of agential freedom. Because of the persisting ambiguity about the term, *freedom,* this statement carries as much confusion as clarity. This ambiguity has plagued theology since the Pelagians and the Augustinians did battle. Pelagius and his successors viewed freedom in a formal, one might say, psychological way. This freedom is the capacity to make choices. The kinds of things that reduce this psychological faculty are external restrictions and internal incapacitations. One kind of external restriction comes from the realm of the social. All political or familial social systems function to limit available choices.

17. In its narrowest sense, idolatry is a phenomenon of the cultus, the worship of a determinate entity as God or the worship of God in a mundane form. But both Hebrew prophetism and early Christian theology expanded the act of idolatry from its cultic context. Tertullian thus says that idolatry is practiced outside the temple and without an idol and historically predates idols and portraits. It is thus not just the making of idols but the worship of a thing. See Tertullian, *De Idolatria,* 27.

Familial curfews limit the choices of the children in a family. Political interdicts in a society limit the choices of its citizens. These restrictions do not destroy the formal capacity to choose but reduce viable possible courses of action to be chosen. Internal incapacitation reduces or eliminates the very capacity to choose. Pathological conditions such as brain damage or psychogenetic neuroses that effect vacillating behavior are examples. According to a rather popular theory, there is no such thing as the capacity for free choice. Free choice is merely an apparent and mistaken cover-up for various physiological and social stimuli. According to this theory, human beings experience themselves as choosing, but the experience is illusory because it is unaware of its own internal and external determinants. Present-day debates over freedom and determinism are about freedom as this formal capacity of free choice.

It should be clear that in Paul, Augustine, Martin Luther, and John Calvin, the freedom that sin removes and salvation restores is not the formal capacity of free choice. In the classical tradition freedom is a comprehensive symbol for the telos of human beings and for their capacity to move toward that telos. Freedom is the power by which agents are able to actualize themselves toward their well-being. If that well-being is defined by such idealities as honesty, knowledge, and love, freedom means the power to realize these things. Its absence is the absence of that power. Thus, freedom is not the formal capacity of choosing but that about the agent that shapes desire and sets its direction. The loss or reduction of freedom is a reduction of dimensional powers of agents, powers of biological conditions, personal being, passions, and interpersonal interaction. And the reduction or enhancement of these powers is not necessarily a reduction or enhancement of the capacity to choose. For instance, we can experience a diminution of the capacity for intimate relations of friendship or romantic love and have no trouble making choices.

How is it that idolatry diminishes freedom? First, it narrows or restricts the way we experience the world. Goods that function to make the agent invulnerable exact a high price. When mundane goods perform a cosmic therapeutic on the hungry heart, they subject agents to a set of rigorous demands. If the idol can defeat chaos, it cannot itself be subject to chaos. Thus, we cannot relate to it as something vulnerable, fallible, or historical. We cannot place it in relativizing contexts. We cannot treat it in attitudes of spontaneity, creativity, criticism, irony, or humor. And we must move through space and time on constant alert against whatever might threaten the idolized good. These attitudes born of fear restrict our capacity to experience mundane goods as they are; that is, in their fragile beauty and their receptivity to creative alteration. Idolatry also constricts freedom because it reduces the powers and dimensions of human reality. It invades and restricts personal being in its temporality and specificity, transforms biologically rooted aggressiveness into malice, and corrupts the elemental passions. With these corruptions of the human agent come radical reductions of the power to move toward ideality and well-being and to move beyond ideality into novelty.

OTHER RESPONSES TO THE TRAGIC

I have contended that evil originates with the agent's attempt to end its discontent and tragic vulnerability. I have also contended that the dynamics this attempts is the dynamics of idolatry. But I do not want to suggest that evil is the only way human agents deal with their tragic condition. Human agents respond to their tragic vulnerabilities in a variety of ways; pathological injury, distractions, and bravado. One type of pathological disturbances appears to come from inadequate copings with the victimizations of historical existence.[18] These responses range from symptoms of stress and minor neuroses and phobias to multiple personality syndrome and severe depressions. So widespread are social and psychologically based pathologies that some segments of our society regard pathology itself as the name for evil or the explanation of evil. In this view the comprehensive human problem is a pathological one and therapy is its redemption.[19]

Distraction is a second way human agents respond to their tragic vulnerability. Available distractions are present in virtually all societies. Distractions dull the aches of discontent. They include chemical alterations (alcohol, nicotine, prescribed pharmaceuticals, and illegal drugs), world-views and techniques that lower self-awareness and effect indifference, and a great variety of groups (cults, religions, hobbies, therapy groups, and social action groups) whose endeavors or group relations help absorb self-preoccupation. Even as psychopathological defenses carry with them a new set of problems that themselves require help, so distractive responses pay a price for what they offer. We are increasingly familiar with the devastations of physio-chemical distractions. We are less self-conscious about the problematic character of distractive world-views, techniques, or group immersion. Criticism of these things tends to be limited to the extreme examples, the outrageously other-worldly philosophy

18. Karl Menninger et al., *The Vital Balance: The Life Process in Mental Health and Illness* (New York: Viking Press, 1963).

19. For a brief and rather technical attempt to distinguish the dynamics of psychopathology from the dynamics of evil, see Edward Farley, "Psychopathology and Human Evil: Toward a Theory of Differentiation," in R. Bruzina and B. Wilshire, eds., *Crosscurrents in Phenomenology* (The Hague, Netherlands: Nijhoff, 1978). For a similar distinction, see also Midgely, *Wickedness*, 60.

or the mind-controlling cult. But distraction in any form is never an adequate way of handling the intolerability of tragic vulnerability. Like idolatry, distraction is fueled by the posture of the refusal of finitude and the insistence on invulnerability. But because we are constitutively and necessarily vulnerable, distraction cannot deliver the desired goods. At its best it makes possible a round of satisfactions and disappointments. The addiction escalates; the world-view becomes ever more extreme; the group betrays. This is why failed distraction is fertile ground for the dynamics of evil; that is, the fanatical, absolutizing of the world-view, the techniques, the group.

Psychopathology and distraction are nonidolatrous responses to tragic existence that produce new levels of problems. But human history also shows a third response. So difficult is this response that we find it expressed more in great philosophies and literatures and outstanding individuals than in widespread social movements. It is the response of realistic acceptance and heroic bravado in the face of ultimate chaos and tragic vulnerability. Unlike psychopathology and distraction, this response confronts and opposes the refusal of the tragic and the insistence on secured existence. Bravado is a way of existing in the world without distraction and without idols. William Ernest Henley's poem catches its spirit:

> In the fell clutch of circumstance,
> I have not winced nor cried aloud.[20]

Bravado has found expression in ancient Chinese philosophy, Roman Stoicism, and present-day humanism.[21] But bravado seems to be more the phenomenon of rare and strong individuals than of communities. This may be because heroism as the accomplishment of self-focused individuals downplays the interhuman, the face, and compassionate obligation. And this is the Achilles heal of heroic bravado. It can promote a callous autonomy indifferent to the sufferings of others and to community.

20. From William Ernest Henley, "Out of the Night That Covers Me," in *Poems* (New York: Charles Scribner's Sons, 1920), 119.

21. Mary Midgely expounds Freud's anthropology as essentially a response of Stoic resignation. See Midgely, *Wickedness*, 164.

7
BEING-FOUNDED

> Courage as the universal and essential self-affirmation of one's being is an ontological concept. The courage to be is an ethical act in which man (sic) affirms his own being in spite of those elements of his existence which conflict with his essential self-affirmation.[1]
>
> The courage which takes this threefold anxiety into itself must be rooted in a power of being that is greater than the power of oneself and the power of one's world.[2]
>
> *Paul Tillich*

The Christian paradigm of the condition of human agents is not merely a paradigm of human evil. The classical texts of this religious faith interpret evil or sin from the perspective of redemption, based on a corporate experience of historical freedom. Writers and editors from the time of the Pentateuch through Paul interpreted human evil in relation to historical deliverance, revelation, divine mercy, Torah, and historical and transhistorical hope. Their assaults on individual and national evils were guided by convictions that God has acted on behalf of the people, that Messiah has appeared, and that the new age has begun. Accordingly, our condition is a mixture of corruption and freedom, and the Christian paradigm includes both of those themes.

It is important to distinguish this paradigm of evil and freedom from its narrative and doctrinal expressions.[3] The Christian movement synthesized a variety of narratives and traditions in a vast cosmic narrative of redemption that takes place through God's activity in

1. Paul Tillich, *The Courage to Be* (New Haven, Conn.: Yale University Press, 1952), 3.
2. Ibid., 155.
3. In *The Symbolism of Evil* and other works, Paul Ricoeur provides a very helpful conceptual map for distinguishing a variety of hermeneutical levels and their vehicles of expression. He distinguishes religious experience itself, cultic confessions, primary symbols (e.g., defilement, stain), myths, rationalized or speculative myths (e.g., the doctrine of original sin) as well as various enterprises of interpretation such as symbolics (hermeneutics), empirics, and poetics. I shall not appropriate this conceptuality as such but I shall make use of some of its distinctions. Thus I distinguish the level of corporate and individual experience of evil with its attending insights, the paradigm in which such finds expression, cosmologizing narratives and myths which interpret the paradigm, and doctrinal responses, negative or positive, to these myths.

history. Drawing on but going beyond Jewish eschatology, Christian theology elaborated this cosmic drama into a projected completion of redemption in the framework of a dual heaven-hell destiny for human individuals. Specific themes pertaining to salvation (justification, sanctification) underwent conceptual refinement. And in the Protestant movement, this refinement included an *ordo salutis,* a systematizing of the steps of the agent's salvation.[4] But we should not confuse the broad structure of the Christian paradigm with the cosmic narrative of divine acts, the eschatological projection of cosmic fulfillment, or the doctrinalization and systematization of specific motifs.

It is important to observe this distinction because the focus of these reflections is on the paradigm itself. Accordingly, I shall not explicate or even presuppose the cosmic narrative (Christology, Holy Spirit). Nor shall I deal with what some regard as the one true meaning of salvation, the apotheosis of human individuals from an earthly to a transearthly paradise. And because my focus is on the paradigm itself, I shall not try to synthesize the various doctrines about salvation that have served as battlegrounds for sectarian disputes. There is, I am convinced, a way of understanding agential freedom not dependent on these things, and that is the theme of this and the following chapters. In the previous chapter I contended that the dynamics of idolatry was the primordial operation in human evil. I now take up the primordial moment of agential freedom, the moment of being-founded.

THE JUDICIAL METAPHOR

In a general and nontheological perspective, the freedom of human agents is a condition of happiness or well-being. However, according to the Christian paradigm, the dynamics of idolatry corrupts this condition and our capacity to achieve it. If this is the case, then freedom comes about only as the power of this dynamics is broken. Thus, breaking the power of these primordial operations of evil requires a primordial operation that transforms this dynamics. The notion of a primordial or founding meaning of salvation or freedom is characteristic of religions of salvation; thus, union (*Nirvana*) in Brahmanism, faith (*Emunah*) in Judaism, seeing (*satori*) in Zen Buddhism. In the Christian tradition a

4. We find the notion of a temporal order of steps of salvation was first promulgated by the Reformed side of the Reformation and was taken up by the Lutheran dogmaticians. For specific accounts of the two versions see the standard expositions of the high or orthodox period of Protestant dogmatics, the late sixteenth and the seventeenth centuries. For the Reformed side, see H. Heppe, *Reformed Dogmatics, Set Out and Illustrated from the Sources,* trans. G. T. Thomson (Edinburgh: George Allen and Unwin, 1950), chaps. 20–22. For the Lutheran side, see *The Doctrinal Theology of the Evangelical Lutheran Churches,* trans. C. A. Hay and H. L. Jacobs (Minneapolis: Augsburg, 1899), chap. 3.

variety of terms expresses the conviction that agential freedom has a moment that all other moments presuppose; conversion, faith, repentance, regeneration, justification. In the classical tradition, these terms are gathered together not just in a quasi-chronology of the sequence of salvation but under a dominating metaphor that correlates well with the monarchical metaphor. Because this metaphor is so dominant in the Christian tradition, and because, at the same time, it contradicts elements of its own paradigm of evil and salvation, I shall begin the exploration of the primordial moment of agential redemption with a critical analysis of this dominant metaphor.

The term "the classical Christian tradition," means in these pages the metaphors and doctrines that survived the early controversies of the Christian movement to become engrained in the liturgy, ritual, doctrine, and piety of Catholic and Protestant Christianity. The contents of the classical Christian tradition are the two-Testament Scripture, the creation-to-eschaton cosmic narrative, the Fall and original sin, Nicene Christology and trinitarian doctrine, and the dual or heaven-hell destiny of the human race. Most of these themes have been the subject of a wide variety of interpretations even to the point of heresy and heterodoxy. Is there a classical Christian tradition concerning the primordial moment of agential redemption? A quick perusal of Christian history suggests there is little consensus about this matter. No momentous controversy pressed the early church to define such a moment. Yet a kind of consensus gradually accumulated over the centuries that found its clearest expression in the material principle of the Reformation, the doctrine of justification by faith. And while this appeared to be a decisive break with Catholic Christianity, most of its contents were in place long before the Reformation.

Since the time of the writings of ancient Israel, religious communities have interpreted the condition of agents and their relation to God through a variety of metaphors. Over the centuries some of these obtained hegemony over the others. In the monarchical metaphor, sin is primarily prideful rebellion against the king of the universe, a repudiation of the authority of the king and [his] commands and laws. Along with this monarchical metaphor of rule came a second metaphor of law whose referent was the king maintaining [his] kingdom through the rewards and punishments of a judicial system. When the Christian movement sought a way to interpret the salvific meaning of the crucifixion of Jesus, it appropriated this metaphor and doctrinalized it into the theory of Christ's satisfaction. The metaphor and the theory presuppose the monarchical metaphor's interpretation of the nature of sin. Sin is a free act of rebellion against the world ruler and thus also against the world order. Even as a human social system risks break-up if it ignores those who break the laws by which it maintains itself and does not proceed to punishing consequences, so the world system would be threatened and with that the integrity and justice of the world ruler if its laws could be violated without consequence. Sin, thus, incurs guilt and calls for punishment. And because sin is not just the breaking of discrete laws but prideful rebellion against the infinite source of law itself, it incurs an absolute guilt that calls for an absolute punishment. And this is what determines the primordial problem of individual salvation, the problem of removing what appears to be an unremovable sentence of condemnation by a monarch-judge whose own inherent attribute of justice prevents adaptation and compromise. If judicial rule were the only metaphor at work to interpret evil and salvation, condemnation would be the end of the story.

But another strain of metaphors for God's relation to human beings is present in the ancient writings, the interpersonal metaphor of the merciful monarch, the betrayed but forgiving spouse. And the satisfaction theory incorporated this strain when it sought the divine motive for the incarnation and crucifixion, the motive of compassion that would find a way to remove the unremovable sentence of condemnation. This combination of judicial and interpersonal metaphors in the theory of satisfaction is the basis for the classical Christian tradition's version of the primordial moment. According to this view, the salvation of human individuals can take place only if both an objective and a subjective problem are solved. The objective problem is the satisfaction of the requirements of justice. It is the problem of acquitting individuals who are infinitely guilty. The subjective or anthropological problem is how individuals can so lay hold of this acquittal that their corruption is transformed. The satisfaction theory attempts to solve the objective problem. And in Protestantism, the *ordo salutis* and the sequence of calling, regeneration, justification, and faith, addresses the anthropological problem. Accordingly, justification is the summary term for the primordial moment. In the judicial metaphor, the primordial problem of sin is guilt and its consequence of infinite punishment, and the primordial moment of freedom is acquittal and the laying hold of or participation in that acquittal.[5]

According to the monarchical-judicial metaphor, God's relation to the world order is analogous to the maintenance of a social system through rule and punishment. The problems with this metaphor are many. Some arise when the metaphor is cosmologized, when elements of the metaphor

5. Laying hold of the acquittal, the benefits of Christ's work, is not just an act of believing in the acquittal. In the Protestant version, it is a *unio cum Christo*, a union with Christ such that one can receive by imputation his righteousness. The union itself is complex and includes adoption, calling, regeneration, justification, and faith.

(laws, sentencing, punishments) are translated into cosmic realities. In other words, the metaphor is transformed into a literalized myth. This cosmologized myth carries with it the two main difficulties of what Paul Ricoeur calls the myth of punishment: the roots of the idea of punishment in needs for revenge, and, the nonequivalence between any offense and any proposed punishment.[6]

Problems also arise with the attempt to make sovereign rule and punishment the controlling imagery for God's being and attributes. There are other root metaphors for God's relation to the world and to human history in the ancient texts. When an aesthetic or creativity metaphor is central, God is the one whose creative power is the condition of the world's fecundity, who lures (to use a term from process theology) the world process toward its best possibilities. When the interpersonal metaphor is central, God is the loving spouse whose primary relation to creatures is care and compassion.[7] These metaphors are more appropriately central because it is in connection with experiences of dependence and experiences of redemption, not experiences of sheer power, that the very notion of God arises in the first place. This is why it makes more sense to say that God is love, goodness, or creativity than to say God is kingly rule.

The most severe problem with the judicial metaphor is that it fosters a distorted interpretation of human evil. This is, in fact, the distortion responsible for the metaphor's hegemony. Metaphors for the divine salvific activity do not drop from the skies nor do they parthenogenetically reproduce themselves. They arise from the way evil and freedom are experienced and they function to interpret that experience. In the Hebraic and Christian tradition, the sacred is known and interpreted in connection with the experience of the hold of evil, its tie with idolatry, and the breaking of these powers. Thus, the primary metaphor for God's relation to creatures arises with the breaking of the power of the dynamics of evil. This turns out to mean the power to live in the condition of tragic vulnerability without insisting on being secured by goods at hand. According to this paradigm, this is what we experience when we experience freedom. And we do not find in this experience of idolatry and its overcoming the elements of the monarchical-judicial metaphor; cosmic

6. Paul Ricoeur, "The Myth of Punishment," in *The Conflict of Interpretations: Essays in Hermeneutics* (Evanston, Ill.: Northwestern University Press, 1974).

7. Contemporary theology not only has subjected monarchical metaphors to criticism but has contended for other primary metaphors to interpret divine attributes and activities. Sallie McFague's *Models of God: Theology for an Ecological, Nuclear Age* (Philadelphia: Fortress Press, 1987) is an extended and rigorous argument for a variety of metaphors which displace metaphors of hierarchy and governance. Wendy Farley's *Tragic Vision and Divine Compassion* (Louisville, Ky.: Westminster/John Knox, 1990) is an argument for compassion as the primary and central metaphor of divine being.

ruler, cosmic law, world order maintenance, punishment. When these elements are permitted to interpret the evil and redemption, their distortive consequences are many: the obscuring of the dynamics of evil and thus the nature of freedom; patriarchal, heteronomous, and authoritarian versions of divine being, and a package of unsolvable theodicy problems. It may be the case that aspects of the monarchical-judicial metaphor have some illumining power. Even so, that metaphor is clearly secondary to interpersonal and aesthetic metaphors in its ability to interpret evil and freedom.

BEING-FOUNDED

If acquittal and participation in acquittal are an inadequate interpretation of the primordial moment of freedom, what is the alternative? Let us recall that the elementary passions converge into a single passion or desire that has a negative underside. This single passion is a striving through goods at hand for whatever can secure subjectivity, enrich and complete its need for reality, and understand and love its being. It is, in other words, a desire to be *founded.* Evil originates when this desire becomes so desperately discontent that it forces goods at hand into the founding role. Accordingly, evil is a kind of weakness, an incapacity to abide chaos and insecured existence.[8] This Hebraic and Christian paradigm of the agent's condition is not just a speculation. It comes from a people's experience of the breaking of the stranglehold of idolatry, the hold of this incapacity or weakness. If goods at hand are in fact unable to found, that which does found is the one thing able to found, the eternal horizon of the elementary passions as an actual presence. Only the creative ground of things can be the meaning of the human being and its world, whether the mystery be targeted by the passion for reality, or by the other yearned for by interhuman passion. Goods at hand and their penultimate satisfactions are not that creative ground and to make them so only perpetuates self-deception and false absolutizings. The eternal horizon as such does not found since it is simply the term for the undesignated referent of the elemental passions. The eternal horizon founds (locates the human being in the face of chaos) only in the form of an actual presence, or in other words, the sacred. Being-founded occurs, then, in the presencing of the sacred, that is, the creative ground of things.

Can being-founded be proved? If proof means direct description, the answer is no. Only world processes and goods at hand lend themselves

8. Mary Midgley, *Wickedness: A Philosophical Essay* (London, Eng.: Routledge and Kegan Paul, 1984) argues impressively for a privational or negative view of human evil. In her view evil is born in weakness, in an insufficiency of motive or a failure of appropriate motives to come together to orient one toward needs of others. See esp. chaps. 1 and 6.

to direct description. And this taps the post-Enlightenment suspicion that religions are either cognitively contentless or their content is supplied by wish fulfillments projected onto the screen of the world. To attempt a description of being-founded and what founds is to court failure from the start. Even persuasive metaphysical arguments for a world ground or fundamental ontologies of the immanent absolute do not describe being-founded itself. Objective arguments of this sort remain outside the order where being-founded takes place, the primordial and existential experience of freedom. In the old texts of Hebrew religion, being-founded occurs in connection with political conflicts, formal symbolic traditions, and radical critical interpretations. What we cannot do is discover in these texts pristine incidents of being-founded in individuals that are so compellingly real and public that they mediate our own founding. Human agents experience being-founded in conjunction with community-mediated exposures of the dynamics of idolatry. Being-founded is, thus, not a discrete apprehension that chases away a worried and insecure world-view but a participation in a historical milieu that existentially mediates the eternal horizon as a sacred presence.

When do agents experience being-founded? When it is interpreted by the judicial metaphor, it occurs when the conditions (satisfaction) of acquittal are met and mediated. Hence, it happens in the attestation of the incarnation, crucifixion, and resurrection of Jesus. This answer presupposes the cosmic narrative and this includes a historical period of pre-sin sacred presence (the Garden of Eden), the subsequent period of fallen history, and the historical drama of divine acts that create the grounds of justification. It also presupposes that suffering and the tragic character of finitude are the results, not the background, of sin. What happens to this answer when human history is approached in the framework of evolution rather than the cosmic narrative of Eden to eschaton? What is the relation to the sacred if there is no literal Eden and nature-corrupting Fall that introduced mortality and suffering into human history? One consequence is that the Christian movement need not work so hard to disguise the obscurantism about world history and evolution that has never completely disappeared. Second, it can acknowledge tragic suffering through the long reach of human history and therefore can explore its role as the background of sin. Third, it can understand the relation between human beings and the sacred and the presence of the sacred as something that is correlated with the capacities and situations of human cultural development.

If the presence of the sacred is understood in historical fashion, there is no Edenic experience of God. That is, there is no period or place in history in which the human form of life experienced the creative ground of things in a mode of utter clarity, directness, and certainty. If human agents have always been tragically vulnerable, they have always resisted that vulnerability and desired unqualified fulfillments. If this is the case, the relation of this life-form to the sacred has always been marked by ambiguity. There is no evidence whatsoever for a historical transition from an Edenic to a fallen relation to the sacred. Nor can we conclude that the sacred withholds its founding presence from the human life form until the events recorded in the writings of ancient Israel or until the appearance of Jesus. The religious cultuses of ancient peoples attest to this presence in their symbolizations of the sacred. What comes with the Hebraic paradigm is the thematization of the dynamics of idolatry behind acts of evil and of an experience of sacred presence that breaks the power of that dynamic.

COURAGE

Being-founded, not partaking of acquittal, is the primordial event of agential freedom. When agents are founded by sacred presence, they experience their existence in relation to that which gives meaning to the totality of things. Being-founded is at the same time an experience of freedom because it displaces radical discontent, the refusal of finite vulnerability, and the insistence on securing. In its negative aspect, being-founded breaks the hold of the dynamics of idolatry. Positively, it is a way of existing as fragile and vulnerable amidst the sufferings and tragic incompatibilities of the world. This way of existing appears paradoxical because it is both a resistance to and realistic acceptance of chaos and vulnerability. Yet there is no true agential freedom apart from this paradoxical posture. What takes the place of this posture when its power is broken? Clearly, it is some sort of courage. The term has its disadvantages. Courage has been defined by warfare, heroism, Stoicism, the knightly code, and the virtue tradition. Any present-day appropriation requires careful differentiations from these frameworks.[9] Yet it is courage, not submission, belief, obedience, or partaking of acquittal, that constitutes the primordial moment of agential redemption. Further, this courage is a complex posture in which three attitudes converge: relativizing, consent, and the risk of being.

Relativizing

The posture of courage contains a powerful negation. This negation should not be confused with the radical criticisms that moral consciousness levels at corrupted social movements and institutions. This attitude of negation is not a critical exposure of oppressions but a relativizing of

9. The most important twentieth-century theological monograph on the theme of courage continues to be Tillich's *The Courage to Be.* In this work courage is a primordial moment in the human response to tragic existence.

finite goods. In the posture of idolatry, we human agents relate to goods at hand through an absolutizing attitude. We are ever on the alert for what might fulfill our elemental passions and secure our being. Played out into policies and actions, this attitude refuses to acknowledge the inherent fragility, corruptibility, and finite limitations of these goods. And it is this attitude that relativizing displaces. Relativizing restores to goods at hand their historical character, thus, their contextuality, their fragility to change and demise, and even corruptibility. And these things make goods at hand incapable of being themselves the fulfillments of the elemental passions. Because relativizing is an existential attitude, it should not be confused with the cognitive conviction or world-view we call relativism. As a world-view relativism is itself a mundane good appropriable by idolatry and the possible referent of the relativizing attitude. The theme of relativizing pervades the texts of Christian Scripture and the classical tradition. We find it in recurring prophetic diatribes on the untrustworthiness of nations and armies, in the author of Job's depictions of the subjection of the awesome powers of nature to sacred power, in Qoheleth's sense of vanity and futility, and in the Thomistic concept of contingency. In the twentieth century, relativizing has its most vocal and eloquent expression in the works of Reinhold Niebuhr.

Consent

The posture of idolatry is a paradoxical relation to goods at hand because it subjects these goods to an absolutizing embrace yet denies their most evident feature, their relativity and limitation. This may be the reason for the instability of idolatry's enthusiasms and why those enthusiasms can turn so easily into ascetic world denial, ennui, cynicism, and despair. Courage contains a similar paradox. It combines a relativizing attitude with an attitude of consent to goods at hand including the world itself. We find this theme in the classical tradition in motifs of the essential goodness of being (creation, the world) and its correlate, the negative or privational character of evil. Thus, the status of goodness extends to the whole range of finitude and embraces both sides of such dualisms as heaven and earth and soul and body. Because of this essential goodness of being, the most formal feature of evil is a reality's departure from itself, a distortion of what is in itself real, valid, or beautiful. For the most part, the classical tradition did not explore how this concept of the goodness of being carried with it a distinctive attitude or way of existing in the world. In other words, it failed to thematize the virtue implied by the goodness of being and the privational character of evil. This failure was probably due to the relatively low place the Hebrew and Christian faiths gave the aesthetic dimension of experience in relation to the moral dimension and to ever-recurring strains of asceticism in the Christian movement. Jonathan Edwards was one of the few thinkers who profoundly grasped the virtue correlative to the goodness of creation. For Edwards consent to being was in fact the very essence of virtue itself.[10]

What is consent? Because the attitude of consent displaces the refusal of finitude, it is tempting to reduce it to its negative aspect. In this aspect, consent to being is a fundamental and existential acceptance of the tragic character of being. The agent consents to the element of chaos at the heart of things, that which resists the ordering and creative power of the sacred and thwarts the human passion for meaning. But limited to its negative aspect, consent is an *apatheia,* an attitude of resignation or acquiescence to whatever happens. If this is consent, it seems more a symptom of the refusal of being or of distractive response than a mark of courage. As an aspect of courage, consent is more like the positivity of aesthetic experience than the negativity of resignation. It is positive because it is an attitude evoked by the reality, goodness, and beauty of being. What do we mean by the essential goodness of being? In its bare and classical form, it refers to the analogy that created being has to the goodness of that on which it depends. Friedrich Schleiermacher reformulated an anthropocentric and negative version of this principle. In his view the goodness of being means that there is nothing about being (or the world order) itself which is essentially incompatible with the development of God-consciousness.[11] I suggest the following reformulation. I am using the term, *being,* here to mean whatever constitutes reality, that is, structures, events, processes, the space-time continuum, and life. But reality or being is not just a random combination of these things but something that takes place in self-initiating and relatively autonomous units that range from cells and microbes to complex macroorganisms such as animals and human beings.[12] We can reformulate Schleiermacher's negative definition of the goodness of being as follows. There is nothing about either the constituents of reality (processes, mathematical structures, etc.) or its self-initiating, autonomous units that is evil in an

10. See Jonathan Edwards, *The Nature of True Virtue* (Ann Arbor, Mich.: University of Michigan Press, 1960), 99.

11. Friedrich Schleiermacher, *The Christian Faith,* trans. H. R. Mackintosh and J. S. Stewart (Edinburgh, Scotland: T. and T. Clark, 1928), 238.

12. In Alfred North Whitehead's speculative philosophy, the *res verae,* the irreducible units of reality, are actual entities or actual occasions which inherit content from the past, have subjective aims, and prehend ideal possibilities. The visible macroorganisms of our world are complex converges of these entities. More than any other, this philosophical account of world process interprets being as constituted by self-initiating entities. Whitehead's account of actual entities is distributed throughout his major work, *Process and Reality: An Essay in Cosmology,* ed. D. R. Griffin and Donald Sherburne (New York: Free Press, 1978).

a priori sense, that is, that engenders or is constituted by the dynamics of idolatry.

Expressed positively, the goodness of being means that the total complex of reality with its self-initiating entities offers to its participants environments that constitute conditions of survival and well-being. Available in these environments are materials appropriate for the well-being of the occupants. The environment is also "good" because it evokes experiences of satisfaction. The environment in which we live is both useful and pleasurable. We human beings experience it as useful when we draw on its resources in pursuit of aims that reflect basic needs. We experience it as pleasurable when we perceive in it variety, beauty, familiarity, and novelty. I do not think this is simply an anthropocentric definition of the goodness of being. An environment that offers the conditions and resources for well-being and satisfying experiences is the meaning of the goodness of being for all living things from cells to primates.

If this is what the goodness of being means, it should be clear that this principle does not exclude chaos, suffering, and tragic incompatibilities. An environment or entity can be useful and pleasurable without being ordered toward the well-being of each and every individual. In fact, without chaos and randomness and therefore incompatibilities and suffering, there can be no self-initiating beings, nothing available for use, and nothing that can give pleasure and meaning.[13] Consent to being is the attitude that guides our ways of using what is available to us, our interest in other self-initiating beings, and our pleasurable perceptions. This is why some degree of consent is never absent in human beings, not even in the most ascetic and world-denying behaviors. And to the extent that we consent to a world of this sort, that is, a world of autonomous, self-initiating beings, we also consent to randomness, accidents, and tragic disproportions. For the environment of such beings can be good only if there is sufficient flexibility in world process to act, perceive, experience, choose, and pursue aims. A "good" world cannot be simply a mathematical structure, an endlessly self-repeating machine, or a kingdom of unbreakable laws. It is necessarily an open world of ongoing creativity, contingent happenings, and incompatible and competing entities and groups. Consent is the existential and emotional acknowledgement of the propriety of these things. Consent does not demand an elimination of resistance to suffering of all kinds or a repression of the desire of elementary passions through or past mundane goods. Cessation of resistance would not be consent but resignation. The repression of passions would not be consent but its opposite,

13. Walter E. Stuerman, *The Divine Destroyer: A Theology of Good and Evil* (Philadelphia: Westminster Press, 1967), describes the mixture of order and chaos as the "Penelopean Web." See esp. chap. 1.

the refusal of the contingency of being. And it is just because consent displaces attitudes of discontent, anxiety, and the refusal of finitude that it is part of the complex posture of courage.

Risk of Being

A third attitude shapes the posture of courage. Relativizing and consent are ways of relating to goods at hand. Their focus is away from the self and on the goods. But one aspect of courage is an attitude about the self as it exists in the world. As flexible, random, and creative, the realities of the world can both offer and withdraw conditions of well-being, items for use, and perceptual beauty. In our environments, we can be surprised, threatened, disappointed, criticized, injured, and killed. Thus the goodness (usefulness, beauty) of the world is a fragile goodness, and to live in the midst of these fragile goods is precarious. We respond to this precariousness in attitudes of self-protection and withdrawal, attitudes that avoid situations that threaten our meaning, integrity, identity, and determinacy. Sensing what our environments can do to us and prompted by the dynamics of self-securing, we withhold commitments, avoid decisions, and restrict our activities to environments that are confirming, predictable, and safe. We do not, in other words, risk our being in the perilous situations of being. It is just this incapacity to risk the being of the self that being-founded displaces when it gives rise to courage. Once the self is founded by the presence of the sacred, it is not turned away from the world (as in refusal) but turned toward the world as a venturing of the self amidst the perils of the world. And while this may include situations and acts of physical courage, the attitude of the risk of being applies to any and all ways the self exists in the world.

Courage, then, is a complex posture that combines attitudes of relativizing all mundane goods at hand, consenting to the essential goodness and tragic character of the world, and venturing one's being in the perilous environments of the world.

FAITHFULNESS

The primordial posture that breaks the power of the dynamic of idolatry is the complex posture of courage. But students of the classical Christian tradition will sense that an important theme has been so far omitted. Granting that sin occurs *coram Deo,* in relation to God, is sin not also against God? Even if we set aside the judicial metaphor and notions of sin as forensic guilt and salvation as acquittal, is there not some sense in which sin is against God? And if this is so, does not the primordial posture of courage involve some positive relation to God? The ancient texts of Israel as well as the songs and liturgies of Christendom are filled with accounts of personal alienation between agents and God. In these passages human beings insult, disobey, disbelieve in, and blaspheme God, and they experience redemption as reconciliation with God. The dominant metaphor of this discourse is not judicial but personal. Does this personal metaphor illumine the character of evil or the founding moment of historical freedom? In what sense can sin be said to be against God and in what sense is the primordial moment of being-founded a moment of reconciliation?

These questions call for extensive exploration of the suitability of personalist discourse for divine being and that falls outside the present project. I shall instead assert briefly what deserves a much fuller analysis. First, the interpretation of the sacred through personalist metaphors is not without basis. We recall that the elemental passion of the interhuman desires through the goods at hand for an other able to give unqualified understanding and affection. In the experience of being-founded, that which founds is this same horizon of the elemental desires in the form of an actual presence. If the presence addresses the passion of the interhuman, it would seem to be in some sense a personal other. Second, if that which founds is the desired horizon of penultimate goods, and if founding does break the hold of idolatry and open human beings to the reality and beauty of the world, then the founding presence is an unqualified goodness. Third, because that which founds, unlike goods at hand, is able to found, it is the center, power, and meaning of being and thus is that on which we and all goods at hand depend. What happens in founding is that the desired eternal horizon is disclosed as the transmundane power and meaning of being which is both good and personal.

What then is the posture appropriate to this founding sacred presence? Because it is the transmundane ground of things, it calls forth a relation and self-conscious attitude of *dependence.* Because this ground of things is also good and in some sense personal, it calls forth an utterly distinctive act and relation of *worship. Worshipful dependence* is the proper and genuine response and relation to the sacred as the personal and good ground of things. And worshipful dependence is the defining content of the term, *faith,* or faithfulness.[14] Faithfulness, then,

14. One of the most extensive analyses of faith, especially as faithfulness and *Emunah* is Martin Buber, *Two Types of Faith,* trans. N. P. Goldhawk (New York: Harper and Bros., 1961). The polemical side of this work and the exposition and criticism of the Christian type of faith (*pistis*) is less persuasive to me than his brilliant analysis of Hebraic faith as *Emunah.* Buber focuses so much on the Christian doctrinalization of faith, its reduction of faith to belief-in prompted by its response to Christological heresies, that he misses the elements of *Emunah* which continued in Jesus, Paul, and the Christian movement. Buber

is the relation that the dynamics of idolatry precludes and that arises with being-founded. And the metaphors that express faithfulness are not society-maintaining metaphors (monarchy and the judicatory) but metaphors of the interhuman.

In what sense then can sin be said to be against God? In the previous chapter I contended that sin's reduction of the horizon of desire to goods at hand altered the meaning of that horizon. In being-founded that horizon is present as God calling forth the posture and relation of faithfulness. And if the eternal horizon is the good, personal, and creative ground of things, sin is a more complex act than simply a mundanizing of the eternal horizon. If the eternal horizon is God and if we insist that goods at hand serve as our center and ground, we misconstrue not only the eternal horizon but God. The classical tradition has called this *unbelief*. But sin is more than an act of misconstrual. When we reduce the eternal horizon to goods at hand, we turn the grounding and securing of our being over to these goods. But if the eternal horizon is God, this act is a way of relating to God. The classical tradition has called this relation *mistrust*. Again, once the idol (the good at hand) is in place, its claims and contents become the law of our being. Nations, causes, world-views, and interpretive schemes become uncriticizable norms, set our agendas, and dominate our actions. The classical tradition calls this displacing of the eternal as God with absolutized normative goods *disobedience*. And if the eternal as God has a personal aspect, these acts of unbelief, mistrust, and disobedience are acts of violation and as such incur guilt. This is not the law-breaking guilt of the judicial metaphor but the alienation which arises in the sphere of relation. Personal guilt is the irremediable obligation created by a failed obligation. And punishment can avenge but never equivocally and legally satisfy personal guilt. Because the eternal horizon is God, the personal and good ground of things, sin has the character of violation and alienation. If that is the case, the primordial moment of freedom must include not only courage but reconciliation. This is what is behind the classical tradition's way of describing being-founded as arising from the divine mercy, compassion, and forgiveness. Being-founded then is not simply a securing presencing of the sacred but a forgiving presencing of the violated (disbelieved, mistrusted, disobeyed) God. And it is from this forgiving presencing that worshipful dependence or faithfulness occurs.

does show the absolute character of faith, an act which does not have a further completion "in God." He also discerns elements of repentance, acknowledgement, loyalty, decision, trust, and the heart all converging in *Emunah*. Thus Gerhard Ebeling says, ". . . Christian faith is not a special faith, but simply faith," in *The Nature of Faith*, trans. R. G. Smith (Philadelphia: Fortress Press, 1961), 20.

Thus, courage, the virtue effected by being-founded, is at the same time faithfulness.

To summarize, being-founded is the primordial moment of agential freedom. Janus-like, it faces two directions and incorporates two transformations. In the one, our incapacity to live without anxious discontent, without idolatry is displaced by courage (relativizing, consent, the risk of being). In the other, our alienating violation of God is displaced by reconciliation and faithfulness (belief, trust, obedience).

8
CORRUPTED HISTORICITY AND THE CREATION OF BEAUTY

> Since according to God's will man (*sic*) is to live on a future basis, he falls prey to nothingness and death in shutting himself off from the future in dread. He cannot bear to look into the void. In order to cling on to himself he fastens frantically on to what he can accomplish. To this end he misuses the created world—that is, he lives on the basis of his works.[1]
>
> *Rudolf Bultmann*

> In a world without beauty . . . in such a world the good also loses its attractiveness, the self evidence of why it must be carried out. . . . The witness born by Being becomes untrustworthy for the person who can no longer read the language of beauty.[2]
>
> *Hans Urs Von Balthasar*

According to the philosophy of human reality in Part One, personal being, bodily life, and elemental passions are major dimensions of individual agents. I began a theological account of our condition with the individual dimension and so far have explored the general dynamics of agential corruption (idolatry) and the primordial moment of its redemption. These primordial dynamics of evil and freedom are powerful enough to pervade and influence the dimensional life of agents. Because idolatry arises in connection with the agent's existential response to its tragic condition and thus shapes the very way it exists in the world, it does not remain sealed off in some part of the individual. Idolatry gains access to and shapes the interrelated dimensions of individual life. And if idolatry permeates personal being, bodily life, and the elemental passions, there can be no real

1. Rudolf Bultmann, *Essays Philosophical and Theological,* trans. C. G. Grieg (London, Eng.: SCM, 1955), 81.
2. Hans Urs Von Balthasar, *The Glory of the Lord: A Theological Aesthetics,* trans. E. Leiva-Merikakis (New York: Crossroad Pub., 1982), 19.

freedom unless being-founded also reaches and transforms these corrupted dimensions. Accordingly, the exploration of individual evil and freedom faces the task of tracking the way the dynamics of idolatry corrupt the dimensions of agential life and what happens when being-founded and the postures of courage and faithfulness re-shape these dimensions.

To use a geographical metaphor, the dimensions constitute a topography of human agency. Psychological and anthropological topographies of the operations and structures of agency are not unusual in the theological endeavors of Christianity and other faiths. The limitation of this metaphor is that it maps human reality on a two-dimensional plane. Another metaphor, archaeology, adds the third dimension of depth and hints at subterranean strata to be uncovered. According to the archaeological metaphor, much of agential life takes place below the acts and intentions of actual consciousness.[3] Dimensional operations and structures serve as a background to the self-aware actions of everyday life. This notion has a commonsense plausibility. We sense that at any given time we are not aware of most of what has shaped our being or even what is in our memories. Topography, archaeology, the unconscious, repression, and the human mystery are all terms that suggest a distinction between our full and ever-changing reality and what we are aware of and use at any given time.

The archaeological explorations of this and the following four chapters are not conducted as speculations about what may be going on in some dark and utterly hidden realm. Their focus is to trace and uncover the roots, the relations, and dynamics of what we actually experience. They are failed explorations insofar as they are unable to discover intuitive and experiential confirmations. We human beings do experience what Aristotelian philosophy and the Catholic tradition call vices and virtues. Self-deception, malice, honesty, and sympathy are not merely speculative concepts or formal categories. Archaeological inquiry attempts to uncover the structures and dynamics at work in these things.

3. Archaeology, a forerunner of deconstruction and perhaps a version of it, became thematic in the writings of Michel Foucault, who saw Friedrich Nietzsche as archaeology's primary originator. In Nietzsche and Foucault archaeology is a tool of historical inquiry. It is necessary not just because any phenomenon contains strata to be uncovered but because the oppressive historical powers of history work to hide the events and concepts that legitimate present corruption. An archaeological method will thus look for those hidden turns of history, turns that may not be prominent and dramatic events but subtle and marginal departures. These turns are behind the deep presuppositions of current knowledge. One could say that archaeology in this sense is a kind of Marxist sociology of knowledge at the service of historical interpretation. See Michel Foucault, "Nietzsche, Genealogy, History," in *Language, Counter-memory, Practice: Selected Essays and Interviews*, trans. D. F. Bouchard and Sherry Simon (Ithaca, N.Y.: Cornell University Press, 1977).

Does human evil affect the way we are related to the past and future and if so what is the result? Is human evil related in any way to biologically rooted anger and aggression? How does the dynamics of idolatry institute changes in the passion of subjectivity? These are the questions of a theological archaeology of agential corruption and freedom.

These explorations are archaeological in a restricted sense. They do make use of a fairly detailed account of the dimensions of human agency and this makes the analysis seem very structural and systematic. Here I must recall that in the philosophy of human reality (Part One), I described these dimensions without exploring their interrelation. Some dimensions are more formal or general than others but this does not mean that some dimensions cause the others. At this point I am content to say that human life is constituted by these dimensions and that they are interdependent, each one influencing and being influenced by the others. This is why I draw back from saying that there is a one-way causality from bodily needs to passions to self-presencing, or from personal being to passions to aggression. These one-way tracks of influence tend to obscure the way the dimensions are interdependent. Because of this unsystematic way of understanding the dimensions, these explorations do not yield a causal sequence of how evil permeates human reality or how freedom occurs. Thus, I shall not try to establish how the corruption of self-presencing causes the corruption of the elementary passions. I do not doubt that the corruption of one dimension does in fact affect corruption in the others and that freedom in one dimension influences freedom in others. But I hesitate to propose a unidirectional interpretation of these influences.

Readers of this text will soon discover that these reflections on agential corruption and freedom fall within what may be called the virtue tradition.[4] The primary insight of this tradition is that specific acts (behaviors, agendas, emotions) of evil and good are rooted in more enduring continuities, ways in which the human individual has taken shape over time.[5] Not only Augustine and Thomas Aquinas but Søren Kierkegaard,

4. The virtue tradition is very much alive in twentieth-century religious ethics. On the Catholic side an important older work is Josef Pieper, *The Four Cardinal Virtues* (Notre Dame, Ind.: University of Notre Dame Press, 1966). Since Josef Pieper, Gilbert C. Meilander, Alasdair MacIntyre, Stanley Hauerwas, and others have written important monographs on the ethics of virtue, see Gilbert C. Meilander, *The Theory and Practice of Virtue* (Notre Dame, Ind.: University of Notre Dame Press, 1984); Alasdair MacIntyre, *After Virtue: A Study in Moral Theology* (Notre Dame, Ind.: University of Notre Dame Press, 1980); and Stanley Hauerwas, *Character and the Christian Life: A Study in Theological Ethics* (San Antonio: Trinity University Press, 1975). On the Protestant side, see William F. May, *A Catalogue of Sins: A Contemporary Examination of Christian Conscience* (New York: Holt, Rinehart and Winston, 1967).

5. According to Gilbert C. Meilander, citing Josef Pieper, virtues are "those excellences which enable a human being to attain the furthest potentialities of his nature." See

Jonathan Edwards and Reinhold Niebuhr are part of the virtue tradition. The embodied self of individuals is not a sheer freedom, a vacuity from which good or evil acts are born ex nihilo. It is a complex of habits (*habitus*), that is, dispositions or inclinations shaped by the convergence of the dimensions. This complex of habits (character) is the continuity or enduring aspect of human being-in-the-world. The classical tradition called the dispositions (habits) shaped by the dynamics of evil, *vices.* In this text they are called corruptions. Those dispositions that arose from being-founded, the salvific impact of divine presence, the classical tradition called *virtues.* In this text they are called freedoms or powers of freedom.

A theory of virtue is one outcome of this account of agential corruption and freedom. The most prominent features of the theory are the following. First, the corruptions and freedoms occur in connection with the dimensions of the human being. Vices are ways human historicity, biological tendencies, and elemental passions undergo distortion. Virtues (freedoms) are powers to effect the proper operations of these dimensions. Second, each corruption originates in the dynamics of evil (idolatry) and this means that response to the distinctive vulnerability of a dimension functions in its corruption. For instance, our response to the tragic elements in our passion for the other functions in the corruption of that passion toward both cynicism and sentimentalism. Further, each freedom (virtue) is a power to exist in the face of the tragic element of the specific dimension. Third, the freedoms are not merely terms for the acts and powers of the dimensions themselves. They do not arise as mere restorations to what the philosophy of human reality describes as self-presencing, determinacy, aggression, passion, and the like. Rather, the freedoms are powers that arise from the effect of being-founded (and thus courage and faithfulness) on specific ways of existing toward the tragic. In other words, the powers of freedom are not just the absence of the dynamics of idolatry but powers of existing in the mode of faith. Creativity, vitality, wonder, and love are not just other names for organic satisfactions or the passions for reality and subjectivity. In other words, this is a theological or theonomous theory of the freedoms (virtues).

FALSE HISTORICITY

Personal being or historicity is the meaning-oriented temporality of individual agents. It includes self-presencing, acts of meaning-as, the coinciding of retentions and protention, determinacy, transcendence,

Meilander, *The Theory and Practice of Virtue,* 6. James Wallace, reflecting his orientation to Aristotle, defines them as traits of human persons that function as indispensable for the goods of human life. See *Virtues and Vices* (Ithaca, N.Y.: Cornell University Press, 1978), 10.

and autonomy. If idolatry arises in conjunction with the way we try to solve the problem of our tragic vulnerability by absolute attachments to goods at hand, it will surely have some effect on our historicity. Idolatry as a way we exist in the world cannot but modify the way we mean things and the way we are determinate and transcendent. Because idolatry is a way of meaning goods at hand as able to secure, it presupposes historicity and our capacity to mean things as. And to relate to goods at hand as securers is at the same time a way of retaining the past and protending the future. Idolatry thus changes our way of being temporal. How does this happen?

Absolutized goods at hand quickly pass into the past. In fact most of what we react to, interpret, become angry about, and struggle on behalf of is already in the past. The contents of the revered nation, the honored guru, and the absolutely true world-view are largely past even if they survive in the living present. For the idolatrous posture clings to these things meant as contents, not as immediate realities in the stream of consciousness, and most contents are not so much directly perceived as remembered. Because they are absolute securers, these past contents take on the status of absolute criteria for what is most real and most important and thus exercise dominion over our responses and assessments. The past thus becomes a hegemony to which we are subject.

How does this hegemony of the past alter our way of having the future? We live toward the future from this subjection to the past. Because the securer (the idol) is a deposited content of the past, fear dominates our relation to the future. The future is the realm of possible threats, criticisms, and changes that can dethrone the securer. Future interpretations may expose the securer's fallibilities, relativities, and corruptions. Future world-views, cultural systems, and gatherings of power may displace the revered nation, the all-sufficient conceptual scheme. Thus, the future must be tamed, its possibilities limited, and its threats neutralized. The idolater moves ever into the future with a defensive weaponry, taking on its contingencies on behalf of the securing past. But this description of the skewing of human temporality is only a very general account of the effect of evil on human historicity. For we human beings are historical not just in our meaning-oriented temporality but in the determinacy of time and place, of race, nation, language, culture, and autobiographical situation and also in the way we transcend these things. The corrupting effects of idolatry spread into these operations as well.

The Corruption of Transcendence

The distinctive temporality of agents is also marked by determinacy and transcendence. Our temporality consists not just in the flowing convergence of the past and the future but in our concrete locations. Thus, instead of being empty, our past and future have specific, located, and culturally formed contents. The future as either an objective realm of possibilities or an imaginatively projected scenario is correlated with a specific past. Determinacy is the contentful, historical concreteness of human beings. It is our specific historical, cultural, and autobiographical shaping over time. Human individuals are determinate at this female or male, African or European, orphan or nonorphan, with a rural or urban past, and mathematical or literary inclinations. Transcendence is our irreducibility to this concreteness, our capacity to surpass it in modes of awareness, criticism, and self-initiation. Transcendence prevents determinacy from being a mere fate, a static content, an external and inexorable causality. Determinacy prevents transcendence from being a mere vacuum, a self-initiation without task, materials, or context. Nor is there ever perfect accord between determinacy and transcendence. An unstable disjunction, an uneasy peace, characterizes their relation because determinacy ever forms identities and continuities which transcendence ever resists and surpasses. Apart from this instability, the corruption of determinacy and transcendence would not be possible. Given that corruption, the benign but functional disjunction between determinacy and transcendence becomes severely distorted. How does this happen?

Transcendence, the content-surpassing aspect of agency, undergoes corruption when it loses its tense relation with determinacy. And it is precisely this loss or separation that idolatry effects. Idolatry arises from our incapacity to tolerate vulnerability, to exist in the face of an ultimate chaos. And we "solve" the problem by making goods at hand our securers against chaos. But what is at hand is not just a set of objects located in our environment but the content of our concreteness and continuity or I-as. The at-hand is what we are as American, religious, ethnic, white, graduates-of, and workers-at. These things do provide relative securities, satisfactions, and fulfillments. *Determinacy* is a summary term for the whole realm of goods at hand and is where the securers, the false founders of meaning, are located. Throughout history determinacy has always been what agents have done evil things on behalf of or in the name of. Determinacy means the tribes, cultures, nations, causes, and symbol systems to which agents offer their loyalties. And when these things must function as nonfragile and utterly good securers, the result is to break the tense relation with transcendence. When that happens, transcendence itself begins to erode. For the determinate as securer cannot bear the self-surpassing postures of criticism, imagination, and self-initiation.

Earlier, chapter 6 described the role of tragic existence in idolatry. Does the experience of the vulnerability specific to historicity, the tense and unstable alienation between transcendence and historicity, lure transcendence toward corruption? Since the dynamics of agential evil (idolatry) effect the corruption of all the dimensions, these dynamics will be at the heart of historicity's corruption. Nevertheless, the specific vulnerability of historicity joins the general fear of intolerable chaos to corrupt transcendence. It appears that the corruption of transcendence proceeds from the deep anxiety transcendence itself evokes. Even in its benign condition, transcendence would sense that its own power of self-shaping is a movement into the dark and the unknown. This is the dizziness Søren Kierkegaard perceived in the self's sense of its own non-necessity and uncertain future. The dynamics of evil plays on and exacerbates this vulnerability at the heart of transcendence. Insisting on release from discontent, the human being immerses itself in its own content, that is, in what it has become as a socialized and culturally specific being. The dark and unknown future flowing from transcendence is replaced by the familiar and safe world of the I-as; by the securings of piety and casuistical prescriptions, the historical glories of the nation, the certainty of beliefs and world-views. Determinacy, then, becomes a temptation and a haven, an invitation for transcendence to escape itself. And this corrupts transcendence because it diminishes the powers of self-surpassing, imagination, and criticism by making them subject to the contents of determinacy.

This flight from transcendence into the determinate does not mean a loss of transcendence. The dynamics of idolatry could not operate if transcendence disappeared. The flight pertains rather to the way we are transcendent. For the transcendence that survives idolatry's influence has more the negative character of an irreducibility than a positive way of relating to the determinate. On the other hand, a kind of narrowing does take place when transcendence is corrupted. In this narrowing the agent is not reduced to an object but to a content. Once we make the determinate, our I-as, into a haven against tragic vulnerability, we narrow our agential reality to our I-as. We permit our maleness or femaleness, our cultural loyalties, our being athletic or aesthetic, blue collar or intellectual to define our reality. This self-reduction is not just an external attitude we adopt toward ourselves. It is something we become, what our reality or being is as a way of existing in the world. Accordingly, reductionism is not merely one among a variety of world-views or approaches to human being: it is also an existential posture that attends the corruption of human determinacy. This, then, is one side of the corruption of historicity, the corruption of transcendence by the idolatry of the determinate, or *false determinacy.*

The Corruption of Determinacy

Determinacy is the space time location, the content aspect of personal being. As a subject matter of the sciences, it is the biological, social, and interhuman legacy and content that makes up the individual's world. From the agent's perspective, determinacy is the agent's own I-as identity. Determinacy's relation to transcendence is neither that of an external tyrant nor a dispensable contingency. It rather supplies transcendence with specific situations of action, a legacy from the past, a source of motivation, and a range of possibilities. As with transcendence, the corruption of determinacy begins when its tie with transcendence is loosened. And this happens when agents turn to their own transcendent aspect as a good at hand that secures. They look not to structure and content but to the powers of self-determination and will to drive away tragic existence and intolerable chaos. Securing goods at hand are not restricted to external entities or contents. The self-making, self-surpassing self is also a good at hand toward which we can adopt postures of awareness, valuation, and hope.

The unstable relation between transcendence and determinacy also plays a role in the corruption of determinacy. Evidence for this instability is the will's ever-present resistance to the determinate. Ernst Becker's expanded version of Freud's concept of the Oedipus complex articulates this theme of resistance to determinacy. According to the psychoanalytic movement, nonrational instinctuality (Freud) or the "limitless organizational expansion from the beginning of the child's experience" (Becker) are severely limited by the prohibitions necessary for familial and societal order. In my view this limitation describes a tension, perhaps a tragic conflict, but not a pathology. But transcendence does resist the bounds placed on it by determinacy. It experiences in its cultural world and its own I-as not the darkness of the unknown but a possible subjugation. This unstable tension, this suspicion about determinacy combined with the experience of intolerable chaos, opens the door to the corruption of determinacy. This resistance to determinacy's possible subjugations now lures human beings into a flight from content and structure into transcendence. Once only a content to be surpassed, determinacy becomes a tyrant to be expelled or fled. Once only a power to surpass content, transcendence becomes the securing thing, able to exorcise the demons of chaos, identified now as the contents of culture, family, tradition, and the I-as. Thus, the uneasy peace between transcendence and determinacy develops into a rupture, a sharp alienation. The resistance of transcendence to determinacy's possible subjugations becomes revolt and repudiation.

How does this defiance of determinacy corrupt our way of being determinate? Separated and repudiated, determinacy takes on the character of sheer heteronomy, an alien and violating power. The human being is thus alienated both from its cultural and historical legacy and from its own I-as. And because the social and the interhuman are borne by the determinate contents of tradition, institutions, and the obligations of the face, alienation from the determinate is at the same time alienation from the face and from the social. In other words, the corruption of determinacy occurs when we think that our own powers of transcending are able to secure us in the midst of tragedy and chaos. Identifying the determinate as itself responsible for our ills, we assume that successful rebellion against this dark and external power will secure us. In the removal of determinacy we look to find our freedom.

Even as the flight into determinacy never removes transcendence, neither does the flight into transcendence remove the determinate. We are determinate as long as we live and breathe. Idolatry effects an altered way of being determinate. Diminished is our capacity to appreciate and enter into the determinate as a realm of goods; the deep riches of aesthetics, the mysteries of the interhuman and the interpersonal, the resources of cultural heritage. Driven away from the determinate into transcendence, we cannot drink from tradition's wells of wisdom or even enter seriously into societal criticism and reform. Alienation from the determinate means alienation from our own I-as, thus from our own gender, race, family, or culture. These things erode before the assaults of a contentless autonomy. The idolatry of transcendence fosters paradoxes and ironies. Absolute value is placed on self- and world-surpassing with little or nothing to surpass. The posture of absolute transcendence pretends to be a radical criticism, but without determinate criteria, it is a bloodless criticism that leaves corruption in place. Nihilism as an existential posture may be an extreme form of the idolatry of transcendence. *False freedom,* the corruption of our way of being determinate, is the other side of the corruption of historicity.

Corrupted Autonomy

Our theme is the corruption of the relation between transcendence and determinacy. Idolatry's alteration of both determinacy and transcendence has both societal and psychological expressions. Highly authoritarian communities and world-views show the suppression of transcendence by their idolatry of inherited contents and customs. On the other side, some periods and cultures (one thinks especially of modernity and technocratic postmodernity) appear to be culturalized phobias of the determinate, eschewing authority, order, continuity, the past, the face, and even truth and reality. The suppression of one side or the other also appears in the psychological dynamics of individuals. Individuals can exist in lifelong patterns of immersal in their I-as and fearing transcendence or in full repudiation of all determinacy.

However, these corruptions of determinacy and transcendence are not simply two separate corruptions. Because they are essentially interdependent, one corruption is also the other's. Corrupted here is simply human historicity, the way we exist as transcending beings in our determinate world. To exist as a transcending determinacy is to be autonomous. Thus the single corruption is a corruption of agential autonomy. In the literatures of theology and ethics, *autonomy* is frequently a pejorative term. It suggests life on behalf of the self alone at the expense of or against anything which is not the self. But with the possible exception of colonies (corals, for instance), most living things have a proper and inevitable autonomy in the sense that they experience the world from their own center and struggle in the world on their own behalf. Human autonomy as we would expect arises in connection with the complexity and dimensionality of agents. However much they are constituted by the interpersonal and social, agents are biologically and passionally motivated individuals. We struggle on our own behalf, experience and interpret the world from the space and time center established by our bodies, and are not indifferent about the status of our own subjectivity and I-as, a concern that Ernst Becker calls self-esteem.

It would, therefore, be a mistake to think of autonomy as simply a narcissistic preoccupation with the self and its experiencings. In most of our everyday experiences, we do not attend directly to ourselves but past the self to worldly situations and contents. Even reflective thinking, (mulling over, solving a puzzle, making a mental list), usually does not have the self as its referent. And when we participate in a conversation, we do not ordinarily attempt to listen to ourselves speak or stand apart and observe how we are reacting. Autonomy is not qualified or reduced by this bypassing of the self in everyday experience. Bypassing the self toward what is other is the ordinary way autonomy functions. In other words, autonomy is a way of existing in the world in which the self-motivated and embodied self bypasses itself toward something else.

Corrupted autonomy is a familiar theme in Western moral and religious philosophies. Scriptures, hymns, poems, epics, and theological tracts are filled with references to hubris, the hardened heart, pride (*superbia*), selfishness, egotism, and narcissism. Extreme expressions of this tradition appear to repudiate autonomy itself as proper and inevitable. Yet, it is important to distinguish between the proper autonomy of human agents and the corruption of that autonomy, the concern of this moral tradition. How does idolatry corrupt proper autonomy? We recall that idolatry arises when agents, unable to tolerate their tragic vulnerability, insist on and find a securing by goods at hand. Thus we press these goods into service of this existential problem. The effect of this salvific agenda or "metaphysical" need is to alter the way the agent is properly autonomous in its world relations. No longer are we drawn past ourselves toward spontaneous participation in what is other. Our insistence on being secured by goods at hand forces the goods at hand (people, tasks, experiences, situations) into becoming our securing utilities. And this way of being oriented to goods at hand closes off our paths to the face whence come our obligations and to the past whence comes our inherited wisdom. Terms like *hubris, pride,* and *selfishness* describe not our proper autonomy but a false primacy the self takes on when its own metaphysical agenda of self-serving structures its world relations.

Throughout these explorations, I have described the dynamics of idolatry as taking place in relation to discrete and external things such as ethnic traditions, nations, and religious traditions. But these examples tend to hide an important feature of those dynamics. For the corruption of historicity is not simply a skewed relation to concrete entities, nor is it limited to something that takes place in a sequence of specific acts. The corruption of historicity is also a way the agent exists through time, a persisting posture of metaphysical hunger. And it is this posture that corrupts both the way we are determinate and the way we are transcendent, thus undercutting our spontaneous surpassing of the self toward the reality and riches of the world.

CREATIVITY

Uncorrupted, historicity is a determinate and transcending (properly autonomous) way of relating to worldly goods. As such personal being is neither idolatrous nor founded in the sacred. According to the Hebraic and Christian paradigm, the only history we know is one already corrupted by the dynamics of evil. Also according to that paradigm, the power of evil is broken not by the pseudo securings of goods at hand but by the one thing able to found, the divine ground of all goods. When this happens, when we exist toward tragic vulnerability through courage and faithfulness, our corrupted historicity is transformed into a new freedom. But the result of this transformation is not simply an uncorrupted historicity, a world relation without idolatry. Being-founded effects a new historicity or way of surpassing the self toward the world that is not merely nonidolatrous proper autonomy. I shall call this new historicity, *creativity.*

Creativity as the Creation of Beauty

As a term for the agent's distinctive temporality, *historicity* is not a specifically moral category. As intrinsic to our very reality it may be a good, a feature of human agency to be valued and pursued, yet still serve both good and evil ends. Creativity too as one of the good features of historicity, is also distinguishable from moral experience. It has to do not so much with what is right and obligatory but with what is beautiful. As an existential feature of agential existence, creativity means the creation of beauty. What does this mean? We face here a matter of enormous complexity, a subject that calls for more than the few paragraphs offered here. I shall reduce the complexity to three motifs: (1) the nature of beauty, (2) types of creativity, and (3) existential creativity or the creation of beauty.

1. The experience of the beautiful is not confined to a group of specially gifted human beings or even to the experience of artistic works they produce. The experience of beauty is an intrinsic aspect of the way human beings experience the world.[6] It is also apparent that since beauty is not an entity, we experience this or that as beautiful, not beauty as such. Nor is our experience of the beautiful limited to occasional dramatic incidents; the memorable sunset, the striking visage. There are elements of beauty in every actual and manifested reality; the flight of the falcon, an animal's call, a tree swaying in the wind. The experience of these things as beautiful is not just the discernment of their function. Neither is it a perception of sheer form; the unit of sound, the shape of a wing. Beauty is what attends the fit of form and function. To experience the manifestation of that fit is to experience beauty. Specific visible and audible events come easiest to mind. The beauty of the falcon's flight is manifest when the falcon's form, its phylogenetically inherited streamlined package of feathers, claws, and wings, unite in an expertise of action. When we say, "That is beautiful!" we refer neither to the static form nor to the function of predation or flying behavior. The expertise manifest in the accomplished synthesis of form and function is what is beautiful. Likewise, the beauty of a human face is

6. Beauty was an intrinsic element in the philosophy of Alfred North Whitehead and thus in subsequent process philosophies and theologies. For Whitehead see *The Adventures of Ideas* (London, Eng.: Cambridge University Press, 1935), chap. 17. See also John B. Cobb, Jr., *A Christian Natural Theology: Based on the Thought of Alfred North Whitehead* (Philadelphia: Westminster Press, 1965), 98ff. In this tradition beauty is not so much a property of things as of experience. See Cobb, *A Christian Natural Theology,* 101. In Continental philosophy and phenomenology, Roman Ingarden and Michel Dufrenne have made seminal contributions to aesthetics: Roman Ingarden, *The Literary Work of Art: An Investigation on the Borderlines of Ontology, Logic, and Theory of Literature,* trans. G. G. Grabowicz (Evanston, Ill.: Northwestern University Press, 1973); and Michel Dufrenne, *The Phenomenology of Aesthetic Experience,* trans. E. Casey et al. (Evanston, Ill.: Northwestern University Press, 1973). The two approaches are actually not very far apart. Dufrenne also argues against restricting the beautiful to the aesthetic realm and defines it as "the truth of the object when this truth is immediately sensuous and recognized," "the true made visible." See Michel Dufrenne, *The Phenomenology of Aesthetic Experience,* lxi. Thus the opposite of the beautiful is not ugliness but the abortive.

not a pure physiognomy but a union of form and expression, of visage and attitude. And we mean the same thing when we say that a human action, character, or virtue is beautiful. Beauty is not just a proper functioning but this fit between function and the reality designed for the function. In living things the fit occurs as a kind of action or accomplishment.

Assuming that beauty itself is a fit between form and function, what happens in the experience of beauty? The experience of beauty has about it a failed cognitivity, a perplexity, an intrigue. A mystery, an element of nonexplanation, attends the apprehension of the fit between form and function. This mystery is why the experience of beauty contains elements of surprise, of something new. Even when we have heard the symphony 50 times before and anticipate its every phrase, we experience surprises on hearing it anew. The experience of beauty also contains an element of pathos. In painting, sculpture, music and poetry, a sense of the pathos and vulnerability in all concrete things (a specific flower, a wrinkled face, a childhood incident) attends the fit of form and function. The pathos of concreteness is what evokes from us emotions of recognition and sympathy so necessary to the experience of beauty. Artistic representations of concreteness show us what once was and will be no more, and when they draw us into that concreteness, they awaken our own sense of ephemerality.[7]

2. Like all terms that float in on the tide of history and culture from centuries of human reflection, *creativity* is profoundly ambiguous. In its most fundamental sense, it is a feature of all living things and of world process itself. Living things exercise beauty when they enact a fit between their form and their function. This exercise of beauty (the coordinated movements of legs in walking, the opening of a bud) is the most general instance of creativity. According to the poet Sara Teasdale, the experience of the beauty of things can be so intense that it places an indelible mark on one's being.[8] Creativity is present in a society's art forms in a secondary and more effortful sense. Exercising beauty or reproducing the world's exercise of beauty may or may not be the primary aim of artists of word, sound, or shape. Whether or not that is the case, all artists experience and reproduce the new. And this reproduction is an exercise of beauty insofar as it effects a fit of form and function. Human agents exercise beauty when

7. See Wallace Stevens' essay "On Poetic Truth" in his *Opus Posthumous* (New York: Alfred A. Knopf, 1957) in which he argues that the poet's task and genius is the articulation of the concrete.

8. Oh, burn me with your beauty, then,
Oh hurt me, tree and flower
Lest in the end death try to take
Even this glistening hour.

The Collected Poems of Sara Teasdale (New York: Macmillan, 1943), 143.

their actions fit form to function, thus in walking, conversation, feeling, and even thinking. But there is a creativity in human life that is neither the exercise of beauty intrinsic to life nor the disciplined creativity of art. It takes place in connection with the world negotiations of personal beings, thus it is the work of our temporality, imagination, and transcendence. This creativity of practical action shows itself when we project alternatives and make decisions, solve technical problems presented by world situations, and when we engage in invention. This is the creativity of *techne*, of *homo faber*, of doing and making. To summarize, agents experience at least three kinds of creativity in the everyday world; the creativity of life itself (the exercise of beauty), the disciplined creativity of the arts, and the inventive or problem-solving creativity of practical action. I distinguish these senses of creativity so as not to confuse them with another creativity, existential creativity or the creation of beauty.

3. In our exercise of beauty, the fit between form and function is partly a creative accomplishment and partly an inheritance from the past. Evolution, early learning, and even training make possible the gracefulness of the runner and even the beautiful use of language. Thus, the exercise of beauty is a creative way of acting out of an inherited, predisposed, and typified fit between form and function. Both artistic and problem-solving creativities take a step beyond the exercise of beauty because they introduce novelties that break the pattern of inheritance and learning. But the focus of these creativities is not on personal existence, the making of the self, but on external outcomes in the self's environment: thus, the opera, poem, or sculpture (in the arts) or the boat, engine, or electronic circuit (in invention). Is there a creativity that like the arts goes beyond inherited patterns but whose material is personal existence and whose outcome is self-making? Is there a creativity of personal being that does not merely display the life-form's inherited fit of form and function but brings about new forms and functions? If there is, the mystery, pathos, and newness would have to do not with the inherited fit of form and function but with the break with that heritage in the sphere of the personal. We are familiar with claims that human beings have an openness to being and are ever moving into the new. But this language does not quite describe existential creativity. Both the exercise of beauty and artistic and inventive creativity involve movements into the novelty. Existential creativity is a person's self-movement into the new *with respect to its own inherited fit of form and function.*

An example is called for. Human agents have the capacity (reason) to grasp abstracted features of things, thus, to identify strings of causes, similarities, differences, and typical patterns of action. Form means the enduring contents of this capacity, the presupposed features of reason.

At the same time, reason is a function (an action) of our personal existence. And something beautiful takes place when the forms and functions of reason come together to accomplish a brilliant demonstration, an insight into the connection between things. Impressive as they are, these outcomes reflect a biological and cultural legacy. Reason is always an embodiment of specific, culturally formed definitions of what is real, true, cognitively possible, and worthy of cognitive effort. And these culture-based incarnations of reason's fit of form and function constitute the enduring contents of agential life.

Can there be a creativity that is more than just the co-option or application of the legacy of the past to new situations? Is there a creativity that might alter the very form of reason which the social past has fixed? Two things would be involved in such an alteration. The deep criteria that determine the form of reason would be changed, the past's determination of what is real, important, and cognitively possible. This alteration involves a creative act of personal existence that reforms the meaning and power of reason. This creative act would not be simply the life-form's spontaneous exercise of beauty but a creation that issues in a new fit of form and function. It is not just an alteration of what is external, a bringing about of something new in the world, but an alteration of the self. In the example of reason, creativity changes the way the past has structured reason's form and function. But everything about the agent is open to this creativity: responsibility, basic loyalties, the interhuman, emotions, and even creativity itself.[9]

Creativity as a Theological Freedom

It is time to connect the themes of creativity and the corruption of historicity. To be active in the world in creative ways is clearly an aspect of historicity. Hence, the corruption of historicity and thus of temporality, transcendence, determinacy, and autonomy is at the same time a corruption of creativity. The hegemony of the self's metaphysical agenda in its world relations corrupts the exercise of beauty, aesthetics, and invention. The powers and functions of these things are not eliminated by this corruption. Human evil has always co-opted the creative powers of reason, art, and invention to promote its idolatrous and oppressive agendas. But existential creativity is not an ontological feature of the human life-form. It is not an existential. The dynamics of idolatry do not corrupt it but rather prevent it from arising in the first place. And the way existential

9. Creativity is the crown of ethics and the redemption of the human being for Nicolas Berdyaev. See esp. Nicolas Berdyaev, *The Destiny of Man*, trans. Natalie Duddington (London, Eng.: G. Bles, 1954), Part II, chap. 3.

creativity comes about is from being-founded. Unfounded and without a center of meaning, our existence is dominated by the inherited fit of form and function. We are open to the future but only to a future structured by or reduced to the forms and functions received from the past. We are self-surpassing (transcendent) in our way of being determinate but the surpassing remains in the inherited framework. To return to our example, we may surpass our epoch's accomplishments in the sphere of reason through special projects but we cannot make our existence over in such a way that we surpass the epoch's meaning of reason we have interiorized. Unfounded, we are dominated by the way our very being is dominated by the legacies of form and function.

The effect of being-founded on the agent's historicity is a new freedom (virtue), namely existential creativity. This freedom is the power to create new fits of form and function in the very heart of our own existence. This is not to say that being-founded directly causes existential creativity. Because of being-founded, courage is the agent's posture toward tragic existence and goods at hand. Courage relativizes the legacies of form and function that shape our existence. And this relativization is not just a world-view but a posture of our very existence. Relativism, we recall, is a fashionable and pervasive feature of the belief systems of modernity and postmodernity. Under its sway, we easily relativize all legacies, all forms and functions, all knowledge and sedimentations of wisdom. But a thematic relativism can be an existential dogmatism, a frozen deposit of presuppositions and form-to-function fits in the center of the individual's existence. Here we have a freedom of world-view but not a freedom to create beauty, to bring about a new, manifestly beautiful fit of form and function in the heart. Unfounded and without the consent and relativizing of courage, we remain bound to fits defined by the legacy of the past. It should be clear that this new freedom is not just another word for proper determinacy, transcendence, or autonomy. It is rather what happens to these things when the human being is founded. Added to the ordinary creativities of making and the exercise of beauty is a new creativity, the creativity of beauty in the sphere of the heart.

Two final clarifications. First, to say that existential creativity arises with being-founded and courage is not to explain that creativity. The relativizing aspect of courage removes the obstacles to creativity by breaking the past's hold on form and function. But why would this breaking carry with it any impulse to create new form and function? At this point we must recall that elemental passions constitute our concrete human existence and these passions have no intrinsic limitation. They press us beyond all limited horizons toward an eternal horizon. Constituted by these passions and released toward the future by courage, our existence becomes a perpetual creation of beauty, that is, of new forms and functions in the sphere of the heart.

Second, the creation of beauty may be a virtue of autonomy but it is not an autonomous virtue. Isolated into itself and cut off from freedoms connected with the interhuman, the body, and the passions, it is contentless and directionless and can become self-destructive and demonic. Separated and alone, creativity is easily appropriated by rationalizations for power and for the abandonment of responsibility. This is the temptation of a (modern) society with an authoritarian, Victorian, and essentialist past. It would make the rupture with past fits of form and function the one and only virtue. But if human agents are dimensional, creativity cannot be so isolated. It takes place not as an isolated freedom but in a complex of interdependent freedoms.

9
THE CORRUPTED PASSION OF SUBJECTIVITY AND THE FREEDOM OF VITALITY

> And there he lay, sick and miserable, malevolent against himself: full of hatred against the springs of life, full of suspicion against all that was still strong and happy. In short, a Christian.[1]
>
> *Friedrich Nietzsche*

> I would believe only in a god who could dance. And when I saw my devil I found him serious, thorough, profound, and solemn: it was the spirit of gravity—through him all things fall.[2]
>
> *Friedrich Nietzsche*

Describing the historicity or personal being of agents is a formalism of sorts. There is little flesh and blood in the concepts of temporality, determinacy, and transcendence. As concrete individuals, we exist in situations through strongly motivated actions, specific moods, and in mercurial swings of emotions that range from elation to despair. Phylogenetically based urges, individual biochemistries, and culturally formed interests all supply motivating directions to our endeavors. Chapter 5 described three elemental passions at work in the scenarios of action: subjectivity, the interhuman, and the passion of reality. If elemental passions are in fact powerful motivations in human life, and if the dynamics of idolatry are in fact a dynamics of the way we exist in the world, it should come as no surprise that these passions can be corrupted by idolatry and influenced by being-founded.

The passions and their corruption is a familiar theme in the classical literatures of both Eastern (e.g., Buddhism) and Western philosophy and religion. We learn about human desire gone awry from the Pali Canon, the David stories in the Hebrew Bible, from Plato, Augustine, Johann Goethe, Jonathan Edwards, Sigmund Freud, and

1. Friedrich Nietzsche, *The Portable Nietzsche,* trans. W. Kaufmann (New York: Viking, 1954), 502.
2. Ibid., 153.

countless others. Passions of power and patriotism have again and again spread armies over vast ranges of the planet. Passions of greed, personal domination, and sexuality have corrupted communities and destroyed families even as repressed passions have fostered resentment, frustration, and depression in countless individuals. The seven deadly sins of medieval piety have more the character of resident passions than overt behaviors.

A Manichean suspicion of world and body has ever gnawed at the vitals of both Catholic and Protestant pieties. Prompted by this suspicion, these movements have sometimes sought the root of human evil in the passions themselves. Thus, the passions are not so much corrupted as corrupting. And when passions are seen to be corrupting, they call for virtues whose function is to repress. To moderns and postmoderns, this suspicion can only seem quaint. So fascinated is technocratic modernity by "freedom" that one almost longs for a new Manicheanism that could at least remember that passions are corruptible. But technocratic modernity cannot acknowledge corrupted passions for two reasons. First, quantifying modes of thoughts and calculative societal relations render the elemental passions invisible. They have no place in the interpretive schemes of modern society. Second, the prevailing societal narcissism (whatever you feel is right) persuades us that biological needs, feelings, emotions, and the like are subject only to psychological and mental health criteria. In this chapter and the next, I shall contend against the repression tradition that elemental passions are tragically structured but not evil and against the prevailing therapeutic world-view that they are corruptible and corrupted.

FALSE OPTIMISM AND DESPAIR: THE BIPOLAR CORRUPTION OF THE ELEMENTAL PASSIONS

Desire for fulfillment is the primary urge of an elemental passion. The underside of this desire is a resistance to what prevents fulfillment. Biologically rooted needs display this negative underside in the capacity for anger and aggression. In the elemental passions, the underside is a struggle against any and all conditions that work against the passion's fulfillment. Desire and resistance point to but do not constitute the tragic structure of the elemental passions, the unclosable disjunction between what the desire wants and what it actually obtains. The reference of the elemental passions is never any specific good or state of affairs in the world. They press past these goods toward an utter securing of the agent's life and meaning, an utter resolution of the mysteries of reality, and an utterly satisfying interhuman relation. The passions are tragically structured because they take place in environments that both promote and oppose their realization. Nor is there ever any certainty that this tension will ever end. They are also tragic because to live in this tension and disjunction is a kind of suffering. Because of the two sides of desire and resistance, the references of these passions are both things desired and various obstacles and conditions that oppose or prevent the fulfillment of desire. And because agents are aware of these ideal and negative references, they develop feelings, strategies, and even theories about them. On the resistance side, agents develop styles of action, policies and strategies, and emotional stances for handling the obstacles and frustrations of everyday life; thus, exaggerated negative expectations, reality-denial, naiveté, and even rationalizations for these things. On the desire side are a range of attitudes and behavior patterns toward the desired; thus, vivid imaginative representations, fantasizing, calculative planning, and low or high expectations of fulfillment. Needless to say, because these distinguishable postures are aspects of the same passion, they tend to reflect and influence each other. Because agents are aware of and respond to their own passions and their references, idolatry effects a double corruption in each of the elemental passions. How does this happen?

Let us recall the effects of the dynamic of idolatry on human historicity. Insisting on being secured by goods at hand, we flee our own transcendence into absolutized determinacy and our own determinacy into contentless transcendence. Since both historicity and the passions described the agent's being-in-the-world, the corruption of historicity will also be a corruption of the passions. Even as the uncertainties and insecurities of historicity are intolerable, so also are the painful disjunctions of the elemental passions. Here, too, we insist on being secured, and in the realm of the passions, being secured means closing the gap between desire and fulfillment. If the gap were actually closed, the tragic structure of the passions would be abolished. And this is just what the idolatrous agent demands. Thus, the mysteries of reality must so reveal themselves that our confusions and our doubts are chased away. Our relation to human others must be characterized by absolute affection based on an unambiguous understanding. World conditions must establish our subjective existence in the face of all perils. This *must* (insistence) does not actually eliminate the gap between desire's aims and realizations. It rather expresses a corrupted way of existing in that gap and in relation to nonfulfillments of desire. What makes this a corruption?

Once goods at hand are pressed into the service of absolute securing, a sharp paradoxical relation develops between the two aspects of the passions, the desires and their resisting underside. Because the desires insist on fulfillment by the goods at hand, they relate to those goods as if they themselves were the eternal horizon. Since no finite good can be its own horizon, no such good can, in fact, fulfill desire. Thus, to insist that it do so has the character of a self-deception, a delusion, a *false optimism* that presides over the attitudes and strategies by which we handle our passions. This optimism influences the way we exercise loyalties and commitments (e.g., to the nation, family, or group) and the way we engage in important undertakings (e.g., our career, our leisure, our friendships). And it fosters all sorts of unrealistic expectations toward the desired goods at hand.

On the other side of the paradox, idolatry corrupts the resisting underside of the elemental passions. What we struggle against is determined by what we desire. If that is the case, our relation to what frustrates desire will surely be affected by the corruption of false optimism. Idolatry, in other words, corrupts the resistance aspect of the passions not directly but through the corruption of how we desire. How does this happen? Recall that the insistence on fulfillment does not, in fact, close the gap between desire and its references. It does not eliminate the fragility of goods at hand. Failure, then, is built into false optimism. This optimism is false because desire must deceive itself about the capacities of the goods at hand to fulfill. Driven by this deception, we must place these securers above the vicissitudes of history and life and bestow on them traits which they do not have. What then happens to resistance and the struggle against what frustrates desire? In spite of the optimistic expectation that the absolutized and securing good has the power to undermine all opposition, its existence remains precarious. This engenders a new and intensified resistance on behalf of the fragile and threatened idol. This new resistance is not the old resistance. Resistance on behalf of the idol is not a relative struggle against the erosions and competitions of world process or society but a defense of the idol (specific culture, the affluent class, the promising career) against all the nasty contingencies that threaten it. The secured but absolutely zealous patriot must struggle ever harder against internal and external enemies. But this absolute resistance is ever a failing resistance, and its outcome can only be disillusionment and disappointment. This experience of the limitation, fragility, and corruption of the securer or idol is existential *despair.*[3]

As the corruption of the resistance side of the elemental passions, despair is a phenomenon of desire. Without deep desire or passion we

3. The *locus classicus* for the theme of despair in Western philosophy and theology is surely Søren Kierkegaard's *A Sickness unto Death: A Christian Psychological Exposition for Upbuilding and Awakening,* trans. Howard and Edna Hong (Princeton, N.J.: Princeton Univ. Press, 1980). According to Kierkegaard, despair is a fever, a sickness, a gnawing of the spirit in which the self cannot bear to be itself and attempts (futilely) to abandon itself. It is a constant vacillation between willing or not willing to be oneself.

could not experience despair. We should not confuse despair with the specific frustrations, disappointments, disillusionments, and defeats of everyday life. Despair is not so much the emotion that attends actual defeat by something at hand as the sense of being betrayed by what is most real, true, and trustworthy. Despair, however, is less a posture toward the past as the future because it projects onto the future a scenario of the fragile idol. Given the defeat of the one thing that could secure, the agent's projected future can only be a scene of defeat. At the deepest level of our passionate existence, we sense the inadequacy of the idol, the intrinsic failure of our attempt to abolish the tragic, and we despair. But despair does not eliminate its counter posture, false optimism, since it depends on that optimism for its existence. This paradoxical posture is the bipolar structure of the corruption of all of the elemental passions. Each of the three passions has its own version of this falsely optimistic and despairing posture. In the present chapter I shall explore the corrupted passion of subjectivity and the freedom of vitality which arises with its redemption.

FALSE HOPE AND ENNUI: THE CORRUPTED PASSION OF SUBJECTIVITY

The corruption of the historicity of agents is a corruption of their temporality in its most formal sense, their way of being determinate and transcendent. But to passionately exist is also to be temporal. And this way of existing in modes of passionate needs and desires is also corruptible. This corruption pertains not just to our mutability but to the way we desire, anticipate, and depend on future outcomes. When the agent pretends that its idol exercises hegemony over the future, its passion for future prospects has the character of *false hope.* On the other hand, when it experiences betrayal by the idol, its passion for its future prospects has the character of existential weariness or *ennui.*

False Hope

Hope is an element in the passion of subjectivity precisely because it is a passion, a desire for what one does not yet have. Hope should not be confused with wishes that things turn out all right. Hope pertains to the agent's very existence or way of existing in relation to itself. It is the desire and expectation that one will be ever one's own self whatever the future brings. However devastating the anticipated events, hope projects not just a defeated and denuded but a responding and resisting person into their midst. Hope is a projecting of one's own historicity into an uncertain and perilous future.[4] Hopelessness, thus, is not just pessimism about a future outcome, but a defeated self projected into the future. Hope and hopelessness concern neither just the agent nor external events and conditions but the power of the agent in relation to events and the power of events over the agent. And, we recall that the passion of subjectivity is a passion both for the agent itself and the conditions pertinent to the agent's meaning and well-being. Thus, the passion of subjectivity and its hope is a way of relation to goods at hand but as projected into the future. The agent passionately desires that the goods of the future will support and confirm rather than take away its being. It is just this relation to the projected future agent amidst its future goods that idolatry invades and corrupts. Idolatry's aim is to bring the passion of subjectivity to an end. The experience and claim of the idolater is that the absolutized and securing goods successfully hold the threats to passion at bay. This of course does not, in fact, happen. The passion of subjectivity does not actually disappear nor does our concern about its future cease. If goods at hand are entertained as securing frameworks, and if the actual conditions for supporting life and meaning remain ambiguous, then a new relation to the future arises. For if goods at hand are in fact genuine securers, they have the power to govern the future. They are able to win the war against whatever comes out of the future to threaten life and meaning. Thus, the false confidence which is an element in the corruption of all the passions is in this instance a confidence about the agent's destiny. It is a confidence that the securing goods at hand exercise hegemony over the future. Nothing in the future can surpass or replace the securing goods at hand. Unsurpassable and invulnerable is the securing nation, political party, belief-system, and religious institution.

Idolatry's effect on hope is to turn it into a false confidence. When we insist that the future can really fulfill our passion for life and significance, our hope is less a projecting forward of our power to exist as an attitude about positive outcomes. This is because in idolatry, the agent is immersed in absolutized goods at hand (idols). These now become the referents of hope with the result that hope, the existential, erodes into a world-view and a belief. It comes and goes with the capacity to believe in certain contents such as immortality or world fulfillment. This is not to say that having such beliefs is the necessary sign of the corruption of hope. The mere presence of beliefs is not necessarily a sign of the operations of idolatry. We can imagine persons who hold all sorts of beliefs

4. This characterization of hope is a brief version of Gabriel Marcel's "Sketch of a Phenomenology and Metaphysics of Hope," in *Homo Viator: Introduction to a Metaphysic of Hope*, trans. E. Craufurd (Chicago: Regnery, 1951).

about wonderful cosmological and personal outcomes whose existential hope is deeply corrupted. And we can imagine persons whose world-views include no such beliefs who live into the future in existential hope. But the corruption of the passion of subjectivity drains hope of its existential element and transforms it into a belief-ful relation to the future. The future means happy outcomes assured by one's securing idols.

False hope, then, is what happens when the passion of subjectivity is corrupted by idolatry. The hope is false because it is the existential projection of one's historicity into a future where happy outcomes are guaranteed by the securer. It is also false because it is a delusion. And this projection is a delusion and self-deception for the obvious reason that goods at hand are unable to rule the future. They cannot head off the threats to life and meaning that come out of the future. Religions, world-views, and corporate entities will not enable us to cheat death, nor can they so organize reality that they themselves are its center, point, and clue. This is a strange delusion because in their commonsense convictions and world-views, agents are of the limitations of finite goods. But the delusion is not a delusion of world-view but of the heart, the location of the passion of subjectivity and its hope.

Ennui

Like all of the elemental passions, the passion of subjectivity has a negative or resisting aspect. The passion for life and meaning is at the same time a struggle against what opposes life or withholds meaning. This aspect of the passion of subjectivity funds negative emotions of disappointment, jealousy, betrayal, and defeat. We experience these emotions when our desires are disappointed. These emotional responses would be absent in a perfect or magic land world in which events and realities adapted themselves to our every wish. They would also never arise if we were utterly without desire. They are harbingers of a future ever mixed with satisfactions and frustrations, a future in which tragic vulnerability continues. Even as idolatry transforms the primary or desiring aspect of the passion of subjectivity into false hope, so it transforms the resisting posture into existential weariness or ennui. At first glance, this does not seem possible. It would seem that false optimism about the prospects of one's very existence simply eliminates all despairing moods about that existence. But absolute exclusions are the properties either of assertions, predicates, and beliefs, or objective states of affairs. Two plus two cannot add to both four and five and an entity cannot be at the same time a turtle and a truck. But human existence is neither an assertion nor an object. We can and do embody contradictory beliefs, and more important, opposing or paradoxical features and tendencies. Thus, the desiring and resisting aspects of the passion of subjectivity are corruptible into contradictory postures. Even in this opposition, they remain dependent on each other. The sense of futility or ennui comes into being precisely because failure is intrinsic to false hope. How does this happen?

Ennui does not arise directly from idolatry but rather from the failure of false hope. It is the disillusion that comes when false hope is betrayed by its idols. In ennui the emotions of frustration escalate into a type of despair, a sense of futility about subjectivity itself. Resistance resembles desire in that its primary reference is the self and its secondary references are conditions or circumstances in which we live. Ennui also combines these two references. The sense of futility is first of all about the self and its prospects and secondly about the worldly conditions of life and significance. Signs of the first and primary reference are the presence of interiorized images of the already defeated self. Signs of the secondary reference are despairing postures toward the conditions of life and meaning.

As the underside of false hope, ennui, too, is a way of existing into the future. What it projects onto the screen of the future is not the victorious and fulfilled self but the defeated self. And this, too, is an existential projection, not a cluster of pessimistic beliefs about objective outcomes. The futility of ennui is a futility of the heart. Even as the corruption of desire takes the form of an exaggerated and self-deceiving hope, so the corruption of resistance issues in an abandoned and despairing resistance. This reduces and subverts but does not eliminate the passion of subjectivity. Ennui is not the absence of resistance but a tired and despairing resistance.[5]

VITALITY

When the dynamic of idolatry invades the human passion for life and meaning, it effects a paradoxical combination of false hope and existential weariness (ennui). I have described the salvific presence of the sacred in the nonforensic notion of being-founded, a presence that graces the human being with courage. Being-founded transforms the passion of subjectivity in two ways; first, it breaks the hold of false hope and ennui; second, it reforms the passion of subjectivity into a new freedom (virtue), *vitality.*

5. In Hebrew and Christian Scriptures the theme of ennui finds its most eloquent expression in the writings of Qoheleth. See the first three chapters of Ecclesiastes. In classical Christian theology, the theme is indirectly present in criticisms of the notion of fate. These criticisms are conducted at the level of cosmology and metaphysics rather than existence and ethics. But the ethical correlate of the category of fate is a posture of resignation. Fate is a category that describes the already defeated self.

Breaking the Hold of False Hope and Ennui

False hope and ennui describe the two-sided and paradoxical corruption idolatry works on the passion of subjectivity. Refusing to live in the disjunction between desire and fulfillment and insisting on the securing of life and meaning, we appropriate goods at hand to establish us against tragic vulnerability. Apart from the presence of the sacred, human agents appear incapable of a nonidolatrous passion for life and meaning. From the presence of the sacred or being-founded comes the one thing that counters that incapacity, courage. And it is courage, the convergence of relativizing, consent, and the venturing of the self, that breaks the hold of false hope and ennui. How does this happen?

The relativizing aspect of courage fosters an insight into the limitations of all goods at hand. This insight undermines false hope's confidence that its passion for life and significance can be fulfilled. Relativizing also exposes the false assumption that securing goods at hand establish and protect the agent in all future scenarios. Relativizing is a posture that grasps the mutability, contextuality, fragility, and corruptibility of both the self and its environing goods. And false hope erodes before the onslaught of this critical posture.

Because existential weariness or ennui is the disillusioned underside of false hope, it too is affected by the relativizing of the references of false hope. However, a mere relativizing would not break the power of ennui. For ennui has already promulgated its own version of relativizing to the point of a sense of futility about the references. Breaking the hold of ennui over human existence requires an aspect of courage that is not just criticism. Courage is also a consent, one might even say, an appreciation of beauty, to the ever-changing panorama of worldly events. This includes consent to the tragic structure of the panorama and thus to the disjunction at the heart of the passion of subjectivity. Consent effects a posture toward this disjunction not as something to be escaped or abolished but as the very condition of self-surpassing, creativity, and the enjoyment of the world.

Vitality as the Freedom of the Passion of Subjectivity

The passion of subjectivity as a human freedom is not merely a release from false hope and ennui. The mere absence of false hope and ennui is simply the uncorrupted passion, not freedom. The passion of subjectivity as such is not a freedom but rather a dimension of agential existence. However, when being-founded and courage break the hold of false hope and ennui, something happens that is not just a restoration to that dimension's operations. Being-founded introduces a power or freedom into the passion of subjectivity that is not simply a resident or constitutive feature of that passion as such. I shall call this freedom that arises with being-founded, *vitality.*

To distinguish the passion of subjectivity from vitality, we must explore what the passion of subjectivity would be apart from the corruption of evil and being-founded. It is true that we have no direct experience of such a thing. We know the elemental passions and everything else about ourselves only under the conditions of history, which is to say, in an already present corruption. At the same time, the structures and operations of the dimensions of agents and spheres of human reality are not synonymous with their corruption. The very notion of corruption not only implies a distinction between what is corrupted and the corrupted state but some awareness of the nature of what is corrupted. Apart from such awareness, corruption itself could never be identified. We can make little sense of the corruption of an interhuman relation if we have no notion whatsoever what an interhuman relation is.

Unfounded, the passion of subjectivity is simply the human passion for a significant or meaningful existence. It is a passion for life and meaning on behalf of the self. And because this is a passion of the agent on behalf of itself, it centers in the agent's embodied self. The passion of subjectivity, is, in other words, a kind of existential solipsism, not in the sense that it refuses to grant reality to what is other but rather in the sense of refusing to grant importance to what is other. To be sure, there are other aspects of human reality and its condition (the interpersonal, the social) that ever draw the agent past itself into world relation. But the agential self dominates the passion of subjectivity. And insofar as the passion of subjectivity is a way of being-in-the-world, objects and goods of the world are its utilities. The life and meaning desired by this passion is the agent's life and meaning. Thus, this passion is directed beyond the agent only to procure the conditions of the agent's life and meaning. This, however, is a benign and not evil utilization of what is other. It expresses not the dynamics of idolatry but the natural existential solipsism, the intrinsic egocentricity of the unfounded passion of subjectivity. Søren Kierkegaard appeals to this egocentric subjectivity when he contends that faith is an impossibility. His question is, How is faith or relation to God possible for a being whose very being is its own primary passion for itself?[6] The question assumes that relation to God requires a passion for God, for something that is other. Needless to say, the problem has no solution when

6. See Søren Kierkegaard, *Concluding Unscientific Postscript,* trans. D. F. Swenson (Princeton, N.J.: Princeton University Press, 1941), 288.

based on two premises: first, God is an external, determinative command; and, second, agency is constituted by a solipsistic or egocentric passion for itself.

Vitality is the freedom that being-founded and courage effect in the passion of subjectivity. What is this new freedom? I recall that one aspect of courage is a risk or venture of the self in the face of an uncertain and threatening future. This is the self's willingness not just to face but to become something new. It is just this venturing of the self that alters the natural solipsism or egocentrism of the passion of subjectivity. As an egocentrism, the passion of subjectivity effects a division between the self and whatever is not the self. This division appears in everyday life as the ever-present choice between serving the self (thus utilizing whatever is other in that service) or servicing what is other (thus abandoning the self). The self is caught between selfishness and altruism. This very situation is brought about by the egocentric structure of the passion of subjectivity. It presupposes that the passion of the human being for itself can exist only at the expense of what is other. But when the hold of false hope and ennui is broken, when the self begins to lose its false primacy and courageously ventures itself, this exclusive relation between the self and what is other is transcended. The either-or of the self and what is other is surpassed. What is this surpassing?

The passion of subjectivity is a passion for life and meaning. When courage and the venture of the self enter the life of this passion, the other is no longer a mere utility for the self. The passion for life is not just a co-option of the other for the sake of one's life, and the passion for meaning is not just a search for a framework for one's own meaning. It is a passion for life itself and meaning itself. Yet vitality is not just a turning away from the self or an indifference to the self's life and meaning. If vitality were that, it would still be dominated by the either-or between the self and what is other. The passion for life itself is a passion to live in the midst of living things. It is neither a passion for the life of others at the expense of the self nor a passion to live at the expense of what is other. It is a passion for the meaning and significance of things as such. Hence, it is neither a passion for the meaning of what is other which is indifferent to the self's meaning nor a passion for the contributions the other can make to the self.

A direct and objective description of this passion for life and meaning itself is almost impossible. Yet, what I am talking about is not merely an inference but an experienced phenomenon. Human beings do experience vitality. We experience a passion for life which is not merely on behalf of the self or on behalf of others. And with that we experience resistance to death, to dullness, to meaninglessness on behalf of something larger than the self. We resist these things as such. So, according to Edna St. Vincent Millay:

> Down, down, down into the darkness of the grave
> Gently they go, the beautiful, the tender, the kind;
> Quietly they go, the intelligent, the witty, the brave.
> I know. But I do not approve. And I am not resigned.[7]

If being-founded and courage returned us to the natural solipsism of the passion of subjectivity, we would remain forever caught in the either-or of a dominant self or dominant other. But being-founded effects a vitality that surpasses this either-or and enables us to exist beyond that division.

Two final comments. Vitality is fundamentally a passion for life and meaning as such. Thus it includes but surpasses the self's passion for itself. It is the exercise of passion on a larger plane. This existence is a new freedom toward both the eternal and the future. Why does vitality effect a new freedom toward the eternal? Natural solipsism or egocentrism (not to be identified with sin or evil) inclines us to the eternal as the ever-present horizon of goods at hand. Idolatry prompts us to insist that our passion for life and meaning be fulfilled and to reduce the eternal horizon to the fulfilling goods at hand under the delusion that the idol closes the gap between desire and fulfillment. Being-founded and courage give the power to exist in that gap in relativizing consent. We are content to exist without possessing the eternal, without receiving from the eternal unambiguous life and meaning. Being-founded then is a paradoxical relation to the eternal. It is a founding that is not founded, a founding that enables an acceptance of an eternal that does not serve our ends and fulfill our passions.

Why does being-founded (and courage) transform the way we have the future? All the elemental passions are ways of existing toward the future but false hope and ennui are corruptions of how the passion of subjectivity exists into the future. Vitality is a relation to the future which is not merely the absence of false hope and ennui. The passion of subjectivity as such is an egocentric passion on behalf of the self. In this natural solipsism, the self's aims on its own behalf dominate its relation to what is other. This too is a way of existing into the future. Because natural solipsism effects a division between the self and its utilized others, agents are anxious and hopeful about what the future will bring. As they attempt to manage and control what happens to them,

7. Edna St. Vincent Millay, *Collected Lyrics* (New York: Harper and Row, 1969), 172.

they are dominated by their own planning and thematizing. But when courage affects a passion for life itself and for living in the midst of others beyond this either-or, the future is not so much a realm of possible utilities as the realm of unfolding life and meaning. Planning, arranging, and thematizing do not disappear (even as passion on behalf of the self does not disappear) but are taken up into a larger passion. For if life itself is not simply a matter of external utilities for the self, then the future is not simply the realm of arranged possibilities. It is as much a gift as is life in the midst of others.

10
THE CORRUPTED PASSION OF THE INTERHUMAN AND AGAPIC FREEDOM

All creatures in the world through love exist
And lacking love, lack all that may persist.[1]
Geoffrey Chaucer

It is characteristic, however, of individual personality that we only become acquainted with it in and through the act of loving, and that its value as an individual is likewise only disclosed in the course of this act. Being an 'object' of love represents, as it were, the only objective status wherein personality has existence and can therefore be manifested.[2]
Max Scheler

The spheres of the interhuman and the social are enmeshed in the life of human agents. But it is important to distinguish the interhuman itself, the sphere of face-to-face relation, from the passion for the interhuman which is a dimension of individual agency. The sphere of the interhuman is the scene of a distinctive corruption, interpersonal violation (see chapter 13). The passion for the interhuman, like the other passions, is corrupted by the dynamics of idolatry. The theme of this present chapter is not the corruption and redemption of the interhuman but of the passion of the interhuman.

THE PASSION FOR RECIPROCITY

A summary of the passion of the interhuman is in order. The sphere of the interhuman is constituted by alterity or otherness, intersubjectivity, and the interpersonal. The interhuman itself is the irreducible event and relation of interpersonal being-together. But the passion of the interhuman is not a desire for these three things. It would not make much sense to say we aspire for alterity. Since intersubjectivity

1. Geoffrey Chaucer, *Troilus and Cressida,* trans. G. P. Krapp (New York: Random House, 1932), 111.
2. Max Scheler, *The Nature of Sympathy,* trans. P. Heath (London, Eng.: Routledge and Kegan Paul, 1954), 166–67.

includes our historical and determinate content, we do in one sense aspire to be intersubjective. But it is the interpersonal that is the reference of a specific and very elemental passion. Why is the interpersonal something agents need and desire? The interpersonal is the sphere of the face, that vulnerable other "I" that evokes compassionate obligation. But the face is not an ontological structure, a predicate or quality of individuality, or even a static relation. It is an event between individuals which awakens the passion of the interhuman. What the face awakens is the desire to be acknowledged, understood, and appreciated by the other and the desire for an other on whom we can bestow acknowledgment, understanding, and affection.[3] Expressed differently, it is a desire that the other perceive and appreciate one's beauty and a desire for others to so appreciate. In the sphere of the interhuman, beauty means more than the bodily manifested fit of form and function. Because we are self-presencing beings, our fit of form and function pertains also to how we think, feel, desire, and act. But we do not ourselves establish these things as beautiful. We depend on others to bestow on these things their status as important, worthy, beautiful. Because this is both a desire to be acknowledged and to acknowledge, the object of this passion is a situation of mutual bestowals or reciprocity.

The passion of the interhuman resembles the other elemental passions in certain formal respects. First, like the other passions, the passion of the interhuman has a direct reference (reciprocity with others) and an indirect reference (the conditions which reciprocity requires). Since human reciprocities depend on relatively stable environments of meaning, custom, tradition, safety, and the like, the indirect reference of the passion of the interhuman is the social. Second, like the other passions, the passion of the interhuman has a resisting underside. The desire for reciprocity carries with it a resistance against those who fail to acknowledge us and against conditions which would isolate us from others. Accordingly, this passion is constituted by a certain instability. Awakened by the face, we desire the other's understanding and appreciation. But under the best of conditions, the other's capacity to bestow or receive these things is very limited. Therefore, attending our relations to others are benign antipathies spawned by disappointments and resentments. These things constitute the vulnerability of this passion which idolatry exploits and corrupts.

3. Throughout this chapter I shall use the terms *acknowledge* and *acknowledgment* as inclusive terms. Acknowledgment includes but is not limited to an intellectual act. Gathered into it are affection, appreciation, and understanding. It is acknowledgment in this broad sense that is the desired reference of the passion of the interhuman.

Finally, like the other passions, the passion of the interhuman is shaped by a natural egocentrism. Natural egocentrism describes the self reference and centeredness of biologically and personally motivated human beings. This egocentrism is the reason the desire for an affectionate reciprocity is not a mere balance between the desire to receive and the desire to bestow. The passion of the interhuman as such is what happens to our historicity and sense of self when it is awakened by the face. It is drawn toward a reciprocity with others which serves the self, a reciprocity on behalf of the self. This egocentrism is responsible for the uneasy alternations between postures of need for the other's affection and the need to bestow affection. And given the unfathomable variations of bodily, cultural, and autobiographical backgrounds, one or the other will tend to dominate the reciprocity. This egocentrism is also responsible for the strong element of utility in the way the other is desired. We should not, however, confuse this benign utility with the attempted management of the other which idolatry effects. This is because our natural egocentrism is not itself idolatrous but is ontologically prior to and the presupposition of idolatry.

FALSE DEPENDENCE AND CYNICISM

The dynamics that shows the effect of idolatry on the other passions also works in the corruption of the interhuman. Inclined to flee the anxiety of tragic existence, we insist on being secured by the penultimate references of the passion. We exist in the delusion that the gap between desire and actuality can be closed. But the desire for the interhuman is a desire for a reciprocity, an interchange between the need to be acknowledged by others and the need for others to acknowledge. In other words, the passion for the other is at the same time a dependence on others both as sources and objects of acknowledgment, affection, and understanding. This dependence or need for reciprocity undergoes corruption from the positive and negative poles of idolatry, that is, false optimism and despair. False optimism transforms the passion for reciprocity into a *false dependence* and despair transforms that reciprocity (dependence) into a posture of *cynicism*.

False Dependence

Dependence is not just a desire but a relation, or a desire that is itself a way of relating. When our need for others turns into an insistence that interpersonal relation secure us against tragic vulnerability, we become inordinately dependent on the other. All things in our environment offer themselves as metaphysical securers. But the good of reciprocity may be the most attractive and alluring good of all. For face-to-face relations with others offer us our most intense relative securings and satisfactions;

thus, the nurture of parents, the affections of friends, and the intimacies of sexual love. If any good at hand could drive off the specter of chaos, surely intimate reciprocity is that good. In the passion of the interhuman, the good at hand is the other at hand.

On the one side of reciprocity, the need of the other's acknowledgment and affection, the false optimism of idolatry prompts us to insist on and expect an absolute acknowledgment. The other is a very special good because of its power to bestow understanding and appreciation; in other words, as the face. Thus, we live in our environments on the alert for others whose beneficent acknowledgments will secure us. The same thing holds for the need for reciprocity, the need for the other as one to acknowledge and appreciate. The face awakens not only the need for the other's acknowledgment but the need to be and act as face, and the need for others on whom to bestow understanding and affection. But altered by false optimism, we become deluded about our capacity to acknowledge, understand, and love.

The passion of the interhuman yearns for reciprocal affection and approval. The primary dependence of human agents on each other is through this yearning. There are, of course, dependencies that arise with biology, nurture, culture, and family. Apart from others we have no biological existence or historical determinacy. But a distinctive dependence arises when the face awakens for intimacy and understanding. Apart from others, not even the relative fulfillments of this passion are possible. Accordingly, when the passion is corrupted into an insistence that these desired reciprocities secure us against the tragic, it degenerates into a passion for an absolute and therefore false dependence. Relative fulfillments of the desire are already relations of dependence. Absolute fulfillments promise a false dependence because, however fulfilling, they cannot bring this passion to an end nor can they drive off the demons of suffering.[4]

4. The reader will recognize the concept of dependence as a central category of Friedrich Schleiermacher's description of piety. In this view the most general structure of our relation to the world is reciprocity, an influencing and being influenced by the world. Reciprocity with our environment is a relative or partial dependence because we influence what we depend on. However, our freedom or self-initiation is not the sort of thing that arises out of a stream of causality. Neither is it something we ourselves bring into being. Hence, our existence as spirit, as self-transcending, is a sheer or absolute dependence. And the sense (feeling, immediate self-consciousness) of this sheer dependence which has no mundane reference is the very heart of piety. When this very formal human structure is subjected to the conditions of history so that its reference is a specific deity or the sacred, piety is a God-consciousness. False forms of God-consciousness occur as human beings identify the reference of sheer dependence with some mundane reality. This being the case, the very essence of sin is a reduction of piety or God-consciousness. For Schleiermacher, then, sin is a kind of false dependence.

I have appropriated this motif of false dependence of Schleiermacher, not as a description of the essence of sin, but as a distortion of one of the elemental passions. My emphasis

Cynicism

The negative underside of the passion for interpersonal reciprocity is a resistance to its failure. We not only desire intimacy, friendship, and affection; we experience disappointment, frustration, and resentment when these things are withheld or when something removes the loved other from our midst. All human relations are thus ambiguous because of this instability. The other may acknowledge or withhold affection from us, and we may or may not withhold or bestow affection on the other. When this passion insists on being secured by the interpersonal, it also distorts its resisting underside. And this distortion reaches both sides of the reciprocity, the being acknowledged and the acknowledging.

Absolutized desire always has failure built into it. To insist that the other fulfill our desire for acknowledgment is to insist on something which must fail. The despair aspect of the passion of the interhuman arises from this experienced failure. This despair is not, however, just a realistic correction of an excessively optimistic expectation. It is the underside of the insistence that the other's acknowledgment establish and be the foundation of our meaning. Thus it does not merely substitute realism for the delusion that an other relation can secure but rather introduces another delusion, namely, that genuine relation is not possible. The two delusions may be logically contradictory but they occur together as existential correlates. This is because the one delusion, the capacity of the other to fulfill the passion, contains the inevitable failure that spawns the other delusion, the incapacity of the other to fulfill it. Together, they constitute a contradictory way of relating to others as both utterly trustworthy and utterly untrustworthy.

The two aspects of the desire for reciprocity are the desire to be acknowledged and to acknowledge. Despair in the one is a deep cynicism about the other's capacity or willingness to acknowledge. In this posture, we relate to the other as one whose motives and self-surpassing empathies are read as machinations of solipsism and narcissism. This cynicism is directed to both the agent's capacity to acknowledge and the other's capacity to receive acknowledgment. In this case the other is

on a fundamental anthropology of desire or passion and account of sin as idolatry prevent false dependence from being sin's very essence. In place of a formal dependence structure of the immediate self-consciousness, I have substituted an account of agency as a self-transcending, passionate desire in the face of chaos and tragedy. Desire rather than dependence is what mediates the eternal horizon. Thus, the dynamics of idolatry originate from the insistence that the desire be fulfilled by the mundane, not from a false way of construing the reference of utter dependence. By focusing on a structural feature of the immediate self-consciousness, Schleiermacher excludes tragic elements of our world relation and misses the role of desire, anxiety, and insistence in both piety and the dynamic of sin. For his theology of sin, see Schleiermacher's *The Christian Faith,* ed. H. R. Mackintosh and J. S. Stewart (Edinburgh: T. & T. Clark, 1928), 259–325.

reduced to something unreachable, an alterity that resists all acts of understanding and appreciation directed to it. In addition, attitudes arise toward the self that are cynical about its own exocentric impulses and spontaneous acts of sympathy, appreciation, and affection. This despair, too, is a delusion because it exaggerates the natural limitations of both the other and the self.

This negative underside of false dependence is a kind of antidependent dependence, a relation to the other which would repudiate dependence. It, too, is a delusion because it would live in a relation to the other as if there were no need and desire for the other, in other words, and no real dependence. Why does this delusion have the character of cynicism? Like the desiring aspect, the resisting aspect of reciprocity is a way of relating to the future. It, too, engenders expectations and typifications of what others are capable of and how they will respond in certain situations. It has the character of cynicism because it repudiates in advance and in an a priori way both the agent's and the other's powers of transcending empathy and genuine acknowledgment. Cynicism, then, is a despairing attitude toward the possibility of genuine relation.[5] Born of disillusionment, cynicism is a reciprocity of suspicion. It suspects that the motives and powers of both the agent and the other are nothing but self-servings or externally manipulated effects. Corrupted by false dependence and cynicism, we want everything and nothing from others. Unrealistic expectation and disillusioned betrayal mark our way of needing and desiring others.

A final point. Because reciprocity has social conditions, the passion for reciprocity is indirectly a passion for the social. It is the social that calls language into being, organizes and stabilizes life, preserves deposits of tradition, and creates institutions. All of these things are needed and employed when individuals relate to each other. This is why the corruption of the desire for the interhuman is at the same time a corruption of the desire for the social. Optimism about the power of reciprocity to secure spills over into an optimism about the social. And the underside of cynicism likewise extends to a cynicism about institutions, traditions, and other features of the social. Here, likewise, too much and too little is expected. What is corrupted here is not the social itself but the passion for the social. Thus the corrupted passion of the interhuman is one of the roots of the actual corruption of the social sphere. Oppression, in other

5. In everyday usages cynicism sometimes means a negating or suspicious posture directed toward anything and everything. In this essay, I restrict the term to a posture directed toward others in the sphere of the interhuman. I reserve the term, *false skepticism,* for the broader despairing attitude toward the possibility of knowledge. Cynicism describes a despairing attitude toward the possibility of reciprocity between the self and others.

words, is abetted by postures toward the social that are governed by this unstable dialectic of false dependence and cynicism.

AGAPIC PASSION

According to the Christian paradigm of agential redemption, the presence of the sacred and the attending posture of courage break the hold of idolatry. But being-founded does more than simply purge the existentials of their idolatrous corruptions. If that were the case, the freedoms (virtues) of human agents would be simply the ontological features of historicity, elemental passions, and biological tendencies. I have also contended that natural egocentrism (not to be confused with idolatry, sin, or evil) governs the elemental passions. This is the self-serving or self-orientation of the agent that remains in operation even when the agent is drawn outside itself toward the world of the other. It is because of this natural egocentrism that the need for the acknowledgment of others is primary to the need for others to acknowledge. Hence, although the passion is awakened for reciprocity by the face, its natural egocentrism prevents it from being a passion for the face. The agent thus desires reciprocity for its own sake and its own fulfillment. Even if the dynamics of idolatry were absent, this passion would swing between being drawn out of itself toward the other (altruism) and a benign utilization of the other (egoism). But the swing itself is a manifestation of the natural egocentrism of the unfounded passion. Both our need to be acknowledged and our need to acknowledge are driven by an egocentric need.

What happens to the corrupted passion of the interhuman when the human agents exist in a posture of courage? We recall that the effect of courage on the passion of subjectivity was to free us from the egocentrism of the passion to a desire for life as such, life in the midst of living things. Courage has a similar effect on the passion for reciprocity. When we exist in a tragically structured world in postures of relativizing consent, we relativize our own "metaphysical" problem of being secured. This does not eliminate our natural egocentrism, our concern for our self and well-being rooted in our biological and historical make-up. It rather takes egocentrism onto a new plane where our desire is not merely on its own behalf but merges with the desires of what is other. On this plane, the agent transcends the tension and even vacillation between the need to be acknowledged and the need to acknowledge. The need for the other's acknowledgment and the benign utilitarian relation it fosters are no longer primary. Freed from the domination of natural egocentrism, our passion for reciprocity is not just egocentrically oriented on our own behalf. What is this new reciprocity which is the reference of the transformed passion of the interhuman?

When courage transforms the desire for reciprocity, the resulting passion is for the face itself. What dominates this passion is not the self's need but what is discerned in the face. We recall that in human reciprocity this acknowledgment is awakened by the face. When courage reduces the dominance of egocentrism, that which only awakened the passion becomes its primary aim and reference. What does it mean to say that we have a passion, an elemental desire, for the face? What is it about the face that draws desire out of its egocentrism onto another plane?

The face displays the mystery of an irreducible otherness, an impassioned vulnerability, and a unique historicity, all of which converge to evoke compassion and obligation. When the face presides over our relations, these things are mutually discerned and felt. But there is something else about the face which attracts and draws us out of ourselves. Jonathan Edwards gives us a clue when he contends that the highest instance of beauty or loveliness is interhuman love and affection.[6] In other words, there is about the face a certain beauty. What makes the face beautiful? I submit that it is the capacity, act, and emotion of relating to others in self-surpassing affection. Affection combines a felt appreciation for the other (for whatever reason) and a felt caring for the other. Human affection is usually displayed in very specific circumstances; caring relations to children, friends, and intimates. It is this capacity
for appreciative caring that the face displays and which constitutes its beauty. Alterity and vulnerability are not in themselves beautiful. There is a beauty about personal being insofar as its creativity, continuity, and determinacy display an accomplished fit of form and function. However, this beauty appeals to our natural egocentrism and does not draw us to the plane where the agent and the other merges. But affection displays a fit between the emotion of appreciative caring (the form) and the relating-acting (function) that evokes from us the same kind of response we have to any beautiful thing. And when the face calls forth a response that mirrors itself, when face evokes face, a reciprocity of mutual appreciation and caring-for, a reciprocity of affection ensues. As beautiful, this reciprocity lures the agent beyond the natural egocentrism that dominates the passion of the interhuman of the unfounded agent.

To return to the thesis. When being-founded reduces the natural egocentrism of the desire for reciprocity by subjecting that desire to the face, it becomes a passion for the interhuman as a relation of faces.

6. Many are the passages in the works of Jonathan Edwards on beauty and loveliness, especially the beauty of virtue. See esp. *The Nature of True Virtue* (Ann Arbor: University of Michigan Press, 1960), chap. 1; and *Religious Affections* (New Haven: Yale University Press, 1959), Part 3, no. 10.

When the passion of the interhuman takes on this character, it becomes agapic passion. I realize that the term, *agapē,* invites endless misunderstandings, but I know of no better term. First, we must be clear that what is under consideration is a passion. Historically, *agapē* is a more comprehensive notion. In its fullest sense it describes not just a passion but a relation of the interhuman. Accordingly, I am distinguishing between agapic passion, the theme of this chapter, and agapic relation (see chapter 13). Second, some interpretations make *agapē* an antithesis of desire.[7] *Agapē* is thus a posture so emptied of self reference as to be utterly indifferent to the positive qualities of its references. The antithesis, then, to *agapē* is eros, desire oriented to objects on the basis of their capacities to contribute to the agent. *Agapē,* in contrast to eros, is oriented only to the other's well-being and is thus determined only by the other's need. But this way of distinguishing *agapē* and desire is simplistic and probably false.[8] To be oriented to the need of the other requires a positive valuing attitude toward the other. Something about the other, (its creatureliness, its livingness, its potentiality, its salvageable content), draws *agapē* toward the other's need. Beneath the pretended indifference of desireless *agapē* is a positive valuing act. Desire of a sort remains in the heart of *agapē,* partly because *agapē* is not without motivation, and partly because of its inability to be indifferent about what happens to what it loves. Against the notion of a desireless and indifferent *agapē,* I would contend that it is the beauty of the face that evokes *agapē,* forgiveness, compassion, and action. For the beauty of the face displays the other's pathetic, vulnerable, and creaturely fit of form and

7. This is the position argued by Anders Nygren in what has now become a twentieth-century classic piece of history and theology, *Agape and Eros,* trans. Philip S. Watson (London, Eng.: SPCK, 1953). Thus Nygren says, "Human love is distinguished by the fact that in all things it seeks its own and prefers to receive rather than to impart its good. Divine love is the direct opposite of this. It seeks, above all, to impart from the fulness of its riches." "Just by seeking what is lost and in itself worthless, God's love demonstrates most plainly its spontaneous and creative nature. 'For sinners are lovely because they are loved; they are not loved because they are lovely,'" 725. The Spanish philosopher, Ortega y Gassett, presents a view of love that at first sight resembles Nygren. That is, he attacks those who confuse love with desire or appetite. It turns out, however, that in Gassett's view, love is in no way indifferent to its object, but is a kind of passion to preserve the other's existence. Love is a journey to the loved in order to be part of the loved, and this implies something about the loved that is drawing the lover. See *On Love: Aspects of a Single Theme,* trans. T. Talbot (New York: Meridian Books, 1957).

8. Nygren seems to have more critics than followers in the subsequent literature on love in the twentieth century. For criticisms of the Nygren view, see Maurice Nedoncelle, *Love and the Person,* trans. Sr. Ruth Adelaide (New York: Sheed and Ward, 1966), 13–19; M. C. D'Arcy, S.J., *The Mind and Heart of Love* (New York: Henry Holt, 1947), chap. 2; and Thomas Gould, *Platonic Love* (New York: Free Press of Glencoe, 1963), 3–6. Gould's criticism is particularly trenchant. "The obvious peculiarity in the Christian version is the surprising demand that we pay no attention to the excellence or foulness, preciousness or worthlessness, of the object of our affections," 166.

function. *Agapē* is not in other words directed to sheer evil, chaos, or inertness. This is not to say that the other in its beauty merits *agapē's* response. The truth in the conventional view is that *agapē* is not an envoy of the agent's egocentrism and what evokes it is not simply promised self-fulfillments.

The conventional view of *agapē* as indifferent to both the agent's fulfillment and the qualities of the other denies an important element in agapic passion. The new freedom of agapic passion is not just a passion to help the other. As such it would still be controlled by the self versus other tension of natural egocentrism. It is a passion brought to a new plane by the face. As a passion it still has a self reference. The desire for a reciprocity of affection cannot be indifferent to the enriching effect of affection. But this egocentric aspect of the passion does not dominate the passion. For in the affectionate reciprocity of the face, intense appreciation and caring-for converge to break the dominance of the self-reference. The agent's orientation on its own behalf continues but is placed in the background by the vulnerable beauty of the other. Paradoxically, this fulfills the agent as it draws the agent beyond itself.

Being-founded then carries desire for the interpersonal beyond the either-or of altruism and egoism. The new plane of this freedom, agapic passion, is the plane of compassionate obligation of the face. This new plane of reciprocal affection is clearly neither the deluded idolatry of false dependence and cynicism nor the plane of egocentric desire on behalf of the self. Desire for reciprocal affection displaces idolatry and presses egocentrism into the background. We can thus see why a passion for the face would affect the corrupted passion for the social. Negatively, this means a diminution of alternating postures of optimism and cynicism toward the social. Positively, it means new postures toward the social itself. For a passion for the face or for reciprocal affection will at the same time engender criteria about the functions and nature of the social. And it will desire social institutions and traditions that permit and even nurture the reciprocities of the face and will resist those which endanger the possibilities of mutual appreciation and caring-for between human beings and between human beings and other living things.

11

THE CORRUPTED PASSION FOR REALITY AND THE FREEDOM OF WONDER

> [Mr. Smallweed's mind holds] the first four rules of arithmetic, and a certain small collection of the hardest facts. In respect of ideality, reverence, wonder, and other such phrenological attributes, it is no worse off than it used to be. Everything that Mr. Smallweed's grandfather ever put away in his mind was a grub at first, and is a grub at last. In all his life he has never bred a single butterfly.[1]
>
> *Charles Dickens*

> Grendel, Grendel! You make the world by whispers, second by second. Are you blind to that? Whether you make it a grave or a garden of roses is not the point. Feel the wall: is it not hard? He smashes me against it, breaks open my forehead. Hard, yes! Observe the hardness, write it down in careful runes. Now sing of walls! Sing![2]
>
> *John Gardner*

THE PASSION FOR REALITY

The desire for life and meaning and the desire for reciprocity with others are not the only elemental passions. Few of us need reminding how important is our orientation to what is real. Our very lives depend on this orientation. We would not live very long if we did not care whether the object bearing down on us was an automobile or a puppy or whether our next step is into a chasm or on terra firma. All living things in fact have some reality orientation. In the case of human beings, the term, *reality,* has a certain ambiguity. Because we are able to entertain meanings and to objectify our situations, we develop criteria for what is real that find their way into institutions and symbol systems. Further, agents internalize reality criteria that reflect their individual perspectives and what they deem to be important. The result is that reality presents itself as something we mean, construe,

1. Charles Dickens, *Bleak House* (New York: Macmillan and Co., 1895), 267–288.
2. John Gardner, *Grendel* (New York: Knopf, 1971), 171.

dispute, and interpret.[3] We develop paradigms that systematize our criteria for reality, and we even disagree about reality's basic genre; whether it is data, information, facticity, structures, events, meanings, or direct manifestnesses. But if reality itself is interpreted and disputed, how can we claim there is a passion for reality?

It surely would be unfortunate if we permitted these unresolved disagreements to obscure a sense of reality which we take for granted in everyday life. We are unable, it seems, to be utterly indifferent about knowledge on which our survival and well-being depend. We exist in our specific situations ever alert to the way things are. And because of our historicity and imagination, our well-being is not just a matter of conditions of physical health and survival but also pertains to whatever enriches our lives. We not only desire food, air, space, and safety but experiences of beauty, surprise, and interhuman pleasure. The term, *reality,* may be unavoidably ambiguous because it covers such a vast range of things having to do with many types of knowledge and experience. On one end of this range are the goods at hand that help us survive and which meet basic human needs. To appropriate these goods calls for sufficient acquaintance with the world so as to handle its dangers and accomplish certain tasks. At this end of the range of knowledge, we desire a knowledge for use and action. And this pragmatic knowledge is as much present in archaic (e.g., hunter-gatherer) societies as in industrial and technological societies. Pragmatic knowledge is not merely survival-oriented knowledge. It pertains to any and all cognitions pertinent to managing our environment for the procurement of well-being.

But the desire for knowledge is not reducible to the desire for environmental know-how. The range of knowledge has another wing. The following experience is not unusual. We try to find out something in order to solve some everyday-world problem (e.g., how to add wiring to a new room or to grow beautiful roses). In the course of our learning how, we become curious about the matter itself and our curiosity reaches far beyond any outcome related to the project at hand. Like Gregor Johann Mendel we may even begin to experiment with the roses to discover more about the mechanisms of gene transmission. And when our efforts are successful, we experience a certain satisfaction simply in the knowledge itself. The satisfaction comes with the experience of knowing, not just the successful management of the environment. On this end of the range of knowledge, there is a desire simply to know, to have things explained, to experience the disclosure of what was merely mysterious or puzzling.

3. For an excellent account of the interpretive and intentional aspects of reality, see Herbert Spiegelberg's essay, "The Phenomenon of Reality and Reality," in *Doing Phenomenology* (The Hague, Netherlands: Nijhoff, 1975).

What is fulfilling about this more aesthetic knowledge is the experience of cognitive meaning, the resolution of a problem, the discovery of a new fact, or obtaining an explanation. On this end of the range of knowledge, knowledge is sought because it is itself a satisfying experience.

The general features of the elemental passions are also present in the passion for reality. First, the passion for reality is directed to immediate or penultimate goods at hand such as the entities, events, and relations of the world system, that refer the passions past themselves to an ever-receding horizon. Second, the desire to know has a negative or resisting underside. Knowledge is not so much a possession as an undertaking, an ongoing struggle that requires constant cognitive negations. This is partly because references of knowledge which are actual and not just ideal are always dense, stratified, complex, multi-dimensional, and changing. They are thus never available to instantaneous and exhaustive intuitions but set ongoing tasks of inquiry which involve excluding, sorting out, and rejecting this or that method or approach. And these exclusions are as much a part of the practical knowledge of everyday life as the focused and technical knowledge of the sciences. Knowledge also has a negative aspect because our cognitive powers (reasoning, imagination, perception, memory, association) are limited and fallible. Hence, knowing requires ongoing critical acts toward our own assumed methods, commitments to past interpretations, and inherited concepts. Criticism, then, is the negative or resisting aspect of the passion for reality and it is present throughout the whole range of knowledge from pragmatics to aesthetics.

Third, the passion for reality is directed both to the self and to what is beyond the self. It is a desire for fulfillments that pertain to the self, fulfillments from a successfully managed environment or from satisfying experiences. But because these fulfillments themselves have conditions in the everyday world, the passion for reality is at the same time a desire for whatever conditions and resources we need in order to know. This desire to know engenders the need for and finally commitments and loyalties to institutions (governmental systems, universities), social systems (sciences, academic guilds), methods (empirical, experimental, intuitive), and categorial and conceptual schemes (Darwinian, Freudian, mathematical, phenomenological, functional). Finally, like all the passions, the passion for reality is egocentrically structured. Accordingly, however much reality draws the agent away from itself into the object of knowledge or the satisfying sphere of beauty, the passion is predominantly on behalf of the self. Egocentrism in the passion for reciprocity shows itself in the dominance of the desire to be acknowledged over the desire to acknowledge. Egocentrism in the passion for reality appears as the dominance of the desire for a managed environment over the desire for experienced beauty and meaning. Thus, the desire for useful facts that contribute to our survival and satisfactions tends to dominate the cognitive relations agents maintain toward the world.

THE QUEST FOR CERTAINTY AND FALSE SKEPTICISM

The corruption of human reason is a frequent theme in Western thought from Plato to Michel Foucault and the Frankfurt School. For Plato, the corruption behind all corruptions is the turning aside of the cognitive eros or striving from its proper object, the good, which is to say the real. And the Enlightenment traced the root of human corruption to the reign of uncritical authority over reason, the antidote for which was criticism and objective evidence. These notions of a corrupted cognitive eros and reason threatened by authority seem quaint to many moderns and postmoderns. Sciences and philosophies of science have convinced us of the fragile status of all cognitive claims. Humanistic sciences and hermeneutics have intensified our awareness of knowledge's paradigmatic and metaphorical character. But the theme of corrupted knowledge is not at the center of a technological and therapeutic society's corporate consciousness.

Contemporary Western societies are not, however, entirely unaware of the corruptibility and corruption of knowledge. Occasional incidents of scientific fraud make headlines. Some authors have tracked how particular sciences have incorporated and abetted Western racism.[4] The Freudian strand of modern psychology has revised the ancient eros tradition in its notion of basic instincts which undermine rationality. Liberation, black, and feminist theologies use Marxist hermeneutics to document how oppressive power co-opts the undertakings of knowledge. But these views are not representative of what prevails in modern governments, industries, universities, sciences, and professions. Nor should we be surprised that there is little awareness of the corruption of the passion for reality in these institutions. A cognitive epoch whose general understanding of human reality blinds it to the elemental passions themselves will have little sense of corrupted passions. In the technocratic world-view, the elements of knowledge are methods, evidences, experiments, hypotheses, discoveries, and problems. Reality means that with which these notions are concerned. This state of affairs itself is an indication of the corruption of knowledge.

4. Sciences, especially biology and anthropology, corrupted by racism and other forms of oppressive prejudice is a frequent theme in the writings of Steven Jay Gould. See esp. his history of the misuse of biology, *The Mismeasure of Man* (New York: W. W. Norton, 1981). See also W. Stanton, *The Leopard's Spots: Scientific Attitudes towards Race in America, 1815–1859* (Chicago: University of Chicago Press, 1960).

Like the other elemental passions, the passion for reality undergoes corruption both as a positive orientation (practical and aesthetic) and as a negating or critical underside of that orientation. I shall call the corrupted desire itself, *the quest for certainty* (cf. John Dewey) and the corrupted negating underside, *false skepticism.*[5]

The Quest for Certainty

I do not attempt in this essay to trace the lines of influence between the corrupted passions. However, the corrupted passion for reality does appear to depend on the corruption of the other passions. Perhaps this is because our cognitive life arises in connection with our pragmatic and experiential transactions with the world, behind which are our passions for subjectivity and reciprocity. To put it differently, our need for knowledge arises in connection with our struggles for well-being and for reciprocity with others. If this is the case, the corruption of these basic world transactions will surely influence the way we yearn for reality.

The passion for reality is an especially fertile field for idolatry because knowledge is so important for our survival, well-being, and enriched experience. Our well-being is connected not just to things, conditions, and events in the world but with understanding these things. And when these things are made to function as securers, our knowledge of the securers takes on a new importance. To be deadly serious about the power of a good at hand to secure us carries with it a deadly seriousness about our knowledge of that good. To desire a securing entity is to also desire a secured knowledge of that entity. The idolatrous posture cannot abide having a securing entity in a cognitively fragile and fallible knowledge. We cannot say to ourselves; I am utterly secured by the institution and belief-system of my religion but I have no way of being sure of this. The securing good demands a securing cognition.

Because the need for a secured knowledge follows the need for the securer, the typical corruption of this passion occurs not in the form of a passion to know everything but a need for certainty about whatever secures. The classical expression of the passion for a knowledge that will remove the pain of existence is the story of Faust. But few people experience the corruption of knowledge as this Faustian hunger to penetrate the universe's mysteries. We experience instead the need to be certain about our world-view, the customs we live by, the holy book we regard as authoritative, the tradition that delivers the truth we live by, or the science or philosophy that provides us with a comprehensive interpretive

5. See John Dewey, *The Quest for Certainty: A Study in the Relation of Knowledge and Action* (New York: Putnam, 1929).

scheme. Thus, the need for certainty embraces not just the contents but the conditions and deliverers of knowledge. Hence, we would be certain not just about truths but about truth-delivering institutions (science, the church), agential powers (perception, reason), and linguistic vehicles (propositions, symbols, metaphors).

The idolatrous act extends itself to the various mediators and carriers of knowledge on which certainty depends. Thus, we absolutize various cognitive goods at hand; the successful method (empirical, hermeneutical, deconstructive), the founding figure of the method, the science or discipline to which we are loyal, the specific piety that provides the presuppositions for believing in an authority. And these postures of certainty co-exist quite easily with intellectual and verbal self-assurances that we are open, undogmatic, relative, and critical. For the quest for certainty is an existential posture that can easily repress its own cognitive absolutism by adopting critical attitudes toward virtually everything.

The dynamics of idolatry modify the passion for reality in much the same way they modify the other passions. Anxiety about our cognitive relations to what secures is a particularization of our general anxiety about meaning and tragic existence. Finding this anxiety intolerable, we would replace it with the posture of certainty. We refuse to exist in the chasm that stretches between the knowledge we desire and the knowledge we obtain. We insist that the eternal horizon of knowledge, the mystery at the heart of things, merge with our cognitive accomplishments. We develop a metaphysical confidence about the capacity of our interpretations of reality to deliver to us what secures or to be themselves the securers. In utter cognitive confidence, we are certain we have discovered history's unsurpassable social system, the definitive economics, the ideal system of government, the absolute religion, the never-to-be replaced scientific or scholarly method for apprehending truth. But the dynamics of idolatry also effect in this passion something quite distinctive. Because of the pragmatic and aesthetic range of knowledge, the agent insists on certainty in both pragmatic and aesthetic types of knowledge.

1. *The corruption of pragmatic knowledge.* In the world of everyday life, the function of knowledge is to help us procure various satisfactions. Remembering the location of desert succulents (for a hunter-gatherer) and discovering how to miniaturize electric circuits are forms of pragmatic knowledge. In a world without evil, pragmatic knowledge would be the relative knowledge agents need to get along in their situations. Technologies necessary to advance medicine might lengthen our life-span and make our lives more comfortable but that is all they could do. But when goods at hand are forced to feed our metaphysical hunger to be secured, a rather strange posture arises toward the pragmatic knowledge of these

goods. The need for certainty produces an anomalous cognitive posture which is at the same time pragmatic (functional) and absolute. If things like medical care, defense systems, and religious traditions constitute the center and clue of our very existence, this awesome accomplishment must be properly known and interpreted. The relative knowledge of environmental managing must also be a certain knowledge.

The absolutizing of pragmatic knowledge has a distortive effect on the way pragmatic and aesthetic are related to each other. Because of the natural egocentrism of agents, pragmatic knowledge has a natural priority over aesthetic knowledge. But when pragmatic knowledge is corrupted by an insistence on certainty, this priority becomes enormously exaggerated. The result is that aesthetic knowledge is narrowed, quantified, and marginalized. Knowledge is virtually reduced to what pertains to the management of the environment. The mediators and instruments of this knowledge—sciences, methods, technologies—are granted the authority to define reality. Reality, thus, is reduced to a region of cognitive management. While it is the case that pragmatic knowledge tends to gain a new hegemony in industrial and technocratic societies, the dominance of the pragmatic side should not be thought of merely in terms of quantifying sciences. Religious pieties and commonsense life orientations also undergo this corruption. When the pragmatic aspect of religious knowledge is corrupted, managing relations arise toward the sacred, faith, worship, and obligations, the effect of which is an indifference to their intrinsic worth, beauty, and truth.

2. *The corruption of aesthetic knowledge.* Knowledge is irreducible to its pragmatic aspect because reality is not synonymous with what is useful. Reality's usefulness is possible only because it has pre-use features that make it appropriable for use. In other words, reality is an impenetrable complex of processes, entities, events, emergings, and relations which manifest a fit of form and function, the apprehension of which is its own reward. If usefulness means simply what evokes pleasure, then it is the case that all knowledge has a pragmatic character. But on the aesthetic end of the experience of reality, pleasure (utility) is in the experience itself, not something else which the experience delivers. Thus, the experience of knowledge as a fulfilling pleasure can be a good at hand and as such can be looked to as something able to extricate us from our tragic situation. And this is the very heart of aestheticism. The cognitive aesthete expects to be delivered by the intensities of cognitive experience. In impassioned participation in the beauties of living things or in the poetical mediation of those beauties, we find our founding meaning.

The aesthetic corruption of knowledge also takes place in connection with relatively broad undertakings, for instance, world interpretation.

For at the aesthetic end of the range of knowledge, we experience meanings and contents which do not pertain simply to the discrete events of everyday life but to ever larger contexts. World-views develop when we apprehend the patterns, repetitions, resemblances, and directions of the world and weave these into myths and symbol systems. On this end of the range of knowledge, we attempt to make sense out of the world. World-views and comprehensive patterns of explanation are not just aids for obtaining well-being. They, too, can occasion intense pleasures and fulfillments. In other words, the experience of what makes sense of the world can itself be intrinsically satisfying.

This broader cognitive experience is corrupted when we insist on being certain about what delivers and maintains the world-view. The passionate need for certainty is directed toward institutions (churches), traditions (of science, piety, casuistry, or doctrine), historical entities (books, creeds), people (leaders, teachers, etc.) and even concepts (revelation, authority, tradition). Accordingly, religions are especially alluring occasions of this corruption. Religions have to do with being-founded, with sacred presence, and therefore with what mediates that presence. Driven by the quest for certainty, religions quickly secure their own knowledge by being certain about themselves, about that in them which mediates the sacred presence: thus, their own holy books, traditions, institutions, and doctrines. But the quest for certainty is not limited to religions. Ardent pragmatists, religious skeptics, corporate executives, exploited and disillusioned nihilistic youth, and sophisticated intellectuals can as easily weave their antidogmatic world-views into cognitive securings walled off from all possible criticism.

As with the other corrupted passions, the lust for certainty is an existential posture and is not merely a matter of beliefs about certainty and uncertainty. Being uncertain, acknowledging fallibility, and asserting the relativity of knowledge are deeply entrenched in both modernity and postmodernity. At the level of beliefs and world-views, most of us are quite ready to confess that we do not know everything, that perception is fallible, that evidences are relative to their mediating instruments, that all empirical knowledge is inexact, and that more can always be discovered. But a corrupted passion is a corrupted way of existing in the world. It is not merely a mistaken belief system but a corrupted posture and existential orientation. Accordingly, we are misled if we think that only one set of beliefs can be a candidate for cognitive idolatry, namely explicit beliefs in a teleologically-ordered nature or in God or a world-ground. Beliefs in the ultimacy of contingency, chaos, and randomness can be so held as to be the final clue to things, the securing cognition, the unsurpassable world interpretation.

False Skepticism

The passion for reality includes a negative underside, a resistance to whatever would endanger our well-being by deceiving us about the way things are. We resist being taken in and deceived. We will not settle for illusions, speculations, guesses, and gambles about whether our food is poisoned or whether the brakes of our automobile are in good condition. In other words, a functioning skepticism is part of our passion for reality. And this skepticism is an important and valuable posture in our ongoing transactions with the world. Desiring reality we sift and interrogate appearances on the assumption that at least some deceptions can be exposed. But when the passion for reality becomes a lust for certainty, the skeptical or critical underside is also corrupted. The lust for certainty insists on and expects a cognitive relation to reality which can never actually come about, a relation in which the absolutized good at hand is mediated by an absolute or utterly fulfilled knowledge. But the insistence that goods at hand really secure always remains only that, an insistence. Realities at hand continue to retain their density and point beyond themselves to an ever-receding horizon. Thus, the desired certainty is always a failed certainty, a certainty which must be constantly re-established, defended, and asserted. Thus enters the despairing side of the corrupted passion. Certainty ever courts disillusion, disappointment, and an abandonment of the very possibility of knowledge. Certainty sets up the knower for betrayal. And when certainty breaks down under the failure of the cognitive object to stand fast, the skeptical underside becomes *false skepticism.* Apart from this corruption, the desire for knowledge and its skeptical or critical underside supplement rather than contradict each other. Although certainty of and despair over the possibility of knowledge are logically contradictory, they nevertheless co-exist as existential postures that pull the human agent in opposite directions.

And now, two clarifications:

1. False skepticism has three references: the self's capacities for knowledge, the world's knowability, and the social and historical mediators of knowledge. These several references of skepticism follow from the complexity of knowledge itself. The elements of knowledge include an act of the agent (operations of consciousness, pre-understandings, perspectivity), contents which are not simply repetitions or projections of the self, and historical mediators. When agents despair of their own capacities for knowledge, they experience a failure of cognitive nerve. And this failure finds expression in whole philosophies of knowledge that contend (cognitively?) that knowledge is circumvented by the biases and perspectives of

the agent. Thus, the operations in the brain, in one's psycho-chemical makeup, or in the cultural environment undermine knowledge by making it the arbitrary result of external causes. This philosophical thesis cannot avoid self-contradiction because it engages in complex analyses and appeals to evidences to make its case. Absolute philosophical skepticism is always a failed skepticism because the passion for reality engenders it and cognitive evidences ground it.

False skepticism also doubts the knowability of the world and the trustworthiness of the mediators and preservers of knowledge. Resembling cynicism's negation in advance of the acknowledgments of others, false skepticism thinks there is something intrinsic about the world that frustrates and eludes attempts to understand it, thus, world process itself undermines the cognitive efforts and status of sciences, methods, traditions, and institutions. When this posture finds philosophical expression, it, too, appeals to a variety of evidences to establish its "truth." Distrust in the historical mediators of knowledge takes several forms. The pervasive element of oppression in human history corrupts and discredits the cognitive delivery of all symbol systems and methods. The abstract, technical, jargon-laden, and guild-dominated results demonstrate that scholarship and the sciences are untrustworthy instruments of genuine knowledge. Criticisms of this sort are clearly pertinent when they are applied to quite specific movements. But they, too, must appeal to the world's knowability to make their case. Hence, they, too, display both a despair of and a desire for cognitive transactions with reality.

2. False skepticism has a narrowing effect on both the pragmatic and the aesthetic ends of the range of knowledge. This narrowing begins when the desire to know is transformed into the lust for certainty. Certainty comes easier when complexity is simplified, when the unpredictabilities of living things are quantified, and when processes and subjectivities are reduced to structures. How does this affect pragmatic knowledge? It is important to remember that pragmatic knowledge carries with it genuine cognitive convictions. Engineers can build things only if they know certain features and behaviors of metals, electricity, and combustion. When pragmatic knowledge despairs of itself as knowledge, it becomes indifferent about its own status as knowledge. Interest turns from knowledge to control. The realm of pragmatic knowledge becomes a realm of reality management. Having power over the conditions of life is the agenda of corrupted pragmatic knowledge. We should not confuse this reduction of knowledge to control with the benign reductions necessary to any specific inquiry, a narrowing intrinsic to all concrete cognitive strategies and procedures.

False skepticism also has a narrowing effect on the aesthetic end of the range of knowledge. When our cognitive nerve fails in relation to our satisfying apprehensions of concrete things, a skeptical posture develops towards the whole aesthetic end of the range of knowledge. This posture refuses to acknowledge that our intuitively satisfying experiences of "the way things are" have any cognitive status. Knowledge is thus reduced to the already reduced sphere of pragmatic knowledge. Once knowledge is reduced to a way of managing the world, the whole spectrum of aesthetic knowledge is turned over to feeling, emotion, and private experiences. The transactions with reality left to agents are transactions with the products of technical inquiry. And since concrete and satisfying cognitive experiences as such no longer have to do with reality, the possibilities of genuine criticism in the realm of aesthetic knowledge are removed. If the transactions of reality management are given primary value, then the agent's aesthetic transaction with the concrete is devalued, written out of what is autobiographically or culturally important.

Imperceptivity

In spite of the pragmatic and aesthetic range of cognitive experience, the passion for reality is nevertheless one passion. And the corruption of this passion has a certain over-all effect on the way agents are oriented toward reality. As certainty presses the passion to narrow its references, the passion itself becomes weakened. To insist on certainty and cognitive success is to narrow the scope and possible contents of knowledge. For the more discrete and manageable is our cognitive undertaking, the easier we can be sure about its results. Thus we reduce the passion's targets to certain genres of things (the definition, the physical entity, the structure), and from this reduction come paradigms of reality and knowledge through which we exist in the world. Thus the agent's reality orientation is determined by acts of focusing, abstracting, fragmenting, and objectifying. As a result, the agent becomes imperceptive to the rich and complex multi-dimensionality of reality.

When the pragmatic end of the range of knowledge is narrowed, we agents become imperceptive toward the concrete, the beautiful, and the mysterious. We lose the sense of mystery because our narrowed cognitive paradigm restricts reality to problems and puzzles. As reality is reduced to what is externally and objectively manageable, we lose cognitive interest in human reality. We cannot take seriously our own concrete intuitions, our aesthetic experiences, even the interpersonal realities of the face. We content ourselves with the surfaces of what is manifest: the easily grasped causality, the one-dimensional method. We become attuned to the mathematical and functional rather than the metaphorical functions of language. We shunt metaphors off to the noncognitive sphere and deny their function in the apprehension of reality. When the aesthetic end of the range of knowledge is narrowed, we become imperceptive toward the pragmatic, the functional, and the objective. Our orientation to reality is corrupted by an aestheticism unable to take seriously anything outside the sphere of the experiential, the personal, and the beautiful. We may be compassionate toward the sufferings of oppressed individuals and groups but our pragmatic imperceptivity blinds us to the agro-economic and political aspects of that suffering. In sum, the price we pay for a narrowed passion for reality is imperceptivity. This imperceptivity is not simply an errant perception, a false reasoning, or a tendency to make mistakes but a narrowed way of experiencing the world. In extreme form, it virtually removes the agent's sense of reality.

WONDER

Like most human desires, the elemental passions are not blind urges but are partly self-conscious and highly nuanced strivings that are carried in acts of meaning, assessment, construing things as, and interpretation. This is why these passions have complex ranges of references and why they can be narrowed or expanded or obsessively or casually pursued. Thus, the passion for reality is not only corruptible (able to be narrowed into a lust for certainty and a despairing skepticism) but is transformable into a new freedom.

Insofar as the passion for reality is, in fact, corrupted, its transformation into a new freedom begins with the effect of being-founded on the lust for certainty and its skeptical underside. When the agent's insistence on being secured by goods at hand is diminished, it has less need for certainty about those goods. One aspect of the lessening of the lust for certainty involves a relativizing of knowledge. Relativizing would seem to be redundant in an age such as ours where relativisms of all sorts are taken for granted. But relativisms can be themselves securing goods at hand held in modes of certainty. And to repeat a point, the lust for certainty and its transformation are existential postures. Courage relativizes the agent's orientation to reality in its convictions about its own cognitive power or powerlessness. From courage comes also the power to consent to a world where knowledge is at best relative and uncertain, and to a cognitive existence in which the gap between the need to know and what finally is known is never closed.

However, this relativized and consenting reality orientation is not itself a new freedom. It may be a knowledge without idols, to borrow a phrase from Gabriel Vahanian, but the mere absence of idols is not a new power of freedom.[6] The elemental passions become powers of freedom (virtues)

6. See Gabriel Vahanian, *Wait without Idols* (New York: G. Braziller, 1964).

only when they are taken beyond their natural egocentrism. What is the natural egocentrism of the passion of reality? All of the elemental passions are strivings on behalf of the self toward what is other than the self. To use the language of Helmut Plessner, agents have both egocentric and exocentric aspects.[7] But the egocentric aspect always dominates the exocentric. This domination occurs in a distinctive way in each of the passions. In the passion for reality, it means the primacy of the need for pragmatic knowledge over the more aesthetic need for cognitive satisfactions that are ends in themselves. Fostering as it does cognitions that satisfy and give pleasure to the agent, aesthetic knowledge, too, is a knowledge on behalf of the self. But the self is more drawn out of itself into the world in aesthetic than pragmatic knowledge. The focus of pragmatic knowledge is on goods at hand which pertain to the worldly conditions of the agent's well-being. And the agent's preoccupation with these conditions at the expense of intrinsically satisfying cognitive experiences is the meaning of the natural egocentrism of the passion for reality. Here, too, we live in an either-or between acting on behalf of the self or surpassing the self for what is other.

The passion for reality becomes a freedom when being-founded (courage) carries that passion's natural egocentrism to a higher plane of existence. The relativizing and consenting aspects of courage begin the transformation by undermining this passion's lust for certainty and skepticism. But being-founded also frees the agent to venture itself, to exist in a relation to things on a plane above choosing between the self and the other. The agent is caught up into a plane where the good is a being-together-with other things, not simply a fulfillment of the other, or of the agent. When the passion for reality is carried to this plane, the agent's reality orientation exists beyond the either-or of knowledge on its own behalf or knowledge satisfying in itself. Openness and participation characterize reality orientation on this plane. The agent does not repudiate itself on this plane. It continues to desire, but what it desires is a way of cognitively being with things. This double posture of openness and participation effected by being-founded is *wonder.*

Openness

Openness is primarily the negative condition of participation. It is what happens to the passion of knowledge when the agent's egocentrism is

7. I owe this reference to Wolfhart Pannenberg, who expounds Helmut Plessner's concept of exocentrism in *Anthropology in a Theological Perspective* (Philadelphia: Westminster, 1985), 34–37. The concept can be found in Helmut Plessner, *Die Stufen des Organischen und der Mensch: Einleitung in die philosophische Anthropologie* (Berlin: DeGruyter, 1965), originally published in 1928.

surpassed. In our natural egocentrism, our reality orientations have a primarily pragmatic character. External goods at hand are sought for the sake of the self's survival and well-being. As itself a kind of openness, pragmatic knowledge can correct dogmatic, hierarchical, and conceptually frozen approaches to reality. But pragmatic knowledge is at the same time a way of sifting and defining reality in advance. The aim of pragmatic knowledge is to sufficiently know the environment so as to procure the conditions of well-being. In the perspective of pragmatic knowledge, the elements of reality are important events, workable methods, available resources, and societal defenses and protections. The reality of pragmatic knowledge may be multi-faceted but the facets are limited to goods that function on behalf of the self. When the venturing and vital self breaks the hold of egocentrism, this domination of goods as utilities is pressed into the background. This does not mean that we no longer strive for the conditions of well-being. Even the most self-denying and self-torturing ascetic cannot utterly suppress such striving. It does mean that as the desire for pragmatic knowledge becomes less dominant, the reality to which we are oriented is not merely types of things pertinent to our well-being. And once we no longer define reality through these types, we can be open to reality's mystery, dimensional complexity, and unrepeatability.

Openness is thus a transcending of the act and posture of organizing reality in advance. It relativizes the pragmatic way of being cognitively oriented to reality. This is why openness is not a desire for simply new types and classifications or new and more adequate evidences. This break with pre-definitions of reality is a necessary precondition of the positive aspect of wonder, namely *participation.*

Participation

The passion for reality is not merely a passion for useful facts. It has a nonutilitarian aspect in which the agent is pleasurably drawn beyond itself into the thing known. Thus, aesthetic knowledge is not just a co-option of things at hand for the sake of well-being but involves perceptions and understandings which are satisfactions in themselves. Our natural egocentrism permits utilitarian knowledge to dominant aesthetic knowledge. But when courage and venturing transform the passion for reality, the desire to know, experience, and enjoy reality becomes the inclusive posture. For what does this vitality-driven passion strive? We recall that cognitive vitality is a way of relating to things on another plane than the either-or of knowing on one's own behalf or knowing for one's own sake. The new cognitive freedom is a desire to understand and experience things in a being-together with them, an engagement which is at the same time an enjoyment. If what is experienced is something living, this enjoyment would be an empathetic participation in the enjoyment of that thing. Knowledge of this sort is both an empathy with and an appreciation of the content (the situation, life, distinctiveness, and even vulnerability) of what is known. In participative knowledge we understand what is other in the mode of empathetic appreciation. Wonder then is not just openness but empathetic participation in whatever is to be known and experienced.

Knowledge of this sort is not absent from everyday life. It is, in fact, a natural accompaniment of some types of human relations. But when egocentrism governs the passion for reality, our experience of participation is restricted to special interpersonal relations. Thus, the agent's cognitive life is separated into ordinary cognitions of things and participative knowledge of the interhuman. But when vitality draws this passion to another plane, this chasm tends to become blurred. And the agent yearns for participative knowledge of whatever is to be known. Participation spreads more and more into all our reality transactions.

What is it about the range of realities or about any specific reality that could tolerate a relation of empathetic appreciation? What is there about reality to appreciate, value, and enjoy? Human others, living entities (a plant, a cell), even ecological complexes (deserts, marshes) all display some degree of accordance between form and function. All of these things have delicate conditions that must be met for them to survive and function as specific entities. Beauty is just this accordance, however partial, of form and function. Because the accordance is ever fragile and ephemeral, beauty always has an intrinsic vulnerability. And it is this vulnerable and pathetic beauty of things that evokes participative knowledge.

What then is the new freedom which being-founded effects in the passion for reality? It is what happens to this passion when the lust for certainty and false skepticism lose their sway when natural egocentrism is taken to another plane. The passion for reality as a freedom is an openness beyond the pragmatic predetermination of reality to reality itself in all of its surprises. It is also a desire to participate in, that is, to empathetically appreciate, what is understood. This two-fold passion of openness and participation is the freedom of wonder.[8] Wonder is the passion for reality transformed by being-founded in the sacred. It is what happens to that passion when courage and vitality move it beyond (but not against) its egocentrism and the dominance of pragmatic knowledge to a desire to participate in reality in its ever unpredictable mystery and beauty.

8. The fullest study in recent decades of the theme of wonder is Sam Keen's phenomenological exploration, *Apology for Wonder* (New York: Harper and Row, 1969). No neat definition of wonder can be extracted from the book but rather a complex phenomenon which he sees as in decline.

SEPARATED PASSIONS AND INTERDEPENDENT FREEDOMS

Until now I have explored the elemental passions separately, focusing on each one's features, corruptions, and powers of freedom. But keeping the passions apart has its price. If the elemental passions are interdependent, each one functions best as a participation in the others. In fact, it is not really possible to think of any of these passions in utter isolation. What would the passion of subjectivity be if we were utterly indifferent to reality and the conditions of reality? How could a desire for reciprocity with others exist without any orientation to reality? And without self-reference and a passion for subjectivity, alterity and therefore true reciprocity would be absent from the interhuman. And without the passion for life and the fulfillments of subjectivity, knowledge is without motivation and function. If these passions are interdependent, then both their corruption and their redemption will affect how they are connected.

Idolatry affects the interconnections of the passions in two ways. First, the dynamics of each corruption contributes to the corruption of others. For instance, false skepticism about the knowability of anything can influence our approach to human others, and cynicism about the face can poison our relations to the whole realm of living things. Second, idolatry has an isolating effect on the elemental passions. It subverts their interdependence and separates them from each other. This is because the act and attitude of idolatry is a focused act. It discovers its securings in specific things and becomes confident that this one thing alone is the center of meaning. This focusing does not prevent simultaneous orientations to a great variety of securers. We seek anything and everything that will drive off the beast that gnaws away at our meanings. But when we locate a securer, we become metaphysically confident toward it and it alone. Our existential posture broadcasts a message: my cultural and ethnic heritage alone, not my culture with other cultures or my culture plus other things, is the center of my meaning. Even if idolatrous dynamics structure all of the elemental passions, we tend to direct ourselves to idols in a piecemeal way. We target specific interpersonal relationships as securers. We develop postures of certainty toward specific mediators of knowledge. Thus, we desire a knowledge whose primary function is to secure, a knowledge thus separated from our passion for life (subjectivity) and the world of the face. We desire a securing reciprocity separated from our attachment to reality and from our historicity.

This dismemberment of the elemental passions is corruptive because the health of each passion depends on its connection with the other passions. Minus an orientation to reality, the *passion of subjectivity* falls back into itself and repudiates its world orientation. Minus the desire for reciprocity, the agent becomes narcissistic and vacuous, estranged from what makes it corporately human. It desires subjectivity without a true subject. When the *passion for reciprocity* loses touch with the passion of subjectivity, it takes on a masochistic structure. No passionate self-reference attends its other orientation, hence, it has nothing of itself to contribute to the reciprocity. When this passion loses its reality orientation, the other it desires recedes into the mists. The agent becomes indifferent to the alterity, the beauty, in other words, the reality, of the other. When the *passion for reality* becomes isolated from the desire of subjectivity, it turns itself over to its object. Indifferent to its own passion for life and existence, this passion becomes bloodless curiosity. And when the passion for reality loses its connection with the interhuman, it exists without the obligations and criteria engendered by the face. It quickly degenerates from genuine knowledge into the desire for control.

If idolatry does isolate these intrinsically interdependent passions from each other, then passions can be true freedoms only if their interdependence is restored. But being-founded does more than simply break the hold of idolatry on ontological structures. It transposes the natural egocentrism of the passions onto the new planes of vitality, agape, and wonder. And with this transposition comes a new level of the interdependence of these passions. Each of the passionate freedoms empowers the other passions. It is vitality that breaks the hold of the natural egocentrism in all of the passions and empowers us to exist beyond the either-or of life on behalf of the self or on behalf of what is not the self. Without vitality, wonder and *agapē* remain trapped in the either-or which egocentrism fosters. We desire reality and reciprocity in a constant vacillation between ourselves and what is other. Agapic passion is what introduces not just an awakened but a passionately desired face into the other two passions. The desire for the face introduces a normative and caring aspect into our desire for life in the midst of living things. And without the desire for the face, vitality and wonder would be empty of their humanizing contents. And without wonder, the desire to empathetically appreciate whatever is experienced, vitality and wonder are deprived of any orientation to what is real. To conclude: being-founded effects not just separated freedoms in the sphere of the passions but a *harmonia* of passionate freedoms.

12

THE CORRUPTION AND FREEDOM OF BODILY LIFE

> This is connected with another striking feature, the ease with which improbable charges are believed against anyone designated as an enemy. . . . When we consider . . . the extraordinary flourishing of violent hostility where no real threat is posed at all, we are (as far as I can see) forced to look for an explanation within. People who seriously believe that they are being attacked when they are not, and who attribute hostile planning groundlessly to their supposed attackers, have to be projecting their own unrecognized bad motives onto the world around them.[1]
>
> *Mary Midgley*

Human agency is a convergence of three interdependent dimensions: personal being, elemental passions, and bodily life. I turn now to the corruption and freedom of the third dimension, bodily life. Aspects are always abstractions. When we reflect on the historicity or elemental passions of agents, we lift these things out of the complex and concrete totality of which they are a part. That totality itself is the embodied human being living in its situation. This is why the corruptions and freedoms of the passions or of historicity never work as independent powers but always *in situ;* that is, in connection with the emotions, motivations, and agendas of an actual embodied human being.

The body of a human agent is not just a thing that occupies space but a unified, functioning field of motivating needs and tendencies. Thus, we do not so much experience our bodies as we experience through our bodies. In other words, we experience our own agency as embodied. Further, to experience through the body is not just to use an instrument but to have emotional responses of fear, anxiety, or enjoyment and to have certain sensations, needs, and tendencies. Body is our biological equipment to survive as mammals and primates and to pursue the conditions of well-being necessary to this particular life-form. Thus we are

1. Mary Midgley, *Wickedness: A Philosophical Essay* (London, Eng.: Ark Paperbacks, 1984), 125.

equipped to breathe, walk upright, procure food, reproduce, defend against predators, and engage in intraspecies fighting.

I am exploring in these chapters the corruptions and freedoms that arise in connection with dimensions of human agency. Yet, these explorations appear to have little to do with the horrors depicted in newspaper headlines: incidents of cruelty, murder, child molestation, and bigotry. Does idolatry have anything to do with what Mary Midgley calls wickedness and Phillip Hallie calls cruelty?[2] As a response to tragic vulnerability, idolatry seems to be more a weakness than a meanness, more a distorted way of existing in the world than an inclination to hurt and destroy. Could it be that human meanness is simply a sickness, a pathology that calls for therapeutic treatment? Is the proposal that the social science professionals handle our meanness and religious professionals handle our inability to cope with tragic existence? This would be an odd proposal if it purported to interpret the Hebraic and Christian vision of the agent's condition. How does this vision pertain to wickedness? In this chapter I shall contend that wickedness or human evil arises from the effects of the dynamic of idolatry on our embodied life. This may sound at first like the old Manicheanism or one of its modern instinctivist versions which make the body the culprit in human evil. I shall argue no such thing. But I shall contend that without some things which the body supplies, we would be incapable of wickedness.

SATISFACTIONS AND OPPOSITIONS: THE BODILY ROOTS OF MOTIVATIONS

In human embodiment, various elements of our biological life converge in the striving of a single organism. Striving is our constant effort to do whatever is necessary to maintain the conditions of life and well-being. Evolution and phylogeny equip all living things for this effort and are the roots of the way members of each species struggle for their specific kind of well-being. Our striving is the striving of a particular life-form. We strive as vertebrates, mammals, primates, hominids, and as a species of hominid. Our biological needs and tendencies are those of this specific evolutionary line. Accordingly, our everyday life actions are guided by desires which arise from the needs and tendencies of our embodiment.

Cultural anthropologists, psychologists, and philosophers never cease to remind us that human behavior is not just the outcome of biological instincts. With self-presencing, imagination, and meaning-orientation has

2. Mary Midgley, *Wickedness* (1986), and Phillip Hallie, *The Philosophy of Cruelty* (Middletown, Conn.: Wesleyan University Press, 1969).

come what we call, history. History has not erased our biologically rooted tendencies but it has taken them up into unfathomable complexities of acculturation and societal life. Thus, our effortful actions of everyday life are never pure displays of genetically rooted drives. This is why we can never reduce human needs to what enables mere survival or the physical conditions of well-being. Thus, while there are strong hormonal elements in our sexuality, our sexual needs and strivings are vastly extended by acculturation, not to mention the complexities which self-presencing temporality and language introduce. Sexual needs vary with high and low valuations of the nuclear family, the role of sex in environments of social power, and the contents of comprehensive myths and pieties. Although the strivings for everyday satisfaction are always more than mere biological fulfillments, they are rarely less. That is to say, biologically rooted tendencies are never very far away from even the subtle forms of human satisfactions. Most of the motivations behind everyday life satisfactions would be paralyzed if their biological roots (survival, physical well-being, sexuality, reproduction, social tendencies) were totally excised.

Biologically rooted striving, like the elemental passions, combines both positive desires and negating oppositions. This double reference is an a priori feature of striving as such. To strive for something is to make an effort to actualize a specific line of possibilities to the exclusion of another line. To strive is to select, sift, and exclude. It is also an effort directed against recalcitrant conditions and opposing forces. The animal predator searching for a meal is struggling against all sorts of things in its environment which would frustrate its efforts; weather, terrain, competing predators, and the eluding skills of its prey. The striving thus includes acts which oppose what would prevent the search. And because of our historicity, our existence in the world through meanings, we are able to develop attitudes and agendas of action toward both what we seek and what we oppose. We can and do symbolize and thematize food, love, and comfort, and also enemies, illness, and death. And the dynamics of idolatry as well as certain freedoms can enter and alter both sets of attitudes. I shall call these two sets of biologically rooted but culturally extended tendencies the *principle of satisfaction* and the *principle of competition.*

The Principle of Satisfaction

For what do we human beings strive? The most formal answer to the question is, we strive for things or conditions that satisfy us in some way. We strive for satisfactions.[3] From the perspective of striving, the desired

3. The seminal modern treatment of the principle of satisfaction is provided by Sigmund Freud under the terms of the pleasure principle, narcissism, and the death instinct. See *Beyond the Pleasure Principle,* trans. C. J. M. Hubback (London, Eng.: The International Psychoanalytic Press, 1922). According to Freud the supreme principle of psychic life

thing must have a capacity to satisfy the desire. What we strive for can be anything and everything we need or think we need. We can strive effortfully to find a good restaurant or to create a just society. Striving is oriented, thus, toward actualizations that satisfy; that is, give pleasure, fulfill a need, or bestow a sense of well-being. Satisfactions are clearly not limited to what yields pleasant physical sensations. They occur in connection with events that reinforce our sense of integrity, build up our self-esteem, support our sense of being significant in our social world, or which move us toward some projected good. This is why self-denying asceticism, self-destructive masochism, martyrdom, and even suicide are not exceptions to but rather indications of the human orientation to satisfaction. The suicide seeks a more satisfying alternative to despair. The martyr finds satisfaction, sometimes to the point of salvation, in the sacrificial act. Masochists find pleasure in their self-inflicted sufferings.

Satisfactions are possible only to the degree that there are things in our environment able to fill our needs. We would be condemned to perpetual cold and hunger (and to instant death) without sufficient sources of warmth and food. Nor would satisfactions be possible if we were so biologically or psychologically constituted as to be unable to experience them. In sum, we can strive for and experience satisfactions because our constitution as needy and desiring beings corresponds with the capacity of our environment to (partially) fulfill these needs. Behind these correspondences and our capacities to enjoy our satisfactions are millions of years of phylogenetic developments. This correspondence or fit between the offerings of our environment and our needs is the biological basis of our natural egocentrism. Biologically rooted but culturally extended urges toward various satisfactions constitute the primary form of our natural egocentrism. Natural egocentrism begins in these primary urges intrinsic to life itself and spreads from there to the elemental passions and the subtle pleasures of human culture. In this primary form natural egocentrism is a natural hedonism, the inclination to the well-being proper to our specific life-form. Nor is there any reason to think of this natural hedonism as evil, sinful, or harmful to human beings. It is simply the

is that "any given process originates in an unpleasant state of tension and thereupon determines for itself such a path that its ultimate issue coincides with a relaxation of that tension, i.e., with avoidance of 'pain' or with production of pleasure," 1. Ernst Becker has expanded Sigmund Freud's notion of the instinctive urge to self-preservation and satisfaction into the major human need which is the need for self-esteem. See *The Birth and Death of Meaning: A Perspective in Psychiatry and Anthropology* (New York: Free Press of Glencoe, 1962), 76–77. For an interpretation of the death-wish and a criticism of Freud's treatment of the pleasure principle as a negative urge for a release from tension, see Midgley, *Wickedness*, 156–57.

self-serving tendency toward a variety of satisfactions which attends our life form.

The Principle of Competition

Striving-for is always at the same time a striving-against. Even sculptors, mechanics, and cooks wage a kind of warfare with recalcitrant materials and unpredictable events. Recalcitrant materials and unpredictabilities are part of the fragile life situation of any living organism.[4] We experience them in the form of ever-present assaults on our comfort and health and as interferences with the environments that mediate the conditions of our well-being. Fragile are both the body in its vulnerability and the resources in the body's environment on which it depends for life and well-being. Fragile and unstable are the things we depend on in the social world. And these instabilities evoke from us not just avoidances of perils but all sorts of oppositions. Members of archaic societies will oppose with whatever means are available the predations of large dangerous animals. Members of technological societies will use chemical warfare against dangerous insects and bacteria.

The oppositions that come with our strivings are not all of one piece. One whole set of oppositions resembles the predatory behavior of other living things. We hunt, gather, harvest, and kill to feed ourselves, and we decimate forests and plunder our planet for the sake of extended comforts, luxuries, and power. But another set of oppositions has a different dynamics. Like other animal species, we are physiologically equipped to oppose members of our own species. We are able to resist or attack human beings who threaten our satisfactions. We are physiologically equipped to compete with each other for food, mates, territory, status, and rights. Being equipped means that our biochemistry makes possible negative emotions of antipathy against other members of our life-form: against strangers, family members, rival villages, or even whole nations and peoples. Our physical make-up enables us to be capable of anger against our own kind. And we should not confuse this angry or emotional antipathy with food-oriented, predatory behavior. We have no emotional antipathy against the chicken we pluck or the fish we catch.

Being biologically equipped to oppose our own kind does not mean that our hormones and enzymes have fated us to murder and warfare. The presence of capacities for anger, for the mobilization of oppositional emotions against others, is not an explanation for the complex conflicts that take place between individuals or groups. This view of simplistic

4. Susanne K. Langer, *Mind: An Essay on Human Feeling* (Baltimore: Johns Hopkins University Press, 1967), vol. 1, 26–27.

biologism and instinctivism assumes that aggression is a positive and independent instinct whose nonfulfillment is a frustration. In this view, our emotional equipment for aggression is like a boiling kettle ever needing to let off steam. In my judgment physiology, ethology, and evolutionary biology have offered evidences for physiological bases for anger and for some parallels between primate and human agonistic behavior. But these evidences do not amount to a demonstration of simple causal relations between human biochemistry and such things as murder and war.[5] As in other primates, aggression and anger are not so much positive instincts or even inclinations as capacities which can be mobilized under certain circumstances. To be sure, physiologically and psychogenetically based pathologies can effect postures of continuing and unfulfillable anger in individuals.

On the other hand, we should not permit negative assessments of biologism to obscure the fact that we are physiologically equipped not just for satisfactions but for oppositions against members of our own species. Yet it is far too simplistic to think of this physiological equipment for opposition as itself evil or the cause of evil. As the underside of the striving for satisfaction, the capacity to oppose is no more evil than the capacity to be fulfilled. Being physiologically equipped for opposition is, in fact, the negative side of our natural egocentrism, which simply means our desire to live and have well-being. Because we desire well-being, we are also ready to oppose, to have antipathy for those who would threaten our mate, our child, or our lives. And this readiness originates not from the dynamics of evil but our evolutionary heritage.

FALSE HEDONISM

Existing in the world as embodied agents, we ever seek biologically rooted satisfactions. And history and experience attest that our biologically rooted desires are not sealed off from whatever prompts agents to agendas of evil. Ancient asceticisms and modern instinctivisms have exaggerated this point into the notion that the body is a powerful puppeteer that works the strings of our behavior. Is the genesis of human evil a problem? Look no farther, says this tradition, evil comes from the impulses our phylogeny has fostered on us. Opposite to this biologism is the prevailing ethos of present-day technocracies. Technocracies appear to socialize their members into thinking that the realm of the body has nothing whatever to do with evil. If there is such a thing as evil at all, it

5. For a similar distinction between aggression and destructivenss as well as a positive view of the functions of aggression, see Midgley, *Wickedness,* 85–90.

arises with our transcendence of the body, our culture-generated psychological needs for self-esteem and social power. Evil can co-opt the body for its agendas of oppression but bodily urges themselves are uncorrupted and uncorruptible. These extreme approaches which either identify or separate the body and evil exemplify the density and ambiguity of the problem. Three questions may help us consider the thesis that evil, the dynamics of idolatry, does find its way to our embodiment. 1. What precisely undergoes corruption when our bodily life is corrupted? 2. How does this corruption occur? 3. What is the nature of the corruption itself?

1. What precisely undergoes corruption when our bodily life is corrupted? Two ambiguities attend the thesis that our bodily rooted desires are corruptible. The first ambiguity arises with the statement that our biologically rooted desires are (morally) corruptible. For at this point the opponents of Manichean views seem correct when they ask how an organic desire, need, or tendency can be something which is corrupt or noncorrupt. To say that such things are corruptible seems to be a confusion of orders. The only corruption that a biological need could possibly undergo would be a biological corruption. Thus, a genetic accident might so alter hormones as to reduce or eliminate sexual needs. A glandular condition may affect the appetite. But these corruptions cannot be themselves moral corruptions, nor can they cause moral corruptions.

The ambiguity at work here is in the use of the term, *desire.* Does desire mean a biochemical phenomenon, an experienced urge toward certain kinds of fulfillment? It should be clear that the elements of biochemistry (hormones, amino acids) have no desires. Desire is a phenomenon of human agency. Even the biologically based needs and tendencies of our life-form take place in the complex field of agential life. As such they are taken up into the agent's existing in the world, experiencing, and responding. Thus, the sexuality of the human agent is never a mere biological fact but a self-presencing way of being sexual. The agent's desire for nourishment is never a mere physiological appetite but a way of being appetitive in a specific society and in specific situations. Because agents experience their biologically rooted desires in connection with their acculturized and symbolized ways of existing, they are able to distance themselves from them. Human sexual desire thus means to desire to *be sexual as.* The desire for safety or comfort is always a desire for a kind of safety, a degree of comfort. We can thematize, symbolize, worry about, and assign importance to desires. Thus, we not only seek the conditions of physical survival: we seek health. And because this health we seek is already reified and symbolized in our culture, it is something we reflect on, make plans about, and assign status to. Thus, individuals, societies, or epochs can bestow on symbolized regions of desire such as physical comfort or sexuality great or little importance. A desire can be on the margin of the agent's complex of values or can be so important that it exercises hegemony over other regions of desire. To return to our question, biologically rooted desires are incorruptible only if desire is construed as a physiological entity or event. As such they would be no more morally corruptible than our skeleton or circulatory system. But if these desires are ways of being-in-the-world, they can be just as affected by the dynamic of idolatry as historicity or the elemental passions.

A second ambiguity about what it is that is corrupted concerns the references of the biologically rooted desires. Because this ambiguity is intrinsic to the phenomenon itself, it is not utterly resolvable by analysis. Does corruption alter the way biologically rooted desires are incorporated into our being (thus, for instance, as marginal or dominant), or, the way the desire is oriented to its reference? This ambiguity is part of the very nature of desire itself. Because desires are transcending ways of existing in the world, they can corrupt either our interhuman, historical, and passionate ways of existing or the way these references are desired. To illustrate, is our sexuality corrupted because sexuality has taken over our being or because of ways we act sexually toward others? We can only say that biologically rooted desires are corrupted in both senses.

2. How does the corruption of biologically rooted desires come about? The temptation to understand by classifying prompts us to treat these desires as isolated aspects of agential life. This sets the task of understanding how these isolated aspects are corrupted by the dynamic of idolatry. According to the model implied by this approach, the dynamics of idolatry spreads like an infection into various aspects of agential life. This model presupposes that the aspects of human reality are adjacent regions rather than interpermeating dimensions distinguishable only by abstraction. But personal being and elemental passions do not exist alongside our biological life. They too have biological roots. Behind all of the elemental passions is the natural egocentrism of our biological being and our orientations to survival and satisfaction. On the other hand, it is also clear that our elemental passions are not absent from the specific needs and tendencies which pertain to the well-being of our organic life. Concerns for reality, for the self's significance and status, and for reciprocity are ever a part of the way we are sexual and reproductive, and the way we seek health, comfort, safety, and nourishment. Because of these interpermeations, the corruptions of the passions function in the corruption of the biologically rooted desires for satisfaction. If this is so, biologically rooted desires are corrupted both by the general idolatrous response to the tragic and by the corruptions of other aspects of

human reality. In other words, postures of ennui (existential weariness), reality skepticism, and cynicism toward others influence our biologically rooted desires. Our needs and tendencies toward sexuality can be distorted by postures of false dependence and cynicism that corrupt the interhuman. Our attitudes toward safety and comfort can be shaped by our lust for certainty.

Like the other aspects of human reality, the biologically rooted desires are corruptible, and what predisposes their corruption is not just their transinstinctual or transcendent element but their tragic structure and its attending discontents. The most formal feature of this structure is the gap that yawns between the unlimited references of these desires and the fulfillments that are offered them. We do, of course, experience temporary and partial nutritional, sexual, and bodily comfort satisfactions. But what we need and strive for and what our environment grants us are never identical. Hence, a kind of suffering, sometimes intense and agonizing, sometimes brief and superficial, attends our biologically desiring life. We also suffer from ongoing discontents that accompany and endure beyond our experiences of satisfactions because we project into the future our need for repeated or better fulfillments whose actualizations are uncertain. Thus, the sufferings and anxieties of our biological striving become part of our general and ongoing demand that our being be secured. They too exacerbate our insistence that our tragic vulnerabilities disappear and our meaning be established. Our biological needs and tendencies have already oriented us to specific kinds of goods at hand. Since these biological needs or desires are not just chemical impulses but needs we experience, thematize, and even institutionalize, they can become reified as goods at hand that hold out promises of distraction and the removal of discontent. Human agents thus look to their own reified and symbolized desires (for comfort, sex, food) as powers able to chase chaos from the heart and from the world.

The biologically rooted desires are neither general orientations to satisfactions nor the specific wishes which guide everyday life. Hunger, comfort, and sexuality fall between general and utterly specific needs. Each of them inclines to its own proper goods and carries with it its characteristic sufferings and anxieties. Accordingly, the dynamics of idolatry can modify our way of existing in each of these tendencies and needs. In each case, what lures us to the good is not simply the anticipated biological fulfillment but the symbolized and acculturized references in which the projected fulfillment is embodied. Thus, in the sphere of sexuality, we look for securing not just in anticipated physiological events but in a myriad of meanings which accrue to these events: meanings (status, function, power) of dating, having children, success, leisure, and career.

In addition, the dynamics of idolatry can also influence and distort the way we are oriented to satisfaction as such. Desiring satisfaction is an intrinsic and unavoidable feature of human life, a feature of our existence in the world. But all features of our existence are at the same time ways of existing. Hence, the way we are oriented toward satisfactions (pleasures, fulfillments) varies from culture to culture, individual to individual, stage to stage in individual development, and even from situation to situation in everyday life. A culture can reify and symbolize pleasure itself in negative or positive ways. To certain degrees we can assess, reflect on, and decide about the place and status of biologically rooted satisfactions. This is why we can thematize and pursue a culturally reified satisfaction as a good able to secure. The moral traditions of both the East and West have voiced the corruptive possibilities of the pursuit of pleasure. In their extreme form these traditions are so fascinated with the corruptive power of biologically rooted needs that they suppress the inevitable facticity and propriety of the whole sphere of embodiment.

3. What is the nature of the corruption itself? What happens to the biologically rooted desires when they are influenced by agendas of self-securing? How do the dynamics of idolatry affect our way of existing as desiring and pleasure oriented beings? The dynamics of idolatry introduce into our orientation toward satisfaction a paradoxical ambivalence. On the one hand, because they must function to secure, the pleasures and satisfactions of our embodiment take on a new centrality that marginalizes or suppresses the face and other aspects of human reality. This new centrality of satisfactions is paradoxical because at the same time it undermines the capacity to be satisfied. The sybaritic life always has a dark side. Paradoxically, the capacity for satisfaction begins to erode when satisfaction is forced to be a securer. At work here is the despairing side of the dynamics of idolatry. And what the despairing side works on is the anxiety specific to our embodied life. When embodied satisfactions are forced into the service of our metaphysical agenda, a new level if not kind of anxiety is introduced. For if our biologically rooted desires and their fulfillments function to secure, the quest for these satisfactions like the lust for certainty turns into a matter of deadly seriousness. Familiar to us all are deadly serious gourmets, bridge players, and sexual athletes who seem to have lost the capacity to enjoy their favorite pursuits. Genuine sexual enjoyment was moot for Søren Kierkegaard's Seducer. Familiar are those so finely attuned to comfort that the slightest frustration is intolerable. Here we have the vacuousness and ennui of the idolatrous aesthete, the wearily aging roué, the utterly cynical sybaritic

youth, and the desperately bored retiree oriented only to the comfortable life. When the embodied satisfactions have to be themselves our securers against tragedy and chaos, we develop postures toward them which eliminate the spontaneities of genuine enjoyment.

For want of a better name, I shall call this paradoxical corruption of our embodied desires *false hedonism.* Hedonism in itself describes the intrinsic and proper orientation of human beings to the satisfactions of their embodiment. It is a false hedonism when we would have our satisfactions themselves be their own eternal horizon. And because it is a posture that erodes the very satisfactions it most ardently pursues, false hedonism is a failed hedonism.

WICKEDNESS

According to the analysis so far, idolatry appears to be more a phenomenon of human weakness than human evil. Lashed by the sufferings and anxieties of life and desirous of meaning and self-esteem, we rush to goods at hand to secure us. But what does that have to do with cruelty, meanness, prejudice, malicious gossip, genocide, and the host of horrors to which history has made us accustomed? To use Mary Midgley's term, what has idolatry to do with wickedness? One modern view which has an ancient counterpart is quite convinced that wickedness flows directly from our biochemically rooted tendencies which we share with animals. Wickedness is the Homo sapiens version of agonistic behavior and aggression which occurs between members of the same species. I have criticized this view in an earlier chapter. However, there is an element in the instinctivist position which deserves serious consideration. If we had no biologically rooted capacity for anger and aggression whatsoever, we would not be capable of what we call wickedness, that is, of postures and actions desirous of harm to the well-being of others. The aggressive underside of our biologically rooted tendencies appears to be, if not a cause, at least a sine qua non, of wickedness. I shall explore how this is so in three steps: the origin of wickedness in the co-option of the capacity for aggression by idolatry, the two basic forms of wickedness (control and malice), and the dynamics of bigotry.

The Absolute Enemy

Our evolutionary past has equipped us with emotions of antipathy and for aggressive acts against our own kind. Animals are similarly equipped for an interspecies fighting which rarely leads to death or serious injury. If our equipment for anger and fighting were so limited, our conflicts with each other would be limited to bluff behavior and to occasional and brief conflicts. What moves us from the limited fighting of most animal species to enduring postures of cruelty and meanness, and to destructive acts directed against groups and whole peoples?

The added ingredient is the dynamics of idolatry, our inability to bear an intolerably chaotic world, our flight from our deep anxieties about meaning, our rush to secure ourselves in goods at hand. In the previous section I described the effect of idolatry on the biologically rooted desires for satisfaction. But idolatry's dynamics also corrupts the negative or resisting underside of our embodied life. In other words, it corrupts our capacity for aggression. To put it more strongly, when idolatry affects our biologically rooted strivings for satisfaction, it mobilizes our capacities for aggression and gives them a new agenda. And with this new agenda, we transgress the built-in limitations of animal aggression which curtail fighting to death and serious injury. How does this happen?

Our biologically rooted needs and tendencies are never so fulfilled as to be eliminated. Human life is an ongoing story of the frustration of these tendencies in the form of recurring injury, illness, hunger, discomfort, sexual denial, and reproductive and familial tensions. Accordingly, to live at all means to constantly cope with and adapt to these frustrations. Adaptations to the frustrations of sexuality have the character of repression. Adaptations to external assaults from other human beings who harm us or withhold satisfactions from us take the form of resentment.[6] Repressions and resentments are not limited to momentary reactions but enduring, self-conscious postures and deep structures of the altered self. Repressions, resentments, and disappointments make up the frustration side of these desires and they mobilize emotions of antipathy which our physiology make possible. It is just this complex of frustrated desires and our ways of adapting to them with the help of our physiological make-up that idolatry enters and corrupts. In other words, idolatry appropriates our biologically rooted capacity for anger, resistance, and aggression, and the result of this appropriation is wickedness.

Even as false hedonism is not a corrupt form of biologically rooted tendencies themselves but of our transcending way of existing in these tendencies, so wickedness is not a corrupt form of the capacity for aggression but a corruption of the way this capacity shapes our transcending way of resisting. Thus, wickedness is not the mere fact or feeling of anger or antipathy as such but a posture of enmity whose dynamics are those of idolatry. What happens when this dynamics alters the resisting underside of biologically rooted tendencies? Negative and resisting

6. The major twentieth-century monograph on resentment is Max Scheler's *Ressentiment*, trans. W. W. Holdheim (New York: Schocken Books, 1972).

tendencies are the underside of positive strivings. Thus, something happens to the way we resist when our positive strivings take on an absolute character. For if a region of biologically rooted striving is our securing center of meaning, whatever interferes with that striving is something that threatens the very foundation of ourselves and our world. In this situation what frustrates desire is not just a relative opponent, a co-competitor with us in everyday life settings. Our opponent now is an enemy, and an absolute enemy. In the relative world of history, the thief who would rob us and the foreign soldier who would kill us are not necessarily attempting an absolute and final violation. But in the absolutized world of idolatry, these acts take on the character of a sacrilege.

New postures arise with resistance to the absolute enemy. Because the other's threat has the character of a sacrilege, its act or presence creates a new set of permissions. For against those who threaten the foundation of things, anything and everything is justified. We do not deal with the absolute enemy with rehabilitative punishments or pragmatically motivated protections of the social order. Those who constitute a sacrilegious threat to our securers have placed themselves above the relative network of goods, norms, and the face. We now have permission to ignore the face of those who would oppose our idol. We owe them nothing but harm and destruction, in other words, enmity. Born in an absolute opposition, enmity carries with it an accusation. It accuses the individual or collective you of threatening the idol. And this accusation gives us permission to wish harm or to destroy.

How are these new postures of resistance related to our phylogenetically rooted capacities for anger and aggression? Enmity, the posture which idolatry evokes toward the absolute enemy, co-opts or makes use of the emotional capacities we have for conflict with our own species. The hormones and chemicals of our physiological make-up are necessary for the experience of fear, anger, and deep antipathy. Appropriating these raw materials, enmity is a kind of emotion, an anger ready to harm or destroy. Wickedness then is an emotional posture and pattern of action which occurs when the dynamics of idolatry appropriate our capacities for aggression for the purpose of resisting absolute enemies.

Control and Malice

To repeat a point, biologically rooted desires and capacities for aggression are taken up into our ways of existence and our self-awareness. As such they enter our stories, traditions, and institutions. Thus, war, violence, and revenge are ever a part of the narratives, celebrations, and self-understandings of peoples and whole epochs. In the sphere of agency, resentments over past wrongs structure the psyche. Opposition against absolute enemies (wickedness) appropriates these social legacies to take on an enduring life of its own. Accordingly, although wickedness originates in the dynamics of positive striving, its existence is not tied to each striving. Our resistances to enemies construed as absolute threats undergo thematizations, create their own agendas, and finally have their own history. Individuals can be so consumed by the enemy's threat that their lives are taken over by complex strategies of opposition against a neighbor, another race, a political movement, a heresy, or a religion. Nations can mount vast campaigns of genocide and destruction motivated primarily by the symbolism of the absolute enemy. Once thematized into symbols and institutions, wickedness always appears to an individual or a people as a good, something which makes things right. Wickedness is a good because destruction of the absolute enemy protects and restores the absolute good, that is, the idol. Two quite different complexes of attitudes occur in connection with our strategies of opposition, *malice* and *control.*

Malice may be the purest though not necessarily the most powerful form of wickedness. For malice is the most personalized form of resistance to the absolute enemy. Malice as a posture displaces pragmatic reasons for opposing the other by narrowing the being of the other simply to deserving-of-harm. The malicious posture does not reduce the other to something nonhuman or to an object, since what evokes malice in the first place is a personalized threat to one's meaning world. This threat is personalized because it issues from the other's presumed devaluation, withholding of praise, or repudiation of the idol; acts that can come only from a self-presencing other. However much harm they might do, earthquakes, bacteria, and even animal predators do not threaten the world of the idols as a world of meanings. We may relate to these things in pathologically exaggerated fears but rarely in malice. Because the absolute enemy threatens the meaning-world of the idol, our antipathy is directed to the origin of its acts of meaning, the person itself. For it is the self-presencing, autonomous other person who can threaten meaning and who can be held responsible. This is why the harm malice desires is not merely a physical harm. Malice is not satisfied to learn that the enemy contracted a cold or sustained an injury. Malice wants the other to suffer in the same personal order in which its threat takes place. The harm and suffering the absolute enemy deserves is a suffering in its own meaning-oriented being, a suffering of rejection, meaning-deprivation, insult, and dehumanization. In other words, it is a suffering effected by malice's own antipathy.

The primary situation of malice is the interpersonal situation, the relation of the face-to-face. This is not to say, however, that malice is not possible toward a corporate object. Agents also perceive corporate others (nations, races, ethnic groups, and families) as threats to the idol. Nor is this resistance to groups prompted simply by fears of physical threats. The corporate other is also a system of meaning, a powerful symbolism whose hegemony would obliterate the agent's securing systems of meaning. Thus, we can and do have postures of malice toward the other as a corporate entity.

The desire to harm or destroy an absolute enemy (wickedness) does not always target known individuals. Campaigns against absolute enemies may be motivated less by personal threats to an idol than by threats to the conditions necessary to our satisfactions. When this is the case, opposition takes the form not of personalized malice but the desire to control. Campaigns of control can be directed to both individuals and social entities. Whichever is the target, the primary motivation is a control of circumstances favorable to the idol. We may fear, oppose, and even want to overthrow a government or political order because it threatens something to which we are idolatrously attached. We may do all in our power to protect the racial and gender imageries which maintain the position of our social class over other classes. The leaders of a dictatorship or of an urban political machine may use any and all tactics (public slander, torture, terror, violation of rights, false imprisonment) to weaken the opposition. By means of psychological manipulation, bribery, office politics, or sexuality, we can attempt to control individuals who threaten our careers, lifestyles, or causes. And intent to control requires little or no personalized malice against either individuals or groups. What dominates control is not so much personal antipathy as the desire to manage an order or system so as to assure absolutized satisfactions. Control introduces a paradoxical element into the dynamics of wickedness because it implies a certain helplessness of the idol. We mount strategies of control because we sense the fragile and limited nature of the idol. Thus we secretly acknowledge that the idol does not really secure. Its power to secure must be constantly re-established, assured, and protected. Thus we must manage our social environment by defeating the other nation, destroying a people, and repressing criticism. We must control other individuals by imposing our private standards on them, by creating dependencies, and by manipulating their fears and desires.

Control is one manifestation of wickedness. But most forms of wickedness combine control and malice. The most powerful and perennial form of wickedness arises in connection with our relation to others identified as alien groups. This comes as no surprise because the conditions of most satisfactions and thus the most powerful forms of idolatry are connected with corporate entities such as traditions, cultures, religions, and nations. When the corporate entity is the securing good at hand, the absolute enemies are the groups that threaten that entity. Thus, we establish and protect our own superior corporate securer by postures which devalue and distort the other race, ethnic group, region of the country, nation, age group, gender, and class. Bigotry is the term for this form of wickedness. Several acts of meaning converge to constitute this posture toward alien groups. First, the alien group and its individuals are given the status of absolute enemies whose very existence threatens one's own absolutely valued meaning world. Second, general features of the alien group are identified and contrasted negatively to one's own group or social world. The other culture is thus barbaric, prone to violence, morally corrupt, or artistically bankrupt. Third, these general negative features are assigned to the individual members of the group, thus creating a rationale for antipathy to and the deprivation of the rights of those individuals. Fourth, each individual is regarded as a mere collection of the group's negative features, an aggregate of inferiorities, and thus deserves the responses of control and malice. Like other postures, bigotry can become reified in both societal and individual dynamics. In society it becomes sedimented into the discourse, institutions, and traditions through which the society understands itself and orders itself. In individuals it becomes objectified in sedimented imageries that guide decisions and carry valuations.

THE FREEDOMS OF THE BODY

To speak of a freedom (virtue) of the body, will have little meaning to some. It is unthinkable to ancient and modern sybarites that the body is anything other than a field of enjoyable or painful sensations. For them the body's freedom is simply its capacity for these enjoyments. To ancient and modern ascetics, freedom comes about only when our penchants for pleasures are repressed or disciplined. Freedom comes only with a defeat of the body. Yet it makes little sense to identify freedom either with bodily sensations or their repressions. The ascetic view seems unaware that bodily orientations to satisfactions and resistances constitute the very life of agents. The sybaritic view appears to be unaware that biologically rooted desires are ways agents exist in the world and thus are occasions of self-making, corruption, and violations of the other. Both views fail to grasp the corrupting effects of the dynamics of idolatry on bodily rooted desires and freedoms that arise as ways of desiring and opposing. Human embodiment is both a fact and a way of existing in the world. The self-making of the agent is in part a bodily self-making. Thus, phylogenetically originated needs and tendencies are taken up into the agent's agendas, aims, and postures. This is why both corruption and freedom can attach to embodiment. Even as both desiring and opposing aspects of bodily striving undergo corruption, freedoms arise when being-founded influences these two aspects. I shall call the freedom of bodily desire, *eudaemonic freedom* and the freedom of bodily opposition, *prophetic resistance.*

Eudaemonic Freedom

We need not dwell on the negative aspects of eudaemonic freedom, the reduction of the power of false hedonism. Descriptions of these aspects in other agential dimensions apply here as well. When being-founded and courage reduce the anxious need to be secured by the references of the bodily rooted tendencies, they return the agent to the natural hedonism of bodily (and cultural) life. Even as the passions of and for subjectivity, reality, and the interhuman are not as such true freedoms, neither is natural hedonism a genuine bodily freedom. As an expression of our natural egocentrism, natural hedonism is neither something evil nor a sign of being-founded in the sacred. Bodily rooted tendencies show a natural egocentrism simply because they are urges and needs of an embodied individual. On this plane they, too, present agents with a choice of either pursuing these fulfillments or abandoning the pursuit on behalf of the fulfillments of others. Caught in this either-or of their natural bodily egocentrism, agents must suspend their own needs and tendencies in order to serve the needs of others.

Recall that one aspect of courage is a venturing or risk of the self onto a new plane. On this plane the agent's natural preoccupations are taken up into the life and reality of what is other than itself. This venturing is a risk because we cannot know what we will become or what will happen to us when we exist amidst claims made on us by larger contexts. When we venture ourselves in the sphere of the interhuman, our desire is for a reciprocity which meets not just our own or another's needs but one in which the two converge. In the sphere of bodily rooted tendencies and needs, the venturing agent strives not simply for that which will fill and end my need but for that whose own fulfillments is the environment of my fulfillments. There does seem to be a difference between desiring either one's own or another's comfort and safety and desiring comfort and safety in the midst of comfortable and safe others.

The self-reference (natural egocentrism) is not abandoned in venturing but is taken up onto a self-with-others plane. The desire for a healthy and clean environment for all living things on the planet is not a repudiation of the biologically rooted desires for comfort and safety. It is not a surrender of the self's orientation to satisfaction. But it does describe a vastly expanded reference of these desires. The ecological posture desires the comfort and safety of the agent in the larger context of the comfort and safety of other living things. Here, too, there is a venturing and risk of the self. For its desire for safety and comfort as part of the safety and comfort of others may limit its specific aims and even call for sacrificial adjustments.

Does being-founded have a direct influence on the bodily rooted desires which transports them to a new plane? Such a notion has the advantage of simplicity but is nevertheless misleading. Bodily rooted desires obtain the new plane of the venturing self on the basis of a convergence of influences. As ways of existing in the world, our embodied needs and tendencies can be influenced by various freedoms (virtues) such as vitality or wonder. However, these freedoms are not simply "caused" but come about in connection with complex interactions between aspects of the embodied self. And it is this totality of interacting passions that takes the way we exist in our needs and tendencies onto a new plane. Thus, our way of (bodily) desiring gathers norms, contents, even imageries from the realm of the face, from empathy with living things, and from the experience of beauty. This new plane is neither a plane of bodily repression nor sybaritic preoccupation but of bodily desire existing in the broader context of the desires and needs of other living things.

Prophetic Resistance

Wickedness is a posture in which our physiologically rooted capacities for anger and aggression are directed toward an absolute enemy. The other's threat to our idolatrized desire evokes attitudes of malice and agendas of control. In wickedness, our natural capacities for aggression direct themselves to a negative idol and, taking on a life of their own, shape lifelong postures of enmity, corrupted imageries, and agendas of harm and destruction. When being-founded begins to replace the false founding of the negative idol, the postures of wickedness weaken. But the absence of wickedness (if that were possible) would not be itself a freedom (virtue) of embodied life. The human being minus wickedness and prejudice yet without courage and the venturing of the self is a being of natural enjoyments and natural anger-abetted resistances. And the freedom which enters with being-founded is neither this condition of natural egocentrism nor its repression.

We have seen how our positive desires can be taken up into the new plane of eudaemonic freedom. In eudaemonic freedom embodied desire expands its references from the self-preoccupation of natural egocentrism to ever-larger environments of living things. Unlikely as it may seem, our capacities for aggression can also be mobilized and transformed into a freedom. The natural egocentrism which prompts our resistances can also undergo a similar expansion. Transformed by courage, our aggressive tendencies are detached from a desire to harm an absolute enemy, and the natural egocentrism behind these tendencies is taken onto a new plane. When we venture ourselves onto the new plane of being with other living things, we expand our self-preoccupations into preoccupations with the struggles going on all about us. We participate in or with the desires and fulfillments of other living things. Empathizing with others in modes of vitality, wonder, and true reciprocity, and even with the face, we are drawn beyond (but not against) natural egocentrism to a plane of mutually interacting preoccupations. We desire our fulfillments in conjunction with the fulfillments of many others. And this expansion alters our way of resisting and opposing. For now we are caught up in the struggles of the other, the pathos of the other's experience. We attend to the things which would harm and destroy other living things. Our oppositions and resistances on behalf of our embodied selves are also on behalf of others. We struggle not only against that which would remove our own comfort and safety, our individual rights, our mates, or extended families, but against threats to our companion living beings. When our way of resisting is transformed into a new freedom, several consequences ensue. One effect of this expanded orientation is that our biologically rooted oppositions (aggressions), become reattached to what we positively desire and cease to have a life of their own. A second effect is that our oppositions become subject to the norms of the interhuman and the face. Thus, the expanded resistance to what opposes the whole fragile web of life becomes a struggle for such things as corporate conditions of well-being, justice, reciprocal social enjoyments, and an opposition against exploitation, injustice, and oppression. This is why this new plane of oppositional existence is a prophetic resistance. It is not a freedom from our biological capacities to resist, from emotions of anger and resentment against what threatens our well-being. But it is an *Aufhebung,* a taking up onto a new plane, of aggression, a mobilization of capacities of resistance for the sake of an expanded, perhaps even social self.

An example is in order. When *human aggression,* a short-cut term for biologically rooted tendencies to oppose and resist, undergoes the corruption of idolatry and turns its rage toward absolute enemies, it is self-evident why it would seek the death penalty for criminals. The fearful and corrupted agent experiences the criminal as an absolute threat to its securing social system. With its natural aggression now having become enmity, the agent seeks simply to harm and destroy the criminal. But there is another posture which also would seek the criminal's death, the pragmatic posture of egocentrism. In this posture, agents seek the demise of certain kinds of criminals because an efficient and economically viable society has no obligation to impoverish itself and endanger the well-being of others on behalf of incorrigible societal members. Prophetic resistance both breaks with the dynamics of idolatry and goes beyond the posture of pragmatic egocentrism. Once courage propels us into the midst of the life of others, the network of living things, our resistance is prompted neither by revenge nor by the pragmatic goods of a specific society. We may angrily oppose the rapist, the murderer, and the oppressor. But prophetic resistance cannot approach these criminals as if there were no face. It cannot embrace a notion of incorrigibility which reduces the other to utter wickedness or to nonhumanity, that is, to something lacking historicity, elemental passions, and transcending bodily desires. The enlarged empathy of prophetic resistance can only oppose and resist in the sense of seeking goods, and this excludes oppositions which remove the very possibility of a criminal's existence in the sphere of the face.

13

ALIENATION AND COMMUNION: THE REDEMPTION OF THE INTERHUMAN

> Both of these kinds of cruelty can hide the face of the victim from the victimizer, can make the victim passive and the victimizer active, for the victim's 'own sake.' But when the face becomes a force, when it can be 'seen' in all the ways people can 'see' people, then the cruel relationship can be changed.[1]
>
> *Phillip Hallie*

> What life have you if you have not life together?
> There is no life that is not in community.
> And now you live dispersed on ribbon roads
> And no man knows or cares who is his neighbor.[2]
>
> *T. S. Eliot*

The individual and the social are the polar terms of a modern dualism created when a social hermeneutic is added to a religious or moral individualism. In theological texts, this dualism appears in such oppositions as justification (of the individual) and the kingdom of God, individual piety and praxis, or virtue and liberation. Human good and evil, then, is either a matter of individual intentions and acts or institutional structures and processes. A twofold moral task arises with this dualism: the sacral reconstitution of the individual through sanctification, forgiveness, and virtues; and the transformation of oppressive institutions. Some social movements and schools of interpretation have taken one side of the dualism against the other, but most modern denominations, their schools, and their theologies find ways to include both. Dualisms tend to arise as corrections of views that stress only one aspect of something, but they are also signs of separation and disrelation. The dualism of the individual and the social fails to recognize

1. Philip Hallie, *The Paradox of Cruelty* (Middletown, Conn.: Wesleyan University Press, 1969), 146.

2. T. S. Eliot, "Choruses from 'The Rock,'" *Collected Poems, 1909–1962* (New York: Harcourt Brace Jovanovich, Inc., 1936, 1963).

a whole sphere of human reality, the sphere of the interhuman or relation. Thus the sphere of relation seems unaffected by both the dynamics of evil and the power of redemption.

The writings of the faith of Israel or the kerygmatic literature of early Christianity called the New Testament do have powerful accounts of the corruption and redemption of both individuals and the social. Psalmists, Gospel writers, and Paul probe the corruption and redemption of individuals. Prophets and apocalyptists expose the oppressions of Israel and foresee the winnowing of the nations. But the texts and literatures of these writings are not exhausted by this duality. The divisions Paul confronts in the churches of Asia Minor are neither individual vices nor oppressive institutional functions but a kind of poisoning of relations. And the communion (koinonia) he envisions is neither an individual nor political redemption. I shall explore the corruption and redemption of relation in the themes of *alienation* and *communion.*

THE REALITY OF RELATION

The interhuman is a sphere of human reality irreducible to either social sedimentations or individuals. It is the face-to-face being-together or relation of individuals as thous that presupposes both the irreducible alterity or otherness of the participants and their already formed interconnectedness (intersubjectivity). Among the spheres of human reality, the sphere of relation is what most easily escapes our attention. Thus, it has been the least thematized of the spheres in philosophy and theology. What makes it so elusive? The social is prominent in the everyday world in the operations of powerful institutions. The social is ever before us demanding our loyalties and evoking our criticisms. Its patterns of causality, functions, and organizations invite empirical and structural analyses. Likewise, individuals are intensely aware of themselves and this awareness has spawned endless empirical and reflective inquiries. The sphere of relation is not something utterly distant from our awareness. It is not a noumenon ever hidden behind what we experience and available only to speculation. But we are aware of it neither as an external entity nor as our own subjectivity. And in a time like ours when reality is either objective or subjective, the sphere of relation is either missed altogether or construed as the social or the agential. And because relations are constituted by both reciprocal acts of agents and enduring patterns, they do seem to be phenomena either of individuals or the social or a combination of the two.

Elusive as they are, relations are as much a part of everyday life as individuals and social structures. Friendships, marriages, love affairs, and parenting are all instances of relations. But to what do these terms refer if not individuals or social sediments? The example of friendship shows us first of all what relation is not. Genuine relation should not be confused with the momentary interactions that constantly go on in the social world; for instance, negotiations with a bank's loan officer. Relation is not the way members of a large group such as an office or labor union interact. Nor is it a term for ways two individuals feel toward each other. Nor does relation describe simply momentary instances in which human beings are thous to each other; e.g., the meeting of eyes between strangers in a restaurant. Nor does relation occur when such meetings turn into extended dialogues. It would even be misleading to identify relation with what Levinas calls the face. For face can be an element in many social interactions which are not relations.

What then is relation? Staying with our example, friendship involves some direct communication, but as a relation it does not cease when friends hang up the telephone or return to their private spaces. Friendship also involves, requires we might say, being together as thous, but this does not mean merely a one time only, momentary encounter. Friendship, and in fact any genuine relation, is constituted by direct communication, the thou element, and some perduring over time. Relation, we might say, is an *enduring way of being-together as thous.* Thus, it is neither a momentary meeting of thous nor the enduring of thou-less social interactions. All of our examples confirm this. In friendship, marriage, and parenting, the participants' way of being thous to each other has become something that endures between them. To use Martin Buber's phrase, relation is the sphere of the between *(Zwischen).*

What enables relation to endure? The enduringness of the between is made possible by contributions both from individuals and from society. There would be no enduring friendships if individuals were incapable of meaning acts, memory, ongoing postures, and deposits of imagery and if there were no social deposits of tradition and language. But these individual and social perdurings are not themselves relation. Somehow the thou element, the being-together as thous, discovers a way to appropriate these resources so as to perdure over time. For a relation of friendship to exist at all, the distinctive meanings, reciprocities, and activities of that specific relation must appropriate societal and individual resources of preserving the past. Yet relation is not merely the perduring of a thou-less social interaction. The thou element is necessary to friendships and familial relations. Friendship has served as our example, but this is not to say that relation is always something satisfying or pleasing. Genuine relation can arise between those who compete with each other even to the point of being enemies. In the case of enemies, the thou element occurs in a conflictual mode that has found a way to perdure through time. It is the merger of the thou with vehicles of duration that constitutes the mystery of all real relation. Relation is mysterious to the degree that this merger eludes our attempts to understand or explore it.

ALIENATION

Not uncommon is the experience on the part of two or more people that "something is wrong between us." What they sense as wrong is not just the flawed characters or stupid acts of the involved individuals but something that lies there between them, a distortion of their "between." Something has poisoned the relation itself. And the scope of this poisoning can extend from a one-to-one relation to whole communities. In spite of this common experience of personal relation, present-day industrial societies seem unable to find ways to interpret the way relation goes awry. The community and literature most aware of relation itself is the therapeutic community. This is not to say that relation is important to quantifying psychologies. But many who are concerned with therapeutic treatment are intensely aware of the mutual victimizations that take place in families and groups. Accordingly, the therapeutic professions have produced texts on the relational elements in psychopathology, family dynamics, and co-dependency.[3] But the therapeutic framework and world-view function to obscure the way relation is corrupted. What poisons relation is biological, psychological, or social pathologies. Excluded then is the possibility that relation might be a distinctive embodiment of human evil. But when we look to the religious community for a correction of this limitation, we find a lack of concern with the sphere of relation as such. To be sure, the religious community's ancient texts are not unaware of the operations of sin and redemption in this sphere. But present-day religious communities (when they have not totally embraced the therapeutic world-view themselves) do repeat the stories and imageries of human evil and redemption. But the prevailing individual-social dualism of these communities inclines them to ignore the sphere of relation or the interhuman. The result is that their primary notions (sin, guilt, prejudice, oppression) are assigned either to individual intentions and responsibilities or to societal processes. Thus, for instance, guilt becomes either a problem of individual feeling or a matter of societal or divine forensics. To conclude, the therapeutic

3. See Harry Stack Sullivan, *The Interpersonal Theory of Psychiatry* (New York: Norton, 1953). Sullivan and the later literatures do address problems which arise between human beings and which pertain to more than simply the dynamics of individuals. However, this more social strand of a psychology and therapeutic has rarely if ever been in touch with the major twentieth-century philosophical articulations of the sphere of the between, that is, with Martin Buber, Alfred Schutz, and Emmanuel Levinas. Thus, the focus of the psychological literature is on enduring but actual dynamics of human interaction. And this places in the background the primary features of alienation, *ressentiment*, and guilt.

community perceives relation but not genuine alienation: the religious community perceives sin, guilt, and resentment but not their location in the sphere of relation. From this situation issues the problem, How can a relation be corrupted by human evil? What form does human evil take when it is neither an agential intention nor a societally oppressive structure? I shall contend that there is a distinctive form of human evil that attends the sphere of relation and shall call it *alienation.*[4]

I spoke earlier of benign antipathies intrinsic to the sphere of the interhuman. These antipathies originate in the incompatibilities and clashes which are unavoidable when self-determining human beings live in proximity to each other. They are benign because they do not arise from or display the dynamics of evil. They effect degrees of separation in relation but they lack what makes separation alienation, namely mutual violation (deprivation of being) and its deposits of resentment and guilt. Accordingly, alienation does not end relation but is a way of being in relation. It does not remove the thou element or its forms of enduring but is a separation of being-together as thous. *Violation* is the corruption of the sphere of relation and its two consequences are resentment and guilt.

Violation as the Deprivation of Being

Violation effects a malignant separation in relation. It is important at this point to notice the difference between violations as individual intentions, postures, or acts of individuals and violation as a structural feature of the sphere of relation. The violating acts of individuals arise from the dynamics of idolatry. They reflect postures of malice and control and they

4. The term, *alienation,* has a long history and has multiple meanings. For a history, etymology, and topology of these meanings, see Frank Johnson, ed., *Alienation: Concept, Term, and Meanings* (New York: Seminar Press, 1973), especially the Introduction and chapter 1 by the volume editor. In general, alienation is a term for the human condition viewed in its problematic character, but it can focus on alienation within the agent, between the agent and the world, or the agent and society. Ernst Becker uses it as a comprehensive term for the human predicament, hence offers his own synthetic theory of alienation in which he gathers up both Sigmund Freud's and Karl Marx's views. See Ernst Becker, *The Structure of Evil: An Essay on the Unification of the Science of Man* (New York: G. Braziller, 1968), Part 2. In Karl Marx alienation arose as a domination of the human being by the world of objects and shows itself in "the failure to develop self-powers by transacting with the world of things." See Becker, *The Structure of Evil,* 129. For Karl Marx on alienation, see Bertell Ollman, *Alienation: Marx's Concept of Man in Capitalist Society* (Cambridge, Eng.: University Press, 1971), 131–36. In Karl Marx, alienation is a comprehensive term for Marxist theory from the standpoint of the agent and describes the devastating effect of capitalist society on the physical and mental states of human beings. Herbert Marcuse continues this theme when he argues that the modern industrial form of alienation is manifest in the merger of the individual's being and self-understanding with the societal system. Thus modern human beings "find their soul in their automobile, hi-fi set, split-level home, kitchen equipment." See Marcuse, *One-Dimensional Man: Studies in the Ideology of Advanced Industrial Society* (Boston: Beacon Press, 1964), 9.

inflict pain and suffering on the other. Alienation and the violation that effects it is a structural feature of relation itself. Acts of violation come and go. The relation of violation is an enduring co-violation of thous. What does this mean?

Violation clearly bespeaks some sort of harm. To violate another individual is to harm, but in what way? Harm to any living thing is a deprivation of its powers to live as its own distinctive kind of being. To violate is to deprive something of its powers of being, its powers of living, functioning, responding, and even creating. If human beings were comprised solely of physically measurable components (an assortment of chemicals, for instance), harm would mean simply the destruction of these chemicals or the conditions on which they depend. But because we are self-presencing, passionate, and embodied, we can be harmed at the point of our existentials, our self-transcending ways of existing in the world. We can be deprived of powers of existence that come with the spheres and dimensions of our reality. We not only can be starved, subjected to pain, and physically incarcerated but also dehumanized, insulted, and manipulated. Acts of this sort deprive us of things needed by the elemental passions; the conditions of subjectivity, the chance to experience and understand reality, and acknowledgment and affection. To be deprived of these things is to have our capacities or powers to exist in the world reduced. Deprivations are what we effect in the being of the other when we withhold acknowledgment and affection, when we falsely accuse, stereotype, and show contempt. In sum, deprivations are directed to the face of the other and they appeal to the face in order to wound the face. In the sense of that which gathers the existentials into vulnerability, the face is what violation violates.

The examples of the preceding paragraph have to do with the violating acts of individuals. These are the violations we experience explicitly in the social world and they provide the clues for what happens when relation is distorted by violation. Relation, a being-together as thous over time, can itself be a deprivation of being. Two or more human beings can be in relation that reduces their existentials or powers of existing in the world. Their very relation can be a sedimentation of violations. Violating acts and postures may continue between them and these acts may symptomize and contribute to the corrupted relation. Does anything endure before and after these acts that is violative? A relation itself is violative when its thous use the enduring materials of the relation against each other. For instance, two partners in a marriage are thous to each other in and through such perdurings as their shared past, sexuality, children, careers, and world-views. They can violate each other in connection with these things and the violation or deprivation of being can restructure the relation. Thus, each one's very participation in this relation is deprivational. More specifically, the way they are sexual to each other can have deprivational effects on each one's historicity, elemental passions, and bodily life including the biologically rooted tendency and need of sexuality.

The dynamics of alienated relation parallel but do not simply repeat the dynamics of idolatry and of social oppression. The dynamics of idolatry arise from how the agent responds to a threatening, chaotic, and painful world. The dynamics of alienated relation originate when evil finds its way to the sphere of relation. How does this happen? Because human evil is not a mere effect of an external cause in the realm of entities, its origin ever eludes us. Yet, there are things in the relation that make alienation possible and lure it into being. Even as idolatry arises in connection with fears and anxieties built into our tragic existence, so alienation has behind it the tragically structured sphere of relation. Relation is already drawn toward separation by the antipathies that attend the unavoidable incompatibilities of everyday life. Even in the absence of evil, the negotiations and relations between agents would be only partly successful. These failed negotiations and antipathies are neither violations nor the causes of violations. But the ever-present separations and benign antipathies play on the doubts of the participants and serve as the rationalization of violation.

In addition, inclinations toward violation are influenced by both agential and societal spheres. From the side of the agent's own self-determination, idolatry can instigate postures and agendas of personal violation. For instance, idolatry can turn the biologically rooted capacity for aggression into postures of malice and agendas of control directed to the other. It can corrupt the elemental agapic passion for reciprocal affection into false dependence and its attendant exclusion and violation of all others. From the side of the social comes another group of influences. The oppressive power of society has already deposited into history institutions of violation: powerful and corrupted discourses, social functions, and patterns of organization which supply the matter and carriers of relation. These already corrupted vehicles are the only things available for thous to appropriate to make relation endure. These two sources of influence on relation constitute passive and active or subjective and external ways of thinking about the origin of violation. On the passive side, relation appears to contract violation from society almost like a disease.[5] On the active side, violation

5. Throughout this essay, I have resisted introducing the issue of pathology, that is, the way in which the spheres of human reality are subject to distortions and injuries connected with a variety of what might be called causes. For a modest and brief effort to distinguish the dynamics of evil from the dynamics of pathology, see my article "Psychopathology and

appears to be perpetuated in relation by the acts of agents. If violation is utterly explainable by these external and agential causes, relation itself disappears into either the life of the subject or the operations of society. But the sphere of thous in relation resists this reduction. Because of the mystery of the merger of thous with carriers of duration, the origin of violation is illumined but not casually explained by these determinations. Violation then is a distinctive corruption of the sphere of the between.

Resentment and Guilt

We human beings are not simply passive to our environments, imprinted by external causes. As agents we respond to what deprives us of being and these responses themselves can shape our determinacy. Insofar as deprivation is not a momentary event but a removal of being, our responses to it are not just momentary adjustments but ways of restructuring or remaking our being. The effect of deprivation on the agent and on relation is not unlike the effect of a physical injury which not only wounds but maims.

Our topic is violation as an alteration of relation. In everyday life, violations can be reciprocal or one-directional where one individual violates another. I shall explore the way violation wounds relation by looking at the effects of violation on both the violator and the violated. In other words, I shall focus on the effects of violations on the agents in relation in order to understand how violation distorts relation. Violators internalize violation in the form of *guilt;* those violated in the form of *resentment.* From these internalized responses arise reciprocal postures which the thou element appropriates and draws into relation. Guilt and resentment are what alienate and wound relation.

1. *Resentment.*[6] Agents respond to the violations of their being by internalizations of resentment. Resentment is a posture, often but not

Human Evil: Toward a Theory of Differentiation," in R. Bruzina and B. Wilshire, eds., *Crosscurrents in Phenomenology* (The Hague, Netherlands: Nijhoff, 1978). I mention this so as not to give the impression that the sphere of relation is somehow sealed off from the effects of pathology. There do seem to be relations and even whole communities which embody strong pathological elements. Thus, childhood abuses can and do result in pathological features that follow an individual throughout succeeding stages of life and in child-to-parent relations of pathologically rooted separation. This analysis of alienation does not exclude this but it does argue against views that interpret alienation as pathology. Insofar as these views are dominated by the so-called medical model, they will see alienation as an effect of certain victimizing causes and redemption as therapeutic intervention.

6. Resentment *(ressentiment)* has its classical formulation in Nietzsche, a formulation elaborated in Max Scheler's work, *Ressentiment,* trans. W. H. Goldheim (New York: Free Press of Glencoe, 1961). For an excellent account of resentment in Nietzsche, see Charles Scott, *The Language of Difference* (Atlantic Highlands, N.J.: Humanities Press International, 1987), 34.

necessarily self-conscious, of antipathy evoked by deprivations of being. As Max Scheler has shown, resentment can be directed not just to individual but to anonymous and corporate violators. Members of racial, gender, ethnic, and age groups respond in resentment when anonymous powers violate them. Violation is possible because self-presencing or personal agents intrinsically resist violation. And this resistance indicates the distinctive way personal being is vulnerable. Physical assaults—the breaking of an ankle—stimulate biochemical responses in the injured limb and even felt responses of pain but not necessarily resentment. Personal violations (which can include physical assaults) invoke resentment because they are assaults on the very personhood of the agent, on self-esteem, determinacy, and transcendence. Resentment structures the self insofar as the violation of personhood creates enduring antipathy that permeates the agent's existentials or powers to exist in the world and shapes its reciprocities with others.

Violation not only elicits the responses and shapes the postures of agents but shapes and alters relation. A friendship can be altered by mutual or unidirectional violations. Because it is an enduring antipathic posture toward others, resentment also alters face-to-face relation. In the sphere of relation, resentment is an enduring wound, a separation of thous. This wound is possible because of the summoning or obligation aspect of the face. The face evokes compassionate obligation to an agent's vulnerability. Face is present in relation as thous sense each others' thouness as a summons to obligation. But when violation occurs, this summons to obligation becomes an accusation. To be violated and deprived of being is to resent and accuse. This resenting accusation not only becomes internalized in the agent's psychic life but it structures the way human beings are thous to each other in their ongoing relation. The violator experiences the resentment of the other as an accusation. And this accusation coming forth from the face enters the sphere of the between and separates or wounds the relation. If violations are reciprocal, resenting accusations from both sides wound the relation.

2. *Guilt.* Resentment rends the interhuman by antipathies and accusations evoked by violation. When we look at violation from the side of the violator, we discover another internalization and rending. To violate the personhood of another, to deprive another of being is to effect an apparently irreparable injury. This irreparable injury or wound in relation is guilt. What is guilt and why does it attend violation?[7]

7. Recent interpretations of guilt range from absolute attacks on the concept (Walter Kaufmann) to defenses. With the exception of Martin Buber, the interpreters of guilt share a common presupposition. They displace it from the sphere of relation in their attempt to understand it. Kauffmann's repudiation of guilt is based on his repudiation of punishment.

We will quickly lose track of our theme if we fail to make some initial distinctions. The theme of guilt occurs frequently in two present-day contexts. First, in the practice of therapy and its conceptual framework, the focus is on problems caused by debilitating feelings of guilt.[8] The locus of guilt feelings is the subjectivity or psyche of the individual. But the problem introduced by violation is not the presence of debilitating feelings but a wounded relation. Second, in the legal system, the focus is on violations not of relations but of laws society has created to maintain its order and protect what it values. The locus of forensic guilt is society not relation. In society the problem of guilt is not a wounded relation but societal disorder and the determination of justifiable penalties.

The guilt that rends relation is neither the presence of guilt feelings of individuals nor the violations of a penal code. It is the name for the consequence of interpersonal deprivation of being and separated relation, the measure of which is neither the intensity of the agent's internalized feelings nor the outcome of legal processes. Interhuman guilt is an actual alteration of the sphere of relation following on violation. What precisely is this alteration? I have already described the wound in relation that enters when the violated respond in accusing resentment. The alteration of relation by resentment is a possibility because self-presencing agents are vulnerable to deprivation and exist toward each other under the summons of the face. When thous exist toward one another as thous, they are summoned by each others' vulnerable and pathetic beauty. As a thou, the other's very existence is a summons to empathetic responsibility. The very reality of a thou asks for recognition and empathy of its thou-ness. The thou, in other words, is a summons of responsibility on whomever enters into relation with it. Because of this claim resident in the face, the violation

In his view deserving punishment is what makes guilt objective. He does think human beings can do wrong, but rejects any notion that wrong-doing deserves punishment. Since punishment is something visited on the agent from society or some external source, Kaufmann locates guilt and punishment in the sphere of the social. See his *Without Guilt and Justice: From Decidophobia to Autonomy* (New York: Peter H. Wyden, 1973), chap. 5. Alf Ross, on the other hand, accepts the premise that guilt and punishment are connected. He thinks this connection is plausible and that punishment should be a logical possibility insofar as a societal system has the right to enforce or retain its order through reproach, censure, etc. Instead of seeing this as an essential tyranny and violation of the agent's autonomy, he thinks that the presence of normative enforcements in a society is the citizens Magna Carta against the State, their protection against tyranny. See Alf Ross, *On Guilt, Responsibility and Punishment* (Berkeley, Calif.: University of California Press, 1975), 98–99. John G. McKenzie hints at but does not develop the theme of the root of objective guilt in the violation of relation. Thus he thinks human beings do violate the moral order and other people and thus are worthy of blame. See John G. McKenzie, *Guilt: Its Meaning and Significance* (Nashville, Tenn.: Abingdon, 1962), 21.

8. For this distinction between guilt and feelings of guilt, see Martin Buber, *The Knowledge of Man*, trans. M. Friedman and R. G. Smith (London, Eng.: Allen and Unwin, 1965), chap. 6.

of thous has the character of an ignored summons, a failed obligation. More than that, violation exploits the fragility sensed in the other and repudiates the claim and summons issued by the face.

When the summons of the face and the obligation it sets are ignored, the violated other makes a new claim on the violator. The violated other is no longer just the one whose fragility and personal being issue a summons to compassionate obligation but the one whose summons was repudiated and whose fragile personal being was violated. Violation thus creates a second summons, namely to rectify the harm, to repair the wound. Because of the face and the summons, the wound is not just in the violated other but is a wound in the relation itself. But this second summons is strangely unique. It is a summons which cannot be answered, a claim which cannot be met, a debt which cannot be paid. If violation was simply an interruption in the realm of objects and external relations, the damage done is conceivably repairable. A damaged roof can be fixed, a lost purse can be replaced. In the legal system, the judge sometimes attempts to rectify the wrong that has been done. A payment is exacted from the drunk driver to the injured client. Attempted rectifications are common in the personal world. The abusing parent attempts to make up to the abused child. One thing is clear in these examples. The rectification is never equivalent to the violation. Pain, injury, insult, and abuse have no dollar equivalents. Even if the attempted remuneration were outlandish, a million dollars paid for a petty insult, it would not remove the second claim created by the violation. Rectifications can never remove the event or the state of affairs in the other of having been violated. They cannot remove the second summons issued by the face.

Violation thus effects an irreparable wound in relation, a wound which endures because of the inability of the violator to answer the second summons to rectify the matter. In the sphere of relation, guilt means this unhealable wound, this unanswerable new claim which violation evokes from the face. This unanswerable claim is just what is sensed by guilt feelings, the affective and internalized aspect of guilt. And if the only thing violators sensed was something easily rectifiable, they would not have guilt feelings, only feelings which attend barter and negotiation. This is why certain kinds of therapeutic treatments can suppress or distract guilt feelings but cannot eradicate the altered state of the interhuman which called them into being. The wound of guilt is not a repetition of resentment. Resentment is the wound that enters relation from the violated's accusation. Guilt is the wound created by an unanswerable obligation brought into being by the violation of the face.

Guilt, like violation, has its own dynamics. Its locus is the sphere of relation but it influences and is influenced by actual human reciprocities of the social world and the psychodynamics of individuals. Agents experience and internalize the wounded relation of guilt as feelings of guilt. Guilt then can join with and alter the existentials or ways of existing in the world and can even bring about or be transformed into pathologies of individual life. Thus, guilt-ridden individuals will experience and treat others through their internalized guilt from which arise enduring patterns of human interaction. The spread of guilt into the self and the reciprocities of the social world in turn influences the sphere of relation, providing ever new materials for the thou-element to appropriate. It should be clear, however, that the degree of guilt awareness or guilt-driven incidents in human interaction is not a measure of guilt itself. Our success or failure to repress feelings of guilt does not determine whether or not our violations are in fact violations or whether they create an unanswerable summons.

To summarize, in the sphere of the interhuman, the dynamics of evil is a dynamics of alienation. Alienation is a rift or separation in the sphere of relation, a wound of antipathy, accusation, and unpayable obligation affected by violation. Both the resentment of the violated and the guilt of the violator find their way into relation itself and are not just internalizations of the participating individuals. Thus, if there is a redemption of alienation, it cannot be addressed simply to the existentials, sins, and lost powers of individuals. It must reach and redeem the sphere of relation itself.

COMMUNION

Human evil in the form of alienation appears to be irreversible and uncorrectable. For no act of good born of remorse, no compensatory payment, can remove the events of violation in the past or the wounding effects of violation relation. Certain reparations can "make things better" and assist our life struggles so as to distract or repress the alienation. But reparations never remove alienation. Yet, something about this description of the permanence and finality of alienation seems not quite right. Familiar are the instances that take place in everyday life where alienation is in fact reduced, wounded relations healed, and resentments displaced. Virtually all human societies contain perduring forms of relation (families, tribes, friendships) which are not simply embodiments of alienation. Human beings do seem to live as thous in relation to each other in various forms of communion, sensitive to the face. Further, the actual healing of the wounds of alienation also occurs not infrequently in human societies.

The healing of alienated relation and the rise of a community of reconciliation are familiar themes in the literature of the early Christian movement. Familiar are the major Johannine and Pauline terms: reconciliation *(katagalle)*, love *(agapē)*, and communion *(koinonia)*. I shall use these three terms to interpret the Christian version of the redemption of alienation but shall not attempt to historically expound and exegete their various meanings in their textual settings. I do hope to explore and interpret the realities to which these terms attest. Communion is simply the over-all term for relation characterized by reconciliation and *agapē*. *Ecclesiality* is the term for the community whose ideal relationality is communion. Reconciliation and *agapē* are not terms for two different things or two stages of redemption. They are simply descriptions of communion from different angles, the one from the angle of the overcoming of alienation, the other from the angle of relation itself.

Prompted by the considerations of systematizing redemption into an *ordo salutis*, Christian theology has often assigned reconciliation and agapic relation to stages of individual salvation. Commonsense would seem to support this view. Differences must first be settled, things made right, before people have relations of love. This chronology of agential salvation also has support from the forensic aspect of the theological tradition. The requirements of divine justice and law must first be satisfied (by atonement) as the condition of our eventual and actual remaking. Accordingly, forensic reconciliation and justification are preceding conditions of agapic relation. But another piece of the Christian paradigm contradicts this priority of reconciliation to agapic relation. Divine love is the basis and condition of the whole drama of salvation. And when human beings become alienated, love is the impetus toward and possibility of reconciliation. *Agapē* in other words is the parent of forgiveness: forgiveness is not the parent of *agapē*. In the following exposition, I shall join with the nonforensic strand of interpretation and shall argue that reconciliation is simply agapic relation as it confronts alienation. I shall try to show why agapic relation is the condition of reconciling forgiveness.

Agapic Relation

Past interpretations of *agapē* place a heavy burden on anyone who would use the term. This burden is the notion that *agapē* is so utterly unique as to be the opposite of all other kinds of human love. A host of unfortunate consequences ensue from this view. If ordinary love involves human desires and emotions, *agapē* must be empty of such. If ordinary love is drawn toward qualities of its object, *agapē* must be indifferent to all qualities, else it depends on considerations of merit. If agapic relation arises only from a special supernatural grace, it must be absent from the ordinary forms of human intimacy. The interpretation I would offer departs radically from this conventional view. At the same time it retains one element of that view, namely that agapic relation or communion is not simply another term for the naturally egocentrical intimacies of everyday life. I shall try to affirm what at first sight seems to be two exclusive views. The first is that agapic relation or communion is a relation of face in the fullest sense of face and is present wherever human beings are thous to each other in that sense. Agapic relation is a relation of both compassionate obligation and mutually appreciating affection. The second is that the beauty to which agapic relation is oriented is not simply the visible beauty of physical form and social function, beauty determined by a society's way of valuing hierarchies of intelligence, morality, and function but is the beauty constitutive of creatures as such.

1. According to the first part of the thesis, agapic relation is a relation of faces in the fullest sense of the word, a relation experienced in familial and other intimacies in virtually all human societies. In preceding chapters I described the elemental passion for the interhuman, its corruption in false dependency and cynicism, and its transformation into a way of desiring the other beyond the hegemony of egocentrism. What *agapē* desires as a passionate freedom is relation in the midst of others in forms of affection and mutual appreciation. Two aspects of the face are present in this reference. The first, articulated by Levinas, is the vulnerable face which summons to compassionate obligation. The second is the beautiful face, the beauty of personhood itself, which evokes affection and caring-for. *Agapē* as a freedom is a passion for the face in both of these aspects.

It is just the face in these senses we find present in the everyday life intimacies of love affairs, friendships, and parenting. Friends are caught up in a relation that draws them beyond their natural egocentrism. They desire and find satisfactions that take place in the "between" in which each participant is fulfilled only as the other is fulfilled. These communions of friendship or of parenting are experienced in a variety of emotions. And these emotions are connected with what makes the other respected, attractive, and beautiful. But we would surely caricature these relations if we claimed that they were based on the degree to which the loved other was meritorious, useful, or pleasure-giving. As genuine relations, they draw the participants out of self-fulfillment preoccupations into the "between." They occur always as gifts individuals make to each other. Communions, relations of self-transcending affection and appreciation, do occur in various human communities. And to the extent that these agapic relations break the hold of false dependence and cynicism and transcend natural egocentrism, they bespeak the presence of the sacred.

Communion or agapic relation is a relation governed by both aspects of the face, the summons to respond in compassionate obligation to the vulnerable face and the mutual appreciation of beauty that ends in affection.

But does not the appreciation of beauty imply that agapic relation is simply a form of eros, a relation dominated by desire and fulfillment? Does it not make worthy qualities (e.g., beauty) conditions of love, thus making agapic relation more a work than a gift? Even as the various freedoms do not abolish but retain an egocentric element, the human being's orientation to satisfactions, so agapic relation does not abolish affection based on desire. Affection and the mutual appreciation of beauty are intrinsic to agapic relation if (1) it is a true relation of thous; (2) it is carried in actual emotions and not just intellectual apprehensions; and (3) it is not utterly indifferent to the being of those in relation. An agapic relation utterly devoid of mutual appreciation is virtually unimaginable. Such a relation would prohibit us from appreciating the fact of the other's existence, the fact of its livingness, its features of historicity, its thou-ness, and its distinctive ways of being these things. Such appreciations occur alongside negative judgments of accusation and repulsion and are covertly at work even in conflicts with enemies. Any view that makes agapic relation indifferent to the being of the other promotes the illusion that the relation yields no satisfactions to the participants, empties the relation of emotions, and has no way of accounting for why the relation is a response to a specific person.

2. According to the second part of the thesis, something draws persons together in agapic relation that is not just varieties of attractions and the pathetic beauty of the face. The mutual attractions of everyday life take place along biological and functional lines. Physiologically based tendencies of bodily life play a part in the affections that attend mating and parenting. Social functions of mutual protection, enjoyment, and play take place along lines of territory, race, sex, ethnic groups, and even age. Genuine affections and even mutual commitments that entail personal sacrifice do arise with these relations. Such relations express a natural social egocentrism, a natural ethnocentrism. And when alienation arises, its healing depends on staying within the criteria for beauty and importance set by these social divisions. Reconciliations do occur in families, among friends, and even in racist and oppressive groups, but they inevitably have the character of restoring the relation to its bases in the societally set criteria of worth. But this is not a reconciliation and agapic relation with the alien other, the other whose beauty is invisible because it does not fit the group's criteria.

The mutual appreciation and affection of agapic relation is not based on these ethnocentric loyalties. Its affection does not arise simply from the appreciation of qualities that follow societally based hierarchies of worth or beauty. Agapic relation does not repudiate actual and visible beauty. To do so would be to repudiate the actual being of the participants. But it does discern, feel, and respond to a beauty and worth which transcend the definitions of natural ethnocentrism. For example, *agapē* reaches out in compassionate obligation to persons in trouble, who are suffering, who are poor, who are victimized. This reaching out is not an indifference to their beauty and worth. If it were such an indifference, it would not be agapic relation but patronizing self-serving or the cold-blooded improvement of an object. But *agapē* senses something about the other simply as a living creature which is proper to support and aid. That something is not simply the abstract fact of need. It is the beauty of the creature as creature, a fit of form and function that comes about with creatureliness itself. In agapic relation we are drawn to that about the face which is not identical with ethnocentric criteria of beauty and worth. We sense a beauty which is not species or culture specific but which is drawn from the larger community of beauty of creatures as such. In agapic relation we sense in each other a worth and beauty behind our manifest limitations, neuroses, and idolatries. Agapic relation thus includes but is not based on the biological functions and social hierarchies of worth. Thus, for instance, if friendship is also an agapic relation, it is not simply based on attractions founded in racial, gender, and national systems of value. This is why the intimate relations of affection that form in connection with societal and natural divisions are not as such agapic relations.

Communion (koinonia) is a transethnocentric and agapic form of human being-together. Communion is a possibility only if the love human beings have toward each other is able to transcend natural ethnocentric criteria of beauty and worth. And what draws us past ethnocentric criteria is the hidden beauty of creatures in their vulnerable existence and livingness. How is that hidden beauty sensed or felt? The same presence that draws the human individual beyond egocentrism to vitality and wonder is needed to create a relation based on the worth and beauty of the creature as such. For there is no creature as such apart from a vast dance of creatures whose tune and rhythm is the presence of the sacred. It is the sacred that provides a frame of reference for worth and meaning as such.

This mutual relation of transethnocentric affection based on a worth and beauty that the sacred communicates to creatures is the meaning of communion (koinonia). The early Christian movement understood itself as a community, an *ecclesia,* in just these terms. Like all human communities, its actual life was rent by alienations. But the criteria which guided its criticism of these alienations were the universal criteria of agapic relation, not the specific criteria of worth and beauty which defined Roman or Greek culture, masters and slaves, or men and women. This is not to say these criteria were absent from the ecclesial community. Patriarchalism and other ethnocentric criteria abounded. At the same time, it is clear that the *ecclesia* refused to define communion in those terms. Thus, in its criteriological sense, *ecclesia* means a community whose ideal is agapic relation or communion.[9]

Reconciliation

The actual human communities we know are environments of alienated relations and not just pure embodiments of agapic relations. As we have seen, alienation describes the rending of relation by violation, resentment, and guilt. I have contended that there are no quantitative equivalents, no reparations, for violation's wounds. How then is communion (agapic relation) possible? The early Christian movement attested to a redemption of the interhuman in its notion of *agapē* and in its experience of communion. But from the very beginning and throughout its history, it has interpreted this redemption by a confusing mix of metaphors taken from the sphere of the social (forensics, law) and from the interhuman (love, forgiveness). Metaphors taken from society's legal system center around desert and punishment and create the expectation that something can happen to satisfy the guilt incurred by violation. The result is that the dynamics of forgiveness pertinent to the sphere of relation is displaced by the dynamics of punishment pertinent to societal ordering. I shall attempt to interpret reconciliation without recourse to the forensic metaphors which have so dominated Christian theology.

Resentment and guilt constitute the wound of violation. The reason this wound is seemingly unhealable is that resentment and guilt constitute an enduring or structural and not just momentary change in relation. A historical being cannot but respond in resentment to personal deprivations of its being, and violations cannot occur without eliciting from the face accusation and an unfulfillable obligation. When thous in relation are violated, the face exercises a new kind of hold or power over their relation. Although we are talking about relation itself, we can best explicate this hold by exploring the way the face exercises a hold over each thou, the violator, and the violated.

First, the face exercises a hold over the violated in the form of resentment. This resentment is not the mere fact of being violated but is an accusation. It says to all violators, personal and anonymous, "You have deprived me of being." The antipathy and accusation of that message is a hold of the face over the being of the violated. It fixes or holds modes of antipathy in the violated and holds the violated in alienation. Second, the face exercises a similar power over the violator. For insofar as

9. For an extended analysis of the transethnic or universal reference of the ecclesial community, see Edward Farley, *Ecclesial Man,* chap. 7, C.

violators are aware of the face at all, they are aware not only of the face of the accusing other but indirectly of their own self-accusing face. They are aware, in other words, of the unfulfillable obligation which now rends the relation. However much the violator may desire a reparation and even attempt to make things right, the violated face continues its resentful accusation. All efforts to pay the bill fail, disabled in advance by the accusation of the face. The face, thus, exercises a power over both the violator and the violated, rending the alienated relation with an unhealable wound.

We are now in a position to explore the one thing that can heal the unhealable wound of alienation. The hold or power of violated and accusing face must somehow be broken. The religious tradition's term for this one thing that breaks the hold of guilt is forgiveness. Forgiveness can mean simply an act or posture an individual directs toward another, a one-way act that occurs not in the sphere of relation but in the intentionality of the agent. But the forgiveness of reconciliation involves both violator and violated in relation. "Forgive us our trespasses even as we forgive those who trespass against us." This prayer concerns relation not subjectivity. Forgiveness enters an alienated relation as a power which confronts the domination of the accusing face. The violated cannot reconcile because of its resentment and accusation. The violator cannot reconcile because of its self-accusation and the unfulfillable obligation that frustrates all reparation. The violated must somehow be released from its resentment and demand on the violator and the violated must be released from its insistence on an impossible reparation. Forgiveness addresses both of these holds of the face. For the violated, forgiveness means a transcending of the accusing face, a breaking of the hold of the power of resentment. For the violator forgiveness means an acceptance of the impossibility of reparation and a transcending of its self-accusing face. Without forgiveness, the violator can never perceive nor accept the transcending of the violated toward the face.

Forgiveness, then, in the sphere of relation is a way of being-together in mutual acceptance which relativizes and places in the background the accusing power of the face. In order to describe forgiveness, I have approached it from the angles of the participating individuals as violators and victims. Reciprocal not one-directional violations bring about human alienation. Thus, when the participants in alienated relation experience forgiveness, they are not experiencing simply something from one side or the other of violation but a merger of two transcendings. In other words, to experience forgiveness is to experience release both from the hold of self-accusation and unfulfillable obligation and the hold of resentment.

How can forgiveness ever take place? How can the awesome power of the accusing face be transcended? It should be clear that forgiveness is not a *causi sui;* it does not generate itself. This is one reason it is not logically or chronologically prior to agapic relation. On the contrary, agapic relation is the possibility and power of reconciling forgiveness. Reconciliation, in fact, is nothing else than the exercise of agapic relation in the situation of alienation. For alienation to be overcome, the power of the face, the hold of accusation, resentment, and unmeetable obligation must be broken. Something other than the hold of mutual obligation must govern relation. But this something else is just what agapic relation is. The something more is the hidden beauty manifest in being a creature that evokes appreciation and affection. Thus, the resenting victim discerns something more in the violator than intentions and agendas of evil, and the violator discerns that the unfulfillable obligation is not an absolute obstacle to mutual affection. Set against the background of creatureliness and the dance of life under the sacred, the face and its response to violation is relativized. In agapic relation human beings relate to each other through a larger, even cosmic background which does not reduce beauty to the territories and hierarchies of ordinary loyalties. They relate to each other in and through their penultimate status as creatures of the sacred and as participants in the reality, goodness, and beauty of being. Like the effecting of powers of freedom in the sphere of individuals, the redemption of the interhuman comes about through the presence of the sacred. Agapic relation or communion is the presence of the sacred in the sphere of thous.[10]

How does communion or agapic relation actually come about? How does it originate? Since redemption occurs from the presence of the sacred, the question is as unanswerable in the sphere of the interhuman as it is in the sphere of agents. No one has access to the way in which the sacred is present in the creaturely. Even the most literal and immediate Christological discourses do not explicate that immediacy. We can, however, explore the origin of communion in a limited sense.

First, because relation is a way thous discover ways of being-together as thous over time, the sphere of relation and therefore of alienation is receptive to the influences of the participating individuals. In their primary form, relations are carried by the ongoing actual reciprocities of individuals and the various postures, intentions, and acts of individuals shape these reciprocities. I have traced how these postures can reflect the corruption of historicity, embodiment, and the elemental passions. In other

10. One of the most important twentieth-century texts on communion, especially as a communion of love, is Dietrich Bonhoeffer's *The Communion of Saints: A Dogmatic Inquiry into the Sociology of the Church* (New York and London: Harper and Row, 1960), 118–36.

words, the dynamics and postures of idolatry affect how we exist toward each other. And these reciprocities provide some of the stuff that the thou element appropriates to make relations endure. Redemption reverses this route of influence. Relation begins to be redeemed when being-founded transforms the corrupted existentials and reciprocities of individuals. The new freedoms such as vitality, wonder, and prophetic resistance become appropriated into the sphere of the "between." One of these freedoms, agapic passion, plays a special role in the redemption of the interhuman. This we would expect because what the thou element needs most of all as an ongoing carrier of agapic relation is the deep desire for the face and for being together in affectionate appreciation. If this passion remains corrupted by idolatry, there will be little or no impetus toward reconciliation. Thus, one source of redemptive influences on the sphere of relation comes from the agents and their new freedoms.

Second, communion rises from the side of the social. In that sphere large and corporate structures (institutions, traditions, and discourses) lend their awesome powers to agendas of oppression. But the resulting corrupted discourses and institutions are never merely outside or alongside of the sphere of relation but are materials that thous appropriate to bring relation into being. For instance, the elements of racism in society's discourses and institutions find their way into the sphere of the interhuman and become the stuff of relation. By the same token the redemption of the social makes available to the thou element institutional materials which promote rather than repress agapic relation. Institutions and their powers thus mediate materials that carry and promote transethnic appreciation and affection.

Neither of these routes of redemptive influence can be said to be the origin of the redemption of relation. If that were the case, redemption would originate entirely in spheres external to relation, thus eliminating the presence of the sacred from the sphere of the interhuman. But the sphere of the interhuman has its own way of being open to the sacred which is not a mere repetition of being-founded or social liberation. Martin Buber, in fact, argues that the sphere of the interhuman is the primary sphere of the divine presence, the reason being that the presence of God is a presence of a thou, a presence in relation. If this is the case, divine activity in the other spheres is secondary and derived. The sacred is present in the sphere of individuals as that which founds and gives courage. Being-founded joins with the dynamics of each individual's historicity and tragic anxieties. In the sphere of the interhuman, the sacred is also a kind of founding because only that which founds the total dance of creaturely things can draw relation past its ethnocentric form to mutual appreciation of the beauty of creatures as such.

14
SUBJUGATION: THE STRUCTURE OF SOCIAL EVIL

Behold, the eyes of the Lord God are upon the sinful kingdom. . . .

Amos 9:8

Bury the unjust thing
That some tamed into mercy, being wise,
But could not starve the tiger from its eyes
Or make it feed where beasts of mercy feed.[1]

Stephen Vincent Benét

With the flock, as is inevitable, it fares ill, and even worse. They are not tended, they are only regularly shorn. They are sent for, to do statute-labor, to pay statute-taxes; to fatten battlefields (named 'bed of honour') with their bodies, in quarrels which are not theirs. . . . Untaught, uncomforted, unfed; to pine stagnantly in fit obscuration, in squalid destitution, and obstruction: this is the lot of the millions.[2]

Thomas Carlyle

The third face of human reality is the sphere of the social. The social is that network of processes and functions by which agents institutionalize their common aims and their life together. It is the inherited context of new agents appearing on the scene. Agents pursue their aims in situations already ordered by generation-bridging institutions as comprehensive as ruling states and economic systems and as specific as families and neighborhoods. Irreducible to agents and their relations, social realities take on a life of their own and display distinctive dynamics of survival and function. At the same time, social entities

1. Stephen Vincent Benét, "John Brown's Body: A Poem," from *Selected Works of Stephen Vincent Benét.* (New York: Holt, Rinehart and Winston, 1927).
2. Thomas Carlyle, *The French Revolution,* vol. 1 (London, Eng.: J. M. Dent & Sons, Ltd., 1906), 10–11.

are not merely autonomous systems of causality isolated from and external to the other spheres of human reality. They are not machines even if their causal patterns sometimes resemble mechanisms. They are open-ended systems in which actions of agents and interpersonal relations contribute to their continual modification.

Because the social is a sphere of its own, it has its own dynamics of evil and redemption. An important strand of Christian paradigm addresses these dynamics. The present chapter continues to explore that paradigm and poses the following question. In what distinctive ways does the sphere of the social undergo corruption and perpetrate evil? In the previous chapters I inquired how evil modified the structures and functions of agents and relations. Similarly in the present chapter, I shall ask how the Christian paradigm of social evil enters and modifies the operations and structures of social systems. The task is to trace how evil originates in these operations, how it finds its way into the machinery of these systems, and how it maintains itself.

That social entities lend their awesome power to the service of evil is a visible fact of human history reported in the classic texts and philosophies of many peoples. At least four quite different ways of interpreting this fact have arisen in the philosophies and religions of the West. The most ancient view locates social evil in a vast cosmic drama in which history is corrupted by demonic powers.[3] According to the second view, the corruption of society proceeds from the actions of corrupted individuals. Thus, the legal system is corrupt because judges, lawyers, and clients are corrupt. War is waged because of the phylogenetically rooted aggressive instincts of individuals.[4] A third view sees societal evil not in moral but in psychological or ontological categories. Society is a realm of corruption because it is an impersonal they whose requirements inevitably violate the instinctual drives (Sigmund Freud) or self-surpassing historicity (Martin Heidegger) of individuals.[5] A

3. The most explicit version of this view is probably that type of Christian apocalypticism which sees human history under the temporary rule of Satan, a view present in the Synoptic Gospels, Paul, and the book of Revelation and which has continued in some form throughout the history of the Christian movement. For this motif in the Christian religion, see the multi-volume history written by Jeffrey Burton Russell. Russell begins his history prior to the Christian movement and continues it through the Middle Ages. Especially pertinent is the first volume, *The Devil: Perceptions of Evil from Antiquity to Primitive Christianity* (Ithaca, N.Y.: Cornell University Press, 1977).

4. Although Dante never really departed from the apocalyptic view of demonic-corrupted history, his great emphasis on the corruptions of the prelates, theologians, and rulers of society suggests this second view. Societal corruption is an outcome of the sins of corrupted individuals. A modern kind of religious conservatism presses this view under the conviction that society would be straightened out if piety and morality characterized the life of individuals.

5. Martin Heidegger's term is, *das Man,* the anonymous One or They. See Martin Heidegger, *Being and Time,* trans. J. MacQuarrie and Edward Robinson (London: SCM Press Ltd., 1962), no. 27.

fourth view associated with post-Enlightenment social sciences and Karl Marx traces social evil to processes intrinsic to social dynamics themselves, thus, to distributions of labor, surplus goods, and the workings of power. The following account of social evil appropriates elements from all of these views except the first. The alienation between agents and social structures appears in the theme of the social tragic which plays a role in but is not identical with social evil. Although individuals are victims of structures of evil, they also make important contributions to society's corruption. And although the dynamic operations of social systems are not in themselves sufficient explanations of subjugation, they, too, have an important function in the working of societal evil.

Interpretations of social evil in this century are not of one piece but range from general theories and comprehensive conceptual schemes (e.g., Ernst Becker, the Frankfurt School) to programmatic and strategic tracts designed to effect political change (e.g., certain ecological studies). In between these poles of generality and specificity are writings which promote the cause of an oppressed group (women, blacks, homosexuals, age groups), writings critical of specific institutions and their policies (education, government), and writings which interpret the corrupted or threatened character of modern industrial societies (Hannah Arendt, Robert Heilbroner, Herbert Marcuse). There are those who reject all genres of social criticism but their own, who would discredit, for instance, all nonstrategic analyses. In my view all of the genres on the spectrum of approaches make distinctive contributions to both the interpretation of the social and to social change. The analyses of this and the following chapter are clearly on the general end of the spectrum. They employ the conceptualities of a variety of social thinkers to disclose the power of the Hebrew and Christian paradigm to interpret corporate evil and redemption.

THE SOCIAL TRAGIC

To be victimized means to suffer at the hands of something, to be negatively and destructively affected by some event, person, or movement. In this broad sense, we human beings are victimized by nature's life-threatening diseases, earthquakes, and droughts. We are similarly victimized by social entities because institutions are not geared to promote the concrete well-being of each individual. There is thus a victimization that comes with the social that is not the effect of evil. The reasons are several. Social reality is actual only in the form of specific social entities such as tribes, clans, villages, families, and nations. And while each of these entities does order the lives of its members, there is no pre-established harmony at work to harmonize the aims of each entity with other entities. A people's migration from a drought-stricken area may threaten the stability of another people. Distributions of wealth and labor and the specialization of roles and skills spawn institutionalizations of leisure, arts, and knowledge. These institutions direct themselves to specific aims and, taking on a life of their own, compete with each other even in the society in which they are located. This problem of competing aesthetic, military, educational, and other institutions is enormously exacerbated in advanced industrial and bureaucratic societies. However self-evidently rational the case is for the importance of each institution, no social system can adequately support them all. No modern government has adequate resources for education, environmental protection, the arts, the stabilizing of its economy, defense, and waste disposal.[6] Nor is a perfect correlation possible between the operations of institutions and the aims and needs of individuals. Since the aims and needs of individuals are never identical, the best even a utopian society can do is to constrain and adjudicate those aims, thus minimizing incompatible and conflicting individual agendas.

The social tragic also means that social solutions carry with them new and ever more frightening problems. Nourishment and health care promote population levels which specific nations and finally the planet as a whole cannot sustain, resulting thus in the pollution of seas and soils and the threatened demise of thousands of species of animals and plants. The leisure and entertainment enabled by technology threaten privacy, silence, creativity, education, and the whole sphere of relation. Because nature is an open and evolutionary process, no environment of nature is without peril, injury, and death. Likewise, there can be no open-ended, fallible, and competing group of social institutions in a social system without victims. It is true that the only societies we know are societies already structured by social evil. But victimizing social incompatibilities, events, and benign alienations would inevitably be part of utopian societies.[7]

6. One of the most detailed depictions of the intrinsic conflicts and exclusions of the institutions of advanced industrial society is Robert Heilbroner, *Inquiry into the Human Prospect* (New York: Norton, 1974). Furthermore, Heilbroner projects into the near future an ever increasing set of conflicts that makes global catastrophe virtually inevitable.

7. There is something about a social entity simply as such that evokes resistance and antipathy. Human individuals rightly sense that even when a social entity, for instance, a profession, a court of law, or a theater troupe, is the source of some good and functions for the well-being of society, its operations are potentially at odds with their own specific well-being and agendas. This is why, I think, that when novels and plays depict individuals as simply representatives of social entities, however good the social entities are, the result is always something ugly and slightly ridiculous. From the time of Charles Dickens to contemporary sit-coms, it is impossible to embody the features of a group (e.g., ministers, actors, politicians, lawyers, the social elite, the young, or the old) into a character and not have an ugly result. Such individuals are ugly because they are mere embodiments of the victimizing "they," even though that "they" may function for the well-being of society.

THE CORRUPTING INFLUENCE OF AGENTS

According to one of the theories of social evil, corrupt agents are the cause of corrupt societies. Legislative bodies are corrupt because of venal politicians, universities because of lazy and lusty professors and visionless administrators. Rejecting the individualism and moralism of this approach, an opposite view argues that social evil has little to do with private morality. Yet if the spheres of human reality interpenetrate each other, each sphere's dynamics of evil will find its way into the others. Even a superficial look at social evil prompts the suspicion that somehow the agendas of idolatrous agents have become entangled in the workings of institutions. Behind the policies and actions of oppression lie self-absolutisms not unlike those that lure agents into absolutizing attachments. Institutions do not, of course, literally fear or absolutize. But many social entities do seem bent on securing themselves at any expense. The policies of many nations do seem to be directed to absolute enemies. Accordingly, the fears and absolutisms of agents appear to have found institutional embodiment. Social entities seem to embody and serve something that looks like the dynamics of idolatry. How does this happen?

There are, it seems, lines of influence between the spheres of human reality. Accordingly, social evil has so qualified the environment into which individuals are born that it shapes individual lives from their beginning. The reverse also seems true. The corrupted postures of agents shape institutions. I contended previously that the goods at hand that promised human beings the most were social goods. For what maintains and delivers the conditions of virtually all human goods are social systems and their institutions. Our search for a good which secures us against the perils of existence comes to rest in the social system. This is why social entities induce such impassioned loyalties.[8] And it is just these loyalties that mobilize our fears of social enemies and our willingness to harm and destroy on behalf of family, tribe, or nation. But loyalty to the social system is only the beginning of a complex dialectic of acts and postures. For social entities are at best only apparent absolute securers. Nations, corporations, and families are fragile and fallible. Like their members, they, too, are subject to the contingencies of nature and history, the limitations of those who guide them, and the threats of other social entities that compete with them. Hence, agents must work hard to assure the security they think they find in their social securers. They

8. In this century the philosopher who saw the importance of loyalty was Josiah Royce. See his *The Philosophy of Loyalty* (New York: The Macmillan Co., 1916). For Royce loyalty, especially loyalty to loyalty, is an important human trait and ethical principle, and not to be confused with group conflict and warfare. He does not sense to any great degree the way in which human evil exploits this trait.

must ever deploy power and symbolic reinforcement to defeat enemies within and without their social systems.

This dialectic of agential effort does not take place outside the sphere of the social, outside of nations, families, and universities. It is part of the machinery of these institutions themselves. Because the security that agents desire is not simply an inner state but a situational state of affairs, their idolatry has a certain entelechy that drives ever toward control of the environment. Thus, the idolatrous postures of agents find expression in actions directed toward shaping the social environment. Idolatrous postures and agendas show up in social entities both as an *infecting of ethos* and as activities of *collusion.*

To repeat an often-made point, there are no isolated individuals, only individuals in intersubjective and reciprocal interrelations. Human agents are so constituted that they need and seek out situations of mutual acknowledgment, communication, and even affection. This being the case, human bodily needs and tendencies, elemental passions, and even curiosities and fears are never mere private phenomena but are strong functions of human being-together. Everyday human life is a constant sharing of values, agendas, motives, and even emotions. Human interactions are at the same time sharings of meanings. And these meanings are not utterly momentary but become sedimented in language and available in the form of the society's prevailing typifications and taken-for-granted stock of knowledge (Alfred Schutz). Fear and respect of a dangerous predator in an archaic society becomes deposited in retold stories and totemic symbols. Accordingly, idolatrous postures and agendas are never simply sealed off into the interiority of each individual self. They are an aspect of everyday reciprocities and the mutual sharing of meanings. They, too, find their way into a group's taken-for-granted typifications and presupposed stock of knowledge at hand and thus into its stories and imageries. Thus the individual's absolute enemy becomes also the shared absolute enemy, the symbolic enemy of the group.[9] The individual's conviction that an ethnic group is inferior is at the same time a shared, typified, and symbolized conviction. In other words, it is a conviction of the social world of shared meanings. *Social infection* describes the spread of the dynamics of idolatry into the shared meanings of the social world.

If social infection is one aspect of the corruption of the social world, collusion is another. Human beings live together in groups and communities not simply in reciprocities of shared meanings but in agendas of

9. An excellent social study of the way discrediting attributes (stigmas) become assigned to individuals or groups is Erving Goffman, *Stigma: Notes on the Management of Spoiled Identity* (Englewood Cliffs, N.J.: Prentice-Hall, 1963). See esp. chap. 1.

cooperative action. They act on each other and they act on other things in cooperation with each other. Let us recall the direction, the entelechy, intrinsic to postures of idolatry which presses toward action and world alteration. Absolutizing postures are never content simply to identify securing goods and absolute enemies. The fragile idol requires constant protection and shoring up. Thus, human beings together do not merely mean their shared idols and enemies but enter into collusions of maintenance and opposition. Racism, accordingly, is never merely a matter of intention and meaning but of collusion and action. It not only stereotypes but subjugates and subjugation requires collusion. If shared meanings are the passive side of the route from corrupted agents to corrupt social entities, collusion is the active side. The aim of collusion is to do whatever is necessary to establish and defend the absolutized social securer. *Collusion* is a conspiracy, acknowledged or unacknowledged, to maintain the securing nation, gender, family, race, ethnic group, or even an in-group of a subculture. Its spin-offs are collusions of opposition and subjugation against whatever actually or symbolically threatens the securing entity.[10]

THE POSSIBILITY OF SOCIAL CORRUPTION

Idolatrous agents contribute to social corruption as their idolatrous postures infect the world of shared meanings and as they conspire to establish their idols and oppose their enemies. But social entities are not themselves agents reciprocally sharing meanings and engaged in conspiracies. The sphere of the social is a sphere of institutions, patterns which organize and maintain human life over periods of time and reaches of space. How is it that institutions could ever be affected by and become instruments of evil? According to social Manicheanism, social entities are intrinsically evil because their very existence violates the self-determination of agents. I have acknowledged the intrinsic alienation perpetrated by social entities (the social tragic) but want to argue that social evil does not consist in this alienation. If social evil is not the social tragic, what then is it? The first step in answering this question is to explore what it is about social entities that makes them corruptible.

Secondary Aims

Let us recall the distinction between an institution's primary and secondary aims. Primary aims are the institution's distinctive reason for

10. The phenomena of both social infection of the world of shared meanings and collusions to maintain corrupted power are articulated more by novelists than social scientists. Given the modern social scientist's determination to be objective and value neutral, this comes as no surprise. Examples of fictional treatments of collusions are Charles Dickens's treatment of the public schools in *Hard Times* and Kingsley Amis's account of what professors can do to an individual in *Lucky Jim*.

being: thus, the directives that preside over a governmental agency, a local chapter of a labor union, or a corporation's research and development team. Primary aims give rise to the institution's specific agendas, organizational pattern, and distribution of tasks. But institutions also embody and promote aims from the larger ethos of their social environment. A corporation can also promote a certain political party; a university may promote (or oppose) civil rights ideals; the book-purchasing policies of a local public library may be oriented to ecology. The secondary aims of institutions tend to be the places of entry for influences from the broader culture and thus from agents and their shared meanings and collusions. The imageries and typifications through which the everyday reciprocities between agents take place do not remain outside of institutions. They shape institutions by influencing and finally constituting their secondary aims. A corporation's general participation in the ethos of a nation's patriotism can embody imageries of fanatical superpatriotism. A university can embody as secondary aims commitments and imageries that promote one gender over another or one race over another. And both the shared world of meanings and the collusions of the members of these institutitions can contribute to the forming of these secondary aims. Groups can conspire to shape an institution toward victimizations which take place within and beyond its boundaries. However, the corruption of an institution does not stop with its corrupted secondary aims. For an institution's secondary and primary aims tend to nourish each other. Secondary aims feed back on the policies and agendas for primary aims. For instance, racism in universities, churches, corporations, and governments influences their way of understanding their primary aims and thus their hiring policies, their selection of constituencies, and their budgetary priorities.

Power

A social entity is not simply a passive recipient of social infection. It also perpetrates social evil. And it is able to perpetrate evil because it is constituted by a power that far surpasses the gathered intentions of its members. The autonomy of a social entity is its tendency to take on a life of its own. A social entity is, of course, subject to the overview of the larger society and its normative culture. But it proceeds by eliciting the energies and commitments of participants who press agendas on its behalf against those of other social entities. And when self-absolutizing imageries infect a social entity's secondary aims, the effect is to isolate it from the constraints of the larger society and from the humanizing criteria of normative culture. Everything from committees with their discrete if not trivial assignments to whole branches of government can press for autonomy and can sell this autonomy in the service of corrupt secondary aims.

According to Paul Tillich, power means the "possibility of self-affirmation in spite of internal and external negation."[11] I would alter this psychologically oriented definition only slightly and say that power is the degree to which a thing is capable of effecting changes in its environment.[12] Social entities and institutions have power in this sense. Institutions are a kind of power because they are ways in which corporate human aims are realized and perpetuated over time.[13] Insofar as things happen in and through them, their very existence is a kind of power. They organize the efforts of their members and influence their larger environments. Without language, symbols, religions, group mores, and traditions, social entities would have no persistence over time. Thus, when agendas of evil alter the primary and secondary aims of a social entity, they co-opt a vehicle of power for purposes of victimization. The victimizing power of an individual is modest compared to the victimizing power of social entities, especially comprehensive social entities that have to do with the very conditions of life and well-being.

THE NATURE OF SUBJUGATION

The analysis up until now has been preoccupied with the contributions of agents to the corruption of social entities and with what makes evil possible in the sphere of the social. But what is social evil itself? What differentiates social evil from the social tragic? Social evil can be defined either by its effects or by its dynamics. The criteria for identifying the effects of social evil are no different from those applicable to agential or relational evil. Social entities are evil if they deprive agents of being, remove their conditions of well-being, and effect suffering as an effect of these acts. Furthermore, the victimizing effects of social entities do not stop with human agents but spread over the larger environment of life-forms. However, evil in the sphere of the social is not

11. Paul Tillich, *Love, Power, and Justice: Ontological Analyses and Ethical Implications* (New York: Oxford Univ. Press, 1954), 40.

12. This definition is borne out by Elias Canetti who argues for the important distinction between force and power. Power is not actual causation but the control of the space and therefore of the possibilities of that over which it is held. His example is the cat who has power over the mouse with which it is playing, even when it has let it go. See Elias Canetti, *Crowds and Power,* trans. C. Stewart (New York: Continuum, 1960), 281–302.

13. For the way a bureaucracy exercises or is constituted as a power, see Max Weber, *From Max Weber: Essays in Sociology,* trans. and ed. Alf Gerth and C. Wright Mills (New York: Oxford, 1946), Part Two. Weber thinks a bureaucracy is the most highly developed means of social power in the hands of those who control it, and he describes how it exercises power through professionalization, secrecy, and other structures and policies.

mere victimization. Benign victimizations are perpetrated even when institutions carry out their ordinary functions. But social entities also can perpetrate malignant victimizations in which they take on a distinctive dynamics parallel to the dynamics of idolatry and violation. What makes the dynamics of social evil distinctive is that it is a dynamics of subjugation. Subjugation occurs when, driven by self-absolutizing imageries, the social entity uses its power to promote itself by victimizing a targeted group. More specifically, subjugation occurs when the particularism that characterizes all social entities turns into the violent utilization of selected groups: races, children, women, and ethnic groups. How does this happen?

Subjugation presupposes an infection of the world of shared meanings. What is the effect of this infection on institutions and social entities? Clearly, social infection does not itself bring about the particularities of history. The territorial locations and special features of differentiated populations, nations, and ethnic groups are not as such signs of infection. Social particularity itself is not evil nor is it the outcome of evil. However, social particularity is the good from which subjugation launches itself. Self-absolutizing imageries and collusions against absolute enemies can co-opt and infect the social worlds of nations, school, villages, races, and age-groups. Self-absolutization can corrupt the shared social identities of human beings.

But why does a group's self-absolutizing move to victimize and subjugate another group? It is willing to victimize because its self-absolutizing removes all elements of the face from its way of perceiving other social groups. For it is the face translated into the imageries of a social world that creates a common world of obligations between groups. And since intended victimization faces the resistance of the other group, victimization requires the violent mobilization of power. A social entity is willing to subjugate when, minus the face, it regards the targeted group as either a menace or a means to its aims. *Subjugation,* then, is a social entity's *utilization* of another targeted group by means of *violence.*

Utilization

All social entities and institutions are historically fragile. Their members sense this and work to help their institutions to function, compete, and endure. Institutions, in other words, build into themselves self-preserving operations. Thus, a church not only perpetuates the "faith once delivered" through ritualistic and interpretative acts but develops ways to preserve and protect these institutional functions. When a social entity maintains self-preserving functions through absolutizing imageries, it will do anything and everything to establish its place, power, and status by making use of weaker groups at hand. One people conquers another and uses selected populations of the conquered as its enslaved servants, soldiers, or even educators. One group which identifies itself by features of physiognomy promotes its well-being at the expense of a utilized laboring group of different color; thus, the Aryans of ancient India, colonizing and enslaving Western Europeans and North Americans, and present-day South Africans. An aristocratic elite creates a system of status along hereditary lines and thereby acquires the service of a menial and lower class. The males of a society create a social system reinforced by primary symbols that remove females from the public realm, the arts, and meaningful careers. Utilization is clearly not the mere fact that differentiations of societal function reflect differentiated abilities. Some individuals are larger, faster, stronger, braver, or smarter than others and accordingly may be elevated to leadership in hunting or tribal rule in archaic societies. But group membership, not qualification, is the basis of utilization and victimization.

Violence

The other aspect of subjugation takes place as groups anticipate the resisting capabilities of utilized groups. Subjugated groups are an intrinsic threat to subjugators because human beings oppose deprivations of their being and resent the arbitrariness of a lower status simply because of their group membership, the mere fact that they are women, black, rural, or elderly. Because of this resentment and potential opposition, subjugation requires mechanisms of violence that anticipate and manage covert and overt resistances. Except in times of overt revolution and in cases of specific law enforcements, the violent aspect of subjugation is more a structural than an eventful and highly visible operation. It is the subjugating group's "readiness to . . . ," and this readiness is expressed in systems of enforcement able to be mobilized when needed.[14]

To summarize, there is a distinctive evil that arises in the social sphere. It occurs when a human group or social entity establishes itself by violently utilizing another group. The resulting inferior status and lowered conditions of well-being go hand in hand.

14. Subjugation is a violence that alters the relation between the agent and the social "they." Even without subjugation, that relation has an alienating character because the anonymity and generality of social aims cannot take into account the individual's personhood and personal aims. But with the unstated violence of subjugation, the they becomes a subjugating they, and they that is not simply anonymously and impersonally over against the agent but which has selected the agent for harm because of some arbitrary feature or membership; that is, because of the agent's gender, race, class, etc. The "they," in other words, takes on the characteristics of an oppressor. It is thus a violent "they."

THE INSTITUTIONALIZATION OF SOCIAL EVIL

According to the analysis so far, evil turns the secondary aims of social entities toward subjugating functions. But this is only the beginning of the corruption of social entities. For when social entities lend the full power of their workings to subjugation, much more is involved than the corruption of their secondary aims. This analysis can do little justice to the complexity of actual subjugation. I can only note that if advanced industrial societies are our subject, subjugation is carried out in the powerful institutions of property and rule and in institutions which carry normative culture. Furthermore, it is important to trace the way in which normative culture functions in the violent utilization of the subjugated group and how subjugation co-opts institutions of property and rule.

Normative Culture

In this essay I have used the term, *culture,* in Talcott Parsons's sense to describe that which gives a social system its sense of direction and which articulates and carries its aesthetic and moral ethos. With normative culture come distinctive institutions whose primary aims include discovering, preserving, and passing on convictions about what is good, useful, beautiful, right, and important. The typical institutions of normative culture are family, education, the arts, and religion. In these institutions are carried the society's normative myths, narratives, and primary symbols. And it is virtually inevitable that the convictions of normative culture have some presence and function in the secondary aims of most institutions.

A thesis is now in order. The imageries and agendas of evil spread to secondary aims of institutions of property and rule from their primary location in the institutions of normative culture. Insofar as the subjugations of social evil infect the shared meanings of the social world, they will restructure the convictions and institutions of normative culture. Normative culture thus takes on and perpetuates symbolisms (e.g., patriarchal mythologies) and traditions of interpretation (e.g., racist ways of interpreting Scripture). And it is the institutions of normative culture that mask subjugation by euphemistic symbols that render subjugated populations marginal if not invisible. Thus, institutions of education develop cognitive modes, pedagogies, and mappings of knowledge that serve subjugation. The symbolisms and organizational structures of religions legitimate the status quo of subjugating power. The result of this corruption of normative culture is that the very criteria that define a society's goods provide a rationale for the violent utilization of targeted groups.

Property and State

The discourse and institutions of normative culture give symbolic and convictional reinforcement to subjugation. But subjugation remains relatively innocuous as long as it fails to reach the institutions that "make things happen," the locations of societal power. Since the formation of the great civilizations several thousand years prior to the Christian era, the two great locations of social power are institutions of property and the State.[15] Even though they are distinguishable aspects of the social system, the two are closely bound up together. Actual subjugation is rarely if ever a merely symbolic act. Behind the assignment of inferior status to a designated group are the actual advantages gained for the group in power. And these advantages invariably have to do with the system of property and invariably require the law enforcements of the State. Actual subjugation then requires using the power of institutions of property and rule. Social evil can have such awesome and seemingly undefeatable power precisely because it becomes a structural part of these comprehensive institutions. Social evil then is not simply the violations that occur between individuals or even the infection of the social world of shared meanings. It is the subjugating functions and structures of institutions of property and rule, rendered normal and right by the corrupted normative culture.

Regimes

When subjugation is reinforced by institutions of property and rule and institutions of normative culture, it is not just spatially pervasive but temporally extended. The very function of institutions is to so order human enterprises that they endure over time and do not disappear with each setting sun. The more comprehensive institutions are, the slower they are to change, and the more they tend to create societal features that persist over generations. In other words, comprehensive institutions of property, rule, leisure, and religion tend to create epochs. Michel Foucault calls these total systems that prevail over an extended time, *regimes,* and the discourse that they bring into existence to serve them, *epistēmes.*[16] Power, then, is not restricted to each institution as a quasi-autonomous social entity but accrues to the total regime formed by interdependent institutions. Regimes of power form from seminal though often hidden events and have structural aspects that endure throughout their epoch. This

15. For an excellent analysis of these two institutions, see Wolfhart Pannenberg, *Anthropology in Theological Perspective* (Philadelphia: Westminster Press, 1985), chap. 8, II. and IV.

16. Michel Foucault, *The Archaeology of Knowledge and the Discourse on Language* (New York: Harper and Row, 1972).

being the case, any actual description of the corruption of the sphere of the social must address the origin and distinctive features of the regime and its epistēme or reigning discourse, a task which Foucault, borrowing from Friedrich Nietzsche, terms *archaeology.*[17]

THE SELF-PRESERVING MECHANISMS OF SOCIAL EVIL

Human evil as violation leaves distinctive prints of alienation (resentment, guilt) on interpersonal relation. Does evil as subjugation leave its own distinctive prints? The question sounds inappropriate since subjugation is itself a kind of imprint, a structural alteration of institutions that works to victimize and deprive. But subjugation does effect certain mechanisms in social entities that look very much like rationalization in individuals and the imprint of alienation in relation. The function of these mechanisms is to maintain the subjugating structure against what resists it by transforming it into something accepted and normal. These mechanisms are an intrinsic structural aspect of subjugation.

As history has taught us, subjugation is often visible and dramatic. We are familiar with societies and epochs victimized by the Ahabs, the Borgias, the Hitlers, and Stalins, societies that practice genocide on their external competitors and their internal scapegoat populations, and societies that exert collectivist control over all aspects of life. But we perceive the subjugating character of these societies more easily from the distances of space and time. Both the subjugated and the subjugating populations of these societies may fail to perceive their social system and their epoch as evil. Most advanced industrial societies would differentiate themselves from these dramatic examples of the misuse of power, from nineteenth-century colonialism, empire-building imperialism, fascism, Big Brother (George Orwell) collectivism, and South African racism. Societies tend to be unaware of their own subjugating structures, and what effects this lack of awareness are mechanisms whose specific function is to render evil banal, euphemistic, and invisible. One mechanism of disguise has to do with the way subjugation is violently maintained.[18] In periods of revolution, transition, and social instability, violence may be very much in evidence. But in stable periods violence is publicly manifest primarily in connection with the pursuit of

17. Specific instances of Foucault's archaeological investigations are his works on madness, prisons, health care, and sexuality. Thus, *The Birth of the Clinic: An Archaeology of Medical Perception,* trans. A. M. S. Smith (New York: Pantheon Books, 1973), and, *Madness and Civilization: A History of Insanity in the Age of Reason,* trans. R. Howard (New York: Vintage Books, 1973).

18. For an excellent account of violence as distinguished from power, see Hannah Arendt, *On Violence* (New York: Harcourt, Brace and Javonovich, 1969), chap. 2.

criminals and self-evidently justified military operations. The masking of subjugation may be partly rooted in the refusal of subjugators to acknowledge even to themselves the victimizing effects of the social system they take for granted. But what disguises subjugation from the subjugated or victimized populations is the embodiment of subjugation in normative culture, that is, in the institutions that mediate morality, value, and importance. When this happens, subjugation appears normal and is something to be taken for granted. Thus, the divisions between the elite and the disenfranchised are symbolized as natural and good. The subjugation of a race is legitimated by myths of natural inferiority which are confirmed by empirical evidences of poor social performances, themselves the offspring of subjugation. Another part of the masking machinery is the routinizing of subjugation into expected and normal roles in the workplace, the family, and the governing body.[19] When subjugation is routinized, it becomes acceptable, taken for granted, and part of the everyday world. At worst it is perceived as an annoyance, a frustration, a minor flaw in an imperfect society which only utopians would try to eliminate. This is what Hannah Arendt means by the banality of evil.[20] Social evil is banal when it is carried out in the routine operations of bureaucracies and other institutions.

Masking is not the only mechanism that maintains evil in social systems. There are also mechanisms of control that anticipate and preempt resistance to and criticism of the subjugation structures. In times of instability and revolt, mechanisms of control are overt, visible, and violent. In other times they are the covert ways in which institutions work to prevent resistance from rising in the first place. Accordingly, institutions of subjugation routinely attempt to constrain social institutions especially concerned with the interpretation of society: the press, the sciences, the universities, and religion. Herbert Marcuse argues that new mechanisms that paralyze criticism have arisen with advanced industrial societies. These include life-styles and mind-sets of consumption and leisure that produce a distracting contentment that eliminates the modes of thinking and interpreting that criticism requires. Thus, the life-style of comfort itself produces a vast indifference to subjugation.

19. Charles Dickens, anticipating the literary muckrakers (B. F. Norris, for instance) of 1930s America, wrote novels about mid-century Victorian England and the effect of the industrial revolution on all aspects of life: the new economics, utilitarian philosophy, education, the court system, religion. A recurring theme is how everyday modes of thought and routine behaviors mask even to the victims the unspeakable daily horrors of life in the schools, the factories, the families.

20. Hannah Arendt, *Eichmann in Jerusalem: A Report on the Banality of Evil* (New York: Viking Press, 1963). See esp. chap. 8, "Duties of a Law-abiding Citizen." Arendt describes Eichmann and others perpetrating horrors by simply going about their day-to-day duties as ordinary bureaucrats.

15
SOCIAL REDEMPTION

> I have a dream that one day every valley shall be exalted, every hill and mountain shall be made low, the rough places shall be made plain, and the crooked places shall be made straight and the glory of the Lord will be revealed and all flesh shall see it together.[1]
>
> *Martin Luther King, Jr.*

Previous chapters describe the redemption of human evil in the spheres of agents and relations. Is the sphere of the social open to redemption? Are deep structures of subjugation redemptively transformable? When societies disguise their subjugating operations, victims experience them as something natural, even as something authorized by a cosmic order. Social redemption is thus perceived to be neither necessary nor desirable. Both tragic and apocalyptic forms of social Manicheanism help maintain this acquiescence. The one identifies social evil with the alienations between agents and institutions; the other identifies history itself with the rule of a demonic power. Our suspicions about these views are aroused when we realize that these songs about resistance as futile reinforce subjugation. The refrain of all social Manicheanisms is, The miseries of subjugation are as inevitable as the perils of nature. Let us bear up under both burdens.

THE POSSIBILITY OF SOCIAL REDEMPTION

Two insights prompt us to turn these suspicions of self-serving social Manicheanism into explicit criticisms. The first is an evident fact of human history, the fact that subjugating powers do fail. Social groups and institutions do undergo corrections and reversals that reduce subjugating elements and bring about more viable forms of social life. To be sure, these corrections are ongoing and relative. In this respect they resemble the redemptions of agents and relations. Social redemption like all redemption is not an all-or-nothing process, at work only if all of human history is perfected. Social redemption means transformation in a certain direction, not a return to Eden or the building of

1. Martin Luther King, Jr., *A Testament of Hope: The Essential Writings of Martin Luther King, Jr.*, ed. James M. Washington (San Francisco: Harper and Row, 1986), 219.

utopia. Subjugation is distributed over myriads of institutions that range from regimes of power (nations, empires, epochs) to local and ephemeral social entities. Redemptive corrections and reversals can and do occur in varying ways throughout this range.

The second criticism of social Manicheanism pertains to how we understand the relation between social evil and the intrinsic features of the social sphere. None of these features requires subjugation as the condition of its existence. However much social evil corrupts social entities, it has no ontological status. That is to say, subjugation is not an a priori feature of institutionality, discourse, primary and secondary aims, divisions of labor, traditioning, or normative culture. A social entity does not have to subjugate in order to organize agential action, exist over time, or produce enduring imageries. It does seem to be the case, however, that the very existence of different social entities involves competitions and incompatibilities that effect tragic victimizations. Nor is there ever absolute harmony between the aims and functions of social entities and those of their participating agents. A similar absence of harmony attends the relations between agents and the events and processes of nature. Yet these incompatibilities are not as such subjugations. And it is because subjugation is not an ontological feature of the social that redemptive corrections can occur. However, criticism of social Manicheanism is only a negative way of understanding the redemptive possibilities of the sphere of the social. The social is not only redeemable, that is, its subjugation reversible, but it can be an environment that correlates with and promotes the freedom of agents and agapic relations. Institutions can contain and sediment imageries that promote courage, wonder, and vitality. Normative culture and social processes can be vehicles of agapic relations.

The possibility and occurrence of social redemption throughout history has not gone unnoticed. It is eloquently articulated in the historical texts of Judaism and Christianity. Prophetic criticism was directed to actual powers of subjugation with the expectation that these powers can be and will be overthrown. Prophetic eschatology anticipated the replacement of present subjugating regimes by future regimes of justice. Influenced especially by Jewish apocalypticism and by notions in the ancient world that pervasive institutions of property and rule were ahistorical manifestations of cosmic realities, the early Christian movement had a more or less fatalistic attitude about the historical redeemability of the "city of Satan" prior to the eschaton. Even so, the Christian movement continued to criticize particular forms of subjugation throughout its history.[2]

2. For an extensive historical study of the early Christian movement that identifies both its patriarchalism and its liberating elements, see Elizabeth Schüssler Fiorenza, *In Memory of Her: A Feminist Reconstruction of Christian Origins* (New York: Crossroad, 1983).

The following exploration of the redemption of the social in the Christian paradigm takes place in two steps. In the first, I focus on the vision or ideal of the social sphere as a sphere of human well-being, thus, theonomous sociality. The issue here is the nature and content of a social order of emancipation and theonomy. In the second, I focus on how this ideal comes about, how redemption transforms the powerful structures and processes of the social sphere.

Emancipation: The Negative Aspect of Social Redemption

Visions of corporate good and well-being, of ideal social order, rarely if ever arise in conjunction with mere speculation about possibilities. They are engendered rather by the sufferings of present subjugations. The actors in these visions are victims who resist subjugation and others who empathetically and strategically adopt their cause. Insofar as actual victimizing subjugations are the context of envisioned social well-being, the articulation of that vision has a negative character that reflects the desperation of the subjugated. By negative I mean that what is envisioned is a liberation from, displacement of, or emancipation from. Negatively defined, the redeemed social order means the absence of subjugation. It is the elimination of the tyrant's boot on the neck, the violation of rights, and of the dehumanizing of scapegoat populations. From the Hebrew prophets to the Frankfurt School and from black theology to feminism, exposers of subjugation engender literatures of protest and calls for emancipation.

Emancipatory movements call for the removal of subjugation in typical and recurring themes. Their literatures passionately describe the pitiful plight of the subjugated, the intense sufferings of victims. They identify subjugating ruling power (kings, church leaders, governments) and systemic structures (the relation of temple and rule, of economy and politics). Post-Marxist hermeneutics exposes the apparently benign discourses and institutions that mask subjugation and remove possible criticism. These themes express what subjugating powers would suppress, the originating events, the euphemistic imageries, and the covert operations of subjugation. And these movements focus on these things not just to understand but to change, to mount agendas of action that would reduce or eliminate subjugation.

Accordingly, emancipation or liberation from subjugation is the way the movements of resistance articulate ideal sociality. The symbolic term, *liberation,* bespeaks the intense and always contemporary desperation of the victimized; the nourishment and medical attention needed this very instant, the pained and self-abnegating self-understanding shaped by the stereotypes of subjugators, the deprivations of cultural resources of beauty and meaning. This is the victim described by Edwin Markham as " . . . . dead to rapture and despair, a thing that grieves not and that never hopes. . . "[3] We should not, however, assume that these negative symbols have no positive content. Positive criteria of human well-being are unavoidably present in the resistance to subjugation and in arguments for emancipation. Some of them pertain to the conditions of physical well-being, to environments of infant survival, bodily growth, and continuing health. The face, the distinctive violability of persons that evokes compassionate obligation, is present in criteria of equality, rights, and agential freedom. All protests against dehumanizing and negative stereotypes presuppose the face. Subjugations of this sort deprive persons of rights by abolishing their claims to be human: that is, their claims to be self-transcending, mysterious, personal, and relational.

But the focus of emancipation is not on these positive criteria but on the sufferings of victimization and the powers that perpetrate them. We should not be surprised that the articulation of positive criteria plays a secondary role in emancipation. Positive criteria originate not in the social sphere but in the spheres of agency and relation. Natural and social conditions may be necessary environments of human well-being, but the criteria for these environments as good or bad come from the physical and personal needs of individuals. This is not to say that there are no criteria for social well-being. But the criteria that do express healthy and functional societies refer back to agents, relations, and the face. This is why movements and literatures of emancipation not only place their causes at risk but court becoming themselves new systemic subjugations when they ignore their own presupposed agential and relational criteria.

Social Theonomy: The Transcending of Centrism

The Christian vision of redeemed sociality is not simply a vision of emancipation, a projected nonsubjugating social order. Nor is it simply the application of agential and relational criteria to the social sphere. The sphere of the social embodies its own distinctive form of human evil (subjugation) and its own distinctive form of social well-being (theonomous sociality). Comprehensive social well-being has found expression in such concepts as justice and in the trilogy of symbols of the French revolution, liberty, fraternity, and equality. But these concepts do not add up to the Christian vision of social well-being. A comprehensive interpretation of

3. Edwin Markham, "The Man with the Hoe," from *The Man with the Hoe and Other Poems* (New York: Double, Page and Co., 1920), 15, 17.

social well-being is closely tied to the interpretation of how the social sphere is corrupted. The interpretation of this corruption I have offered in this volume focuses especially on how something parallel to the idolatry of agents finds its way into the operations of institutions. This means, specifically, that the tragic conflicts and the natural centrisms of institutions (of home, village, nation, ethnic group) are corrupted into self-absolutizing centrisms. Theonomous sociality then has to do with how a society manages and transcends its tragic conflicts and its natural centrisms.

Two tragic aspects are structural features of the sphere of the social. According to the first, institutions create victims when their good and ordering functions compete with each other. Societies shower victimizations on their members from their very efforts to adjudicate, defend, educate, distribute wealth, preserve freedom, and constrain power. The resulting sufferings and victimizations are not necessarily the products of subjugation. But insofar as these victimizations are inevitable outcomes of the fallibilities, contingencies, and competitions of social entities, we cannot expect redemption to eliminate them. To do so would mean eliminating the autonomies, powers, and functions necessary to the very existence of social entities. Social evil arises when, however we account for it, the autonomies and aims of social institutions become absolute, when they seek their goods by designating other groups as simply their means or their enemies. Thus, the autonomous powers intrinsic to institutions become instruments of subjugation. If this is the case, a redemptive community (or group, institution) must not only find a way to pursue its goods without subjugation; it must relativize and constrain its institutions in their autonomous functions and find a way to maximize their cooperation.

The second tragic aspect of the social is the inevitable noncorrespondence or benign alienation that characterizes the relation between agents in their self-surpassing historicity and the requirements set on them by the social as an anonymous and impersonal "they." This alienation is an intrinsic and not accidental feature of the relation between agents and institutions. It is not, however, a timeless essence but a historically dense and variable reality. Accordingly, this relation of noncorrespondence can vary from destructively authoritarian to relatively supporting relations. The social "they" can be a demonic "they" that grinds over and preempts rather than enhances the potentialities of agents.[4] Emancipation addresses the demonic and authoritarian functions of institutions and works

4. See Paul Tillich's essay, "The Demonic," in *The Interpretation of History,* trans. N. A. Rasetksi and E. L. Talmey (New York: Scribner's, 1936). An excellent account of Paul Tillich on the demonic can be found in James Luther Adams, *Paul Tillich's Philosophy of Culture, Science and Religion* (New York: Schocken, 1970), 229–34.

to reduce or eliminate the destructive they. Institutions can arise that promote rather than violate the personhood of their agents, that acknowledge rather than repress the relations and reciprocities of the sphere of relation. These chastened and self-relativizing institutions of a redeemed sociality can never end the inevitable disharmony between their societal functions and the aims of agents or the suffering that attends it. But they can pursue their functions so as to take into account and promote the historicity and creativity of their participating agents.

So far only one point has been made. Social redemption means a chastening and relativizing of the self-directedness or autonomy of social entities. Only in this way can they make room for the aims of agents and reduce the competition among themselves. But such a redemption calls for a certain transcendence on the part of social entities. How is this possible given the fact that institutions do take on a life of their own and thus create their own distinctive organizing patterns, discourses, corporate memories, and distributions of power all in service of their primary and secondary aims? How is this transcending possible given the particularistic and centrist orientation of social entities which orient their functions to specific times, places, and constituencies? It is after all just this particularity that attracts the loyalties and mobilizes the energies of agents. I contended earlier that institutions are turned toward idolatrous aims when their agents absolutize the ethnic, social, and other functions they serve. The natural centrism of institutions, that is, their natural particularity, is where the dynamics of institutional evil begins. To say that a social entity is evil means that its self-absolutizing way of being particular drives it to forms of subjugation. It subjugates on behalf of an absolutized human race (homocentrism), males (patriarchalism), the State (superpatriotism), or the ethnic group (ethnocentrism). Even if natural centrism were not corrupted, it so constitutes social entities as to make it virtually impossible for them to transcend their aims for broader concerns. The deep dynamics of social evil becomes operative when the natural centrism of a social entity, its tendency toward an isolated and autonomous pursuit of aims, is transformed into self-absolutizing subjugations. This is why the redemption of social entities is not just the removal of subjugating structures but the rise of a community able to transcend its own natural particularity or centrism. How can a social entity pursue its primary aims and the goods of its particularity and at the same time take into account the broader criteria of face and relation?

A thesis is in order. Social entities can transcend or surpass their natural centrism only when their secondary aims reflect criteria and serve goods that are irreducible to any particularity. The basis of this transcending is the same for social entities as it is for agents. Social entities need something like being-founded, a reference to and presence of the sacred, to press them beyond their natural autonomy and particularity. The resulting transcending cannot be a repudiation of location, territory, or specific cultural content, else it would mean the destruction of the social entities themselves. Transcending means taking up *(Aufheben)* the aims and goods of particularity into agendas oriented to the well-being of broader environments. Only the sacred can lure social entities away from their self-absolutizing centrisms because the sacred is the one reality not identifiable with the good of any particularity of place and time.

What can founding mean when we apply the term to social entities? In its full theological sense, this *founding* is the presence and activity of the sacred in the arena of human history.[5] As with nature or the spheres of agents and relations, the presence of the sacred is an adjudication of incompatibilities and a creative luring toward ever new and enriched levels of being. A natural theology would attempt to show that the unfolding conditions of the well-being of the social sphere require this adjudicating, luring presence. I shall only contend at this point that the sacred, the unspecifiable and unlocatable transcendent, is implicitly if not thematically indicated when human beings resist their subjugation, when they criticize the absoluteness of any centrism, and when they work for institutions that harmonize with each other and promote the interests of agents. In sum, the redemption of the social means both emancipation from subjugation and the emergence of forms of sociality in which autonomous particularity is relativized and transcended and which are thus enabled to incorporate broader criteria of well-being and the face. This sociality is a theonomous sociality because the power of its relativization and transcending is the power of the sacred.

THE PROCESS OF SOCIAL REDEMPTION

In the previous section I offered an account of the Christian vision of theonomous sociality. Is this vision simply utopian literature? The redemption of institutions does seem to be a fact, however ambiguous, of history. Can anything be said about the way this redemption occurs? Does the Christian vision include not only an ideal what but the how of social redemption? Is there a theonomous way of expecting, planning for, and effecting this redemption of the social sphere? Does the Christian interpretation of the human condition have anything to contribute to the way we resist subjugation and act to effect theonomous institutions? All these questions call for an affirmative answer. The Christian

5. A recent and very helpful theological reflection on this topic is Peter Hodgson's *God in History: Shapes of Freedom* (Nashville: Abingdon, 1989).

paradigm of good and evil does effect our ways of understanding how social redemption happens.

Consider the following thesis. Social entities and institutions are redeemed when the redeemed relations and shared meanings of the social world permeate the secondary aims of institutions. Considered as a negation, this thesis fosters criticism in two directions. First, it opposes the view that redemption changes imageries, typifications, and reciprocities but is unable to reach and alter institutions. The positive implication of this criticism is that social redemption is political and thus calls for strategies that address entrenched institutional power. Second, it opposes the view that social redemption is simply a matter of political, institutional change, a view that presupposes either that the shared meanings of the social world are irrelevant or that their alteration follows automatically on political change. The positive implication of this criticism is that social redemption is superficial and even destructive if it does not reach the social world of shared meanings. Together the two implications assert that the power of subjugation can be reduced by political and economic change but theonomous sociality will arise only when the secondary aims of institutions are permeated by a transformed social world.

The Redemption of the Social World of Shared Meanings

One of the outcomes of the rise of advanced industrial societies is a kind of fatalism about institutional change. According to the quantifying modes of thought of these societies, the sphere of the human is constituted by two types of entities: institutions knowable according to the laws of their operation, and, individuals knowable according to the laws of their behavior and their physiology. Absent in this faint remnant of an old dualism is the social world itself with its dense and messy reciprocities and deposits of meaning. Insofar as agents are defined as entities behaving in social systems, they are more or less helpless products of powerful institutions. Change is a matter of the autonomous dynamics of these institutions. A less quantifying approach would quickly discover not only the sphere of the interhuman but the shared meanings and reciprocities that take place in institutions. Furthermore, this duality of autonomous social systems and individual behaviors is sure to miss the very phenomenon of social evil. For social evil as subjugation arising from self-absolutizing centrism permeates institutions by way of meanings at work in everyday reciprocities and typifications. And any program of institutional change that ignores these shared meanings of the social world invites a recorruption of its newly liberated political and institutional forms. Thus, the successful revolution of the North American colonies from their colonizing parent left untouched a set of shared meanings that justified and perpetuated slavery. Thus, racism and continued subjugation persist alongside external legal and political emancipations of North American blacks. Thus, dehumanizing imageries and postures about women persist after the initiation of policies of enfranchisement and equal pay. The redemption of the social sphere must somehow reach and alter social evil in the sense of the infected social world and acknowledged or unacknowledged collusions. The redemption of the social sphere calls for two quite distinct but interrelated undertakings, both of which we find in the history and literature of the Christian movement: radical criticism, and, the creation of communities of redemption.

1. *Radical criticism* is a comprehensive term for all attempts to identify and discredit the subjugations of a social system. We find it in many literary genres. Hebrew prophets connected the poverty of their time to ruling structures and even foreign policies. We find it in the works of poets (Steven Vincent Benét), playwrights (G. B. Shaw) and novelists (Charles Dickens). Natural (Carl Sagan, Jonathan Schell) and social (Thorstein Veblen, C. Wright Mills) scientists engage in radical criticism from within their location in their sciences. Whatever the genre and location, radical criticism is always a kind of hermeneutics. It interprets contemporary situations under criteria that pertain to the well-being of various life-forms.

Radical criticism is also a hermeneutics because its exposure of subjugations calls for a special focus on language. Language attends virtually everything that happens in the social world. Cooperative tasks, reciprocal communications, and enduring relations all draw on deposits of meaning and require linguistic acts. And subjugation becomes part of the social world only when targeted groups are symbolically identified, stereotyped, or even removed from the ordinary network of meanings. Because the language of corrupted institutions helps mask subjugation by making it normal, and because the transcending of centrism requires its own symbolization, critical hermeneutics uses language both to expose and discredit and to create new imageries.

What critical hermeneutics exposes are the ways in which a group's deep symbols, narratives, and everyday usages serve subjugation. Subjugating language includes but goes far beyond the negative stereotyping of "inferior" and threatening groups. It sediments the heroes, leaders, and savior figures into the society's corporate memory. It renders subjugating events into neutral and technical jargon and stereotypes into humor and euphemisms. Because subjugation also operates by withholding status, power, and rights, it uses language to render the subjugated group invisible and thus to reduce its reality and power. We know that marginalization has taken place when the experience, history, and particularity of a people or gender is absent from a society's prevailing discourse. Until recently, it would seem that blacks, women, and other subjugated groups have no history. On the basis of prevailing masculine pronouns, it would seem that women have no existence. Further, subjugating groups foster world-views on the everyday discourse of the society in which the hierarchies of subjugation are made rationally self-evident. And because subjugating societies have a poor corporate memory about the events from which subjugation originated, one function of radical hermeneutics is to uncover these repressed events and stimulate the "dangerous memory" of the subjugated.[6]

Exposing the subjugating functions of language is not the only task of radical hermeneutics. Social entities which transcend their particularity toward broader criteria require more than simply a purge of their oppressive symbols and failed acknowledgments. If institutions are to be environments that promote the freedoms of agents and agapic relations, their secondary aims must somehow incorporate criteria of the face. This can happen only if these aims are influenced by narratives, myths, world-views, and linguistic conventions that mediate those criteria. For the face is not reducible to any one particularity and natural centrism. And if the secondary aims of institutions are totally faceless, the institutions degenerate into self-absolutizing and self-serving autonomies. This is why radical hermeneutics is not just linguistic criticism but world interpretation. And one aspect of world interpretation is the attempt to discern and bring to expression the face. And since the face is located in the sphere of the interhuman or relation, a hermeneutics concerned with subjugation and redemption is particularly concerned with the discourse and events of this sphere.

To say that social redemption requires a discourse that serves theonomy and connects with the face is not to say how this happens. We do see, however, in the course of human history both the building and eventual decay of such discourses. All human societies have stories and primary symbols that expose subjugation and create transcending institutions. The ancient texts of Hebrew, Jewish, and Christian religions contain powerful exposures of subjugation and imageries that connect the face to institutions of rule (monarchy) and worship (synagogue, *ecclesia*). These texts pose tasks of retrieval for critical hermeneutics. But the appropriateness of this retrieval does not preclude

6. See Sharon Welch, *Communities of Resistance and Solidarity: A Feminist Theology of Liberation* (Maryknoll, N.Y.: Orbis Books, 1985), chap. 3.

the continued rebuilding of discourses that connect institutions with the face.

2. The second requisite for the redemption of the social world is the creation of *theonomous communities.* Communities are necessary for the redemption of the social world for two reasons. First, the criticism of subjugating structures will have little enduring effect if its bearer is the occasional isolated agent. Corrupted social worlds are enduring infections of the social world that show up in acknowledged or unacknowledged collusions to subjugate. These infections and collusions are so entrenched that only communities of resistance can displace them.[7] Only communities can take radical criticism beyond simply momentary protests to deposits of meaning that endure in the social world. Only in communities do we have an enduring locus for the new and dangerous memory of the repressed events that brought about subjugation. And it is the liberating imageries of communities that expose the masking of subjugation by making it appear normal.

Second, the enduring transformation of the social world of shared meanings requires an environment that embodies and preserves the obligations of the face. Redemption thus goes beyond emancipation and requires a displacement of subjugating imageries with imageries that promote the transcending of centrism on behalf of the well-being of the total environment. But imageries are not momentary events of speaking. They endure over time and function in the meaning-structures of the social world. And that which carries these enduring imageries and makes them available to new generations of agents are face-to-face communities. Neither criticism nor world interpretation would have any lasting character without embodiment in communities whose primary aims are to be environments of redemption. And apart from such communities, there is little possibility that redemptive transformation will ever reach the social world of shared meanings. Prophetic individuals may plant seeds of criticism and attestation to the face but without the soil of communities, the seeds have little chance to take root. Political changes might be effected but the deep structures of social evil will remain.

The Redemption of Institutions

I have distinguished two aspects of the process of social redemption, the redemption of the social world of shared meanings and institutional change. I make this distinction only to argue that social redemption is

7. Present-day theological feminism offers an account of such a community. See Rosemary R. Ruether, *Women-Church: Theology and Practice of Feminist Liturgical Communities* (New York: Harper and Row, 1985).

more than institutional change. However, the distinction will hinder as much as it helps if it posits two separate steps of social redemption or two separate entities to be redeemed. The social worlds of shared meanings and institutions have no independent existence from each other. Assuming that social redemption involves a criticism and replacement of taken-for-granted typifications and imageries in the social world, how is it that institutions are transformed into environments that promote agapic relations and agential freedom? Or to put the question differently, how does the alteration of imageries and typifications affect institutions? I shall address this question first in a formal way and then move to the distinctive problem of social redemption that has arisen with new powerful institutions of property and rule in the global village.

To begin with a thesis, the hegemony of primary aims over institutional life prompts institutions to resist redemptive change. Primary aims draw institutions forward through time, organize their various units, and mobilize the energies of their participants. Primary aims are what institutions explicitly attend to. Corporations are oriented toward making profits, football teams toward a winning season, and schools toward pedagogical activities. Accordingly, institutions naturally resist attending directly to their secondary aims. Too much of this attention is usually a risky distraction from the institution's primary business. Secondary aims are part of the taken-for-granted background of institutional life, not the foreground of planning and activity. This hesitance to attend to secondary aims is exacerbated when secondary aims serve subjugation because of the dynamics at work that mask subjugation and preempt in advance any resistance to it.

Unless a social entity's primary function is to subjugation, redemption is not going to mean a destruction of its primary aims. Rather, the redemption of social institutions means an alteration of the secondary aims that advance subjugation and of the way these aims influence the primary aims. Thus, if institutions are to be redemptively transformed, their resistance to reviewing their secondary aims must be confronted. They need to transfer their invisible secondary aims from the suppressed background into the visible foreground. This process of exposing unacknowledged and unattended secondary aims of institutions resembles in some ways the psychoanalytic exposure of powerful but repressed psychological dynamics of individuals. But in the case of institutions, what it means to turn attention to secondary aims is not a coming to consciousness. After all, institutions are not conscious subjects. It means that the various units in the institution that process its primary aims are mobilized to deal explicitly with the secondary aims. In other words, the secondary aims become thematized items on the institution's agendas of action. This thematization must somehow reverse the institution's indifference to its secondary aims. The institution must be persuaded to engage in the unnatural act of giving its energies and organizations to assessing its secondary aims, a task which seems to risk the survival of the institution by turning it away from its primary aims. But an institution whose secondary aims have effected racist structures and operations can be redeemed in its racism only by a self-transcending and explicit placing of racism in the foreground. And the way an institution does this is in connection with its actual agendas and operations.

But it is clear that agendas and operations do not simply alter themselves. Something is necessary to effect this attending to secondary aims, this placing of covert subjugation on the agendas of institutions. It is doubtful that the effecting of this strange self-critical institutional activity will come about from a mere leakage of influence from the surrounding social environment. The redemptive change of institutions requires a precipitating agent, a vanguard of cooperating agents who have become aware of the subjugating character of the secondary aims and who work to assist the institution to thematize and deal with the problem. This vanguard may or may not be a structural part of the institution itself.

The above description of the redemptive change of institutions is formal and abstract. The actual workings of institutions in history do confirm the description. Vanguard communities and movements have facilitated theonomous socialities in specific times and places. But even small and temporary social entities are recalcitrant to social redemption because they are always interwoven into larger systems of property and rule. In this respect something seems to have happened in twentieth-century advanced industrial societies that makes them virtually unredeemable.

Familial, educational, religious, and aesthetic institutions of normative culture mediate to society at large the primary criteria for interpretations of well-being, of the good, the right, and the beautiful. In pre-archaic societies, in social systems like those of ancient Egypt, Greece, and Rome, or in medieval Europe, economics and politics are continuous with the normative culture. Ideals of justice and the holy are not absent from these institutions of property and rule. This is not to say that these institutions are utterly determined by such ideals, or that they themselves have no influence on the institutions of normative culture. Rather, there is sufficient contiguity between these institutions and the ideal-mediations of normative culture to ground appeals for their reform. An ancient or medieval monarch can be criticized and even deposed under ideals of justice.

Since the industrial revolution and the rise of industrial societies and technocracies, the relation between institutions of property and rule (economics and politics) and normative culture has undergone a dramatic change. Property and rule occur in new and increasingly globalized social entities, for instance, corporations and governmental bureaucracies, which live a life of their own above the workings of normative culture. The old contiguity between economics and politics and the normative culture is replaced by powerful and autonomous social entities. A virtual abyss has developed between the aims and criteria of institutions of property and rule and the criteria of well-being (good, right, beauty) of the normative culture. The subjugations that structure a modern society are still part of the secondary aims of corporations and governments, but there is little or no mediation that passes from the institutions of normative culture to institutions of economics and politics that could alter corrupted secondary aims. The exception to this is the continuing power of the legal system over governments and corporations, a system that continues to assess both individual and corporate behaviors under ideals that have their distant root in normative culture. But the legal system is now itself cut off from normative culture. Its orientation is to past legal precedent, not the powers of the sacred or the face. Thus, in modern industrial societies, a proposal that a business review its secondary aims under criteria generated by religious, moral, or aesthetic traditions could only provoke amusement and contempt.

How this abyss, this noncontiguity, has come about between institutions of power and normative culture is historically complex. I surmise at least the following. 1. In most Western countries religion has undergone de-establishment, and this carries with it the de-establishment and relativization of the moral traditions which religion fostered on society. This pluralization of moral and religious traditions privatizes and separates these traditions from the public sphere and its institutions. 2. The new global economic interdependence is creating an institution (the multinational corporation) that exists above all specific societies and thus above any specific normative culture. 3. The welfare of individuals and of all specific social entities increasingly depends on the health of the economic system and thus the multi-national corporations, with the result that the many criteria of normative culture are displaced by or become subject to the one criterion of the bottom-line.

The relation between institutions of rule and property and normative culture is not just a separation but a reversal of functions. Now the institutions of rule and property create the ethos, the ideals, the rules of the game, even the myths and primary symbols for the institutions of normative culture. Thus, management efficiency and therapeutic become the criteria and subject matters of churches, schools, and even arts. In this way the institutions of property and rule become the "normative culture" for education, family, and religion. In these conditions, normative culture has little role to play as a transcending source of criticism and remaking of institutions of rule and property.

This isolation of the secondary aims of institutions from normative culture or the subjugation of normative culture by institutions of rule and property seems to undermine the very conditions of social redemption. It tempts us to a renewed social Manicheanism, a fatalist posture that abandons social criticism and the expectation of social redemption. And it confronts us with the problem of how the social entities of advanced industrial societies ever can be redeemed. Yet redemptive social changes do continue to happen. Corrupted political systems give way to reform. Subjugating symbolic systems that have ruled for millennia (for instance, patriarchalism) begin to erode. Even old and frozen collectivisms show signs of thaw. And vanguard communities continue to bring radical criticism and testimony to the face, to corrupted social entities, and to institutions.

16
REDEMPTIVE COMMUNITIES

> Like a shunt every social relation leads back to the presentation of the other to the same without the intermediary of any image or sign, solely by the expression of the face. When taken to be like a genus that unites like individuals, the essence of society is lost sight of.[1]
>
> *Emmanuel Levinas*

This essay has explored the way human evil and good alter agency, relation, and society. But there is something unsatisfying about simply assigning things to their respective locations, in this case to three spheres. Analyses of this sort leave us discontented at several points. First, any mere distribution of something into compartments appears to be a formalism that has little to do with what is concrete and actual. Distributed into three spheres, evil and redemption thus are lifted above the unitary actions of living human beings. Second, assigning evil and redemption to spheres postpones and calls for an inquiry into their interspherical unity and interrelation. We still need to explore the intrinsic interconnection of the spheres and thus the interconnection between evil and redemption in each sphere. Thus, for instance, how are the ways evil and redemption work in each sphere influenced by how they work in the other spheres? A third discontent arises from the conviction that a vision of evil and redemption should have something to do with passionate practice. Assuming for the moment that the tracing of redemption in three spheres is plausible and illuminating, how does this analysis direct us to strategies of change?

This final chapter cannot ease all of these discontents. I shall, however, take up the issue of the mutual influences between spheres. The first two sections of the chapter address the way evil and redemption are shaped by the way the three spheres interact. The third section moves in the direction of the concrete when it contends that it is evil itself that separates the spheres and that their reunion is a matter of redemption. It contends, further, that this reunion takes place under the criterion of the face. Because the unifying of the spheres occurs through the spread of the face to the spheres of agency and the social,

1. Emmanuel Levinas, *Totality and Infinity: An Essay on Exteriority,* trans. A. Lingis (Pittsburgh: Duquesne University Press, 1969), 213.

redemption originates in the sphere of the interhuman and is promoted by face-to-face communities, a theme taken up in the final section of the chapter.

THE INTERCONNECTIONS OF THE SPHERES OF HUMAN REALITY

Discovering how the three spheres of human reality are interconnected is more difficult than discerning the spheres as such. Individual agents, face-to-face relations, and social institutions are all part of our everyday world. To experience the world at all is to experience these things. But the way these things are interconnected is not a matter of direct experience. We should not be surprised at this. To understand things in their relation to each other requires access to and grasp of the larger system or entity whose reality and rules set the parameters of the relations. We would make little progress toward understanding how the circulatory system and organs of reproduction are related in human beings if we had no inkling of the organic entity of which these two things are parts. It is just at this point that our inquiry into the interconnection of the three spheres begins to falter. We quickly discover that there is no entity of which these things are parts. This may be why so many interpretations of human reality select one of the spheres, for instance, the individual (as an organism, or as personal) or society, as the comprehensive entity in which all else is located. For sociobiology, human reality means individual organisms of the species, Homo sapiens, disposed by their evolutionary heritage toward certain delimited types of individual and social behavior. For some strands of continental philosophy, human reality means a distinctive form of personal agency (subjectivity, being-there, for-itself, or consciousness-of) to which adhere sociality, other-relations, and world relations.

I would contend that human reality does not coincide with any of the spheres. Nor is it an entity like an organic body or thing. Whatever its destiny and relation to the sacred, human reality is something that has evolved as one of this planet's life-forms. Accordingly, the three spheres coinhere not in a discrete entity but in this distinctive life-form. Agents, interhuman relations, and societies are spheres of this planetary life-form. When we would describe the distinctive way this life-form perdures over time, we use the word, *history*. When we would describe its distinctive way of becoming self-aware and intercommunicative, we use the word, *language*. When we would describe it as a system of interacting agents, we use the term, *social world*. History, language, and social world are examples of comprehensive terms we use to describe this distinctive life-form as we view it from different perspectives. Human reality then is a comprehensive term for a distinctively temporal, linguistic, and interactional life-form. This is the reality in which the interconnections of agents, relations, and the social take place. Is any one of the spheres so primary that it is the entity of which the other two are parts, the cause or explanation of the other two, or the unity of the three? A case can be made for all three of the spheres so to function. Human reality surely depends on the existence of individuals whose organically rooted motivations and actions are necessary to both relations and institutions. Even the alterity necessary to the sphere of relation is a sign of the irreducible, self-surpassing historicity of individual agents. And apart from the activities of individuals, there are no actual social institutions, only nonliving skeletons of some past sociality. But interhuman relation as the condition of shared meanings and a shared world is the basis for the reality postures of agents. Furthermore, the operations of institutions are not just the effects of the acts of individuals isolated from each other but of agents in relation who share meanings and interpretations. Yet individuals are what they are only because they arise in societies that shape them from the time of their origin, and they have no existence prior to or outside that shaping. And in order to exist at all, face-to-face relations must appropriate available social sediments and vehicles that enable them to endure through time. We must conclude, then, that all of the spheres are primary, necessary, and unifying of human reality. However much each sphere is irreducible to and unexplainable by the other spheres, it nevertheless depends on them for its existence. This essential interdependence of the three spheres is their primary interrelation and the presupposition of their mutual influence. Systems of influence can range back and forth between the spheres only because they are already mutually intertwined.

The three spheres are not only intrinsically dependent on each other but are open to each other's influences. Various sorts of causalities flow from each sphere to the others. This flow of influence is evident to commonsense or everyday world experience and it constitutes much of the subject matter of the social and psychological sciences. We observe how aggressive individuals can affect their familial, tribal, or even national environments. We trace certain features of social life to biologically based organic drives of individuals. And the postures and agendas of agents influence and alter the face-to-face relations of intimacy and friendship. Alienated, intimate, pathological, and passionate relations influence the lives of their participating individuals and the social systems in which they participate. And institutions are comprised of structures and processes that constrain and shape both relations and agents. This is why the social sciences can discover correlations between forms of institutionality and agential behaviors. There is no single meaning of causality in this flow of influences between the spheres. Causality or influence can mean simply contextuality, motivating elements, statistical correlations, external, and even violent determinations. Each sphere "causes" in the teleological sense when it provides aims or goals for the other spheres and in the more external sense when its movements directly effect changes in those spheres. Furthermore, the ways in which the spheres exercise influence vary from sphere to sphere. Agents influence institutions in different ways than institutions influence agents. Agents influence relations and social entities through actions informed by their passions and their transcending historicity. Relations influence especially through the evocation of the face. Social entities influence through storage, symbolization, transmission, and the power of collusion.

In addition to being interdependent and interinfluential, the three spheres also transcend influence and dependence. To say that a sphere transcends another sphere means, negatively, that it is not the mere product of that other sphere's causalities and that its own momentum and complexity absorbs and surpasses what shapes or constrains it. Positively, transcending means that influences or causalities originate from within that sphere. Agents, relations, and social institutions are never mere outcomes of something. Agents transcend and surpass through their historicity. They respond, resist, and create. In the sphere of relations, the face transcends because it evokes vulnerability and compassionate obligation. Social institutions transcend by a perpetual open-ended adaptation to new situations. To summarize, the three spheres of the human life-form are interrelated by institutional interdependence, reciprocal influencings, and mutual irreducibility and transcendence.

THE INTERSPHERICAL DYNAMICS OF EVIL AND REDEMPTION

Because they are located in the spheres of human reality, evil and redemption will partake of the entanglements and mutual transcendings of those spheres. Thus, the primacy of each sphere in its own order carries over into evil and redemption. We can, accordingly, argue for the primary importance of socially entrenched evil and liberation. This argument properly appeals to the natural primacy of the social sphere and contends that corrupted sociality undermines and subjugates individuals and relations from the start. Accordingly, liberation is primary to all other redemptions. But institutions and the social also depend on face-to-face relations, hence we can argue that the corruption and redemption of these relations is primary to the social. And because institutions and relations depend on the passions and actions of individuals, redemption begins with the self.

Human evil in each of the spheres influences and is influenced by the operations of evil in the other two. Accordingly, social subjugation and alienated relations play a twofold role in the idolatry of agents. First, they add an element to the agent's experience of tragic existence. I have drawn an artificial and misleading picture of tragedy and suffering by abstracting it from human evil (Part One). The tragic is only formally and abstractly the intrinsic incompatibilities that structure the spheres. It is true that vulnerability, incompatibility, benign alienation, and grief constitute relations and that even nonsubjugating social institutions perpetrate suffering. But much of what presses human beings to the desperate attempt to secure themselves is the suffering they experience from social and relational evil. In this way social and relational evil intensifies suffering and is an intrinsic part of the dynamics of idolatry. Second, corrupted relations and subjugating social evils influence the idolatry of agents because they are preceding environments of evil into which agents are born and grow.

Yet similar streams of influence flow from idolatry and social subjugation to the sphere of relation. Subjugating and unjust social institutions contribute to the resentments, guilts, and mutual violations of persons in relation. And idolatrous attachments to goods at hand based on the passion of the interhuman presses participating agents into violating relations. Thus, evil occurs in human reality as this reciprocal exchange of influences between agential, relational, and social spheres.

These exchanges of influence between the spheres take place not simply in a general way but in connection with the specific and distinctive evils of each sphere. Idolatry is never something general but is a cluster of unfreedoms in agents, postures of envy, imperceptivity, and malice. It affects the agent's being-in-the-world and that includes ways of being in relation and being in institutions. Specific unfreedoms predispose the agent to violation and its alienating guilt in different ways. Further, an unfreedom (for instance, malice), will itself be modified and intensified by acts of violation in relations and by participation in subjugating social structures. The self-masking powers of subjugating movements exacerbate imperceptivity and blind agents to the oppressive elements of its environment. The subjugating structure of a society (for instance, racism, already present and taken for granted), will assist idolatry-prone agents to locate their absolute enemies and scapegoats. Subjugation itself has many forms and these can be further corrupted by specific unfreedoms or specific forms of alienated relation.

Similarly, redemption in each of the spheres influences and is influenced by the redemptive transformations of the other two. This interdependence of redemptive transformations in the spheres is the counterpart of the interspherical operations of evil. If redemption were limited to agents, it would be defeated from the start by powerful influences of corrupted relations and subjugating institutions. This is why interpretations that limit redemption to one of the spheres are not only abstract but have themselves corrupting effects. Individualistic redemption tends to be a rather cruel moralism, indifferent to the subjugation of scapegoated peoples and even insensitive to the pains and vulnerabilities of relations. When redemption is limited to institutional change, it tends to become a cruel politics, a justice machine oblivious to the miseries, idolatries, and even rights of individuals.

Streams of influence from one sphere to the others are necessary for the redemption of the human life-form. And these influences are carried by the entities and processes specific to each sphere. Transformed passions (freedoms) such as courage, vitality, wonder, and agapic passion influence the way agents participate in specific relations, the way we are friends, mates, parents, males, females, and lovers. They also influence the way we participate in institutions. Influences also pass from transformed social systems to agents and relations. The defeat of a subjugating power and the turning of an institution in the direction of justice redemptively affects the shared meanings of face-to-face relation and influences the postures of agents in the direction of the freedoms. In the texts of early Christianity that report the kerygma or preaching of Jesus, the expression for redemption that appears to embrace all three spheres is the Kingdom of God.

To say that evil and redemption are borne by deep structures and processes that reflect the reciprocal influencings of the spheres is to say that they are *historical.* Human evil is never a discrete and isolated corruption, a demonic inhabitation, or a piece of human ontology. It is a network of occurrences that varies with every agent, situation, and period of time. The actual interaction of the spheres is never a mere structure, essence, or repetition. An agent's posture of enmity will always reflect the subjugations and relations of that time and place and will be embodied in the agent's unique autobiographical and developmental situation. The same holds for specific relations and institutions. Redemption, too, is historical, taking place in unrepeatable situations of specific times and places. Thus, redemption transforms institutions in a specific social system that is never the mere repetition of the past. Its agential freedoms arise in connection with the unique biological heritage, psychological history, face-to-face relations, and ever-changing situation of each person. The same holds for the redemption of relations. In sum, redemption's entrance into the network of interconnected spheres varies as situated agents and social entities replace each other in the open-ended marches of historical time.

THE ALIENATION OF THE SPHERES AND THE REDEMPTIVE POWER OF RELATION

Because the spheres of human reality are interdependent, the distinctive corruption of each sphere is conditioned by that of the others. Does evil have any effect on the way they are related? Can the way the spheres are related be itself subject to corruption? I described the spheres as having a certain independence from each other. Can that independence become an isolation, a disrelation, a disharmony? The way redemption transforms human reality shows us this is the case. For redemption rarely if ever occurs as a total harmonization of the spheres. Movements of redemption and their paradigms characteristically center on one of the spheres. Nor is this focus necessarily a pseudo redemption. Individuals do experience being-founded, courage, and the freedoms amid the horrors of subjugating social systems. For instance, American black religion powerfully embodies these things in both the time of slavery and the present. And societies do undergo revolutions that correct centuries of oppression and restore some justice to the social system yet continue to foster impoverished relations and bleak agential lives. Redemption in the full sense of a harmonization of the spheres tends to be more an eschatological hope than an actuality.

But why this disconnection? Human beings can experience redemption in one but not all of the spheres because the spheres never merge into a single identity. This is why a world-view, piety, or theology can value one sphere over the others. But the limitation of redemption to one of the spheres bespeaks more than this formal possibility. For this limitation is not a neutral or trivial issue but something that serves human interests. For instance, restricting redemption to the spheres of agents and relations serves the interests of the subjugating powers of society. If redemption really does mean something that affects all the spheres and thus their interconnections and influences, then one of the effects of evil is the separation of these spheres and the telos of redemption is the correction of that isolation. Accordingly, criteria for human good pertain not only to each sphere (criteria of biological and psychological well-being, face-to-face relations, and societal efficiency and justice) but also to the functioning of the three spheres together.

Harmony is the criterion for this comprehensive redemption only in the most formal sense. We must qualify then the principle that each of the three spheres is primary in its own order. For that which redemptively unites the spheres of human reality does not arise outside the spheres but in connection with one of them. *That which unites the spheres in the cause of human good is the face.* The face is the deep criterion for all of the spheres because of the role the interhuman plays in both the sphere of agency and the sphere of the social and because it is the humanizing criterion that structures both of those spheres. The functions, agendas, and powers of social systems and their institutions produce no criteria for their own limits or for how they co-opt and treat agents nor do agents as agents produce criteria for their treatment of each other. Minus the interhuman and the face, individuals use institutions for their individual purposes, and institutions deploy individuals for their agendas. It is only because of the interhuman and the face that individuals transcend their subjectivity toward others in compassionate obligation. It is the face that shows the other as one who can be murdered, violated, and manipulated, and as one to whom we are responsible. The face is the agent's own face discovered in the alterity of the other and the other's face experienced in the agent's own sphere.

The face is a criterion for individual agents because one of the agent's elemental passions is for communion with the other. The life we want and need, even the reality we lay claim to, requires the sphere of the interhuman and the face. The face is a criterion for the sphere of the social because, apart from the vulnerabilities, needs, and obligations of agents in relation, the goods that institutions promote can only deprive and victimize. The goods they promote under the forgetfulness of the face are the goods of the ant colony, the military operation, and the bureaucracy; the goods of order, efficiency, survival, and power. Agents and their well-being are not an intrinsic concern of social systems as such. Apart from the face, social institutions are oblivious to agents, compassion, and obligations. Institutions can and do embody these notions, but only because the face has obtained some power and presence in their workings.

There is then a primary sphere among the three spheres. This is the sphere of relation (the interhuman) in which is born the criterion of the face and which turns all the spheres toward the good of human reality. And this discloses a deeper sense in which the three spheres are corrupted by human evil. Evil not only works in each sphere in a distinctive way; it exploits the irreducibility and transcendings of each sphere to effect a disconnection from the face. Face-to-face relations, agents, and institutions all degenerate when they lose connection with the face. This means there is a deeper meaning of redemption than simply the spread of redemptive influence from one sphere to the other. In this deeper sense, redemption means reconnecting the spheres to the face. In each of the spheres, redemption mediates the power and presence of the face. For this power and presence of the face is the condition for the spheres to work together to promote human good. Formally speaking, the three spheres occupy and interact in human reality, the human life-form, but in actuality these interactions take place in specific social systems connected to agents by bonds of loyalty. The isolation of the spheres from the face originates here in the actual dynamics and conflicts of power. Specific races, genders, classes, ethnic groups, and even nations, infected by the idolatries of their agents, lose their connection with interhuman criteria. Specific idolatries prompt agents to refuse responsible action in their relations and social environment. Thus, the dynamics of evil at work in the spheres effects isolation between the spheres. And the dynamics of redemption press social entities toward openness to a criterion broader than themselves, the criterion of the face.

The problem is that the face is experienced along the lines set by the natural centrism of social units. How then can the face be a criterion that ranges not only over the three spheres but beyond the units of social loyalty and identity? What would ever open a specific people beyond its natural familial and group discernments of the face to compassionate obligation toward any and all others? How can the face be released from its capture by the determinacies, loyalties, and commitments of specific social locations? The face transcends these regions only if it manifests something that pertains to the good of the total human life-form, and, beyond that to the good of all life-forms. In the Christian paradigm of redemption, the transregional face is experienced in connection with the experience of the sacred. It is the presence of the sacred, thematized or unthematized, that restores the unity of the spheres by drawing situated peoples to transcend (but not repudiate) their self-reference. It is the sacred manifested through the face that lures regional (familial, national, tribal) experiences of the face toward compassionate obligations to any and all life-forms.

COMMUNITIES OF THE FACE

According to the argument so far, sacral mediation of the face is what draws self-absolutized social entities beyond themselves to larger settings of human good. The face, we recall, is itself located in the sphere of relation. How, then, can the face influence or be present in the other spheres? The question is stated improperly. For the face must be intersphericaly present if the spheres are really interdependent. However, the way the face is present is as an element in the face-to-face relations of particular groups or social systems; families, clubs, offices, and ethnic gatherings. Even institutions whose primary aims have to do with violation and victimization have codes of interpersonal loyalty and familial and friendship relations. To restate the question, how can the face be mediated to agents and institutions, given its natural entrapment in regional intimacies and loyalties?

If the face is ever to function beyond the limitations of regional loyalties, it must be communicated in the form of a transregional criterion. If this does not happen, compassionate obligation follows the lines established by natural centrism and natural human intimacies. But how can human beings become oriented to the universal face that attends any and all agents and peoples? How can we ever be drawn by a face not borne by the known, trusted, and safe other? The communication of the universal face calls for a distinctive social and historical mediator, the *community of the face.* The community of the face is not any and all community but a distinctive kind of community.

It is necessary at this point to distinguish between social groups that are not communities, communities, and communities of the face. Face-to-face relations take place in all actual groups, but in groups that are not communities, these relations are not central to their primary aims. A community is a social group in which face-to-face relations are valued and pursued for their own sake. Face-to-face relations are part of the raison d'etre of a village, therapy group, and some kinds of schools. Accordingly, in most instances, a small village is a community and a staff of researchers is not. And where there are face-to-face relations, the face has some sort of presence. However, the mediation of the face is not part of the primary aims of either noncommunity social groups or communities. These social forms can mediate the face beyond themselves, but it is not part of their primary aims to do so.

A *community of the face* is a community whose raison d'etre as a community is the mediation and attestation of the universal face. The mediation of the face to resisting agents and subjugating institutional powers requires attestation. Its power as a criterion must find expression in symbol, narrative, metaphor, and persons. Its criteriological relevance calls for relating it to the life of agents and to institutions, and sets tasks of interpretation and exploration. Furthermore, the primary form of the spread and mediation of the face is not thematic explication but relational embodiment. But the embodiment that will communicate the face to any and all persons cannot simply be one which restricts compassionate obligation to a regional loyalty. The face ever points beyond such boundaries, and a community that embodies and attests to that universal reach is oriented to any and all life-forms. Insofar as the experience of the face as a transregional criterion is connected to the experience of the sacred, the attestation to the face will at the same time be an attestation to the sacred. And the embodiment of the face will occur through the ritualization of the sacred.

Historical types of communities of the face and of the sacred have arisen in connection with Hebraic and Christian communities. This is not to say there are no others. The *ecclesia* of the Christian movement has embodied the translocal and transethnic reference of the face and the sacred. At the same time, its actual mediating social forms have always been mixtures of communities of the face and natural centrist communities that serve racial, ethnic, and gender loyalties. In spite of this history, *ecclesia* stands for an ideal type of community of the face in the sense that its primary aim is to embody and attest the face for any and all and to press all autonomous and local social powers to open themselves to the face. The need for translocal redemptive communities of the face should not be discredited simply because of the historical failures of this actual religious movement called Christianity. The dynamics of human evil continue to infect all historical forms of human community. Thus, however ideal their self-understanding and noble their calling, all actual communities of the face will be mixtures of continued subjugation and redemptive attestations.

This thesis that redemption reaches the spheres of human reality through communities of the face has two important implications. Those who take one side or the other in the debate over the political versus the spiritual mission of the Christian movement may resist these implications. The first implication is that the communities (congregations?) of the Christian movement are not primarily institutions of political change. Like all communities the community of the face will have a political-institutional aspect. It is not an institution of political change because its primary aim does not compete with or work to replace any of the society-maintaining institutions of the social system. If its primary aim is to attest and embody the face as such, it cannot at the same time be the State, a political party, a leisure organization, a society to promote physical and mental health, or a school of public or private education. Its calling is not to be these institutions but to communicate the face to them. To say that the *ecclesia* is transpolitical, transaesthetic, or transtherapeutic is to invite misunderstanding and even exploitation by the self-protective agendas of subjugating powers. These powers maintain themselves by infiltrating and corrupting communities of the face and by isolating those communities into private, innocuous, and nonpolitical spheres of individual morals and consolations. But history has shown us that the attestation of the face has a powerful political content. To say that the community of the face is not itself the state is not to say that its attestation has no relation to politics. Rather, attesting to the face addresses all human institutions because it holds before them criteria from the sphere of relation that expose the workings of evil and the possibilities of freedom.

The second implication is that the Christian community is not primarily a community for agential change. This implication may find more resistance than the first one because, according to the conventional view, the church's role in "salvation" is to mediate the resources (revelation, divine forgiveness, true doctrine, moral tradition) to individuals. Against this view, I contend that the redemption of individuals is a secondary aim of the ecclesial community of the face. Like institutions, agents constitute a distinctive sphere of human reality which human evil works to isolate from the face. The very existence of a community of the face is a displacement of that isolated sphere. The reality of this community is not the mediation of resources to separate agents but of agents-in-relation under the face and before the sacred. To be sure, this embodiment (koinonia) of the face into relation has a redemptive effect on agents. But both spirituality and politics are offshoots of this primary reality.

It goes without saying that if redemption has anything at all to do with what is actual, it exists as some sort of practice. But the term, *practice,* too, is tracked by ambiguity. This ambiguity arises because each of the spheres of human reality sustain their distinctive practices. Thus, practice can mean the actions and even the postures of agents, the strategic and political operations of institutions, or the interactions of people in relation. Communities of the face properly engender various kinds of practices pertinent to both agents and institutions. However, I have argued that community of the face is primarily a community of relation. Is there a practice that arises in connection with the sphere of relation? Does the role of the community of the face in redemption call for a distinctive meaning of practice? It is clear that a distinctive practice arises with all actual communities of face-to-face relations. Passively understood, this practice is a participation in the relations that constitute the community. Actively understood, a community of the face calls forth strategies and activities oriented not just to that community's self-maintaining functions but beyond itself to the spheres that human evil would separate from the face. These practices include agential and corporate actions, corporate rituals, education, resymbolizing, knowledge-oriented inquiries, and many other things. Here, too, there is a discipline of practice for communities of the face that parallels agential and political disciplines. And communities of the face show degeneration and decline when these disciplining practices lose their orientation beyond the community and when they no longer reflect the criterion of the face and the sacred. Thus, education, preaching, and ritual in the church can be co-opted by subjugating powers or regional loyalties of the church's location. They can be absorbed into the masking operations of subjugating groups. At the same time communities of the face can critically turn back upon themselves to renew the distinctive disciplines of their practice under their own criterion of the face.

INDEX

(Boldface type denotes pages on which terms are defined.)

Printed in the United States
23779LVS00006B/106-204